P9-CRD-944

Not for Profit. All for Education.

Oxford University Press USA is a not-for-profit publisher dedicated to offering the highest quality textbooks at the best possible prices. We believe that it is important to provide everyone with access to superior textbooks at affordable prices. Oxford University Press textbooks are 30%–70% less expensive than comparable books from commercial publishers.

The press is a department of the University of Oxford, and our publishing proudly serves the university's mission: promoting excellence in research, scholarship, and education around the globe. We do not publish in order to generate revenue: we generate revenue in order to publish and also to fund scholarships, provide start-up grants to early-stage researchers, and refurbish libraries.

What does this mean to you?
It means that Oxford University Press USA published this book to best support your studies while also being mindful of your wallet.

Not for Profit. *All* for Education.
As a not-for-profit publisher, Oxford University Press USA is uniquely situated to offer the highest quality scholarship at the best possible prices.

OXFORD
UNIVERSITY PRESS

TEN LESSONS IN
INTRODUCTORY
SOCIOLOGY

Lessons in Sociology

Series Editors: Kenneth A. Gould and Tammy L. Lewis

Twenty Lessons in Environmental Sociology
Kenneth A. Gould and Tammy L. Lewis

Ten Lessons in Introductory Sociology
Kenneth A. Gould and Tammy L. Lewis

Twenty Lessons in the Sociology of Food and Agriculture (forthcoming)
Jason Konefal and Maki Hatanaka

TEN LESSONS IN
INTRODUCTORY SOCIOLOGY

SECOND EDITION

Kenneth A. Gould

Brooklyn College of the City University of New York

Tammy L. Lewis

Brooklyn College of the City University of New York

New York   Oxford
OXFORD UNIVERSITY PRESS

Oxford University Press is a department of the University of Oxford. It furthers the University's objective of excellence in research, scholarship, and education by publishing worldwide. Oxford is a registered trade mark of Oxford University Press in the UK and certain other countries.

Published in the United States of America by Oxford University Press
198 Madison Avenue, New York, NY 10016, United States of America.

© 2018, 2014 by Oxford University Press

Library of Congress Cataloging-in-Publication Data

Names: Gould, Kenneth Alan, author. | Lewis, Tammy L., author.
Title: Ten lessons in introductory sociology / Kenneth A. Gould, Brooklyn
   College of the City University of New York, Tammy L. Lewis, Brooklyn
   College of the City University of New York.
Description: Second edition. | New York : Oxford University Press, [2018] |
   Includes bibliographical references and index.
Identifiers: LCCN 2017007202 | ISBN 9780190663865 (pbk. : alk. paper)
Subjects: LCSH: Sociology.
Classification: LCC HM585 .L495 2018 | DDC 301—dc23
LC record available at https://lccn.loc.gov/2017007202

To two of our favorite public sociologists:

C. Wright Mills and George Carlin

Neither the life of an individual nor the history of a society can
be understood without understanding both.
C. Wright Mills

Some people see things that are and ask, Why?
Some people dream of things that never were and ask,
Why not? Some people have to go to work and
don't have time for all that.
George Carlin

Table of Contents

Annotated Table of Contents

The origins of sociology are discussed, with special attention to the founding fathers of the discipline: Karl Marx and Friedrich Engels, Max Weber, and Emile Durkheim. The text also highlights some key theorists who have largely been left out of the sociological canon, including W. E. B. DuBois and Charlotte Perkins Gilman. Sociology was founded during a time of tremendous social change, and the foundations of the field reflect the attempts of early sociologists to understand the shift from an agrarian to an industrial society. Some of their key concepts that continue to be used in the field today are elaborated, such as class conflict, social facts, and the iron cage. Three main goals of sociology are outlined, and the differences between the scientific and postmodern points of view are described. The logical relationship between theory and data is discussed as a key component of sociological analysis. Three research examples are discussed in depth to illustrate the differences among qualitative, comparative, and quantitative studies in sociology. The examples show some of the ethical issues raised in research. They also elaborate how researchers go about getting research subjects, and how this varies in terms of whether the researcher is doing ethnography, case studies, or surveys.

Part 2   What Unites Us?

3.   Socialization and Culture
Stella M. Čapek

This lesson invites the reader to develop a sociological perspective on how a person acquires a sense of self through the process of socialization. It begins with the question "Who are you?" and some observations about how one might answer this question differently depending on one's age, cultural experience, and location in society. It looks at how sociologists define culture and proceeds through a sampling of relevant sociological theories that include the symbolic interactionism of Charles Horton Cooley and George Herbert Mead, the dramaturgy of Erving Goffman, and views of the self as a consumer in a globalized world that draw on the perspective of the Frankfurt School and, more particularly, Herbert Marcuse's concept of repressive desublimation. The lesson also examines the impact of social movements on the self, using the examples of the slow food movement and more traditional social justice movements to explore how the self has agency and can be involved in change. Along the way, it provides many examples and opportunities for the reader to reflect on identity and the self (including one's own) and how it develops as a process of interaction with culture and society from childhood through adulthood. The lesson makes the case that sociologically understanding the development of self and its patterned relationship with social structure provides meaningful insights into the constraints and opportunities present in our lives and liberates us to make good choices in the future about who want to be and how we want to shape the society in which we live. The closing sentence of the lesson returns the reader to the question posed at the beginning—who are you?—but with the benefit of a more systematic, sophisticated, and interactive understanding of the dialogue of self and society.

4.   Social Institutions

Naomi Braine

This lesson provides a conceptual introduction to social institutions, as both a focus for research in sociology and a conceptual framework for thinking about social processes. The main social institutions in contemporary society are education, family, economy, politics, religion, health, and media. In basic terms, social institutions are the structures that enable a society to create and sustain a collective social life from day to day and year to year; they answer the question, "How do we do _____ around here." In more sociological language, social institutions are systems of shared behaviors, beliefs, and social norms that organize the major areas of social life and provide the structures within which members of a society manage their lives at all levels, from the personal to the workplace to the government. Throughout the lesson, social institutions are discussed at different levels of society, from individuals and social networks (micro level) to hospitals, schools, and organizations (meso level) to the government, corporations and social policy (macro level). The lesson starts with an overview of social institutions at different levels of society and then provides an in-depth exploration of health and marriage to guide students through more focused analyses of specific institutions.

Part 3   **What Divides Us?**

---

5.   Race and Intersectionality

Janine Kay Gwen Chi

The goal of this chapter is to discuss the multifaceted ways in which race affects our lives. Integral to this discussion is the fact that there is not a single person in this society—or any society, for that matter—who remains unaffected or untouched by the realities of race. This lesson takes a nonconventional approach to the study of race and race relations. Rather than examining the topic through the experiences of different groups, the lesson is organized into ten lessons that address key issues ranging from the sociohistorical construction of race through the realities of residential segregation to global migration and citizenship. As such, studies relying on different sources of data are utilized, such as quantitative demographic data and in-depth ethnographic fieldwork. The lesson tackles common misunderstandings and assumptions of race and race relations by relying on a number of different bodies of literature on interracial attitudes, immigration, and nationalism. This strategy attempts to correct existing approaches to the topic by allowing readers to develop an understanding of race as a perspective or lens rather than as a traditional object of study.

6. Class and Intersectionality

Brian K. Obach

Class is one of the most important social factors that sociologists study. Generally, class refers to one's position within the economic system. Class status can be defined in terms of income and wealth or on the basis of related characteristics, like educational attainment or type of employment. One's social class position profoundly shapes the experiences that individuals have and the kind of life they will lead, whether it be one of desperation and an ongoing struggle to secure even the most basic necessities; one of comfort, security, and luxury; or something in between. Class is also closely related to power, with those of higher class having more ability to influence state policy and the economic well-being of others. While many people think of one's economic standing as a product of individual character and ambition, class must be recognized as a social system that exists outside of any individual. Economic systems can vary in their class structure with greater or lesser degrees of social inequality and opportunities for individual mobility from one economic status to another. While some sociological theories suggest that the class system serves an essential function in society, most sociologists view poverty, vast economic inequality, and impediments to social mobility to be problematic. Relative to most other economically developed capitalist democracies, the United States is characterized by a great degree of class inequality and a high rate of poverty. In 2010 almost one in six Americans lived in poverty. More than one in five children lives in poverty in the United States. While individuals have some capacity to alter their economic condition, the structure of the economy and government policies play a large role in fostering or limiting opportunities for economic mobility. Many policies in the United States, such as education funding and health-care policy, tend to reinforce existing inequalities and limit opportunities for individuals to move up in the class system.

7. Gender, Sexuality, and Intersectionality
Nancy A. Naples

This lesson describes the changing sociological imagination of sociologists who study gender and sexuality. It describes the different theoretical perspectives and illustrates these different approaches with exemplary studies. Sociologists of gender and sexuality apply a sociological imagination to a wide range of topics including gender socialization of children and heteronormativity (the presumption of heterosexuality), the significance of culture in constructing gender and sexuality, discrimination and economic inequalities, violence against women, the diverse experiences of gender nonconforming and trans people, and political activism. The lesson also highlights how the development of the sociology of gender and sexuality are important and intersecting fields of study that were fostered by the activism of feminist sociologists and queer activists and scholars. Before many women entered the field, the sociological approach to gender focused on sociobiological explanations of differences between men and women and heteronormativity. Taking their lead from the women's movement, especially from feminists of color, sociologists of gender insisted that gender was socially constructed and that it intersected with class and race in such a way that it contributed to a diversity of experiences among women. As scholarship on the social construction of gender expanded, different understandings of the social construction of gender included the attention to the intersection of gender, sexuality and race, and other social categories. The notion of intersectionality has become one of the key concepts in the academic fields of sociology, women's studies, critical race, and queer studies.

Part 4   How Do Societies Change?

8. Forces of Social Change
Jason Konefal

Social change is ubiquitous. But who drives social change, and how do societies change? This lesson examines these important questions from a sociological perspective. First, the macro models of social change in sociology are outlined: the evolutionary and dialectical models. Each model presents a very different understanding of social change. In the evolutionary model, social change is conceptualized as a process of adaptation. In contrast, the dialectical model views social change as a conflictual process among competing groups. Second, insights from the different theoretical traditions in sociology that help to understand social change are reviewed. These include how the structure of society enables or constrains social change. How people in their everyday interactions affect social change and how access and control over information and knowledge affects social change. Third, the actors who drive social change and the practices that they use to change society are examined. These include the state, corporations, social movements, and experts. Lastly, examples of social change in action are presented. Nested analysis is used to show how social change takes place from the individual to the global level. At the individual level, how individuals contribute to social movements, the role of leaders in changing society, and whether consumption changes society are examined. Examples of environmental justice, racial justice, and environmental conservation movements are used to discuss social change at the local, national, and global levels. Specifically, the case of Love Canal and environmental justice is used for the local level, Black Lives Matter for the national level, and efforts to stop tropical deforestation for the global level.

9. Global Dynamics

Kenneth A. Gould

Sociologists commonly refer to the period of the late twentieth century and the early twenty-first century as an era of globalization. The sweeping set of social changes associated with globalization were made possible by developments in communication and information technology like communication satellites, computers, the Internet, and cell phones. The results have been a number of changes in social organization that have occurred on a world scale. These changes include an expansion of world trade, the transnational production of consumer goods, the emergence of a global culture and global social norms, a growth in the power of transnational corporations as social institutions, increased international migration, the development of global social movements, and new threats to our global environment. The globalization of society in recent decades impacts what you wear, what you eat, what you buy, where and how you work, what you watch, what you aspire to, and even what you choose to study in college. Understanding where globalization came from, how it is organized, what social changes it involves, how it effects you, and how you can affect it is the subject of this lesson on global dynamics.

If this book is available for sale, please contact the Oxford University Press Global Academic

10. Public Sociology: The Task and the Promise

Michael Burawoy

C. Wright Mills argues that sociology works at the intersection of history and biography. This lesson shows how the idea of public sociology—a sociology that engages with communities beyond the academy—arose from and developed with the author's own experience with a changing world. Public sociology was and continues to be rooted in US sociology but even more so in other countries where professional sociology is weaker. Public sociology can only be understood in relation to critical, professional, and policy sociology, and this lesson explores these connections.

Introduction and Acknowledgments

Kenneth A. Gould and Tammy L. Lewis

We both teach Introduction to Sociology. As academics working in a public university, we think teaching this class is one of the more important things we do to contribute to our society. We believe in the promise of sociology as a way of producing knowledge and as a way of understanding the world we live in. While we would like all of the students who take introduction to sociology to become sociology majors, the statistics suggest that only one in ten students will go on to be majors. With that in mind, we have constructed this book to be useful for both the eventual sociology major and the student who will only take one sociology course in their college career. This is an introductory book, but it is a challenging book; it is not "Sociology for Dummies." We have designed this book in a way that we hope will help you to gain critical insights from the discipline of sociology. Our intention is that this book will help lead you to find your sociological imagination so that you can apply it in your daily life as an engaged citizen, whether you become a professional sociologist, the president of the United States, a professional athlete, a retail store manager, a physician, or something else. We believe that the sociological imagination, well applied, has the power to both liberate the individual and to improve our collective quality of life as a society. We really, genuinely like sociology, and we hope that our enthusiasm is at least a little bit contagious.

Part of what drives our work are the dual concerns with (1) fighting the "endarkenment" (more on this in a moment), and (2) making social science accessible and meaningful to the engaged public. We first heard the term "endarkenment" watching satirist Stephen Colbert on the *Colbert Report* in a segment titled "Welcome to the Endarkenment" (July 22, 2012). The term encapsulated what we have, for years, jokingly and seriously called "the decline" (short for "the decline of Western civilization"). Colbert used the term in reference to a political platform that stated, "We oppose the teaching of . . . critical thinking skills." To our minds, the declining quality and outcomes of the educational system in the United States is a serious concern (see Council on Foreign Relations 2012). By teaching the logic of social science and the connection between observations and claims, we hope to fight this trend. This book emphasizes how to understand the connection between data and claims and how to assess the claims being made by others. By doing this, we hope to generate students (and, over the long term, leaders and publics) who ask questions such as, "How do we know that's true?" rather than simply accepting what they read on the Internet or watch on YouTube. Despite its declining popularity among both conservatives and liberals, we believe in science. We believe in knowable facts. We believe in data-based decision-making. We worry when our national discourse is led by opinion makers whose opinions do not match empirically verifiable reality, especially when the consequences lead to decisions and public policies that negatively affect the majority and benefit the few. Our belief in public sociology leads us to think that sociology really can be used to make the world a better place, by facilitating more critically analytical and engaged publics, and a sound knowledge base from which to generate sound policy.

One of our primary goals for this book is to engage students in critical thinking about the society in which we live. *Ten Lessons in Introductory Sociology* and *Thirty Readings in Sociology* are designed to raise sociological questions, apply a sociological lens, illustrate how data are used, and present core sociological topics in an engaging and accessible way. The book is organized around four questions: (1) Why sociology? (2) What unites society? (3) What divides society? and (4) How do societies change? This book and the companion reader aim to show the relevance of sociological research and analysis to students' lives.

We conceived this book but could not have done it on our own. We thank our coauthors, all excellent teachers and researchers, committed to the collective project of teaching the next generation of critical thinkers and leaders. We would also like to thank the reviewers who gave us valuable feedback, especially Josh Gamson. The following reviewers provided invaluable feedback for the first edition: Toby Ten Eyck, Michigan State University; Rachel Whaley, Southern Illinois University; Amy Holzgang, Cerritos College; James Vela-McConnell, Augsburg College; Robert McAuslin, Washington State University; Deborah Thorne, Ohio University; and Keo Cavalcanti, James Madison University. The following reviewers gave us helpful feedback for the second edition: David Brown, Illinois State University; Theodore Ekechukwu, Austin Peay State University; Kimberly E. Fox, Bridgewater State University; Daniel Kreutzer, Metropolitan State University; Gail Murphy-Geiss, Colorado College; Alan J. Spector, Purdue University Northwest; Susan Wortmann, Nebraska Wesleyan University; and three anonymous reviewers.

Thanks to the members of our family, from whom we have gained insight and understanding of the diversity of experience, perspective, and trajectory that comprises our social world. As crazy as they are, they keep us grounded in some important ways that we think are reflected in our work and in this book. And special thanks to Anna and Isabel, who manage to simultaneously keep us young and make us old. A special thanks to Isabel for helping us distill the reviewers' comments on the second edition.

Our editor, Sherith Pankratz, is committed to providing students with high-quality material. She and Oxford University Press stand committed to fighting the endarkenment. Oxford University Press is a not-for-profit publisher, and we think that is an important model in a time of high-cost, high-debt, high-profit higher education. A special thanks to Sherith for her faith in the work, her intellectual stand, and her patience.

We would also like to thank our colleagues in the Department of Sociology of Brooklyn College of the City University of New York. As a team of teachers and scholars deeply committed to the promise of urban public higher education, they are truly inspirational. Finally, we thank our students and colleagues, past and present, at the City University of New York, Muhlenberg College, St. Lawrence University, Denison University, University of California, and Northwestern University. Teaching is a collaborative enterprise, and this book reflects much of what we have gained in our years of collaborations.

References

Council on Foreign Relations. 2012. *U.S. Education Reform and National Security.* Independent Task Force Report No. 68. New York: CFR. http://www.cfr.org/united-states/us-education-reform-national-security/p27618

Changes to the Second Edition

Throughout the second edition, authors have updated data, examples, and websites and made more explicit connections to *Thirty Readings in Introductory Sociology*. In addition, the following list highlights the more significant changes to each lesson based on feedback from reviewers:

Lesson 1: replaced the food box to discuss fast food.

Lesson 2: adds discussions of the roles of W. E. B. DuBois and early female sociologists in the history of sociological theorizing and adds a chart comparing conflict theory and functionalism.

Lesson 3: the discussion of culture is extended.

Lesson 4: includes descriptions of the five central social institutions; increased focus on the privatization of government functions; and updated to address the legalization of same-sex marriage and implementation of the Affordable Care Act.

Lesson 5: greater focus on Latino/a and Asian and multiracial experiences; new section differentiating racism, prejudice, and discrimination; and discussion of Black Lives Matter.

Lesson 6: greater focus on Weberian concepts of class.

Lesson 7: sexuality was added to the lesson, which had been "Gender and Intersectionality." It is now "Gender, Sexuality and Intersectionality." This lesson has the most changes of all of the lessons with significant sections added that address LGBTQ issues and two new boxes: one on the beauty myth and one on the gender pay gap.

Lesson 8: new box on Fight for $15; new section on Black Lives Matter and the role of social media in social movements.

Lesson 9: new boxes (one on immigration and one on the production of iPhones) and a new section on international migration.

Lesson 10: more integration with the sociological imagination to link back into the book's introduction.

About the Contributors

Naomi Braine is an Associate Professor in the Sociology Department at the City University of New York, Brooklyn College. Her primary teaching areas include research methods, social policy, drug use, and the sociology of public health, primarily through the lens of the HIV epidemic. Prior to joining the faculty at Brooklyn, she worked in the nonprofit health research sector and consulted for community-based organizations and the New York State Department of Health. Her research interests include HIV prevention as a social and structural process, drug use, gender and sexuality, and collective action.

Michael Burawoy teaches sociology at the University of California, Berkeley. He is past president of both the American Sociological Association and the International Sociological Association. His lesson on public sociology further details his sociological biography and interests.

Stella M. Čapek is Professor of Sociology in the Department of Sociology/ Anthropology at Hendrix College. She teaches courses on environmental sociology, social change/social movements, medicine and culture, urban/ community sociology, images of the city, the sociology of food, sociological theory, and an interdisciplinary creative writing course on nature writing. She has also taught courses about sustainability and ecotourism in Costa Rica and in the US Southwest. She is especially interested in interdisciplinary environmental studies, environmental justice, ecological identity, social constructions of nature, and sustainable community design. She has published articles on environmental justice, tenants' rights, urban/ community issues, local interactions with wildlife, health and environment, green design, ecological identity, and transnational social justice collaborations, along with some creative nonfiction. She has co-authored two books, *Community versus Commodity: Tenants and the American City* (1992) and *Come Lovely and Soothing Death: The Right To Die Movement* (1999) in the United States and has written an organizational history and manual for social change titled *Building Partnerships That Work: Grassroots, Science, and Social Change, The Endometriosis Association Story* (2006). She is an active member of the American Sociological Association, The Society for the Study of Social Problems, The Society for the Study of Symbolic Interaction, and the Association for the Study of Literature and the Environment. Besides her academic interests, she enjoys hiking, yoga, creative writing, weaving, dance, playing folk music, and learning everything that she can about building a socially just and ecologically sustainable world.

Janine Kay Gwen Chi, Associate Professor of Sociology, is currently Chair of the Department of Sociology and Anthropology at Muhlenberg College, a small private liberal arts college in Allentown, Pennsylvania. There, she teaches a variety of courses, such as Introduction to Sociology, American Ethnic Diversity, Inequality and Power, and the Sociology of Nations and States. Her research focuses on the ways in which ethnic and cultural politics intersect with nation-building projects and have involved the application of contemporary theories of citizenship and cosmopolitanism to study recent restaurant industry and food trends. She received her doctorate in sociology at the University of Washington, Seattle in 2003.

Kenneth A. Gould is Professor of Sociology at Brooklyn College of the City University of New York, and Professor of Sociology and Earth and Environmental Sciences at the CUNY Graduate Center. In addition to Introduction to Sociology, he teaches courses in environmental sociology, globalization and sustainability, and environmental justice. Gould's research examines the responses of communities to environmental problems, environmental social movement coalitions, the role of socio-economic and racial inequality in environmental conflicts, and the impacts of economic globalization on efforts to achieve ecologically and socially sustainable development trajectories. He is co-author of *Environment and Society: The Enduring Conflict* (1994), *Local Environmental Struggles: Citizen Activism in the Treadmill of Production* (1996), *The Treadmill of Production: Injustice and Unsustainability in the Global Economy* (2008), *Green Gentrification: Urban Sustainability and the Struggle for Environmental Justice* (2017), and co-editor, with Tammy L. Lewis, of two other books in this series: *Twenty Lessons in Environmental Sociology* (2015), and *Thirty Readings in Introductory Sociology* (2017). His most recent work examines the impacts of oil development on the environmental protection and development trajectories of Belize. He is past chair of the Environment and Technology section of the American Sociological Association.

Arne L. Kalleberg is a Kenan Distinguished Professor of Sociology at the University of North Carolina at Chapel Hill. He received his B.A. from Brooklyn College and his M.S. and PhD from the University of Wisconsin at Madison. Kalleberg has published more than 125 articles and chapters and a dozen books on topics related to the sociology of work, organizations, occupations and industries, labor markets, and social stratification. His recent book, *Good Jobs, Bad Jobs: The Rise of Polarized and Precarious Employment Systems in the United States, 1970s–2000s* (2011), examines the growing precarity and insecurity of work and the polarization of jobs with regard to earnings as well as noneconomic rewards such as the control people have over their work activities and schedules, especially in balancing work and family. His major current projects include a book about the differences in precarious work and its consequences in six rich democracies (Denmark, Germany, Japan, Spain, the United Kingdom and the United States), an historical study of institutions and inequality in the United States, and a study of the mobility out of low-wage jobs in the United States. Kalleberg is a fellow of the American Association for the Advancement of Science and served as the secretary of the American Sociological Association in 2001–2004 and as its president in 2007–2008. He is currently the editor of *Social Forces: An International Journal of Social Research*.

Jason Konefal is an Associate Professor in the Department of Sociology at Sam Houston State University. His research examines the relationship between political economic structures and practices and opportunities for social change. Specifically, he is interested in how neoliberalization and globalization are affecting governance processes and possibilities for equality, justice, sustainability, and democracy in food and agriculture. Dr. Konefal's recent publications have appeared in the *Journal of Rural Studies, Agriculture and Human Values*, and *Organization & Environment*. With Maki Hatanaka, he is the editor of a forthcoming book in this series, *Twenty Lessons in the Sociology of Food and Agriculture*.

Tammy L. Lewis is Professor at Brooklyn College of the City University of New York and Professor at the CUNY Graduate Center in Sociology and Earth and Environmental sciences. In addition to Introduction to Sociology, she teaches courses on urban sustainability, social movements, environmental sociology, and research methodology. Her research examines alternatives to development and sustainability, with a focus on Latin America. She has conducted research in Belize, Brazil, Chile, Costa Rica, Ecuador, Nicaragua, and Peru. She is author of *Ecuador's Environmental Revolutions: Ecoimperialists, Ecodependents and Ecoresisters* (2016) and co-author with Kenneth A. Gould of *Green Gentrification: Urban Sustainability and the Struggle for Environmental Justice* (2017). With Gould, she is the co-editor of two other books in this series: *Twenty Lessons in Environmental Sociology* (2015) and *Thirty Readings in Introductory Sociology* (2017). She co-authored her first book, *Environment, Energy, and Society* (2002), with Craig R. Humphrey and Frederick H. Buttel. Her work has appeared in *Conservation Biology, Social Science Quarterly, Teaching Sociology*, and *The Chronicle of Higher Education*, among others. She is the chair of the Environment and Technology section of the American Sociological Association.

Justin Sean Myers is Assistant Professor of Sociology at Marist College. He received his PhD in sociology from The Graduate Center, City University of New York, his M.A. in Sociology from San Diego State, and his B.A. in sociology from Sonoma State University. His research utilizes historical and qualitative methods to understand how social and environmental inequities are created, reproduced, and challenged through the food system, with an emphasis on how low-income communities and communities of color are utilizing food to address environmental injustice and political and economic marginalization. His work has documented the efforts of food justice organizations to challenge cultural assimilation, mass incarceration, and gentrification through urban agriculture programs, community mobilizations against Walmart and for unionized grocery stores to create good jobs so people can afford good food, and how public-sector grocery stores may be able to increase food access in low-income communities when private-sector grocery stores are unable to. This scholarship has been published in *Agriculture, Food and Human Values, Environmental Sociology*, and *Geoforum*. He is currently writing a book on the food justice movement in Brooklyn, New York.

Nancy A. Naples is Board of Trustees Distinguished Professor of Sociology and Women's, Gender, and Sexuality Studies at the University of Connecticut (UConn). Her scholarship on gender and citizenship, social policy, immigration, community activism, and feminist methodologies includes publication of two sole authored books, five edited collections, over 60 journal articles and book chapters, and many book reviews and other publications. She is editor-in-chief of the five-volume *Wiley-Blackwell Encyclopedia of Gender and Sexuality Studies*. She received the 2008 Faculty Excellence Award in Research (Humanities/Social Sciences) given by UConn's Alumni Association, the 2010 Distinguished Feminist Lecturer Award of SWS, the 2011 Feminist Mentor Award from SWS, the 2011 UConn's College of Liberal Arts and Sciences' Excellence in Research Award for Social Sciences, and the prestigious Jesse Bernard Award from American Sociological Association.

Brian K. Obach is a Professor of Sociology and the Director of the Environmental Studies Program at the State University of New York at New Paltz. He earned his PhD from the University of Wisconsin at Madison. Obach's research and teaching focus on environmental sociology, social movements, the sociology of food and agriculture and political economy. He is the author of *Organic Struggle: The Movement for Sustainable Agriculture in the United States* (2015) and *Labor and the Environmental Movement: The Quest for Common Ground* (2004). When he is not teaching or conducting research, Obach spends his time hiking the beautiful Shawangunk Ridge and playing in the all-professor rock band, Questionable Authorities.

List of Tables

List of Figures

List of Boxes

PART 1

WHY SOCIOLOGY?

Most students don't come to college wanting to be sociology majors, in part because they don't know what sociologists do. Sometimes confused with psychology or with social work, sociology is a unique way of viewing the world that is distinct from those perspectives. While psychologists focus on the mental state of individuals, and social workers help people navigate social services, sociologists attempt to understand what makes society possible at a broader scale. Sociologists ask: What are the underlying forces that hold us together as a society? What connects us as individuals to one another? What are the seen and unseen structures that enable us to cooperate to achieve our basic human needs? Sociologists also examine the limits of human society. Why do social groups come into conflict? How are differences reconciled? How to we create social change to address social problems? In short, sociologists examine broad patterns in social life.

For many students who were raised in the United States, a sociological view of the world does not come naturally. We have been taught to understand ourselves individualistically, as unique and special. We are taught that our successes and failures are our own and that anyone can (and should) work hard to raise themselves up by their bootstraps and achieve anything that their natural abilities will allow. A sociological view of the world, what is called "using your sociological imagination," requires you to temporarily put aside an individualistic interpretation and instead, take a look at the bigger picture to understand individuals' "social location." For instance, what is a person's race, class, gender, nationality, age, and so on? Knowing an individual's social group memberships can tell you a lot about that person without even knowing them. Sociologists study social hierarchies that place certain groups above other groups and the ways these shift over time. Based on our understanding of social structures and social forces, we recognize that it is easier for individuals from certain groups to pull themselves up by their bootstraps than others. While we are taught to believe that our society is a meritocracy, the reality of life in the United States suggest that both social location *and* individual choices are important components of understanding people's lives and experiences. A sociological way of looking at the world asks us to consider the ways that society enables us and disables us based on our social location. It forces us to see that our fate is not entirely in our own hands because we are part of something bigger than an individual. This can sometimes be uncomfortable.

Sociology developed as an academic discipline in the midst of the industrial revolution in an effort to understand the big social changes that were affecting everyone. We continue to examine society to understand why we cooperate, go to war, degrade the environment, attempt to improve the environment, promote marriage equality, resist marriage equality, and so on. The questions we ask are aligned with the times that we live in. Sociologists seek objectivity in answering these questions and we have developed tools to scientifically assess what is happening in the social world. You will learn about some of these in the chapters that follow.

When you are surrounded by vehicles moving slowly down the road, do think of yourself as traffic?

The Sociological Imagination

Kenneth A. Gould
Tammy L. Lewis

INTRODUCTION

On the first day of class, we tell our students that only one in ten students who take introduction to sociology become majors. A lot of you sitting here are taking this course because it is a college-wide requirement. Our goal is to make the most of our time with you. If you finish this book understanding the sociological imagination, we are confident that you will see the world in a different way from this semester forward. Obviously, we're proponents of a sociological view of the world. If we weren't, we would not have spent years in graduate school studying sociology or years teaching it. We definitely would not have taken the time to write this book. In this lesson we will explain some of the things that originally got us excited about sociology and tell you about sociology's promise.

When I (Tammy) went to college, I didn't know what I was going to major in. I had spent some time in religious schools of two very different types that had instilled in me a sense of civic duty and a concern for social justice. I had a general sense that I wanted to help others and make things better. To me and my college academic advisor, a psychologist, it made sense for me to try out an introduction to psychology course. I took that class hoping to find my major and calling. I learned a lot and took a few more psychology courses, but they did not satisfy my urge to make things better on a broad scale. I could see that if I majored in psychology and perhaps became a psychologist or a social worker that I could possibly help individual people with their individual problems, but that wasn't what was really driving my desire to help others. I kept thinking that even if I could help a poor immigrant woman reconcile her issues with her mother or help secure child care for her son, she would still be a poor immigrant woman with a life that was not easy. It turns out that I was more interested in how being poor and an immigrant and a woman shapes someone's circumstances, and I wanted to figure out if and how those conditions could be altered to make things better for groups of people, not just individuals. Being a practical person, it seemed to me to be a more effective way of making things better.

Growing up in the United States, I wasn't taught to think about my life or the lives of others in the context of "groupness." We have an ideology that says that individuals shape their own outcomes. I was raised with the idea that if I worked hard, I could be just about anything I wanted to be (though my grandfather was disappointed that, since I was a girl, that I would not be able to play football.) Nevertheless, the nuns at my Catholic school and the teachers at my Quaker school put a wedge in that individualistic "American dream" thinking to suggest that I also had an obligation to those less fortunate than me. When they spoke of the less fortunate, they weren't referring to those who didn't work hard enough. They spoke of those who worked very hard yet, due to some forces beyond their control, would not ever be able to work hard enough to achieve the upward mobility that the American dream promised.

My second semester of college, I took introduction to sociology. I still didn't know what sociology was at this time, but I knew someone taking the class and I had heard the teacher was good, so I tried it. We read Karl Marx and learned about his concern for helping *classes of people* (well, really just one class: the proletariat). The level of analysis had jumped from individuals to groups, and I was hooked. The focus wasn't on helping one individual worker with his or her problems but understanding the plight of workers in general and figuring out how they could come together to collectively improve their opportunities and quality of life. If they succeeded, their quality of life would be better. This spoke to me.

SELF AND SOCIETY

One of the key relationships that sociologists examine is the relationship between the individual self and society. A key theme of an introduction to sociology course is that individuals affect and are affected by society (see Figure 1–1). We are largely taught about the top arrow: individuals shape the world around them. Sociology looks at this. For now, we want to focus more on the bottom arrow, because it is the one that we tend to focus on less. Society affects the individual. We use the term "society" as shorthand for the many social forces that affect our lives, such as the social institutions (such as families, schools, economy, politics) and our social group memberships (such as race, class, ethnicity, gender). Our historical era also shapes who we are. Sociology asks two key questions: How are individuals shaped by society? And how do we, in turn, shape society? When we use the word *shape*, there are a few ways this can be interpreted. One is as "reproduce." How do we as individuals reproduce society? In other words, how do we maintain society? One way we do this is by carrying out what we've learned from our social institutions and social group memberships. If you simply follow the practices and traditions that you were taught when you were growing up, you are reproducing the society that came before you. This is one way that we maintain social continuity. A second way to think of the word "shape" is to "change." How do you as an individual change your society? What do you do that is different than what came before you? How do your practices

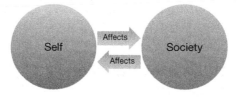

Figure 1–1 Dynamic Relationship between Self and Society.

change social institutions and social membership? Figure 1–1 is a very simple diagram, but the possibilities that lie within it are complex.

Another way that sociologists talk about the relationship between self and society is by using the terms "agency" and "structure." **Agency** refers to choices that individuals make. It implies that individual actors can exert their power to make something happen. For instance, you have some agency in terms of your grades. You can choose to put effort into your schoolwork or not. On the other side, the "society" side, we talk about "structure." Structure is shorthand for **social structures**, such as social institutions, social **norms**, and other invisible rules that guide our lives (and is the subject of most of this book). We have less control over social structures. For instance, your race and class have likely shaped the educational opportunities that you've had to date. Whether you went to a good elementary school or a not so good one is largely shaped by such structures. You didn't have much control over that, though your parents (using their agency) probably tried to get you into the best schools within their structural constraints. Sociologists call the tension between agency (what we can individually control) and structure (social constraints and opportunities that are beyond immediate individual control) the "structure–agency debate." Again, in the United States, we tend to believe that we have a lot of agency. As sociologists, however, our job is to examine structure to understand how it limits and enables agency.

Agency would appear to be based on individual traits—what we think of as character or personality, or our "nature." Sociologists debate "nurture versus nature," and we think that nurture (or upbringing or **socialization**) has a lot to do with people's actions. That said, we can all think of families in which siblings are very different. Big parts of their upbringing—their nurture—may have been largely the same, but it resulted in big personality differences. If you have brothers and sisters, how similar or different are you? Difference suggests that there's something about your elemental selves that makes you respond to situations differently. Those are individual traits, and they influence how you face the world and use your agency. There's more to agency, however, than your individual self. Your group membership has an influence on how much agency you have. For instance, in the early 1900s, men in the United States had more agency (power, control, and initiative) over their own lives than women had over theirs. Men could do more to affect change in society than women could. Of course, this has changed, which also shows that society is not static: it changes over time. Think of other groups whose power has risen and fallen.

Part of what we want you to see here is that even agency—the thing that we have most control over—is affected by social structures.

THE SOCIOLOGICAL IMAGINATION

Much of what we've been explaining about the relationship between structure and agency, and society and individual, was given a name and described by sociologist C. Wright Mills as *the sociological imagination*. In "The Promise," the first chapter of his book *The Sociological Imagination*, Mills (1959) introduces the term and argues:

> *The first fruit of this [sociological] imagination—and the first lesson of the social science that embodies it—is the idea that the individual can understand his own experience and gauge his own fate only by locating himself within his period, that he can know his own chances in life by becoming aware of those of all individuals in his circumstances. In many ways it is a terrible lesson; in many ways a magnificent one. (6)*

(Note that Mills is using all masculine references. He was writing in 1959, and that was the social norm at the time.) To explain how this works, Mills distinguishes personal troubles (personal problems) from public issues. A personal trouble is a problem that an individual experiences whose source is the individual's actions (their agency). A public issue is when a lot of people have a problem because the source of the problem is public or social. In other words, the source of the public issue has something to do with social structures. Let me give you an example that is a spin-off of an example that Mills uses: if you lose your job because you mouth off to your supervisor, that's a personal trouble. If you lose your job because your company is relocating to China because the labor costs there are cheaper and the plant you work in is closing, that is a public issue. Often, these things aren't so clear-cut.

Mills discusses the examples of unemployment, divorce, war, and life in the metropolis. Let's look at unemployment, since it is of particular importance in our current era. Do you know someone who's unemployed? We do. We've got relatives and friends who are educated, able, and hardworking but do not have jobs. Why is that? Is it due to their personal characteristics? Is it because they are uneducated? No. Because they are incompetent? No. Because they are lazy? No. One of our friends with a master's degree in biology from a top institution, who has years of experience in the field as an adjunct instructor and is dedicated to her profession, cannot get a job. She's been trying for years since being laid off from a place where she worked for two decades. Sadly, she doesn't have a sociological imagination and largely blames herself for her predicament. She's trapped in what Mills calls a private orbit. He says:

> *Nowadays men often feel that their private lives are a series of traps. They sense that within their everyday worlds, they cannot overcome their*

> *troubles. . . . What ordinary people are directly aware of and what they try to do are bounded by the private orbits in which they live; their visions and their powers are limited to the close-up scenes of job, family, neighborhood.*

What can we tell our friend from a sociological point of view? First, pay attention to the news. Look at the rate of unemployment and also the numbers that aren't shown, such as those discouraged people who have stopped looking for work. She is not alone. This is a public problem. There is a social explanation to what's going on. We are currently recovering (slowly) from a major economic recession. This is part of a historical moment that is much bigger than just individuals. In our globally connected economy, what's happened with the housing bubble in the United States and in China with low wages and in Europe with the Euro debt crisis affects individual workers everywhere. Millions of people did not suddenly become lazy, incompetent, and uneducated. Something else, outside of their individual selves, changed. The sociological imagination pushes us to understand the world in social rather than individualistic terms.

To see the big picture, it is critical to objectify ourselves. Using our sociological imagination, we objectify ourselves as a character in history. Devoid of personal characteristics, we compare the individual to others in their same social situation (in other words, in the same social groups). This allows us to see the individual as one of many and not completely in control of their personal destiny. Mills sees this as terrible, because it shows us our personal limits. He also thinks that it empowers us, because it shows us our place in history and what we can do to shape history. What does this mean for our friend the biology instructor? Well, first it means that she can stop blaming herself for her predicament. Second, it suggests that to find a solution, she might look to what others in her social group are doing to solve the public trouble. She might get involved in a political campaign. She might help organize an adjunct instructors union. She might decide to deal with the problem individualistically by taking her social security early at a reduced rate. The sociological imagination does not direct us to use it in any particular way. It empowers us with a view of the bigger picture and makes our choices clearer. Peter Berger, another American sociologist, suggests that when one has the sociological perspective, like puppets, we can look up and discover the contraption that's been controlling us. Obviously, we're not like puppets. We have some control, but the idea that there's a social force acting on our individual behaviors is a key lesson of sociology. **Sociology** asks us to look for social rather than individualistic explanations. It asks us to move beyond our private orbits to examine how history and institutions affect us.

The sociological imagination asks us to examine the relationship between private troubles and public issues. Take a minute now to reflect on your life. Think about a few of the most difficult personal problems or private troubles that you or someone you know (e.g., family, friends) has faced over the last several years. All of them, no doubt, feel very personal. Stretch your mind now. Employ your new sociological imagination. Might any of these problems be public issues? In other words, are any of these troubles related to larger social issues in society? What might the connection be between your private trouble and the public issue? Take a problem that you think was a result of a public issue. Think about how your biography, history, and group membership influenced the situation. Are the factors involved with the private trouble and public issue universal (in other words, did everyone face them)? Do they vary by group membership—race, class, gender, ethnicity, culture, age, immigration status, or sexual orientation? How would this situation and solution be different for someone who lived in another era, another culture, or another place or who had a different identity or location in the social structure (race, class, gender, etc.)? How was the problem resolved? Individually? Socially or publicly? If the problem was resolved individually, how might the resolution have been different if it had been resolved socially or publicly? If it was resolved socially or publicly, think about how the long-term effects of the public issue may have been altered by the social or public solution. Push yourself here to begin to develop your sociological imagination. We'll continue to ask you to do so throughout this book.

What promise does sociology hold for you? Sociology will force you to question things you take for granted. It should make you feel a bit uncomfortable. Part of its aims is to scrutinize and uncover things that seem natural or that seem inevitable. While we may grow up thinking that we have free will and make choices based solely on our individual preferences, sociology shines a light on how your society and your group membership shapes many of what you thought were *your* attitudes, values, preferences, tastes, and life choices. In some ways, this is very disempowering; it may make you feel like a cog in the machine. It shouldn't, though. There's another side to it. Once you're able to see the influence that social forces have on your behaviors, you will be able to distinguish between the choices you thought you had and the ones you truly have.

Some of the questions we will ask in this book are very personal and will have an impact on how you see yourself. We'll ask, what is the relationship between the individual and society? How does group membership (in terms of race, class, and gender) shape our personalities? Our life choices? The constraints and opportunities we face? Some of the questions are more outward-looking. For instance, we'll examine social change and ask how societies got to be the way they are today. Indeed, this was a question that the very first sociologists asked (more about this in the next lesson). We'll ask, what about society can be changed? Can we influence the direction that it takes? If so, how? Beyond the very practical reason of fulfilling a requirement for your associate's or bachelor's degree or preparing for your MCAT exam, this course should also help you see your place in the world: How your society has affected you, and how you can shape your world.

WHAT AFFECTS YOU?

Sociology is a way of looking at the world. Looking at the world with your sociological imagination turned on allows you to see the people, institutions, and events around you in a new way. It allows you to contextualize how a particular person, in this moment, is being impacted by larger social forces and historical trends. Looking at the world, your life, your family, your community, and your country in this way is a little weird. It's not how most people experience things. In some respect, the sociological imagination makes you a bit of an outsider in that you are not only in the moment but also observing the moment, analyzing the moment, and reflecting on the moment through a sociological lens. For instance, most people, when they are stuck in traffic, see everyone around them as being "traffic." With your sociological imagination turned on, you might understand that *you* are traffic. You are traffic for everyone else around you. You are actively making the thing you are experiencing as traffic. You might also wonder why there are so many cars here now. Where is everyone going? Why at this time? Who decided to put a highway here, and why doesn't it allow enough space for everyone to get where they are going quickly? Why isn't there more mass transit? If there is mass transit, why don't people use it? Couldn't we organize our comings and goings better so as to avoid us all sitting here in traffic being annoyed thinking about traffic? That's what looking at the world sociologically is like. A warning: the sociological imagination can make you a little annoying to be around. You might be watching TV with friends when a commercial comes on for underarm deodorant. Everyone else may just see pretty people, hear a catchy jingle, and read a memorable slogan. You, on the other hand, might wonder out loud, "Why does this company want to make me think I smell badly?" You might turn to your friends and say something like, "See how they try to tear down your self-esteem by making you insecure about how others perceive you and then tell you, you can fix what is wrong with you by giving them money for their product?" Your friends are already looking at you like you might be out of your mind. You go on: "Look at how she looks at him now that he uses the deodorant. Suddenly he's attractive to her. That's so shallow, not to mention heterocentric. And why do they have to be white? Are only white people sexy?" You've lost them. Now they are thinking, "Hey, sociologist, maybe you'd have more friends if you'd just be quiet, watch the show, and maybe use some deodorant." Of course, individual results may vary. The point is that a sociological imagination allows you to make the connections between everyday experiences and larger social forces (like economic structures), the interests and actions of institutions (like corporations), the impacts of social norms (like gender roles), and the operation of power structures (like racial hierarchies). Once your sociological imagination is turned on, it is hard to turn off. We've never figured out how to do that, actually.

For most, the really empowering part about developing a sociological imagination is the ability it provides you to make deeper sense of your own life. Rather than experiencing your life as simply a series of individual experiences intersecting with other people's series of individual experiences, you start to see how your time, your place, your social position, and your group memberships shape your experiences and your interactions with others. In that sense, sociology is a way of making sense of your own life. You are living a life and creating a biography within the context of a particular time and place—a history—that you did not create nor ask for. You were born into a family not of your own choosing, in a particular society that defines a family in a particular way. Is your sense of who your family is rooted in a nuclear family or an extended kinship network? Does your family live all together in a single dwelling, or is it spread out across the entire planet? Are you genetically related to your family, or is your familial affiliation constructed differently? How many, if any, dads do you have? What does the relationship between fathers and children involve? What are the roles, norms, obligations, responsibilities, and rights associated with that relationship? The ways in which families are socially constructed and understood varies over time, across cultures, and within societies. And you entered a particular family, in a particular place, at a particular time, which has a major impact on how you construct your own identity and on how you understand who you are and what your place within the family is.

Your family exists in a **culture**, or maybe even two cultures, or between cultures. You may be a part of a family with strong cultural norms. Those cultural norms transmit sets of values to you as you learn what is right and wrong, what you should and should not do, and who you can and cannot be. Your culture is specific to a time, place, people, history, and tradition. You may find yourself under pressure to maintain centuries-old traditions or under pressure to construct completely new family roles. Figuring out who does the housework in a family with same-sex parents in the twenty-first-century United States is likely to be more problematic than figuring out who was to do the housework in a family with different-sex parents in the nineteenth-century United States. That issue would be addressed differently in twentieth-century Tanzania or China and in different ways in different parts of that century. Culture changes, norms change, and expectations change, and they impact how you understand yourself and your world. You know what your family expects of you, and much of what it expects is shaped by the social world external to your family. What will the neighbors think? What will your teachers think? What will the police think? Should you get married? To whom? When? Should you go to college? Get a job? Join the military? The answers to these questions that you come up with will be shaped by the family that you have been a part of, the culture(s) that family reflects, and your relationship to that. Even your decision to accept or rebel against your family's expectations and cultural norms is shaped by your particular society's understanding of what it means to accept or rebel, the rewards and sanctions associated with

FOOD FOR THOUGHT
UNDERSTANDING OUR FAST-FOOD NATION
Justin Sean Myers

Think about your eating habits. Are you eating a lot of on-the-go meals? Are you using the microwave to heat up breakfast, lunch, and dinner? Does ordering delivery or the drive-thru beckon because you are squeezed for time or too tired to go grocery shopping? Would you rather eat out at a fast food or casual dining restaurant than make a meal from scratch? Odds are yes, and you are not alone.

The United States has witnessed what could arguably be called a revolution in eating over the past half-century. We have traded home cooked meals at the dining room table for TV tables and to-go meals, highways and drive-thru hamburger joints, and eating out on Friday nights. In the 1970s fast-food consumption constituted around 3 percent of the average American's daily diet. Today it constitutes over 12 percent. Consuming more fast food is just part of this change. U.S. households spend a lot more money on food made outside of the home then they used to. In 1970, 25.9 percent of all food spending was on food prepared away from home. Today it has increased to over 44 percent, the highest level ever recorded.

How do we explain this transformation though? Do we just chalk it up to the sum of millions of isolated individual actions, or do we shine a light on the variety of social, cultural, familial, environmental, political, and economic factors that shape our food choices? A sociologist wouldn't focus solely on the individual's actions to explain this change but would begin to investigate the social conditions that have changed since the 1970s. A sociologist would ask: What are the structural relations creating *paths of least resistance* that make eating food made away from home far more likely to occur today than fifty years ago? Current research at the national level points toward several factors: a larger percentage of women working outside the home, more dual-earner households, smaller family sizes, higher household incomes, more convenient and affordable fast-food options, and increased marketing and advertising by fast-food companies.

Increased consumption of food away from home is therefore dependent on an infrastructure of everyday life that pushes people toward choosing such foods. For instance, the *stalled revolution* within gender relations played a strong role in the movement toward consuming food made away from home. The mass movement of women into the workforce after the 1950s occurred alongside men's refusal to share the work of preparing breakfast, lunch, and dinner. As a result, women juggling the *second shift* of paid work outside the home as well as cooking for the family sought time-saving solutions to food preparation and found them in on-the-go meals, options that were now more affordable for families with two incomes and fewer mouths to feed due to declining family size. Yet, this movement toward eating food made outside the home was itself premised on a transformation in the food service industry, whose economic model is premised on agricultural surpluses. The rise of fast-food companies would not be possible without a capitalist agricultural system prone to systemic overproduction of corn, wheat, and soybeans, tendencies that are supported through federal subsidy structures that subsidize the price of corn, wheat, and soybeans. This combination

Food for Thought *continued*

of market and state practices has created an environment of cheap beef, chicken, and pork, as the low-priced corn, wheat, and soybeans are fed to these animals to fatten them up, which in turn has created relatively affordable fast food and on-the-go meals. The omnipresence of fast-food options is subsequently reinforced by their constant marketing and advertising as solutions to a fast paced life where we are constantly on the go.

The movement of women out of the home and into paid employment, men's refusal to cook dinner, a food system whose massive surpluses keep food cheap, and increased access to and marketing of fast food are all important for understanding the structural roots of the increase in eating food prepared away from home. Consequently, through the sociological imagination eating such foods is understood as a "public issue" of social structure rather than a "private trouble" of the individual, and a result not solely of our own making but a choice we are pushed toward based on the world in which we live.

Sources

Hoschild, Arlie. 2012. *The Second Shift*. 3d ed. New York: Avon Books.

Nestle, Marion. 2013. *Food Politics: How the Food Industry Influences Nutrition, and Health*. 3d ed. Berkeley: University of California Press.

Simon, Michelle. 2006. *Appetite for Profit*. New York: Nation Books.

US Department of Agriculture. 2014. "Food-Away-from-Home." http://www.ers.usda .gov/topics/food-choices-health/food-consumption-demand/food-away-from-home. aspx.

rebelling or accepting, and the cultural forms which rebellion or acceptance may take. For instance, you might choose to reject many of the social norms or rules that your family and community have imposed upon you. Your society has established forms of rebellion for you to adopt. You can get something pierced, get a tattoo or two, dye your hair a distinctly unnatural color, and wear an ironic T-shirt. You can even go to events where hundreds of rebellious people like you come together and display their very similar expressions of difference from the established social norms. You might think of this as one of a number of "rebellion kits" that society has prepared for your use. Mainstream culture in any society has its social norms and so do its subcultures that respond to that mainstream culture. The rebellion options for a young gay college student from a middle-class suburban, white Christian family in twenty-first-century America are quite different from the rebellion options for a similarly positioned person in Uganda. Family, culture, and geography matter sociologically in the shaping of your life and life course.

Geography also matters in some sociologically interesting ways. The skill sets you develop living rurally are very different from the skill sets you learn as an urbanite. And your socialization into those skill sets—that is, how you learn what you need to know to get by—is shaped by your geographic location.

Did you grow up going fishing with a family member? Did you grow up going to the art museum with a family member? Did you learn how to snowmobile as a child? Did you learn how to surf? The ecosystem you grow up in shapes how you understand your place in the world and how you negotiate it. Did you grow up playing Little League baseball? Did you grow up playing stick-ball in the street? Did you move to the United States and have to figure out what baseball is? Did you grow up playing ice hockey? Did you grow up with farm chores? Did you grow up taking the subway? Baseball, hockey, surfing, snowmobiling, fishing, farm chores, and subway riding are all things socially created before you got here and that you learned or did not learn, largely depending on where you found yourself on this planet. And depending upon how much you've moved or traveled in your life, you may find yourself as a freshman in college meeting people who have never gone fishing or never been on a subway for the first time in your life. You should talk to them and find out what it was like to run through the spray of an open fire hydrant in the street to cool off in the summer, or to jump in the swimming hole, or run into the ocean, or to have never been near enough water to do any of those things. Where you learn to live your life, and where you do live your life, matters for your understanding of what it means to live a life.

Place on earth matters, and place in history matters. The time or era into which you were born and in which you will live your life deeply impacts the social constraints and opportunities you face. Look around your introduction to sociology classroom and consider who wouldn't be in college if this were two hundred years ago: women in the United States did not have access to higher education then, so everyone in your class would be male. Looking around your class today, it is likely that most of your classmates are women, as women's college attendance now exceeds that of men. History has altered gender norms, roles, and rules over time. Two hundred years ago, college was primarily for the wealthy privileged elite. If you or some of your classmates are not part of the top 1 percent in wealth and income in the country today, you can see the historical impacts of the creation of public colleges and universities, scholarships, loan programs, and the socioeconomic need for a more broadly educated working population. Is everyone in your class white? Most African Americans were denied access to higher education before the Civil War and lacked access to many colleges and universities until these institutions were forcibly desegregated in the civil rights era of the 1950s and 1960s. African Americans are still underrepresented in college, as are Latinos. Only recently has Latino college attendance exceeded that of African Americans. If you are going to college with a racially and ethnically diverse student body, you are having a very different experience than college students had two hundred years ago. People who came before you, acting individually and in groups, changed social conditions in ways that altered what going to college would be like for you.

Today, about 32 percent of Americans complete a bachelor's degree, and women earn about 52 percent of those. Fifty percent of Asian Americans, 32 percent of whites, and 22 percent of African Americans complete bachelor's degrees. If you lived in the Russian Federation instead of the United States, you would be more likely to complete an associate's degree or higher. If you lived in Portugal, you would be less likely to earn a degree past high school. You probably did not decide for yourself if you would live in the United States, Russia, or Portugal, but the fact of where you happen to find yourself living either increases or decreases the chances of you going to and completing college. Your race, class, gender, the country you live in, and the era into which you were born have all played a role in landing you in an introduction to sociology college course—one that has a different mix of students than college courses had two hundred years ago. Who goes to college two hundred years from now—and whether going to college even exists two hundred years from now—will be determined by people creating, affecting, and being affected by a series of complex social forces operating over time. Based on two hundred years of historical trends, we might expect college to become something more broadly available across all classes and races and genders and places. However, with tuitions going up, student aid going down, the number of women in college increasing, and the percentage of nonwhites attending college increasing, we might expect college in the United States to become the domain of only very rich women of color. What is important to remember in terms of the sociological imagination is that what landed you in college is not just your intelligence and motivation alone. Your family expectations and position, your culture, your race, your gender, your socioeconomic class, the country you live in, and the historical era into which you were born all have played a part in determining whether college would be an option for you and whether you would be willing and able to access that option. Taking a class about the sociological imagination should help you to understand how you came to be taking a class about the sociological imagination. It might also make your head spin a bit. That's okay. It gets better.

SOCIOLOGY IS A SCIENCE

Sociology, the systematic study of society, is a science. That may sound a bit strange since sociology does not look much like chemistry, physics, biology, or the other so-called natural sciences. Science is a hunt for patterns. Natural scientists hunt for patterns in the natural world and then try to explain those patterns. For instance, the sun comes up once every 24 hours. The pattern of the sun rising every 24 hours is observable, measurable, and therefore empirically verifiable. It is an observable natural fact that the sun rises every 24 hours. The series of observations that resulted in accepting the pattern of sun rising as fact comprise natural science data. Systematically collected observations revealed a pattern in the natural world. Social scientists do much the same thing in their observations of the social world. For example, when unemployment rises, domestic violence increases. The pattern of the relationship between increases in rates of unemployment and increases in rates of domestic violence has been studied by sociologists. Data have been systemically collected, and the relationship has been observed across time and place. As sure as the sun comes up every 24 hours, you can count on domestic violence going up when unemployment increases. The relationship between unemployment and domestic violence is an observable pattern in the social world. Our knowledge of that relationship as a social fact is the result of the systematic study of the social world. In this case, it is a measurable, empirically verifiable pattern and one that illustrates the intersection of biography and history. The chance that you will personally experience domestic violence is affected by your community, state, and country's rate of unemployment at any particular historical moment. Scientists hunt for patterns and have established specific methods for making observations, collecting data, and analyzing that data. Lesson 2 of this book will introduce you to the methodologies that sociologists use to hunt for patterns in the social world.

The hunt for patterns is only part of the scientific enterprise. Natural scientists usually don't stop at just identifying patterns in the natural world; they also want to explain those patterns. Why does the sun come up every 24 hours? For a long time, people believed it was because the earth stood still in the middle of the universe and the sun revolved around it on a set path at a set speed. That was a theory, a framework for understanding why the observable natural fact of regular sun rises occurred. It took a lot of corollary scientific observations of other patterns (the apparent movement of the stars, planets, etc.) to figure out that that theory was wrong. It turns out that a better theory is that the earth is rotating at a regular speed, so that the sun does not actually "rise," but the earth turns. That theory has been so extensively tested through a wide range of methods of observation and data collection that most of us now accept it as a natural fact. You can thank the intersection of your biography with this particular history that believing that the world turns and the sun does not revolve around it won't result in your being imprisoned or killed for heresy by your dominant social institutions. If you found yourself living at a different time (six hundred years ago) and a different place (Europe), your beliefs and the consequences of your beliefs would in all likelihood be quite different.

Like natural scientists, sociologists seek to explain the patterns they observe and develop theories to organize those explanations. Why would higher unemployment lead to greater incidence of domestic violence? That is, what could be going on in society to link high unemployment to higher rates of domestic violence? Is there a causal relationship? How could unemployment cause domestic violence to increase? Let's think through this together. First, if people are unemployed, they are more likely to spend more time at home instead of being away at work. If people are at home together more, the chances that everything that people sometimes do together—laugh, cook, make love, hit each other, and so on—will go up. People don't have a reason or a mechanism to report incidents of laughing, cooking, or making love to institutional authorities, so we would not know if these increased with unemployment. (We have good reason to believe that they actually don't). With a little more insight, we might propose (or hypothesize) that unemployment leads to feelings of frustration and anger at the individual level and at the family level. As families experience economic stress, anxiety increases, and people vent these feelings of anger and frustration on each other. Sometimes that venting may take the form of physical violence. That sounds like a reasonable theory or explanation for the pattern we observe between unemployment and domestic violence. Like figuring out why the sun rises every 24 hours, we would need a lot of corollary scientific observations of other patterns to figure out if our theory is right or wrong. We might have to interview victims and perpetrators of domestic violence to find out if the economic stress of unemployment was central in a high percentage of incidents. In doing systematic interviews with a representative sample of victims, we might discover that alcohol and other drug use was also a factor. In fact, much sociological research has been done on this pattern, and sociologists are quite confident that they understand the factors and relationships that produce increased domestic violence from higher unemployment. If you had had this insight into the relationship between economic trends and personal troubles 150 years ago, you might be remembered today as a revolutionary thinker (see Emile Durkheim). Today, understanding that such a relationship between personal troubles and public issues exists now only qualifies you as an introduction to sociology student. Let's look at a couple of examples of how sociologists have analyzed the relationships between personal troubles and public issues using a **nested analysis** approach.

NESTED ANALYSIS

Corporation Nation

Charles Derber, a sociologist at Boston College, has written about what he calls the "anxious class" in his book *Corporation Nation: How Corporations Are Taking Over Our Lives and What We Can Do about It* (Derber 1998). Now, anxiety is something that we experience individually. We all know what it feels like to be anxious, and anxiety would appear to be a very lonely, isolating, individual-level phenomenon. So how could a "class" be anxious? What Derber is writing about when he examines the anxious class is changes in the global economy. So, how do changes in the global economy create anxiety in individuals, and what could these individuals have in common to lead Derber to call them a class? He starts by locating the anxiety-ridden in their historical context. He argues that American middle- and upper-middle-class workers are experiencing job and socioeconomic status anxiety in a way that they didn't in an earlier era. That is, he analyzes why the particular time and place that people find themselves in now creates anxiety.

In the early post-World War II era in the United States, the middle class expanded. Industrial jobs boomed, unions were strong and delivered high wages and good benefits to their blue-collar members, US-based corporations dominated the global economy, and they hired white-collar managers and delivered upper-middle-class salaries. Certainly, for white males with middle-class and upper-middle-class jobs, things looked pretty good. Job security was high, and expectations of upward social mobility were realistic. It was reasonable to expect that you would keep your job working for the same firm and that you would move up in the workplace hierarchy, earning better money, buying a house and a car or two, and sending your kids to college. It was easy to believe that this was because Americans worked hard, were diligent, dedicated, God-fearing, law abiding, and had strong traditional American values. If there was anxiety to be had by this class, it was not related to job security or the economy. Being a sociologist, Derber notes that this happy condition of this class was not solely because of the hard work and strong values of its members. At that historical moment, American industrial expansion had peaked partly due to the government effort during World War II to expand our production capacity. Our potential European and Japanese industrial competitors found their factories and infrastructure in postwar ruin. A postwar baby boom rapidly expanded markets for consumer goods. Labor unions had gained strength under the government support of the New Deal as the country had struggled to pull out of the Great Depression prior to the war. That is, a set of social factors external to individual workers, or even to an individual class, created conditions under which the American economy could thrive. This was specific to an historical moment (and therefore is unlikely to be reproduced in the future). For the most part, Americans had low levels of economic anxiety, but this was not primarily a result of their own individual attributes and abilities. It was an easy time for individuals (at least for white males) to find themselves successful and to take personal credit for that success. That is a moment in history that many white males today wish they could return to.

Derber contrasts that historical moment with the end of the twentieth century. In that moment (and ours), industrial jobs were leaving the United States rapidly, American manufacturing was in decline, companies were downsizing, both blue-collar and white-collar workers were being laid off, and union membership was dropping. People who had grown to expect that if they worked hard and followed the rules they would keep their good paying jobs and maybe even move up the economic hierarchy found themselves out on the street. People became anxious. Their economic expectations were suddenly out of sync with their economic realities. People lost their jobs and then lost their homes. If they kept their jobs they found their wages cut, their benefits reduced, and their jobs contingent, temporary, or constantly under threat of elimination. They couldn't send their kids to college or had to take on massive debt to do so. Savings disappeared. Personal debt went up. People wondered what was going on. What had happened? These were the same Americans who worked hard; were diligent, dedicated, God-fearing, and law abiding; and had strong traditional American values. Unemployment went up but not because people had suddenly become lazy, incompetent, or uneducated. It was a difficult time in which to think of oneself as successful. People blamed themselves. Derber, however, links the emergence of widespread economic anxiety among the American middle and upper-middle classes to changes in the global economy and to changes in social institutions. In particular, he identifies the rising power of corporations as social institutions relative to the declining power of labor unions and the state (government) as a primary cause of the social conditions that created individual anxiety for people. As communications, information, and transportation technology changed, corporations found it easier to operate globally. They no longer needed to maintain good relations with American workers in American towns or to rely on Americans having good paychecks to create American markets for American consumer goods. They could move production and jobs to other places in other countries where labor was cheap and unions couldn't organize to deliver job security and benefits to their members. Suddenly, industrial enterprises that had been fundamental to the postwar American economy were being moved out of the country. Jobs don't leave by themselves; somebody has to decide to move them. And corporate executives decided to move American manufacturing jobs out of the country, leaving American workers bewildered. General Motors shut down plants in and around Detroit. People who had been automobile workers their whole lives, and who expected their kids to be able to get good jobs in the industry too, found themselves in a society with dramatically fewer auto manufacturing jobs. Other corporations threatened to leave if communities, states, or the federal government didn't give them tax breaks or subsidies. Corporations sought wage cuts and benefits cuts from unions and threatened to further reduce employment if they did not get them. And as union membership declined, the relative power of corporations increased. They pressed the government for **deregulation**. Deregulation allowed corporations to do more of what they wanted, which was to increase profits by keeping employment low, wages low, and benefits low. They moved toward flexible workforces, meaning that jobs were temporary and workers could be added and let go at a moment's notice. And as jobs became flexible, temp services became the largest employers. The American middle and upper-middle classes found themselves not knowing from day to day if they would have a job tomorrow, or have health insurance for themselves and their families, or if they would be able to make the rent or mortgage next month, or send their kids to college, or make the car payments, or find another job. They became the anxious class—and if they lacked a sociological imagination, they blamed themselves.

As sociological research has revealed, economic anxiety increases alcoholism and drug use, divorce rates, domestic violence, dropout rates, and suicide rates. The families and individuals that experience these very personal feeling troubles may or may not realize that they are a symptom of larger social trends. It is not obvious that the relative increase in the power of corporations as social institutions can lead to increases in the likelihood of drug addiction or suicide. Certainly, there are a lot of factors

SOCIOLOGY AT WORK
WORK AND THE SOCIOLOGICAL IMAGINATION: LAYOFFS AT PILLOWTEX
Arne L. Kalleberg

The textile city of Kannapolis straddles the border of Rowan and Cabarrus counties in North Carolina. Founded in 1887 by the Cannon Mills textile company, Kannapolis was not incorporated until the 1980s; in the 1970s, it was the largest company town in the United States. In 1985, Fieldcrest Mills acquired Cannon Mills, changing its name to Fieldcrest-Cannon, and became the world's number-one manufacturer of towels and blankets. In 1997, Pillowtex (a pillow manufacturing company based in Dallas, Texas) bought Fieldcrest-Cannon's blanket manufacturing operations. In 2003, Pillowtex went bankrupt and closed the plant. Over 4,800 workers were laid off. This was the largest single layoff in North Carolina history and attracted a great deal of national attention.

Many of the laid-off Pillowtex workers had worked at these plants their whole lives (the average length of employment there was 17 years), and had parents and even grandparents who worked there too (42 percent had a relative who also worked at Pillowtex). Nearly half of these workers had not completed high school, and their average age was 46 years. Seventy percent were unwilling to relocate out of the geographical area in search of a new job. It is not surprising, then, that these workers had great difficulty getting other jobs, due to their relatively low levels of education, age, and long-term attachment to a particular employer and locality due to family and other social reasons (Beatty, Longman, and Tran 2004).

These Pillowtex workers did not become unemployed because they lacked motivation, didn't want to work hard, or had low education. We cannot explain the unemployment at Pillowtex on the basis of any of their individual characteristics. Their unemployment was not their "private trouble," but rather represented what C. Wright Mills referred to as "public issues."

Explaining why these workers became unemployed requires us to use a nested, multilevel analysis. The Pillowtex workers became unemployed because of changes that have taken place in the textile industry as a whole in recent years as well as in this particular company. Advances in automation and technology in the manufacture of textiles meant that fewer workers were needed to produce towels, blankets, and other fabrics. More liberal trade policies made it easier for global companies with lower wage costs to compete with American companies. Globalization and technological change encouraged American companies to offshore the manufacture of textiles to countries with lower costs of production and labor standards and made it easier for them to do so. Management mistakes, such as poor inventory control and taking on too much debt, further weakened the company financially. Moreover, Pillowtex was based in Dallas and so did not have the kind of commitment to the local community and its citizens as did previous owners. All these structural factors combined to encourage Pillowtex to file for bankruptcy protection and to cease operations in Kannapolis.

Source
Beatty, M., D. Longman, and V. Tran. 2004, April. "Community Response to the Pillowtex Textile Kannapolis Closing: The 'Rapid Response' Team as a Facilitative Device." North Carolina Employment Security Commission. www.unc.edu/depts/econ/PlantClosure/beatty_longman.tran.pdf.

at play for any single individual or family. But individuals and families live their lives in specific historical moments, and in specific places, and those moments and places have tremendous influence over our life courses. Being a hard-working autoworker and United Auto Workers member in Detroit in the 1950s did not lead to the same social outcomes for you and your family as being a hard-working autoworker and United Auto Workers member in Detroit in the 1980s. Derber's sociological analysis shines a light on the changes in technology, the global economy, and institutional power relations that shaped an historical moment and the lives of the people in it.

Derber uses what sociologists call a **nested analysis** to demonstrate how historically significant macro-level changes in the global economy and institutional power relations impact the personal biographies of individuals living in a particular historical moment. In a nested analysis, the individual is understood as being located within a family, and the family is understood as being located within a community, and the community is understood as being located within a country with particular institutional arrangements, and the country is understood as being located within a global world. That is, the web of social relationships that connect each level to each other is illuminated by noting that each level, from micro (individual) to macro (global), exists in a specific social context. Nested analysis is an approach you will find employed throughout this book to shed light on the relationships between biography and history, micro-level social phenomena and macro-level social forces, and your life and the specific time and place you are living it. Derber's nested analysis of the social impacts on individuals of a distinct historical moment is illustrated in Table 1–1.

Table 1–1 offers a simple illustration of how changes at the macro level toward global competition and global production facilitated changes in

Table 1–1 Nested Analysis of Two Historical Moments in the American Economy

	Post-World War II	Late Twentieth Century
Global	US industrial expansion Europe and Japan disabled	Global competition Global production
Institutions	US companies dominant Strong labor unions Strong US government	Transnational corporations Weak labor unions Deregulation
Communities	Strong, place-based manufacturing	Deindustrialization
Families	Secure employment Upward mobility	Anxious Contingent labor
Individuals	Optimistic Feeling successful	Pessimistic Feeling failure

the relative power of social institutions (corporations, unions, and the state) at the national level. It notes that changes at the global and institutional levels facilitated changes at the community level toward deindustrialization and that produced micro-level (family and individual) anxiety as work became less secure. This cascade of social change finally increases the chances that people will feel pessimistic about their economic future and that they are failures personally. Of course, people have agency, and individuals can do things on an individual level to increase their own chances of success. However, your likelihood of landing a good job in the steel mill goes down when the steel mill moves to another country, and the chances of getting a second job at the call center is reduced when the call center is moved to another country as well. Your ability to do well in college is reduced if tuition rises out of your reach or when student loan programs are cut. That does not mean that you can't get a good education or get a good job—but it does mean that fewer people will, even if the number of great potential students and great potential workers goes up. You can control some of the factors, but the sociological imagination will help you to be aware that jobs and college are things that any particular society, at any particular moment, does or does not make available, to more or fewer people.

Families That Work

A second example that demonstrates nested analysis looks at the American family. In *Families That Work: Policies for Reconciling Parenthood and Employment,* Janet C. Gornick and Marcia K. Meyers (2003) examine the problems that families have faced since the 1960s and 1970s when there was a sharp rise in women's employment. Prior to that time, the "traditional family" had a gendered division of labor: men earned income in the workforce, and women raised the children at home. Since women have entered the workforce (not simply out of desire but also out of economic need), issues have arisen that American society has not yet completely addressed. Gornick and Meyers focus on three social problems. First, child well-being has declined. Second, working parents are overburdened. Third, there continues to be gender inequality in the workforce. The authors use quantitative data to support their claims. For instance, they track aggregate measures for child well-being such as birth weight, school achievement, hours of television viewing, teenage pregnancies, and so on. A quantitative approach like this, using numerical information, allows us to see broad patterns in family life in the United States. Based on this approach, the authors argue that the way we have structured the dual demands of employment and caregiving in the United States fails families, both parents and children. Does it have to be this way? How can we make it better?

This piece is an excellent example of demonstrating the differences between addressing a public problem privately versus publicly. The response to these problems in the United States is for each family to work out their own solution. Some families use private child care, some families work non-standard hours so that one parent can always be home, some families are simply overburdened and children are left alone, and many families suffer from poverty. These are private solutions to a social problem. As Americans, we tend to think of ourselves as independent, and we try to deal with these things on our own, with varying degrees of success. Other countries that are also dealing with the same social problems have taken different approaches—more public, collective approaches.

Gornick and Meyers compare twelve high-income, industrialized countries in terms of their public policies toward families and the outcomes for parents and children. The strategy of using comparative data enables us to see that the way that we do things in our society is not the only way to address social problems (or not address them, as the case may be). See Figure 1–2. This shows that in the United States, parents are more likely to work on evenings and weekends than in other nations for which Gornick and Meyers have data (Belgium, Luxembourg, Germany, France, the Netherlands, and the United Kingdom). While parents in other nations also do this kind of split-shift parenting, it is most prevalent in the United States. In Belgium, the comparison group with the lowest numbers, only 5 percent of parents work in the evenings, and 12 percent during the weekends. The US rates are more than twice as high, with 12 percent working evenings and 28 percent working over weekends. Comparative analysis opens our eyes to possibilities about alternative social arrangements. It also enables us to see relationships between causes and consequences. In this case, we see that women entering

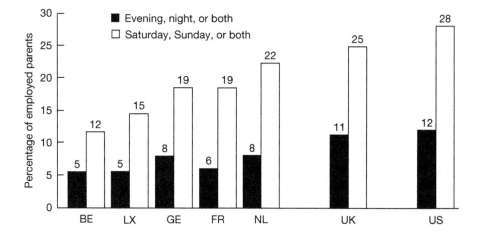

Figure 1–2 Prevalence of Evening, Night, and Weekend Work Among Employed Parents, 1997.

In *Families That Work: Policies for Reconciling Parenthood and Employment.*

© 2003 Russell Sage Foundation, 112 East 64th Street, New York, NY 10065. Reprinted with permission.

Table 1–2 Nested Analysis Comparing Two Types of National Responses to Address the Public Problems Created by Dual-Earner Families

	United States	Some European Countries
Global	Women enter the workforce; new dual-earner families create social problems (declining child well-being, overburdened parents, gender inequality in the workforce)	Women enter the workforce; new dual-earner families create social problems (declining child well-being, overburdened parents, gender inequality in the workforce)
Institutions	Limited public responses to "public issues"; private solutions including working nonstandard hours, paying large sums for private child care of questionable quality, and self-care for children	More extensive public response to "public issues," including "publicly regulated and financed paid family leave, regulation of working time, and public early childhood education and care policies" (Gornick and Meyers 2003, 13)
Families and individuals	Economic insecurity and poverty; overburdened parents; lack of parent–child time; women earn less than men; low-quality child care; poor school achievement	Greater economic security; parents have more time with children, especially in early years; smaller wage gap; child-care quality regulated; higher school achievement

the workplace caused problems in many high-income, industrial societies. From this point, we can continue the analysis to see that some countries responded to this with public policies to address the problem, and some did not. Public policies included "publicly regulated and financed paid family leave, regulation of working time, and public early childhood education and care policies" (Gornick and Meyers 2003, 13). Did the policies make a difference? Was there a consequence? In this case, policies matter. Where policies were enacted, they improved the lives for families; where they were not, problems persisted and worsened (see Table 1–2). Public solutions were better for families than the private solutions that the United States currently uses.

The nested analysis used by Gornick and Meyers allows us to see how our individual circumstances, such as having or being overburdened parents, are a consequence of larger social forces, such as lack of social policies to support families. In 1971, when President Nixon vetoed the bipartisan Comprehensive Child Development Act (that would have created universal child care), he changed what the experience of balancing family and work would be like for generations of Americans. Public policy matters for private lives.

CAREERS IN SOCIOLOGY

We believe there is intrinsic value to possessing the sociological imagination. It enables you to understand your life and the lives of those around you with greater depth. But does that pay the rent? What kind of career can you have with a degree in sociology? This is a question our students ask a lot. There are a few ways to answer this. The first way is to focus on the skills that sociology students learn. You will learn to read critically, collect and analyze data, and write reports. In most sociology programs, you will learn how to use computer applications, such as SPSS and SAS, to analyze quantitative data. These skills can be applied to many types of work. You could use them as a retail store manager, a government analyst, a private sector market researcher, or a nonprofit fundraiser. A second way to answer this question is to think about the topics that are the focus of sociology. We analyze social problems, try to disentangle issues related to stratification and inequality, and seek to understand the causes of social change. Students turn these concerns into careers in journalism, public policy, and working for organizations that advocate for social change. Other students love doing research. We have former students who work for think tanks and government agencies doing primary data collection and analysis. Some students go on to get PhDs and become sociology professors. If you're interested in learning more about this, the American Sociological Association produces an online guide to careers in sociology that elaborates on these topics and presents research about the types of jobs recent sociology graduates across the United States have today. We've included that and some additional websites at the end of the chapter that you can use to look up existing job opportunities.

THE REST OF THE BOOK

We have organized this book into four sections that correspond to themes commonly taught in introduction to sociology courses: (1) Why Sociology? (2) What Unites Us? (3) What Divides Us? and (4) How Do Societies Change?

The first section, "Why Sociology," has two lessons—the one you're reading (Lesson 1: The Sociological Imagination) and Lesson 2: Theory and Methods. The goal of the first section is to introduce you to a sociological way of thinking and to explain how sociologists do sociology. This lesson introduces some of the organizing principals of the book: the concept of the sociological imagination and what we mean by "nested analysis." These ideas are intended to orient you to a sociological perspective in which individuals' actions can be understood in the context of larger social processes, such as institutional, national, and global change. This lesson, and the ones that follow, also provide examples of work done by sociologists that represent qualitative analysis and quantitative analysis. Lesson 2 will expand upon qualitative and quantitative analysis and how we collect data to find patterns in social life and how we develop explanations for those patterns. Lesson 2 also provides you with a brief history of the discipline of sociology, which has existed as a formal academic discipline for less than two centuries.

The second section of the book is titled "What Unites Us?" The two lessons in that section explain the social mechanisms that maintain society from one generation to the next. Lesson 3: Socialization and Culture looks at how individual personalities are shaped by culture. It examines the arrow of the diagram in Figure 1–1 that points from society to the individual: How did you get to be the way you are? What makes you a part of society? The second lesson, Lesson 4: Social Institutions, examines a few of the major institutions that organize our day-to-day life. You may not think about it much, but our society has figured out how to deal with many issues that could make our day-to-day life troublesome. We produce goods, such as food, clothing, and shelter (economic institutions); we keep some degree of order (legal and political institutions); we take care of sick people (health institutions); and we teach our future generations how to maintain the system, through families and educational institutions. If we can try to make visible some of these underlying structures of society, we get a better understanding of why it is that we wake up every day and do the things we do. This section focuses on the social glue that makes day-to-day life possible. It also recognizes that society, culture, and social institutions are not static. They change and force us to consider the implications of change. For instance, some questions you might consider include: How does the increased use of social media influence childhood socialization? What are the consequences of the changing definition of the family?

The third section, "What Divides Us?" contains three lessons: Lesson 5: Race and Intersectionality, Lesson 6: Class and Intersectionality, and Lesson 7: Gender, Sexuality, and Intersectionality. We hope you're wondering what intersectionality means! We'll get to that later. For now, let us put these chapters in the context of the sociological imagination. When Mills asks us to consider our fate by considering the fates of others in our same circumstances (in other words, look at others in the same groups that you are part of), some of the main groupings in our society are race, class, and gender. Sociologists can tell a lot about individuals if they know their race, class, and gender. Obviously, there are other social groupings that also matter. For instance, we could also talk about religion, age, or political party. We have chosen to discuss the categories that we think make the biggest difference in terms of social stratification. By **social stratification**, we mean, how people are ranked in society. We urge you to think about other social groupings in regard to stratification, too. The concept of **intersectionality** forces us to think about how our membership in multiple groups affects who we are and where we fall in the stratification system. Does race, class, or gender have a bigger impact on one's life opportunities? These lessons address questions such as: Is the significance of race in the United States increasing or decreasing? How does increasing economic inequality affect democracy? Why is there gender inequality in wages?

The final section of the book asks "How Do Societies Change?" While the second section of the book argues that there is a lot of continuity in social life, this section focuses on how large-scale social changes occur. As we know from the example of Derber's work in *Corporation Nation*, as broad social changes occur, these changes also impact social institutions, communities, families, and individuals. Lesson 8: Forces of Social Change examines some of the major causes and consequences of social change with a series of examples focused on the United States. In the next lesson, Lesson 9:

Global Dynamics, social change is examined at the global level. This chapter makes connections cross-nationally. It explains how an era of globalization has made it possible that actions taking place halfway around the globe can have consequences for you. The final lesson of the book, Lesson 10: Public Sociology, looks to the role of sociologists in creating social change. Some questions that this section raises include: How and why does social change happen? Will countries become more or less alike due to globalization? What control do we have over social change? How might we shape the future?

A few more things. You might have noticed that there are eleven authors of this book. We're authors of three of the chapters, and the coeditors of the volume. Why did we go about gathering nine other sociological experts to write the other lessons and boxes? Well, you might have noticed that the idea of "society" is a pretty broad concept. We think so. As such, the field of sociology is very diverse. It has numerous subspecialties. It is impossible to be an expert in all of the areas of sociology; for that matter, it is really difficult to pick out which of the many subfields should be presented in introductory sociology. You can't fit it all into one course. You have to pick and choose what's important for students to learn first. In addition to our own ideas about what's most important to include after collective decades of teaching sociology, we also had some help figuring this out because a number of sociologists have actually studied this.[1] We invited experts in the various fields we believe are most important to contribute from their field of specialization. In this way, we hope to bring you the most important topics taught by experts in the field, who we also think are great teachers and communicators. At the introductory level, you may not be able to read expert-level work, so we asked each sociologist to pitch their lesson to the introductory-level student.

There are some specific elements that you will find in each lesson of this book. First, each author incorporates the sociological imagination and nested analysis. Second, they use examples that are relevant to you. Third, each lesson has examples of sociological studies that include qualitative and quantitative data and analysis. Fourth, each lesson contains a box discussing how the chapter theme relates to the topic of work, titled "Sociologists at Work," and a box discussing how the lesson relates to the topic of food, titled "Food for Thought." To help you study, we've bolded key words in each lesson. At the end of the book, we have a combined index and glossary that defines key terms. To help you apply and think about the work in the context of your own life, each lesson has discussion questions. The main points of each lesson

---

[1] Caroline Hodges Persell, Kathryn May Pfeiffer, and Ali Syed (2007) interviewed leading sociologists to find out what the most important principles they wanted students to understand after taking an Introduction to Sociology class. Persell and her collaborators compared their findings with three other analyses of content in sociology: (i) Wagenaar's (2004) survey of members of the Section on Undergraduate Education of the American Sociological Association (ASA); (ii) the ASA's (2004) report *Liberal Learning and the Sociology Major*; and (iii) Grauerholz and Gibson's (2006) analysis of 418 sociology syllabi published by the ASA. The topics covered in the ten chapters of this short book are those that are considered important by a majority of these sources and are ones we consider critical in our own introductory courses.

are quickly summarized in a "Take-Aways" list. Each lesson also lists websites and readings for further research. Finally, because the world is shifting and words alone cannot capture the richness of social life, each lesson starts with a photograph to help you visualize what these concepts mean in the real world. We ask you some questions about the photo in the beginning of the lesson. At the very end, we offer you our reflections on the photo. There's a subfield of sociology called "visual sociology." We couldn't fit in a whole lesson on it, but we thought we'd at least give you a taste. Enjoy!

Lesson Take-Aways

- Sociologists examine the relationship between agency (what we can individually control) and structure (social constraints and opportunities that are beyond immediate individual control).
- The sociological imagination is a perspective that allows us to understand an individual as the product of their history and biography. It helps us understand individual behaviors as shaped by larger social structures: historical context and group membership (such as our race, class, gender, nationality, sexual orientation, etc.)
- Sociology is the systematic study of society. It uses the scientific method to ask questions and collect and analyze data to identify and understand social patterns.
- Nested analysis situates individuals within the larger social contexts that they are located, including family, community, country, and so on. Nested analysis connects micro-level social phenomena (what happens at the individual level) to macro-level social forces (historical trends and social structures).

Discussion Questions

1. In what ways have social structures and social institutions shaped the choices that you have made? How have they shaped the big choices, such as your decision to attend college? How have they shaped the little choices, such as what you had for breakfast this morning?
2. C. Wright Mills argues that the life of an individual can only be understood in relation to the history of a society. In what ways has the history of your society shaped you as an individual? What historical events or processes seem particularly important to your life course now?
3. List a few personal troubles that you or people close to you have had. Can you connect those personal troubles to public issues? Are there ways in which public policies affected the way people close to you resolved those troubles?

Sources

Berger, Peter L. 1963. *Invitation to Sociology: A Humanistic Perspective*. New York: Anchor Books.

Derber, Charles. 1998. *Corporation Nation: How Corporations Are Taking Over Our Lives and What We Can Do about It*. New York: St. Martin's Griffin.

Gornick, Janet C. and Marcia K. Meyers. 2003. *Families That Work: Policies for Reconciling Parenthood and Employment.* New York: Russell Sage Foundation.

Grauerholz, Liz and Greg Gibson. 2006. "Articulation of Goals and Means in Sociology Courses: What Can We Learn from Syllabi." *Teaching Sociology* 34(1): 5–22.

Mills, C. Wright. 1959. *The Sociological Imagination.* New York: Oxford University Press.

Persell, Caroline Hodges, Kathryn May Pfeiffer, and Ali Syed. 2007. "What Should Students Understand after Taking Introduction to Sociology?" *Teaching Sociology* 35(4): 300–14.

Wagenaar, Theodore. 2004. "Is There a Core in Sociology? Results from a Survey." *Teaching Sociology* 32(1): 1–18.

Related Websites

American Sociological Association: www.asanet.org

Careers in Sociology: www.asanet.org/career-center/careers-sociology

CollegeGrad.com: www.collegegrad.com

Contexts: www.contexts.org

International Sociological Association: www.isa-sociology.org

Idealist: www.idealist.org

Society for the Study of Social Problems: www.sssp1.org

USAJobs: www.usajobs.gov

LESSON 1, PHOTO REFLECTION:

Cars and trucks filling the Brooklyn-Queens Expressway.
Photo by Ken Gould

An individual trying to get to work or school by car on a crowded thoroughfare experiences themselves as being stuck in traffic. Collectively, such individuals *are* traffic. You may choose to use private cars, public transportation, a bike, or walk to work or school, but the availability and ease of access to those options is largely determined by decisions made by others. Government policies, corporate influences, and other institutional actors have produced social patterns that shape when people will go to work or school, how close or far they may live from work or school, who can afford various transportation options, and where roads, rails, bike lanes, and buses will go. We chose this photo to represent the intersection of biography (your commute) and history (the construction of highways) and the relationship between private troubles (your being late for school or work) and public issues (how can we better manage our societal need to move people from place to place?). If you were the photographer, what picture would you take to represent the sociological imagination?

How would you study the police?

2

Theory and Methods

Tammy L. Lewis

How do sociologists know what we know? How is sociological knowledge different from what your grandmother tells you about "how those types of people are"? In what ways is it more or less valid than what you and your friends see and experience when you're out on a Saturday night? What are the goals of sociology? This lesson focuses on what sociologists do—how they ask questions, how they gather information to answer those questions, and how that information is used to find patterns in social behavior. Lesson 1 explained sociology's dominant lens—that is, a sociological way of thinking. Lesson 10 will describe how sociological findings are and can be used in the "real world." This lesson explains the practical means by which sociologists generate knowledge and produce generalizations about the social world.

SOCIOLOGISTS START WITH REAL QUESTIONS

Sociologists live and work in the real world, and we are affected by the social problems that we encounter on a regular basis. The topics we choose to examine often reflect our lived experiences. No surprise to C. Wright Mills, we are affected by our history and our biography. For instance, as an undergraduate sociology major looking for a topic to research for my senior thesis, one that spoke directly to me was the problem of pollution along the New Jersey shore. Every summer when I was growing up, my family would spend a week at the beach. Over time, going to the beach became less and less appealing as each year the news reports (and our own eyes) showed syringes and human excrement washing up on the beach. In my lifetime, I had seen a once very clean beach become disgusting. How could this change be explained? What was happening to tourism? To businesses reliant on tourism? What efforts were being made to improve the beach quality? Who, if anyone, was involved in these efforts? What were their motivations? Would they be successful? These questions became the basis of my senior thesis, and led me to a career as a sociologist who studies the environment, social movements, and sustainable development. Alas, C. Wright Mills would urge

33

me to examine my personal career trajectory in the context of the historical period in which I lived (one of increasing ocean pollution) and in the context of the social group(s) of which I was a member (upper-middle-class white Pennsylvanians who vacationed at the Jersey shore).

The founders of sociology were also motivated to address issues that they confronted based on their lived experiences in a particular historical moment. Sociology became an academic field in the late 1800s. Key to sociology's emergence were Karl Marx (born in Germany, 1818–1883), Emile Durkheim (born in France, 1858–1917), and Max Weber (born in Germany, 1864–1920). These three academics witnessed tremendous social change in their lifetimes. Europe was industrializing. The economic shift from agricultural work to factory work was accompanied by broad social changes: large numbers of people moved from the country to the city to work. Religious beliefs were challenged by science. People who had been ruled by aristocracies were gaining political power through democratic rule. The new field of sociology emerged to essentially ask: What just happened, and what's going to happen next? Sociologists didn't necessarily agree on the answers to these questions. For example, Marx saw the changes as potentially for the better, while Durkheim worried about what had been lost. In short, the first sociologists were attempting to explain their lived experiences, which coincided with the transition from "traditional" society to "modern" society. Another German sociologist, Ferdinand Tönnies (1855–1936), called this the shift from *gemeinschaft* (rural, kinship-based, values guided, collective community; translated simply as "community") to *gesellschaft* (urban, commercial, artificial, individualistic society; translated simply as "society").

There were reasons to be skeptical about the future. Along with the rapid industrialization and urbanization came poverty and disease. The industrial working class was extremely deprived. People worked long hours but were still hungry. There were no labor protections. Children worked in the factories. The "founding fathers" were not immune to these conditions. Karl Marx, who lived in London, lost three of his children to disease when they were infants.

THE FOUNDING FATHERS OF SOCIOLOGY AND THEIR LEGACY

The work of the founding fathers of sociology still shapes the types of questions that are asked and the logics that are used to understand patterns in society. As such, we will lay out a few of their key ideas. As you hopefully are already anticipating, as the social world has changed, so have the questions that sociologists ask about it.

Karl Marx is probably best known for his critique of capitalism. In 1848, he and his collaborator, Friedrich Engels, wrote "The Manifesto of the Communist Party." In this piece, they wrote of two "great hostile camps," of "two great classes." These two sides were the bourgeoisie (the capitalist owners of the "means of production," such as factory owners) and the proletariat (the industrial workers). Marx and Engels interpreted the history of humans as a history of conflict between the "haves" and the "have-nots," with the economy being the central engine of change in society. Over the history of human society—through tribal society, slavery, feudalism, and capitalism— the economic system defined the relationship between classes. They argued that this relationship between oppressors and oppressed shapes the rest of the social system (such as families and the political structure) and is justified by dominant ideologies (in other words, ideas about the way the world should be) that made extreme inequality seem acceptable. Marx and Engels argued that, historically, social change occurred through class conflict. Marx and Engels predicted that capitalism (the economic system) would create intense class conflict and that this conflict would create change in society. They believed that the change would eventually lead to workers taking control of production and that a new classless system, communism, would arise in which society's economic needs would be met without oppression. Another important work, *Capital*, published in German in 1865, further analyzed capitalism, socialism, and class struggle.

Other key themes from Marx and Engels's collaborations included ideas about the alienation of workers, class consciousness, the role of ideology in maintaining inequality, and more. Today, this way of looking at the world forms the basis of a school of thought called **conflict theory**. This perspective assumes that social change and conflict are normal, expected aspects of social life. When there is social order, conflict theorists look to sources of coercion and domination that make it appear to be such. Conflict theorists regard conflict as the main source of social change. C. Wright Mills's work followed in this tradition, as do many contemporary sociologists whose main interests focus on unequal power relationships in society. Contemporary issues, such as record income gaps between the rich and poor in the United States and Europe and the movements for social change to address these gaps (such as the Occupy Movements and the Bernie Sanders's presidential campaign in the United States), are the subjects of such analyses.

Max Weber (pronounced "Vaber"), a German founding father, was especially interested in understanding history and the causal factors that led things to be the way they were. He believed **rationalization** was the dominant trend in human history. In Weber's view, he saw a shift over time from human behavior that had been driven by values, traditions, and emotions to behaviors that were instead directed by rules and regulations set up by the bureaucracies of modern society. Weber writes extensively about **bureaucracies** in *Economy and Society* (published in German in 1922). Bureaucracies have written rules that establish how institutions will function; they set up operating procedures that in theory require that everyone is treated the same. This has pros and cons. Take, for example, your experience registering for classes. The plus side is that you know there is a procedure for signing up for classes. You don't have to rely on having a relative who works in the registrar's office to sign up for a class that you want to take. You don't have to worry that you won't be able to enroll in a class because you're a woman, gay, or Hispanic. These are the pros. But say you go to sign up for a class you need to graduate, and it is already full. The bureaucracy won't let you sign up, even though you beg and plead and make sure they know that you're a straight-A student, you need this class, and you can't afford to pay for the additional semester you will need to be in college to get the course. If the class is full, it is full. Those are the rules. You see the downside.

In Weber's most famous work, *The Protestant Ethic and the Spirit of Capitalism* (1905), he analyzes the factors that led to the development of *rational* capitalism (as opposed to *traditional* capitalism). He focuses on rational capitalism, but he sees rationalizing trends in all matters of social life, including science, law, and politics. Whereas Marx and Engels understand the emergence of rational capitalism as a stage in the human struggle over material resources (meaning over tangible items, such as factories, goods, and wages), Weber thinks that rational capitalism was the outcome of ideas, particularly religious ideas. Weber links the ideology of Protestantism (specifically Calvinism) to human behaviors in the economic system (the practices of saving and reinvestment) to explain the emergence of a modern system of capitalism. To make a lengthy argument brief: in traditional capitalism (not under the influence of Calvinism), profits could be spent to enjoy life. As Calvinism emerged, that changed. Calvinists believed that they should work hard to earn profit and those profits should be reinvested. The reinvestment and subsequent accumulation was considered a Calvinist's ethical, value-based duty. Calvinist believed that capital accumulation was a worldly sign from God that a person was "chosen" for salvation. Hard work, saving, and reinvestment became known as the Protestant ethic. Thus, religious beliefs led to reinvestment, which allowed for the accumulation of capital, which allowed for modern/rational capitalism to expand. In this way, Weber argued that the origins of our economic system stem from ideas—specifically, a sense of religious duty. The idea led to changes in the economic system.

Weber found that over time people simply continued to reinvest and accumulate capital for the sake of accumulation (being rich), and the connection to the religious motivations (being chosen) was lost. He finds irony in this and describes human action as trapped within an "iron cage." Today, the system of modern, rational capitalism shapes our economic behavior. While people once participated in this system to demonstrate that they had been chosen by God, today we simply participate without that meaningful connection. Weber might look upon us as robots performing tasks without good reason.

Whereas Marx and Engels are optimistic, Weber is not. He does not see history as progressing, moving us to a better place. Instead, he sees us as trapping ourselves in an iron cage, living mechanical lives through bureaucratized institutions. If you've ever seen the opening to the TV series *Weeds*, which shows a California suburb with clone-like people performing the same tasks over and over, this is what Weber predicted: "Little boxes on the hillside, little boxes made of ticky tacky, little boxes on the hillside, little boxes all the same." The theme song to *Weeds*, "Little Boxes," goes on to discuss the conformity and disenchantment of the people: "And the people in the houses, all went to the university, where they were put in boxes, and they came out all the same. And there's doctors and lawyers, and business executives, and they're all made out of ticky tacky, and they all look just the same." Weber sees the rationalization process as dehumanizing. Over time we have moved from actions based on emotion, superstition, and magic, to actions based on logic and efficiency. Again, this has costs and benefits. One of the biggest costs is dehumanization. This is what contemporary sociologist George Ritzer has explained as the "McDonaldization" of society. He asks, where's the magic?

Another area that Weber contrasts with Marx and Engels is on his understanding of **stratification**—that is, how the various strata (layers) of society are divided. Marx and Engels had a very simple view of stratification: society is divided by economic class. People are either owners or workers. Weber's view is more complicated. He looks at stratification by class (much like Marx's view), status (referring to how much prestige a person has), and party (referring to how much power a person wields). You'll learn more about this in Lesson 6: Class and Intersectionality. For now, what's relevant is that Weber examined stratification in terms of the economic system and also in terms of politics and culture, thus enlarging and complicating ideas of stratification.

Émile Durkheim was the first French sociologist. His contributions were both theoretical and methodological, and his scientific studies legitimized sociology's acceptance as an academic discipline. He wrote several classical books, including *The Division of Labor* (1893), *Rules of the Sociological Method* (1895), and *The Elementary Forms of Religious Life* (1912). His best-known book is probably *Suicide* (1897), in which he looks at the phenomenon of suicide—what most people would consider the most personal of acts—as a social act. Durkheim uses quantitative reasoning (discussed later) in a way that had not systematically been applied to suicide throughout Europe or to social phenomena generally. He shows that suicide rates varied regionally and that they corresponded with the religions of the regions. Protestants had higher rates of suicide than Catholics. He further argued that the variation could be explained by the degree to which individuals were integrated into society by their religions. Thus, social groups that have high degrees of social integration have lower rates of suicide than groups whose members are loosely integrated. Therefore, suicide isn't something completely individualistic. Where people live and what groups they belong to help determine whether they are more or less likely to commit suicide. Though Durkheim focused on religion's role in integrating individuals, other social institutions, such as work and school, can also play integrating functions.

One of Durkheim's main concerns was with how social order is maintained. Durkheim believed that it is our human nature to be insatiable and therefore we are perpetually unhappy because we cannot have more, more, more. Society is our protection from our nature: it is an external, regulatory force that limits human desire. Our reliance on forces external to us actually saves us from ourselves, in Durkheim's view. Social expectations—for example, religious laws—can be a force that regulates our behavior. Durkheim saw these external forces as critical to society. Related to this, Durkheim develops the concept **social fact**, which is central to sociological thinking. A social fact is something that exists externally and independently from any individual and cannot necessarily be seen, but it has a force on an individual's actions. A simple way of thinking about this is a social norm. It is something that exists outside of people and has a very real influence over how social beings behave. Values and social institutions have similar sway over individual choices. For instance, there are certain ways of behaving in a classroom that are unspoken. You don't smoke in class. You don't sit on the floor. You raise your hand when you have a question. You take notes when the professor lectures. You haven't necessarily chosen consciously to abide by these rules. You take them for granted, and they seem "natural." These social facts maintain individual behaviors so that we know how to act in given situations, and thus society is reproduced.

Here let us point out the concerns that drove Durkheim's work. Whereas Marx sought a revolutionary and utopian future, Durkheim appeared to long for the past. His work examined how society could establish and maintain social order and cohesiveness. To his mind, in the past, religion had served as the cement that held society together and gave it structure. But, if religion's influence as a social fact was declining, Durkheim fretted, what would take its place to create maintenance, connection, and stability for society? He feared modern chaos. He was likewise concerned about how individual desires could be controlled so that they did not upset the balance between the individual and society.

Durkheim's analysis of social phenomena led to the development of social theories within a school of thought called **functionalism** (see Table 2.1). Like Marx, Durkheim was a macro theorist. That means that he tried to make sense of society in a broad sense, not on a small scale, such as through specific one-on-one interactions between individuals. For Durkheim, society looked like a functional whole, made up of various parts. Another functionalist, Herbert Spencer, compared society to the human body and explained the parts of society as different organs in the body—each with a specific role to play. Functionalists ask how the various social parts work together for the good of the whole by examining their uses (their "functions") for society. For instance, what do the brain (schools), the heart (hospitals), and the stomach (agriculture) do for the body (society)? Functionalists examine two types of functions: **manifest functions**, which are the goals that are explicitly stated, and **latent functions,** which are consequences of actions that are not immediately apparent but which exist nonetheless. For instance, education is a social institution, an important "organ" in the social "body." Its manifest function is to educate youth to be productive members of society. A latent (hidden) function is that it is an institution that reproduces inequality, with poor children going to poorly funded schools and having poor outcomes and rich children going to well-funded schools and having positive outcomes.

When certain actions have negative effects on society, they are called dysfunctional. Dysfunctional aspects of the system can lead to changes in the system, according to functionalists.

Another important claim that functionalists make is that shared values and norms create a consensus that holds society together. You should already be starting to see that conflict theorists and functional theorists have very different ways of looking at the world. When conflict theorists detect consensus, they believe that it is a result of repression by the haves and that the have-nots are being exploited. Stratification is also viewed very differently. For instance, while conflict theorists see the conflict between the haves and the have-nots as a potential driving force for social change in society, functional theorists, instead, have analyzed the functions that inequality has for society as a whole. They argue that a reward system like capitalism, which produces inequality, actually ensures that the most important jobs, such as that of a physician, will attract the most talented only by offering the highest rewards (highest incomes). They further argue that inequality serves society by ensuring that there is a group at the bottom of the hierarchy that is willing to take low-paying jobs cleaning toilets and doing other undesirable tasks and that the group at the bottom will also buy undesirable products, such as stale bread at a discount, which all ensure that society functions. The functionalist perspective was dominant in US sociology in the 1940s and 1950s and included some important theorists in American sociology, such as Talcott Parsons (US-born, 1902–1979) and Robert Merton (US-born, 1910–2003). With the social changes of the 1960s and the questioning of whether there truly was some consensus underlying American society, functionalism came under attack.

Table 2–1 Comparing Conflict Theory and Functionalism

	Conflict Theory	Functionalism
View of society	Conflict shapes social life; society is divided between the "haves" and the "have nots"; change occurs through struggle	Society functions for the good of the whole and is held together by shared values, consensus, and cooperation; problems in society (dysfunctions) can lead to social change
Key concepts	Class struggle, class consciousness, stratification, inequality	Functions (manifest and latent), dysfunctions, values
Types of research questions	What are the causes and consequences of inequality? Who benefits and who loses from various types of inequality (such as in schools, housing, access to environmental amenities)? How are structures of inequality maintained and how are they changed?	How do various social groups (such as schools, religious organizations, subcultures) instill values in their individual members? How do values change over time and how does that affect social institutions? How can societies function when there are competing sets of values?

FOOD FOR THOUGHT
WRITING SOCIOLOGICALLY ABOUT FOOD
Justin Sean Myers

So you need to write a paper for a sociology class and you know you are interested in the topic of food, but you don't know where to start. There are several things to keep in mind. First, think about what level of analysis you want to study food at: the *micro*, the *meso*, or the *macro*. Do you want to understand why people are going vegetarian, vegan, or raw? This is *micro*; you want to talk to people and understand the meaning they give to their eating practices. Maybe you want to know how school systems are trying to institutionalize healthy and green lunch programs. This is *meso*; you want to understand how a social institution is changing its organization of food procurement, preparation, and distribution. Or you might want to know the larger social trends shaping the industrialization and globalization of food commodity chains over the last century. This is *macro*; you want to know the long-term economic and political structures shaping the actions of individuals, social groups, and social institutions.

Each of these different levels of analysis would involve engagement with different social groups, asking different research questions and obtaining data in different forms. The *micro* processes of identifying as a particular food consumer could be handled through ethnographic or in-depth interviews rather than mass surveys. The *meso* processes of institutional change could be engaged in through blending ethnography and in-depth interviews of people within these institutions, determining how they understand and explain the shift, locating these actions in relation to policy moves at the federal and state levels toward local and fresh sourcing of food, and explaining why the government is moving toward local food. The *macro* processes of food industrialization during the twentieth century could be obtained through quantitative data produced by the government, think tanks, academics, and journalists, such as the number of farmers, the size of farms, farm yields, crop diversity, and ownership rates of tractors and harvesters.

On the other hand, if you are interested in why students on your campus are not eating at the new salad bar, you could conduct a university-wide survey and gather quantitative data to determine which factors—price, convenience, availability, taste, healthiness, sustainability, worker rights, and so on—shape student eating choices. You could then share this data with the university to make the salad bar a success. Likewise, if you want to know how the industrialization of agriculture has affected farmers where you live, you might want to do qualitative research involving ethnography or semi-structured interviews. This qualitative data will be much richer in terms of flesh-and-blood people and will speak to what is going on in your geographic region, but remember that this data may not be generalizable to all farmers nationally or globally.

Whether you do qualitative or quantitative research or focus on the micro, the meso, or the macro, it is important to also think about the theoretical frameworks that will shape your research. For instance, an ethnography grounded in the Marxian conflict perspective might inquire into the class consciousness, or lack thereof, of restaurant workers. This framework might investigate whether restaurant employees identify as workers with collective interests or as competitive individuals seeking to maximize their own self-interest. What factors produce this self-identification? In addition, this framework could investigate the methods that employers and managers utilize to cultivate a pro-company workforce and disrupt or prevent unionization attempts by workers. Does management utilize racial or gender differences between the kitchen staff and the wait staff to create wedges between workers and prevent unionization? These are just a few of the questions, methods, or theories you could use, but it should be enough to get you thinking about what you want to research and what data collection method you could utilize to answer your research question.

There's much more that could be written comparing and contrasting the founders of sociology. If you major in sociology, you will take at least one course on sociological theory in which you will read these theorists and debate their ideas.

MISSING FROM THE CANON

Questions of sociology change over time, much as the conditions of the social world change. The development of conflict theory and functionalism, along with numerous other schools of thought (such as symbolic interactionism, critical theory, feminist theory, and postmodernism, among others), continues to this day. As society changes, so do our questions about it. We are responsive to the social world. We live in it. The founding fathers asked questions of their industrializing period. In his book *Social Theory: The Multicultural and Classic Readings*, social theorist Charles Lemert (1999) discusses the "second great period of social theory" (14), starting sometime in the late 1950s. What this historical period had in common with the classical or founding period of sociology was that it was a time of great social change. Lemert states of this period: "We live in a time of confusion wrought every bit as much by the successes of modernity as by its failures" (18), a time when society questioned a "unified dream" (7). Globally, Western dominance was weakened as colonies gained their independence, and formerly oppressed peoples could speak, which shook up global ideology. Alternative realities presented themselves and opened paths for change. The civil rights and women's movements in the United States reoriented daily life, encouraged new ways of theorizing about the world and led us to reassess the past. Within the academic discipline of sociology, we re-examined the contributions of academics beyond the "dead, white, European founding fathers" represented in the sociological "canon;" canon meaning the set of work commonly accepted as defining key aspects of the discipline.

Of particular note was the introduction of W. E. B. DuBois's (1868–1963) work into sociology classes. DuBois was the first African American to earn a PhD from Harvard University. He was a professor at Atlanta University and a civil rights activist who was one of the founders of the National Association for the Advancement of Colored People (NAACP). He produced a groundbreaking study, The Philadelphia Negro, which was the first of its kind to systematically examine African Americans in postslavery urban America, in part collecting data using door to door surveys and interview methods. His book *The Souls of Black Folk* is becoming part of the sociological canon of this century. A key concept from that book that resonated in the postcivil rights era was the idea of **double consciousness**, which was used to explain an African-American perspective on the world. DuBois ([1903] 1990) writes, "It is a peculiar sensation, this double-consciousness, this sense of always looking at one's self through the eyes of others, of measuring one's soul by the tape of a world that looks on in amused contempt and pity" (8). DuBois predicted that a key issue of the twentieth century would be "the color line," and, indeed, the importance of "race" has persisted in society and been an object of study for sociologists.

Despite DuBois's contributions, US sociology did not consider his work central to the field. Aldon Morris, sociologist and author of *The Scholar Denied: W. E. B. DuBois and the Birth of Modern Sociology*, writes of his education (in the 1970s):

> *My undergrad years were full of intellectual excitement as I encountered the scholarship of Karl Marx, Max Weber, and Emile Durkheim. . . . Still I felt there was an intellectual lacuna because Du Bois' scholarship [that he had read in junior college] and worldwide racial inequalities were not topics of analysis. Their absence from discussion seemed particularly perverse at a time when protest and revolutions were forcing white oppressors in America and around the world to confront the color line. (Morris 2015, xiv)*

Importantly, DuBois's work examines race at a time (post-Reconstruction) that racial issues dominated US society. However, as Morris argues, dominant structures and individuals in US sociology did not embrace DuBois and his ideas until much later, after the civil rights movement had shifted our thinking. Here, we are able to do a sort of "sociology of sociology," in which we apply our sociological imagination to understand why some theorists, theories, and concepts gain credence at various times in history and at other times do not. Through the work of DuBois and others, early theorizing about "race" is becoming integrated into sociology's canon.

Similarly, "female sociologists" of the late 1800s and early 1900s in the United States were not, and are still not, entirely part of the canon. Feminist sociologists today point to important sociological theorizing done by Harriet Martineau (1802–1876), Charlotte Perkins Gilman (1860–1935), and Jane Addams (1860–1935), among others (Lengermann and Niebrugge-Brantley 1998). For instance, Charlotte Perkins Gilman, in her book *Women and Economics* (1898), argues that due to the sexual division of labor (whereby men work outside the home and women in the home), women are economically dependent on men and are thus unequal. Her work outlines strategies to alter this arrangement, such as collective day care, so that women can work outside of the home, and women and men can be equal. These early female theorists are underrecognized in their contributions, in part because of discrimination in the workplace (they were not hired for faculty positions) and because of more overt sexism within the professional association of sociologists (Deegan 1981). The women's movement of the 1970s created a space for these early female (and feminist) theorists to be analyzed and their works to be recognized. Through these efforts, sex and gender analyses in sociology are no longer on the margins but part of everyday sociological work.

Contemporary society is going through another period of upheaval and social change that we predict will lead to new questions and new theories. As you will see in Lesson 9, globalization and the technological changes that we are currently experiencing creates another such period that is rich for reviewing where we've been historically and theorizing about where we're headed.

MULTIPLE GOALS OF SOCIOLOGY

August Comte coined the term "sociology" in 1838 and defined it as social physics, a science of society. Early sociologists believed that the scientific methods that were being used to understand the natural world could also be applied to learn about the social world to understand how and why human events occur. They were optimistic that if this worked, sociology could be used to rectify society's ills, such as poverty and war. In this way, sociology is an Enlightenment-influenced discipline. This view of sociology is called **positivism**, which, rather than referring to its optimistic outlook, promotes the belief that through systematic empirical observation, law-like statements can be made about the social world in much the same way that the natural sciences identified laws of nature.

Sociologists have considered how it is that we can study society at the same time we are shaping and being shaped by it. Social science has long asked the question of whether social science can be "objective." Max Weber's classic response to this question was made in 1918 when he became the editor of the journal *Archiv*. Weber argued that the goal of social science is to examine what is, not what ought to be. Weber believed that if society could decide on its values (what ought to be), social scientists could determine the best means of achieving such goals. As a science, sociology can compare the consequences of certain actions, but its role isn't to decide what should be done. So, for example, if society believes racial housing integration is a desirable goal, sociologists would be able to best determine how to create racial housing integration. For Weber, it is important to make the distinction between the sociologist as citizen (deciding what should be valued) and the sociologist as scientist (applying methods to determine the best means at achieving values). Weber acknowledges that sociologists are embedded in society and what we choose to study is inevitably connected to social values and the important questions of our era. Our values come into play in deciding what is worthy of our scholarly attention. For instance, for me, environmental degradation seems to be a pressing issue to our planet and its peoples. This is not something that I decided individually. My era has shaped my attention to this issue. Weber's view on this subject is in sharp contrast to Marx's view on such things. Marx argued that the philosophers have studied the world, but the point is to change it. This perspective is taken up in the final chapter of this book focused on public sociology.

Sociology as a Science

Part of what makes sociology a science is that sociologists use a systematic process to access information to uncover some truth about the social world or at the least some understanding about the trends and patterns in social life. Calling sociology a social *science* implies that it follows a method of asking questions about the social world, constructs theories that answer the questions, tests those theories to see if they hold up to evidence, and thus comes to a logical answer to the question that is based on verifiable facts. Observations lead us to support, refute, or refine theories, and, from that point, we build knowledge. This research process is the same one that is followed in the natural sciences. Figure 2–1 simplifies this research cycle: theoretical claims are evaluated based on data; data are used to correct and refine theory; refined theories are evaluated with new data; and the cycle continues to produce better and better explanations about how and why things happen in social life.

Theory and methods of observation, thus, complement each other. When we *do* sociology, we start with a question about the real world. To answer questions, we sometimes start with existing theories—that is, logical explanations of social processes or causal explanations about how and why events occur, and we sometimes begin with data or observations. The data are systematically gathered using research methods. We gather data related to the social processes we are studying. When we start with a theoretical proposition and test it by making observations, we call that deductive reasoning. When we start with observations and attempt to make generalizations (theoretical explanations) based on what we observe, we call that inductive reasoning. Theories are tested and refined based on observations. Observations also yield new propositions

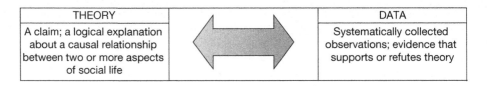

THEORY		DATA
A claim; a logical explanation about a causal relationship between two or more aspects of social life		Systematically collected observations; evidence that supports or refutes theory

Figure 2–1 Reciprocal Relationship between Theory and Data.

(theories) to be tested. What we call **methods** are systematic procedures that sociologists use to make observations (gather data) and refine and test theories. Thus, the two—theory and method—go hand in hand. They contribute to each other. To verify theory, you need observations. To make sense of multiple observations, you need theories. This is all pretty abstract. In a few pages, I'll walk you through some examples so that this relationship becomes clearer.

Sociology as Understanding Meanings

This very scientific and positivistic view of sociology is contrasted by social constructionist and postmodern views within sociology. Some sociologists argue that "science" per se is not the goal of sociology. Instead, the goal of sociology is to uncover social understandings and meanings. These viewpoints force us to ask if there is a Truth (with a capital "T") out there for sociologists to know. Is there one reality that sociologists can capture? For some things, maybe yes, and others, definitely not. There can be various realities or meanings regarding a situation based on one's point of view. Much of what we experience in the world is socially constructed. What that means is that the understandings that we have about certain things are social products that are created by social actors (with more powerful social actors playing larger roles in how things are defined). Let me give you an example. In post-World War II America, a smokestack was understood as progress. People associated it with industry and jobs—positive meanings. However, today, a smokestack means pollution—a negative connotation that has come about from social learning and education about the human health effects of industrial production. The social item (the smokestack) didn't necessarily change, but the way we defined the situation did. The socially constructed meaning of "smokestack" changed. Both of these realities about the smokestack are true in that both of them were perceived to be true by society. Since society continually changes, so does our reality and our truth (with a lowercase "t"). That is not to say that reality and truth are always moving targets. There is a material reality out there that was true in both periods: carcinogens being emitted from smokestacks have negative health effects for humans. Truth, then, is socially determined in some cases but not all. While we may never arrive at absolute truths in sociology due to the nature of the social objects that we study, we are closer to Truth when multiple observers agree about some fact and that fact holds up to scrutiny over time. This is called intersubjectivity.

Sociologist Howard Becker delivered the presidential address to the Society for the Study of Social Problems titled "Whose Side Are We On" (Becker 1967) that relates to the social constructionist perspective on sociology. It's a really interesting speech that I recommend that you read; in short, what he argues is that when you're doing sociology, it matters whose side you take. By that he means that if you're studying a hospital, you have to figure out if you want the patients' point of view or the doctors'. If you're studying schools, do you study principals or students? Do you study the police or the boys in gangs? In social life, there is a "hierarchy of credibility" (Becker 1967, 241). We tend to give more credence to those whose ranks and roles are higher in the stratification system (like the doctors, school principals, and police). Sociologists often disrespect the established social definition of a situation by studying those with less power (like the patients, the students, and the boys in gangs). These people tell us information that often contradicts what we think we know about a situation. For instance, a patient might tell us an unbecoming story about how a doctor interacted with a nurse. A gang member might tell an incriminating story about what a police officer said during a stop-and-frisk. People with social rank have a stronger voice in defining what is "real" in social life; however, there are multiple understandings based on social rank. Like Weber, Becker believes that the sociologist should be explicit about whose side he or she is on since you must always study the social world from someone's point of view. Becker's discussion also leans toward the scientific view of sociology in that he believes it is critical to explain how you did your work (your method of collecting and analyzing data) so that it could be replicated. Replication of research is part of the scientific method of testing and refining theory.

Scientific and postmodern views are at two ends of the spectrum of sociology's goals. In an excellent overview of research methods, *Constructing Social Research,* Charles Ragin (1994) argues that the primary goal of social researchers is "to identify order and regularity in the complexity of social life" (31). We look for patterns to make sense of social life. This fits both the scientific and postmodern perspectives. In Table 2–2, we organize three main goals of sociology (though there are many other ways we could classify the goals). In this configuration, sociologists do social research to (1) understand unique phenomena, (2) understand causal relationships, and (3) uncover broad trends and patterns.

The goals and questions of our work often determine how we go about gathering information to answer the questions. Our work begins with questions and from that point we determine how to make observations. Some questions lend themselves to gathering quantitative data (i.e., numerical data), and some questions lend themselves to gathering qualitative data. In general, quantitative data are better for theory testing and understanding broad patterns. When we want to understand broad patterns, it is also important that we make a lot of observations. Qualitative data are better for understanding meanings, getting into the mindset of the participants, and understanding an event in-depth. To do this sort of work, we must evaluate situations in great depth and thus typically get a lot of rich data about one or a few events. Table 2–2 provides an overview of the relationships among goals, theories, and research strategies. The next section elaborates on an example of each.

Table 2–2 Relationships among Goals of Research, Role of Theory, Strategies for Gathering Data, Sample Size and Method, and Examples

	Primary goal of research		
	Understand unique phenomena	Determine causal factors related to a given outcome	Uncover broad trends and patterns
Key strategies for gathering data	Qualitative; participant observation, interviews	Comparative; construction of case accounts through various means: interviews, analysis of existing documents, historical analysis	Quantitative; survey research, content analysis, analysis of existing quantitative data
Role of theory	Generates theoretical propositions that can be examined through other studies; inductive	Can generate new theory or test existing theory	Typically used to test existing theory; deductive
Number of cases and level of depth	Typically one or a few cases (or communities) are analyzed in great depth; small N	Typically multiple cases are analyzed and compared with sufficient depth to draw out key characteristics related to variables of interest; medium N; diversity of cases	Typically large numbers of cases are analyzed to understand rates of behaviors or relationships among variables; little depth; large N
Sampling method	Nonprobability sampling; purposive sampling; snowball sampling	Depends—what is critical is having variation among the cases to logically evaluate causal mechanisms	Probability sampling
Example	*Ain't No Makin' It: Aspirations and Attainment in a Low-Income Neighborhood* (MacLeod 1995)	*Don't Burn It Here: Grassroots Challenges to Trash Incinerators* (Walsh, Warland, and Smith 1997)	*Class Counts: Comparative Studies in Class Analysis* (Wright 2000)

EXAMPLES: QUALITATIVE, COMPARATIVE, AND QUANTITATIVE STUDIES IN SOCIOLOGY

Qualitative Example: Ain't No Makin' It: Aspiration and Attainment in a Low-Income Neighborhood *by Jay MacLeod*

I use this book (MacLeod 1995) in my Introduction to Sociology courses because it is a terrific example of qualitative research. The author, Jay MacLeod, was a student when he started this research, which I think is inspiring, and students love reading this book. MacLeod examines the "achievement ideology"—the idea in American society that success is based on merit and that "any child can grow up to be president" (3). Through work he was doing while a sophomore in college, MacLeod meets some low-income high school students who don't buy into the ideology. They don't believe it's true for them. They are, in fact, quite pessimistic about whether the system will deliver for them. They think that the American dream ideology is a farce. MacLeod, a middle-class kid, is really struck by this, and he wonders if lowered (what he called "leveled") aspirations "represent a quitter's cop-out? Or does this disqualifying mechanism suggest that people of working-class origin encounter significant obstacles to social mobility?" (4). He wants to understand the relationships between individual aspirations and whether they make a difference in terms of life outcomes. The questions that he asks are brought about by direct observations that he makes in the course of his life.

MacLeod took an **ethnographic approach** to his work. There are other terms for this type of work, such as participant observation and fieldwork or field study. Ethnographers immerse themselves in their research communities. This type of observation is like what natural scientists do in the field (imagine birdwatchers in the rainforest). However, "qualitative field study differs from other research methods in that it features researchers themselves as observers and participants in the lives of the people being studied. The researcher strives to be a participant in and a witness to the lives of others" (Lofland, Snow, Anderson, and Lofland 2006, 3). MacLeod started research where he was. He was already engaged with the boys of the community through his work. This "getting in" process—gaining access—can be difficult in many circumstances when the researcher isn't trusted or accepted by the group being studied. MacLeod was aided by already being known and trusted through his role as a counselor in a youth program in the community.

The way he picked his research subjects (what sociologists call a **sampling method**) is by choosing to study the boys he was already in contact with. In ethnography, researchers often have a **key informant**, a connection in the community who provides important insider information that helps the researcher gain access to others and get a better understanding of what he or she is observing. From the key informant, MacLeod learned about other boys in the community, interviewed them, and went on to spend time with a larger group. This is called **snowball sampling**: one participant tells you about another participant who you can interview and so on. We also call this **nonprobability sampling**. A nonprobability sample is not necessarily representative of the population of interest. It is in contrast to probability sampling, which is an attempt to get a representative sample and is discussed in the quantitative research example.

MacLeod's research goals were "to understand the aspirations of older boys from Clarendon Heights" and to tell the stories of boys who are not often heard (10). MacLeod found two groups of boys: the Brothers and the Hallway Hangers, both of whom were poor, living in public housing, and attending the same deteriorating school. The difference between them was that the Brothers were black and were optimistic about their future; the Hallway Hangers were mostly white and "despondent about their prospects for social mobility" (6). Did their aspirations make a difference in where they ended up in life?

SOCIOLOGY AT WORK
WORK AND THEORY/METHODS: THE CASE OF OVERTRAINING
Arne L. Kalleberg

After I graduated from college, the best job I could find was as a file-finder at an insurance company in New York City, where the only real challenge was to look constantly busy while doing very little. I was overtrained for this job and didn't enjoy it. Yet I couldn't figure out why I was unable to find a better job with a college degree. So, I decided to go graduate school to learn about sociology to understand why people like me with a college degree were stuck in jobs for which they were overtrained. This experience illustrates an important thing about how sociologists come to study particular issues: they reflect on events in their own lives or puzzles that they would like to solve.

To explain overtraining, I first needed to find a theory. Grand theories—such as those advanced by Marx, Weber, and Durkheim—were too general. Instead, I turned to a "middle range" theory: the idea of status inconsistency. This theory states that people experience stress when their statuses are inconsistent: for example, a teacher (who has relatively high occupational status) who is not paid well (and has a low economic status) may suffer from status inconsistency. I reasoned that overtraining was a form of status inconsistency (i.e., high education but low education required for the job) and that this should produce stress in the form of lower job satisfaction.

I then sought to find some data that would enable me to test this theory. I found a recent survey of 656 male office and factory workers in Wisconsin (see Kalleberg and Sørensen 1973). This survey contained information on a person's level of education, his occupation, and his level of job satisfaction. I then developed a measure of how much education his occupation requires and compared that to the amount of education he had. I considered workers who had more education than their job required to be overtrained, while those who had less education than their job required to be undertrained. Using statistical analysis, I found that people who were overtrained were indeed *less* satisfied with their jobs than other workers (since their expectations for getting a job that utilized their education were not fulfilled), while those who were undertrained for their jobs were *more* satisfied (perhaps because the realities of their jobs exceeded their expectations).

My empirical findings confirmed my theory. The results also had practical implications for policy, in that it underscored the importance of people having jobs that "fit" with their expectations and educational investments. In other words, people are happiest when their expectations match reality. This finding led me to do further research to understand why some people are better able than others to find jobs that fit their expectations. Understanding this helped me not only to contribute to sociological theory and research on an important problem related to work; it also enabled me to comprehend better my own experiences as a young college graduate.

Source
Kalleberg, Arne L. and Aage B. Sørensen. 1973. "The Measurement of the Effects of Overtraining on Job Attitudes." *Sociological Methods and Research* 2(2): 215–38.

MacLeod lived in Clarendon Heights and spent time with the two groups (totaling 15 boys), participated in their activities, and interviewed them over a period of one year. He says, "Much time was spent with these peer groups during all four seasons and at all hours of the day and night" (9), and "field notes, a record of informal discussions, and transcripts of taped semistructured interviews with each boy (individually and, on occasion, in groups) make up the main body of the data" (9). **Semistructured *or* semistandardized interviews** are different than survey interviews in that the researcher begins with a set of questions that he or she uses as a guide but asks them in a conversational discussion in which he or she is prepared to be flexible to see if the interviewee might take him or her in a direction he or she had not accounted for. This opens the researcher up to find unexpected results. Survey questions are not designed in this way. They are inflexible and scripted. MacLeod studied a relatively small number of cases (15 boys, two peer groups, or one community, depending on how you look at it) to try to understand what effect aspirations had on the boys. The material he collected is **qualitative data**. He analyzed their words and their stories about their lives and tried to find patterns between aspirations and outcomes. Though he did not perform a quantitative analysis, which would be focused on numerical data, we could imagine a quantitative study that looked at social mobility in the United States. It might ask, what percentage of people move up in class standing over their lifetimes? What percentage move down? Stay the same?

To this point, I haven't mentioned theory. A large part of MacLeod's book is telling the boys' stories in their own words. This is one of the reasons that my students like it so much. They say reading the transcriptions—words right from the boys' mouths—is like reading a good novel. The parts of the observations and interviews that MacLeod presented were carefully chosen, however, to speak to some theoretical concerns. In the second chapter of the book, MacLeod laid out five competing theories that explain the role of schools as reproducers of class. All of the theories show how school reproduces class position; however, the theories differ in terms of their explanatory mechanisms. MacLeod used these theories to sensitize him to relevant data. He chose parts of the interviews that relate to each of these theories, and in the conclusion of the book, he explained how his data supported and refuted various aspects of the theories. (I won't tell you how the story ends up; I hope you'll check out this book for yourself.) In 2008, MacLeod published a follow-up edition (the original was published in 1987), in which he interviews thirteen of the original boys to see where they ended up.

How do researchers like MacLeod protect their research subjects? It isn't always easy. There are numerous ethical issues to address. Students who take my qualitative research methods course read the part of MacLeod's appendix called "Fieldwork: Doubts, Dilemmas, and Discoveries." In this section, he elaborates on the grey ethical areas of fieldwork. For instance, what should he do about the illegal activities he witnesses? What should he do when the boys ask him to buy beer for them? What about more serious problems such as pregnancies and beatings? What about when he was questioned by the police as the sole witness to a shooting? These were all situations he faced and are extreme examples of the complexity of being both participant and observer.

Sociological research in general has the potential to pose numerous ethical problems. Our professional association, the American Sociological Association, has guidelines regarding the ethics of research. In addition, institutions that conduct research, including colleges and universities, are required by the federal government to convene institutional review boards (IRBs). The purpose of an IRB is to evaluate the ethics of proposed research projects—in particular, to ensure that research subjects are not harmed by the research process and to ensure that the potential harm is outweighed by what is to be learned through the study. The history of the development of IRBs is an interesting one. The Nuremburg trials shined a light on the experiments that Nazis did on humans during World War II. These raised critical issues about protecting human subjects. Questionable practices by the US government also made it clear that some standards were required. See, for example, the Tuskeegee syphilis study carried out by the US government, the Milgram study conducted by psychologists, and the Tearoom Trade study, the result of a sociologist's work. Your college has an IRB. If you do independent research that uses human subjects in the course of your academic career, you'll need to be cleared by your campus IRB.

Returning to the point of the example of *Ain't No Makin' It*, when researchers ask questions that are about understanding specific processes or groups of people, qualitative, ethnographic studies are often most appropriate. These studies provide rich insights into small groups. The drawback of these studies regard questions of generalization. How common are the experiences of the boys that MacLeod studies? Are the same social dynamics at work in Seattle and Chicago? Does it apply to girls? Can we make generalizations about American society based on this small sample? If we want to understand how common this is, it is necessary to look at bigger, more representative samples of the population. When doing sociological research, it is important to match the type of question you're asking with a suitable method and acknowledge the strengths and limitations of various methods.

Comparative Cases Example: Don't Burn It Here: Grassroots Challenges to Trash Incinerators *by Edward J. Walsh, Rex Warland, and D. Clayton Smith*

The next example of research (Walsh et al. 1997) shows what types of questions you can answer when you increase your "N." When sociologists talk about N, we're talking about the sample size, or "number" of cases. If you're studying one community, we say you have an N of one. When, as in the case of *Don't Burn It Here*, researchers are studying eight communities, we say they have an N of eight. As a general rule, when you are doing research with small Ns, you are generating theories to be tested by others. When you are doing research with large Ns (say, thousands of participants in the case of survey research), you are testing theories and making generalizations.

Comparative case studies, which have a middle-level number of cases, can be used to test, refine, and generate theories. Comparisons are set up to figure out why a certain outcome happens in some cases but not in others. For instance, in *Don't Burn It Here,* the research team wanted to find out why proposed trash incinerators are sited (built) in some communities but not in others. The researchers looked at three communities that were sited with incinerators and five communities that successfully kept incinerators out of their "back yards." (You've probably heard the term NIMBY, which stands for "not in my back yard.") Waste incinerators are not something anyone wants in their back yard. Why do they end up in some communities but not others? This type of question lends itself to comparative case studies.

In trying to determine what key elements (independent variables) had an effect on whether an incinerator was sited, Walsh et al. (1997) looked at existing social science theories for guidance. This aided them in identifying what types of data they should collect for each case. For instance, based on other studies the researchers thought that citizen resistance would prevent incinerators from being sited. From a well-established theory about resistance movements called resource mobilization theory, they were able to hypothesize that "the higher the target community's socioeconomic status, the greater its resources for challenging such a project were likely to be" (44); thus, they knew when collecting data that they would want to learn about the community's socio-economic status. They could then compare the socio-economic status of communities that got incinerators and those that did not to see whether the resource mobilization theory was supported. This was one of a number of variables based on existing theories that they would test. In addition to what they identified from the existing theories, they also learned some things by looking at the details of the cases, the data. For instance, activists told them that early organized resistance prevented an incinerator from being sited and that the size of the proposed incinerator also mattered. This sort of data could contribute to refining existing theories, if they held up across a systematic investigation of cases.

Unlike MacLeod's study, in which he selected cases based on a community he knew and wanted to know more about, the sampling method in comparative case studies needs to be more systematic. First, the researchers needed to define what they meant by a "case." Cases can mean many things: a case can be an individual, a family, a neighborhood, an organization, a school, a city, a state, a nation, and so on. In *Don't Burn It Here,* they defined the cases geographically as the area within three miles of a proposed siting, in communities with organized resistance. They limited their cases to three states where there had been considerable siting controversies in the late 1980s: New Jersey, New York, and Pennsylvania. Then researchers select comparisons with a purpose. In *Don't Burn It Here,* the researchers are very clear about their case selection: they were sure to pick cases where the incinerators were sited and places where they were not.

Once these sites were selected, the researchers needed to collect relevant data. They didn't just collect all of the possible information they could; they were focused. Case studies are not a data-gathering technique per se. There are lots of ways to learn about a case. One is ethnographic, as we learned from *Ain't No Makin' It*. Elements of that method were used in constructing these cases, but the data collection was more specific. For each of the eight cases, the researchers conducted semistructured telephone interviews with people who were for and against the incinerators. They also conducted focus groups (interviewing small groups of people at one time) to learn about the key issues. In addition, they constructed a newspaper file of each controversy. The data gathered through these methods were related to key variables from the theories and then compared. What were the similarities and differences? Were there patterns of variables that were similar in the sited versus the not sited cases?

This study has a noteworthy element: in addition to the data collection techniques previously described, the researchers also conducted telephone surveys of people who lived around the areas where the incinerators were proposed to be sited. This is a method that generates **quantitative data,** meaning that the data collected through the surveys could be summarized and compared numerically. For instance, the researchers could compare the percentage of people who were against the incinerators in each of the eight sites and could evaluate whether that made a difference. This adds the ability to generalize, not necessarily because it is quantitative but because they were able to study a large number of people (a large N) who were selected in a way in which they were representative of the community (called **probability sampling**). That is not typically a part of comparative case studies, but it is one that makes this analysis strong. When you take a research problem—in this case, whether an incinerator will be sited—and study it in multiple ways (ethnographically, through case studies and through surveys), it is called **triangulation**. Your results are stronger because you are able to examine and confirm results in a variety of ways.

The conclusion to this study is nuanced. They found support for aspects of some theories but not others. They are able to show what combination of variables are more likely to be associated with incinerators being built and what combination leads to incinerators being shelved. The social world often does not follow exact laws. Social science is a probabilistic science, which means we can make predictions based on odds of what will probably occur, given our best science. Walsh et al. (1997) conclude by refining the various theories they borrowed from. They also suggest other ways that their work can be generalized. Though they are focused on incinerators, they suggest that the work can be extended to siting of "toxic waste facilities, nuclear power plants, nuclear waste dumps, prisons, and other comparable projects" (259), what environmental sociologists call LULUs—locally unwanted land uses. The authors conclude with two practical memos that summarize the findings: one with advice to grassroots activists resisting LULUs and one to country officials considering siting them. These memos illustrate the practical uses of sociology. The researchers show what sociology as a science determined about the sitings; they constructed the memos to show how citizens, with values, can choose to use the work.

Quantitative Example: Class Counts: Comparative Studies in Class Analysis *by Erik Olin Wright*

Our final example (Wright 2000) looks at a quantitative study. Quantitative research is well-suited to questions about broad social trends and can be used to make generalizations to large populations. Erik Olin Wright's research concerns fit the bill: he wants to know how the social class structure has changed over time in the United States and other countries.

More so than in the other types of research we have discussed, sampling is one of the most critical aspects to getting quantitative research right. When we do quantitative research, we are typically selecting a subset of a large population, called a **sample**, to make generalizations about the **population**. It is critical that the sample be representative of the population. In other words, it should be a microcosm of it. When I teach this, I use the example of making soup. When you're making soup and you want to figure out how it tastes, you give it a good swirl and then try to collect a spoonful of well-mixed, representative soup. The pot of soup is your population, and the spoonful is your sample. The way we get representative samples of individuals to represent a population is by using techniques called probability sampling. I won't go into detail here. What you need to know is that by doing probability sampling, we are able to make good predictions about trends in the population by only surveying a relatively small number of people. When the next presidential election comes around, look at some of the polls that use probability sampling. The pollsters are able to make very good predictions about the election outcomes even though they only survey one to two thousand likely voters (the sample). The key is that they use probability sampling to generate a representative sample of who is actually going to vote (all voters are the population). In the 2012 election, Nate Silver of the *New York Times* FiveThirtyEight blog gained notoriety by assessing a wide range of polls and using quantitative social science methods to almost perfectly predict the election outcome, including which candidate would win each state. In the 2016 presidential election, the polls were very close, but most predicted a Hillary Clinton presidency. I'm writing shortly after that outcome and pollsters are just beginning to do the work of figuring out what went wrong with their predictions. Hillary Clinton received more total votes than her opponent, but the electoral college votes gave Trump a victory. You can bet that the pollsters are looking to their sampling strategies to understand why their samples did not accurately predict the votes of the population (everyone who voted).

Back to *Class Counts*. Wright is interested in understanding the economic shift from an industrial economy based in manufacturing (making things) to a service economy based on selling services, such as haircuts, hotel stays, and trading stock. His book covers many countries, including Australia, the United Kingdom, Canada, Sweden, Norway, and Japan. In this discussion I will focus just on Chapter 3: The Transformation of American Class Structure. This chapter seeks to understand how the class structure of the United States has shifted over time from 1960 to 1990. He frames the research theoretically: Who is more right in their predictions? Traditional Marxists or postindustrial theorists? Marx's theory suggests that the working class would expand and become "deskilled" over time. Postindustrialists (also called postmaterial theorists) hypothesize that the service economy would create more skilled work and workers gaining control over their work lives. To examine this question, Wright uses data from US Census reports (taken every ten years) and a telephone survey of 1,498 employed workers in the United States. This is a large N study. There are many nuances to this study, but the big finding in this chapter is that the working class in the United States has gotten smaller, thus refuting Marx's prediction. The data do not support that aspect of Marx's theory. Wright does not end with that observation, however. He asks several other questions based on his finding: While the US working class has gotten smaller, has the global working class grown? Does the unit of analysis need to shift from the nation to the globe? What would that show? When we talk about unit of analysis, we are referring to the level of analysis. In Wright's study, he could have studied individuals, but he aggregated data to study nations' economies. In his conclusion, he's suggesting that he should shift the unit of the analysis to the globe to understand how class structure has changed in an era of globalization. This is the nature of research—results yield new questions, which yield new results, and our knowledge about the social world grows.

One of the strengths of quantitative research, such as survey research, is that you are able to describe the characteristics of a large population. Wright can be fairly confident that his research is adequately describing the class structure in the United States in a way that MacLeod cannot. MacLeod's research on the boys has limited ability to generalize. A weakness of quantitative research, however, is that it is fairly superficial. Wright is able to understand how job sectors in the economy changed, but he is not able to tell the stories of individual workers and how or why their employment situation may have changed. We get broad strokes and big pictures, but mechanisms of change and the meanings that individual actors attribute to those changes are difficult to ascertain through survey research. MacLeod's ethnographic approach is much better at getting at the meanings that the boys gave to their behaviors. Again, a theme in discussing research strategies is that your goal or question must match your research strategy.

CONCLUSION

This chapter discussed the origins of sociology, its founders, the relationship between theory and methods, and three specific research examples. If you go on in sociology, you will take at least one class in theory and one class on methods and will learn even more about the intricacies of research strategies and the relationship between theory and methods.

Lesson Take-Aways

Three main points summarize your takeaways:

- Sociologists study the society in which we live; as such, we use our sociological imaginations to ask questions that are socially relevant to our time period and lived experiences. That doesn't mean we can't be objective.

- Sociology emerged in the mid-nineteenth century amidst great social change. The founders of sociology asked questions about the causes of social change, about what forces hold society together, and about how society is stratified. Contributions by theorists that focused on race and gender are increasingly being recognized as part of the foundation of sociological theorizing. The questions asked by early sociologists continue to be addressed by contemporary sociologists even as we ask new questions that arise in this era.

- To answer sociological questions, sociologists build upon existing theories and use systematic methods to gather and analyze data. We don't have one method that fits all research problems; instead, methods are matched to our research goals and the research question.

Discussion Questions

1. Think about some of the social issues that affect your life: for instance, student debt, globalization of the economy, and the role of technology in relationships. Use your sociological imagination to think about why these issues speak to you. What types of research questions might you ask about them?
2. Building on the research questions you raised in question 1, consider hypothetical responses based on what you know about the founders.
3. How might you gather data to address your questions? What patterns do you think you'd find? What causal relationships? Can you anticipate any ethical issues?

Sources

Babbie, Earl. 1986. *Observing Ourselves: Essays in Social Research*. Prospect Heights, IL: Waveland.

Babbie, Earl. 2013. *The Practice of Social Research*. 13th ed. Belmont, CA: Cengage Learning.

Becker, Howard. 1967. "Whose Side Are We On?" *Social Problems* 14(3): 239–47.

Berg, Bruce L. 2009. *Qualitative Research Methods for the Social Sciences*. 7th ed. Upper Saddle River, NJ: Pearson.

Deegan, Mary Jo. 1981. "Early Women Sociologists and the American Sociological Society: The Patterns of Exclusion and Participation." *American Sociologist* 16(1): 14–24.

DuBois, W. E. B. 1990. *The Souls of Black Folk*. New York: Vintage Books.

Farganis, James. 2010. *Readings in Social Theory*. 6th ed. New York: McGraw-Hill.

Healey, Joseph F. 2012. *Statistics: A Tool for Social Research*. 9th ed. Belmont, CA: Wadsworth.

Jones, James H. 1992. *Bad Blood: The Tuskegee Syphilis Experiment.* New York: Free Press.

Lemert, Charles (ed.). 1999. *Social Theory: The Multicultural and Classic Readings.* 2d ed. Boulder, CO: Westview.

Lengermann, Patricia Madoo and Jill Niebrugge-Brantly. 1998. *The Women Founders: Sociology and Social Theory: 1830–1930.* Boston: McGraw-Hill.

Lofland, John, David Snow, Leon Anderson, and Lyn H. Lofland. 2006. *Analyzing Social Settings: A Guide to Qualitative Observation and Analysis.* 4th ed. Belmont, CA: Thomson/Wadsworth.

MacLeod, Jay. 1995. *Ain't No Makin' It: Aspirations and Attainment in a Low-Income Neighborhood.* Boulder, CO: Westview.

Morris, Aldon D. 2015. *The Scholar Denied: W. E. B. DuBois and the Birth of Modern Sociology.* Oakland: University of California Press.

Ragin, Charles, C. 1994. *Constructing Social Research.* Thousand Oaks, CA: Pine Forge.

Ritzer, George. 2010. *The McDonaldization of Society.* 6th ed. Thousand Oaks, CA: SAGE.

Walsh, Edward J., Rex Warland, and D. Clayton Smith. 1997. *Don't Burn It Here: Grassroots Challenges to Trash Incinerators.* University Park: Pennsylvania State University Press.

Wright, Erik Olin. 2000. *Class Counts: Comparative Studies in Class Analysis (Student Edition).* Cambridge: Cambridge University Press.

Related Websites

American Sociological Association's Section on Methodology (resource page): http://www.asanet.org/communities/sections/methodology/resources

American Sociological Association's Section on Theory (links page): http://www.asatheory.org/soc-theory-webpages.html

Bureau of Justice Statistics: http://bjs.ojp.usdoj.gov

Institute for Social Research, Social Science in the Public Interest: www.isr.umich.edu/home

Pew Research Center, Pew Global Attitudes Project: www.pewglobal.org

US Census: www.census.gov

LESSON 2, PHOTO REFLECTION:

Police lining the streets to patrol the Tell Trump We Are #HereToStay Rally and March, New York City.
Photo by Tammy Lewis.

One goal of sociology is to identify patterns in the social world. Sociologists ask questions that arise in real life, such as: Why do people become police officers? Why are there more male police officers than female ones? Do police officers have a racial bias in their decisions to make arrests? Are certain types of policing, such as community policing, more effective at deterring crime? Theories provide us with testable propositions that can be evaluated through observations. You might propose that people become police officers because they come from families of police officers. To test that proposition, you would need to collect data. There are a number of ways you could do this, such as interviewing police officers or distributing surveys to them. Based on the data you collect, you could refine your theory and make generalizations about why people become police officers. If you were the photographer, what picture would you take to represent theory and methods.

PART 2

WHAT UNITES US?

It is pretty amazing to consider that on a daily basis, without much thought, large numbers of people cooperate to have their needs met and help other people have their needs met. There are parts of our society that operate like a well-run machine. For instance, students don't wake up every morning and have to figure out what it is they are supposed to be doing (on most days). Instead, our behaviors and activities are, in part, automatic. Students know what to do, where to go, and how to behave, as do most of the other people around you. There's a script. It is not by accident that all students know when and where to go to class each day, what to do while they're in class, and what the expectations for them are when they leave class. We live in a highly organized society that has written and unwritten rules about what it means to be a college student. The written rules pattern much of our behavior. For instance, you might receive a class syllabus that states that attending your Introduction to Sociology class is required. That written rule will (hopefully) get you to attend all of the class periods. The unwritten rules and expectations also shape our actions. For instance, you don't make phone calls to your mom when you are in class, nor do you smoke in class (there's probably a written law about that). Sometimes these rules are broken and when that happens, the rule-breaker will be laughed at and receive some dirty looks from classmates and the professor. This is all to say that we have shared sets of expectations about what is and isn't appropriate behavior, and when we break the rules, we get negative feedback. We don't decide these things on our own. Society, which precedes us, has established sets of guidelines that we learn and, for the most part, follow.

Sociologists study what these rules are, how we learn the rules, and how we reproduce or attempt to change the rules. The process of learning the rules is called socialization. The rules are part of what we consider "culture," and these rules are embedded in social structures that we call social institutions. Although each one of us has our own unique features (what we might call personality), we largely learn how to act based on what is and isn't acceptable in the societies in which we live. The shared set of understanding serves us as individuals (e.g., we know what to do on a daily basis, we know how to be students) and allows us to function as a society (e.g., we know how to cooperate, we educate our next generation). Different societies have different expectations and teach different sets of rules. However, the underlying social structures serve the same functions: they unite us, allow society to cooperate, and allow society to reproduce itself. These social structures have proven to be incredibly durable but can change over time. Ask some older people what their college education was like. What's endured? What's changed?

In what ways might our built environments affect who we are?

3

Socialization and Culture

Stella M. Čapek

INTRODUCTION: WHO DO YOU THINK YOU ARE?

Who Are You?

I f I asked you this question, where would you start? Suppose you had to list three to five things that best describe who you are. What would be on your list? In fact, let's make this real instead of hypothetical. The ideas in this chapter will make more sense if you actually try this. So please take a moment right now—grab a piece of paper and write down five things. *Who are you?*

I am:

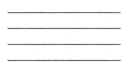
(You don't have to write in this book; this space is for your imagination.)

Finished? Whatever your answers turned out to be, they will be intriguing to a sociologist. For one thing, no matter how unique you are, you're likely to have quite a bit in common with others who come from a similar social background, culture, and generation. Often you share the same "cultural bubble"—it might include music, fashion, memorable historical events, technology, key values and beliefs, or knowledge of a certain city or geographic region, among many other things. Common cultural patterns might be as general as your use of English rather than Spanish or Arabic to express your thoughts or as specific as your taste in food, what you think your body should look like, your assumptions about romantic love, and your future occupation(s). These patterns are often invisible to you because they're so familiar that you don't "see" them. Sociologists, on the other hand, look for these patterns everywhere. We call them **social structure** because every society has persistent, identifiable patterns of relationships. Learning to see social patterns is an important skill. It helps us understand how things work and how social groups relate to each other. At the same time, on a more personal level, it puts us in a better position to make conscious decisions about who we want to be and what kinds of patterns we want—or don't want—to be part of in the future.

This chapter will invite you to think about what we call **socialization**—the process of taking on the values and practices of your culture(s). What is culture? We use this word all the time, but what does it mean to a sociologist? **Culture** is a rich, multifaceted, and sometimes contested concept, and sociologists don't all agree on one definition. In the broadest sense, culture refers to everything that we make as human beings—for example, ideas about right and wrong, a new piece of music, language and symbols, a pair of shoes, a social movement, or the latest piece of technology. Here's one—rather formal—definition: "Culture is the accumulated store of symbols, ideas, and material products associated with a social system, whether it be an entire society or a family" (Johnson 2000, 73). Simply put, culture has a historical component (it accumulates over time) and consists of products that we make (ideas and material objects) in small and large groups. If you think about it, this covers an enormous amount of territory. How do sociologists make sense of such a broad set of possibilities?

If we select just one piece of this "territory," non-material culture (the ideas that we produce), we can map out certain significant categories like norms (i.e., rules for behavior) and values (i.e., general beliefs, such as "democracy is good"). We notice that some norms (called mores) are taken very seriously and punished heavily when violated—for example, the prohibition against murder. Other norms (called folkways) are everyday rules about politeness and convention—for example, how you do (or don't) greet passing strangers on a city sidewalk or what you are expected to wear in a certain situation. Violating a folkway might bring laughter, ridicule, or anger, but usually the consequences aren't dire. These categories are interesting because a closer look at their content reveals that they vary greatly across time and space. For example, killing is more accepted under certain conditions (e.g., serving in the military or acting in self-defense). This might raise the questions: Who made these rules in the first place, and why?

It's important to note, too, that although many people speak of culture (e.g., American culture) as if it were one unified entity, in fact, culture is made up of many smaller subcultures (like the cultural bubble mentioned earlier). Depending on when and where we were raised, certain things seem "normal" to us, and we tend to judge other practices—often negatively—through our own value system. The word for this attitude is **ethnocentrism**, and we all have some amount of it. Because this can create blind spots in research, sociologists try to cultivate an attitude of **cultural relativism**; that is, we try to understand ideas and actions through the eyes of those who are practicing them. In fact, sociological research is a good antidote to ethnocentrism, because it exposes us to the rich diversity of the world's populations and meaning systems. This is enormously important in a world that is easily divided by fear—for example, a fear of immigrants as people who might take away jobs, increase crime, or foster terrorism. Since culture is constantly evolving, the analytical categories that sociologists develop help to capture both what is persistent and what is changing in our social structures. The field of sociology, too (like all academic fields), is a kind of culture that evolves over time, so new concepts and definitions constantly make their way into our sociological dictionary, giving us names for patterns that we didn't notice before or perhaps that didn't exist earlier. For example, recent theories pay more attention to how material objects (e.g., buildings, computers, a door handle) have "agency" and how they shape what we do even though they're not alive in a human sense.

Here are a couple more definitions of culture to consider. Sociologist Ann Swidler defines culture as "a 'tool kit' of symbols, stories, rituals, and worldviews, which people may use in varying configurations to solve different kinds of problems" (Swidler 1986, 273). This highlights how we work out "strategies of action" in our everyday lives, using culture as a kind of tool kit. Sociologist Howard Becker defines culture more specifically as "the shared understandings that people use to coordinate their activities" (Becker 1986, 15). These are useful ways to think about culture, emphasizing shared knowledge as a kind of pragmatic map for action that we use to make sense of the world. But while culture brings us together, it can also be an instrument of domination since some groups clearly have more power to shape and impose their culture than others. This power might be purely economic, or it might be based on what sociologist Pierre Bourdieu calls "cultural capital"— other kinds of social "assets" like education, appreciation for art, cosmopolitan travel experience, and manners, among other things (Bourdieu 1979). Culture can be something that we *have* and something that we *do*. It exists outside of us and inside of us at the same time. We'll see that culture is part of a dynamic process that is deeply entwined with the emergence of our self and, often, with issues of power.

So how does culture get inside of us, and how do we come to play a role in the invisible social structures mentioned earlier? To get an answer, we'll go back to the earliest stages of a child's life since all of us begin to learn about who we are when we are still very young. At that age, we're not too aware of how our society (e.g., family, friends, media, teachers, and others) is shaping us. But people respond to us all the time, sending signals about social expectations. In other words, they're socializing us. For instance, if we play games that focus on cooperation, as happens in some societies, we'll get a different message about what it means to be good and successful than children who learn to value competition. As we grow older, we develop a more distinct and conscious sense of self (as you probably demonstrated when you made your list at the beginning of the chapter) and perhaps become more aware of the influence of others. Sociologists are especially interested in how our self emerges and changes over time. There are many layers to the socialization process since there is more than one culture in any society, and, besides that, we don't just passively take in values. We embrace some and challenge others, especially as we get older. Or, to put it another way, we have agency (i.e., we can actively resist or shape the patterns in our society), but we're also constrained by social structure in particular ways. Thus, socialization is quite a complex process, and our self always contains unique elements even as it is shaped by outside social forces.

What is your "self" anyway? Is it something that you just have inside you, a kind of essence that makes you who you truly are? This is a commonly held notion about the self—it sits somewhere "in there" (in your head? somewhere in your chest?). But we'll see that a sociological understanding of self is different from this. To sociologists, the self is a *process*, a dialogue, something that changes all the time based on social interaction and cultural influences. It has lots of different components, and it never stops developing as long as we live. This doesn't mean that we don't have any firm foundations or stable aspects to our identity, but it does mean that we're constantly being shaped through socialization (and, just as important, *re*socialization since life is a continual social learning process; we will talk more about resocialization later).

To understand the self, we'll use a variety of sociological theories. Some of these work best at what we call the micro level, where the focus is on small group interactions (e.g., parents and children, a group of friends, a pair of lovers, a neighborhood gang, a doctor and his or her patients, etc.). **Symbolic interactionism** is one such theory: it's a micro-level theory that studies how the self develops through symbolic communication with others over the course of a lifetime. Another micro-level theory that we'll consider is dramaturgy, which sees human beings as actors who learn to play convincing roles and engage in what Erving Goffman (1959) calls "impression management." On the other hand, when we encounter the Frankfurt School's ideas about the "culture industry" in capitalist societies or consider social relationships in the global political-economic system, we'll be focused more on macro-level patterns that involve large group interactions. We'll have a chance to reflect on how identity is shaped by consumerism and globalization as well as movements for social change. Regardless of the level of the theory, all of them have at least one thing in common—they'll enhance our understanding of the self, culture, and socialization (and your answers to the "Who am I?" question). We'll consider plenty of examples along the way to make it clear how theories apply to everyday life.

A major goal of this chapter is to help you develop what sociologist C. Wright Mills calls the sociological imagination—that is, your ability to see how unique elements of your identity are linked to social and cultural patterns, from the micro level to the macro level. What's exciting about sociology is that it can help you notice how you're connected to social groups that you've never paid attention to—maybe the people in another country who sewed the clothes that you're wearing, the groups that made the rules about what kind of information goes on the outside of a soft drink can that you're holding, or whether you're able to recycle that can. Sociology can also help you understand parts of yourself that you've probably never had a chance to think about. This is an empowering kind of knowledge that allows you to make more conscious decisions about the social patterns that you want to be part of. Let's take a sociological look at the self.

TOOLS FOR UNDERSTANDING THE SELF: QUALITATIVE AND QUANTITATIVE INSIGHTS

How do sociologists study the self? To get beyond mere opinion, we use a carefully designed research process whose goal is to study society and culture in an unbiased and systematic way. How do we tackle something as complicated (and often invisible) as the self? One option is to systematically observe social interaction between people, either as a participant or observer. Two of the theories we'll explore—George Herbert Mead's ideas about childhood socialization (i.e., symbolic interaction) and Erving Goffman's concept of social interaction as performance (i.e., dramaturgy)—are based on observing people in their everyday lives. Even though we can't see inside a person, we can learn a great deal through careful and regular observation. Qualitative sociologists generally use observation, interviewing, and a variety of sources and social artifacts (things that people have made) to study culture and society. Much of our later discussion will draw on this qualitative approach.

On the other hand, many sociologists are interested in collecting quantitative data, usually based on surveying representative samples of large populations. An example of a quantitative approach is the Twenty Statements Test (TST) developed by Manford Kuhn and Thomas McPartland (1954). The TST is a survey instrument designed to measure key ideas about the self and to permit comparisons not only within the survey group but also across different generations. I used a very short version of this idea at the beginning of this chapter to invite you to think about your own identity. The TST asks participants to write down twenty statements in response to the question "Who am I?" The answers are coded and translated into numbers so that the responses are easy to compare. Remember what we said earlier about the cultural bubble that shapes the experiences of each generation? The TST has helped sociologists understand how it changes and how it influences the self.

Louis Zurcher (1977) describes one such key discovery in his book *The Mutable Self*, published in the late 1970s using data from the TST. His sociological study documented a shift over time in college students' responses. Earlier, their self-concept seemed to be relatively stable and linked to social institutions like family and organizations like churches and clubs (e.g., "I'm a Boy Scout"; "I attend the Methodist church"; "I want to be an engineer"). But Zurcher noticed a new trend that is still visible today: institutionally linked identities like memberships in organizations and expectations of having a certain job were less important, and students' self-definitions were more individualistic and based on the moment (hence the title "the mutable self"). Today when I ask for self-descriptions from my students, I'm more likely to get something like: "I'm a vegan, I love to travel, I like the color green, and I'm passionate about _____ (fill in the blank: a type of music, changing the world, etc.)." Some students mention careers and organizations, and many mention their families, but their identities appear to be more subject to change from moment to moment. And, there's often a sense that they're inventing themselves as they go rather than following pre-established rules.

If we think about some of the massive social changes that were happening in the United States in the 1960s and 1970s, it isn't surprising that identities began to shift. As we'll see later, dramaturgist Erving Goffman might refer to this as a period of "improvisation" during which the **social script** was changing. As social rules became more flexible, the self was increasingly experienced as a constantly changing personal accomplishment. This idea is also heavily marketed to us by the advertising industry, which is very busy selling us products to accomplish this task. Closer to your own generation, the expectation of having one job or living in one geographical area for a lifetime began to vanish, adding even more improvisation to one's life path. This may feel entirely natural to you, but a sociological imagination would reveal that the self hasn't always been viewed in this way, and in some places and social circles, it still isn't. A mutable self leads to an enhanced sense of freedom on one hand ("I can be anyone I want to be"), and increased anxiety on the other ("But who am I?"). Sociology can help us make sense of changes like these and offer important insights into the social context of our lives. Let's turn now to some key sociological ideas about how the self is formed, using the theory of symbolic interactionism.

THE SELF AS DIALOGUE: SYMBOLIC INTERACTIONISM

The theory of symbolic interactionism focuses on how human beings shape each other through ongoing symbolic communication, beginning with gestures that we learn as infants. As we learn, we constantly interpret messages coming to us from others. The messages could be words, body language, silence, a text message, a television image, or some other form of communication, but in every case, we try to "read" what the message means and consider how to respond to it. A well-established body of research shows that without social interaction and communication, children don't develop anything that we would recognize as a sense of self. They have no language, and even their body language is different from other children. It appears that social interaction is as crucial as food, water, and shelter. Language and signals from others are what give us our bearings and connect us to our cultures.

The symbolic interactionist Charles Horton Cooley used a simple but powerful concept—the **looking-glass self**—to help explain this. Cooley suggested that, just as we look in a mirror to check our image, we look out into our surrounding social environment to get feedback about who we are. This usually begins with immediate family and grows to include a wide variety of other "agents of socialization." Our social mirror (and our imagination) expands with the number and variety of contacts that we have. Some of these are direct, face-to-face relationships, but others, increasingly, come from a broad range of electronic media including advertising, television, the Internet, and the various forms of networking that we have come to call "social media." All around the globe, we are much more exposed to indirect socialization from these media than in the past. Since we're electronically linked in previously unimaginable ways, we need to include these in an updated concept of the looking-glass self.

It's important to be aware that the social mirror is powerful regardless of whether it is accurate. For example, a beautiful, intelligent child might be surrounded by people who perceive him or her negatively (notice how a movement to support the rights of transgendered people has challenged, or problematized, "him" and "her" categories). Unless the child gets different feedback, these messages will be taken as truth. Likewise, we tend to take as "normal" whatever we grow up with, until we are old enough to see (in a different, broader social mirror) that others do things differently—for example, practices relating to food, gender and family, sexuality, political beliefs, religion, and many other things. Think for a moment about how your social mirror has changed over time and what kinds of messages you have received from it. For example, have you been praised, more often than not, for who you are, how you look, and what you do? Or has your "social mirror" planted doubts and made your way more difficult? Quite often, the answer is "both."

Here's a true story that might help us think about social mirrors. It's about a small boy's first encounter with a negative perception of his skin color. Growing up in a mostly Latino neighborhood in Los Angeles, his brown skin didn't stand out as anything unusual until he began to attend a preschool with children of other races and ethnicities. When he came home from school, his family noticed that he was rubbing and rubbing on his arm. His mother asked him what he was doing, and he said he was trying to rub the brown off, looking for the white underneath. He was getting the message somehow that white was the better color. In as simple (and heartbreaking) a way as this, the power structure of the society came home to him, and he learned that his color didn't match what was signaled as "normal." What happens to such a child? The answer will have a great deal to do with his overall social mirror (including family, friends, teachers, and others) and what it encourages him to do with this piece of knowledge.

As I pointed out earlier, the advantage of sociology is that it helps you to see how you fit into a larger social pattern. That includes both positive elements of identity as well as problems that might feel devastating because they seem unique to you. It often turns out, though, that even this seemingly unique aspect of your self has much in common with many other human beings. The sociological imagination allows us to see how our personal problems connect with these larger social patterns. It's not only an interesting analytical concept, but it can also literally save lives. It offers perspective, combats isolation and self-blame, and offers an avenue for joining with others to change the society. You can probably see how such a perspective could benefit the boy previously described.

Thinking about our past socialization is an interesting and revealing exercise, but it has limits—first, because we're not very aware of the indirect socialization that comes our way, and, second, because most of us don't remember our earliest socialization experiences. For example, my parents were immigrants to the United States, and I grew up speaking two languages. I don't remember much about how I learned either one—it seems to me that both were just there, always. I don't remember anything about the complicated and awkward process of learning to master two languages (and cultures), but my mother later told me about it. She helped me "see" that child that I couldn't remember, and her recollections shifted my sense of self a little bit, as new information and perspective almost always does.

Symbolic interactionist George Herbert Mead (1934), in his classic work *Mind, Self, and Society*, developed key theoretical concepts that shed light on the social learning process that we experience as children. In fact, he developed many of his ideas by observing his own children playing. His theory of socialization includes the social mirror idea but adds two elements: (1) developmental phases, and (2) two components of the self, **the "I"** and **the "Me."** To Mead, the self is not a thing but rather a process that develops through interactions with other human beings. So, the self isn't located "inside" of you or me. Mead would say it emerges in the space *between* myself and another human being and *only* there. Having no social interaction literally means having no self. You can see how different this is from views of the self as innate or, perhaps, genetically determined. It's also a radical-sounding idea in places like the United States, where people learn to value and focus on individuality rather than on a "relational" self.

Mead's self is not only relational, it is also made up of two key components—a person's impulsive, spontaneous behavior (which Mead named the "I") and the rules, or "voice," of society (which he named the "Me"). The I and the Me exist in tension and in dialogue and shape our behavior in an ongoing way. Let's explore this idea a bit more. All human beings have impulses that prompt us to get what we want. For example, you might see something that you want to buy, eat, or possess in some way, and your impulsive voice (the I) says, "I want that right now!" Unlike Sigmund Freud (whose ideas about the id, ego, and superego you may be familiar with), Mead saw the impulsive self in a mostly positive light, as the seat of our creativity and a source of novelty; at the same time, he recognized that its focus on immediate gratification needed to be shaped by the rules of society. So, as a child learns what the social rules (i.e., norms) are, he or she acquires an inner voice, the Me, that serves as a reminder of these rules. According to Mead, once we have both an I and a Me, the rest of our life is a kind of moment-to-moment dialogue between the two, as the Me attempts to direct the impulsive I, and vice versa. For Mead, this dialogue, or inner conversation, is what constitutes the self.

Here's an especially important point: the I–Me dialogue lets us see *ourselves* through the eyes of *others* (i.e., through the rules and expectations of society). To Mead, this ability to take ourselves as an object and to reflect on our past and future behavior is the key to the socialization process. It's also what distinguishes us from infants and, perhaps, animals (although we're still learning a great deal about animal consciousness that challenges our earlier ideas). If you have a pet—say, a dog, a cat, or a horse—he or she can find a way to tell you "I'm hungry now!"; "I want attention now!"; "I don't like what you just did!"; or "I reeeaaaaaallllllly like what you're doing!" But your pet can't tell you, "Yesterday, when you did that, I had a real problem with it" or "Tomorrow at 3:00 I'm going to be very hungry if you don't leave enough food." Because human beings can stand back and think about (and, crucially, talk about) the future and the past, our communication has enormous flexibility. According to Mead, the Me part of the self (the part that we internalize from society) is what gives feedback to the I (impulsive and always stuck in the present tense) about the past and future. As a result, we're able to make thoughtful choices about our actions. For example, I might tell myself, "The last time that I broke that social rule _____ [fill in the blank here], things didn't go so well for me." Think about how this might apply to you—maybe you overate, overslept, engaged in a relationship that you wish you hadn't, or just lacked some important information that would have made you behave differently. Sometimes we'd rather not have this Me voice—it can be very unwelcome, especially when we're enjoying ourselves. But the I–Me dialogue gives us valuable perspective and helps us function in a society that contains other people and rules that make our communities work. Of course, the rules may not work for everyone, or they may not be fair. We'll discuss later how the self is related to social change.

So, when and how do we acquire our self, exactly? According to Mead, we go through three developmental stages—a preparatory phase, a play phase, and a game phase. When we're small infants, we're focused on immediate gratification. If we're hungry, we cry for food. A baby embodies the impulsive (unreflective, always present-tense) voice, the I. Over time, though, the infant is drawn into a broader range of social interactions. She or he begins to imitate gestures that people make—perhaps waving, smiling, or making certain simple motions. Mead called this early imitative stage phase "preparatory" because the child is trying out social behaviors without knowing much yet about what they mean. But, over time, through social interaction with others (usually the parents and immediate family), the child's impulses come to be at least partly governed by social rules. He or she gradually learns to imagine the social realities of others and to play roles that reach beyond the rather simple "I want this, and I want that" world.

I can promise you that when you do sociology, you'll notice these processes happening all around you all the time. For example, while I was writing this chapter, I spent some time in a medical waiting room. A young father and his somewhat impatient son (somewhere between age two and three) were also there. Their conversation went something like this:

Boy: Can we go back there?

Dad: No, it's not our turn.

Boy: Why can't we go back there?

Dad: Because someone else is having their turn.

Boy: Who?

Dad: I don't know.

Boy: [Jumping off the chair excitedly] Let's go see!

Dad: No, no, we have to wait.

Boy: Why?

In this situation, the dad was patiently giving his very young son information about how he was expected to behave. Later, the boy said, "Have a nice day!" to someone and was disappointed when the person didn't respond. He asked his father loudly, "Why doesn't he say something?" His dad soothed him, telling him that not everyone answers. Still later, the boy made everyone in the waiting room laugh when he asked his father "What's the name of that place where I go to get shot?" (meaning "get a shot"—but he didn't quite have the language down yet). The boy's eagerness especially reflected the I impulsive voice, but the conversation with his dad was giving him perspective about how things worked socially (the Me). And, because he was so young, it was easy for him to get a smile out of the adults in the room—one of the many rules of interaction that sociologists find interesting.

The Me voice begins to develop especially during a second stage, which Mead referred to as the "play" stage. We know that the urge to play is found in many animals, not only human ones—for example, there are delightful films, using hidden cameras, of bears and dolphins and other animals playing. Mead recognized that, apart from the pure joy of it, play is an important social learning experience. In the play stage, a child begins to act out roles based on individual people (i.e., significant others) that he or she has noticed. These need not be actual people—for example, they often include storybook, movie, or cartoon characters. Children act out these roles as they understand them in their imagination, often playing dress-up and making up stories and dialogues. It's a lot of fun to watch these interactions if you happen to be around children.

Here are a couple of examples. One of my students remembered going through a phase of being fascinated by the Teenage Mutant Ninja Turtles, especially the character named Raphael. He loved playing this role and even had a little costume. One day he wandered away from his parents at an event, got lost, and had to ask for help. When the announcement came over the microphone "We have a little boy named Raphael who is looking for his parents," his relieved parents knew exactly what was going on (even though his real name was Patrick). As for me, I remember playing at being movie stars with my little girlfriends, with plastic high heels, a fake mink stole, and candy cigarettes (yes, smoking was much more attractive, glamorous, and socially accepted then). I also remember reading a child's book about archaeology and wanting to dig up golden treasures. My mother let me excavate a small piece of ground just outside the house. I actually dug up an

FOOD FOR THOUGHT
SOCIALIZATION AND YOUR (FOOD) SELF

Justin Sean Myers

Physiologically, human beings must eat food. This is biologically determined. But there is no biological script that tells us what to eat or not to eat. Culture—the values, beliefs and norms regulating social behavior—is the intermediary between our need for food and our actual food practices. Culture sets the boundaries or rules regulating what, how, and when we eat. Which plants or animals are seen as edible or inedible, which parts of the plant or animal are framed as edible or inedible—all of this is decided through social interactions with family, friends, media, religion, and nationality, among others.

In the United States today, the choicest cuts of meat are between the head and the tail, including chuck, rib, short loin. tenderloin, and sirloin, while other body parts are ignored, such as the feet, tongue, brain, tail, and snout. This is not true for all cultures. The national dish of Scotland is haggish, which generally is sheep's stomach filled with a mixture of sheep's heart, liver, lungs, onion, oatmeal, and spices. Regional cuisines within the United States also demarcate cultural difference. For instance, Rocky Mountain oysters are generally bull testicles, but can also be pig or sheep, that are covered with flour, deep-fried and served as an appetizer. Then there is Brunswick stew, which emerged in the southern United States and is a vegetable soup consisting of tomatoes, beans, corn, okra, and generally the game meat of squirrel. Both of these regional cuisines are rooted in the people and landscapes of those areas. Rocky mountain oysters emerged out of a Western cattle ranching culture, and Brunswick stew was born from a hunting and foraging culture in the Appalachian forests.

It is important to understand how cultural practices shape your own "food self" and help construct your own "food boundaries." In the United States eating dogs is socially taboo, while in many Asian countries dogs are a part of cuisine. The difference is not in the object itself—dog is plenty edible—but the social beliefs, values, and norms attached to the practices. When dogs are socially constructed as part of the family, they are anthropomorphized, which leads to the act of eating household pets being viewed more as a form of cannibalism than omnivorism. Likewise, the boundaries separating weeds (inedible) and crops (edible) are arbitrary. Farmers and gardeners in the United States frame mugwort, amaranth, and lamb's quarters as invasive weeds. On the other hand, mugwort is a staple in Korean culture as part of a soup called ssuk, amaranth is synonymous with Jamaican culture as the dish callaloo, and lamb's quarters was vital to the premaize agriculture of Native Americans.

Now take a breath and think about your own food practices. What cultural foods, be they local, regional or national, do you partake in? Which social actors (e.g., family, friends, religion, mass media) have had the most influence in shaping these practices? How much power or say have you had in shaping your food self?

After thinking about these questions answer this statement: "My favorite food is _____." In answering the statement, be sure to connect all the invisible strings—the artifact—an old metal doorknocker, a winged figure that must have fallen off of the house during some earlier renovation. Fantastic! I had no idea what a real archeologist did, but I was enjoying "being" one. That's quite typical of the play phase, where the child is only *beginning* to imagine being someone else. Of course, later I learned that it takes a lot of preparation and hard work to be an archaeologist, and I took a different path. I still have an interest in archaeology, though, and I still have the little winged figure. It's quite beautiful and reminds me of the excitement of unexpected discoveries.

Mead found the play stage fascinating because while the child is trying out new roles, the self is undergoing significant development. As we imagine what it would be like to be somebody else (even if it's a Teenage Mutant Ninja Turtle named Raphael), we start to figure out what we look like to others. Like Cooley's social mirror, the Me gives us feedback about this. One of my colleagues, who is both a professor and a mother, saw this happening very clearly with her three-year-old daughter. Her little girl often cried when her mother left for work, a difficult situation for both of them. Then one day, just before she left the house, her daughter suddenly announced: "OK, now *I'm* going to work, and *you* cry!" Such role-playing showed that she was able to step out of her own role and imagine what it might be like to be somebody else (the mom). Playing at being a grown-up changed her perspective on the situation. Mead would say that the Me is what gives her context, social skills like language, and even a capacity for empathy (which, after all, is based on trying to imagine what something feels like to somebody else). She doesn't know that she's doing all of this, of course, but socialization is in full swing. As we become more aware of the society around us, the Me voice takes up residence, you could say, inside us, evaluating situations and offering perspective as part of a lifelong conversation.

Language plays an enormous role in the socialization process, but we're mostly unaware of it—it's one of those invisible structures that we mentioned earlier. As an infant, you're born into a social group that already speaks a certain language, and you will, in most cases, learn the language quite effortlessly. But if something interferes with this process, or if you learn a second language through travel or study, you will begin to notice the difficulties of translation—some words and concepts just don't exist in other languages. The rules are different, too. Some languages (many) distinguish between saying "you" formally and informally, but English, for example, doesn't have that distinction. Some languages, like Chinese, are more tonal, rely- ing on pitch as well as pronunciation. Physical gestures and body language are often part of the words we learn. It's easy to insult someone without intending to by making the wrong physical gesture. And it's easy to commit laughable errors in somebody else's language. I remember that while spend- ing time in Costa Rica, I made a mother and her young son laugh very hard when I told them in Spanish (not my native language) "I am very married" (*casada*) when I meant to say "I am very tired" (*cansada*). A sense of humor is a good thing to pack when you're traveling. I'm sure you have your own examples of awkward language situations. The point is, we usually don't pay attention to language and how it shapes our interactions until we have to. But language is, at every moment, part of our socialization process.

Consider this example of a young boy on a long car trip with his three siblings, testing out what he has learned about language. His father, who is doing the driving, is getting impatient with the children's arguing. He stops the car and tells the four children, "OK, if you have anything to say, say it now. Whatever it is, just go ahead and say it, say anything you want. And then we're going to be quiet." He asks each child if he or she has anything to say. When he gets to the youngest—let's call him Tommy— Tommy (about four years old at the time) says, "Shit." His father pauses for a moment and says, "Do you have anything else to say?" Tommy says, "Shit shit shit shit shit." There's a moment of tense silence in the car, and then everyone laughs. Tommy had already learned that this was a bad word, but he enjoyed saying it. He cleverly bent the rules by accepting his father's invitation to "say anything." Do you think that the impulsive I won out in this situation? It's possible. Or maybe he knew that because he was still little, he could get away with it. The Me probably gave him some perspec- tive, helping him play out in his mind whether he was likely to be pun- ished. For example, he was already learning that he could disarm others by making them laugh. Not surprisingly, as an adult he is a successful writer who continues to use humor as an important element of his work. The I–Me dialogue is creative, not just restrictive, and not by any means a simple or always predictable process.

To complete our understanding of the self, Mead identified a third and final stage of socialization (although he would remind us that socialization is a lifelong process). He called it the "game" phase. Now the child no longer only acts out single roles of significant others, but learns how to play roles that are simultaneously connected with many others at every moment. For example, in a game of tag or basketball, a child must be constantly aware of how she fits into the group of other players. Earlier, during the play phase, she might have wanted to act out the role of a famous basketball player and endlessly shoot baskets, but now she has to master the art of being a team player. Mead saw this as both valuable practical experience and a metaphor for how we learn the rules of society more generally (he referred to this as the "generalized other"). In this stage, the Me becomes more connected to a bigger picture, made up of a network of social relationships.

Although we have focused mostly on children so far, as mentioned earlier, the self is always a process, always *in* process, balancing impulse with a broader perspective under changing circumstances. Some moments of transformation are obvious, as in so-called rites of passage that celebrate or mark some change in our life. Common examples are birthdays, graduations, marriages, turning twenty-one—I'm sure you can think of others. In contrast to our original childhood socialization, **resocialization**, or the learning of new identities, happens at many points in our lives. Becoming a college student, committing to vegetarianism, learning to ski, getting a job, moving to another city, learning to use a new piece of technology, being diagnosed with a chronic disease, having a child, losing a spouse, graduating from law school, joining the military, coming home *after* being in the military, becoming a senior citizen—the list of resocialization possibilities is almost endless because it's part of a lifelong process.

A rather dramatic recent example of resocialization involved a young man who was a leader in a white racist hate group, one of many such US groups monitored by a social justice organization, the Southern Poverty Law Center (SPLC). Because of some significant people in his life, he experienced a change of heart and wanted to put his past behind him. The trouble was that he was tattooed all over his face and head and upper body with hate messages and symbols. Maybe because his story was so noteworthy, the SPLC helped to pay for the painful and elaborate process of getting the tattoos removed. He has since worked to challenge racism in US society. Most of the time the resocialization process is more subtle than this, but it always involves learning a new way to be in the world. Mead's contribution was to make this process visible.

To sum up, Mead's theory of symbolic interaction helps us make sense of how society gets into us and how we adapt to social conventions and also resist them. If we think about it a little bit more, we're also likely to see that we can critique Mead's framework in a number of ways. What if, for example, you grow up in more than one culture, as happens to many children? Which Me do you listen to? What if the Me that you learn (the voice of society) devalues who you are, especially if your identity is not mainstream? And, interestingly, what if you live in a capitalist society that encourages you to shop impulsively as much as possible? How might the I–Me dialogue shift or experience distortion in that case? We'll have a chance to think about these and other issues later. In the meantime, we'll explore another micro-level theory that also focuses on symbolic communication and offers some more tools for understanding socialization and the development of a self.

THE SELF AS ACTOR: DRAMATURGY AND IMPRESSION MANAGEMENT

Sociologist Erving Goffman developed a theory known as "dramaturgy" that offers intriguing insights into social behavior. In his classic work *The*

Presentation of Self in Everyday Life (Goffman 1959), he drew on theater metaphors to help us understand the roles that we play in society—hence the name "dramaturgy." Key concepts include the actor, audience, props, script, improvisation, front-stage and backstage performance, and a few others that we'll discuss later. Although he focused less on the development of young children than Mead, Goffman would agree that we learn to do "impression management" at a very early age. In other words, we learn that when we do certain things, we win the approval of our "audience" (initially our immediate family). Based on the feedback we get (you can see how this relates to the social mirror concept and the I and the Me), we learn to perfect our role performance, just as a theater actor would, so that we will "have our act together" and won't be judged negatively. As in Mead's theory, this process continues over the course of a lifetime and varies depending on situations that we find ourselves in.

Because acting is usually associated with deception, dramaturgy might strike you as a rather cynical or superficial view of human beings. Usually, when someone implies that someone else is acting or calls them "manipulative," it's an unflattering term. Goffman would simply point out that we respond to social messages all the time and that we have a stake in being seen in a positive light; therefore, we work very hard to make sure that others see us this way. This work, which actually takes considerable energy, is not something that we think about much. Our routine, everyday behavior becomes almost automatic, so sometimes it takes an outsider—perhaps a child who has not yet learned the rules or a visitor from another culture—to spot what we are doing, to notice the effort involved, and to ask questions about it. In fact, another micro-level sociologist, Harold Garfinkel (whose approach is called ethnomethodology) encouraged his students to break social rules when they studied social interactions, so that people's invisible expectations about social structure would become very obvious, along with the work they do to "keep things normal." Think, for example, about some of the rules for public spaces—not speaking to people in an elevator even though you are physically standing very close to them, not noticing a homeless person who is trying to get your attention, averting your eyes from someone who is missing a limb, or ignoring that someone just burped loudly at a formal dinner. A child will wonder why we don't do the seemingly natural thing, which would be to interact or at least to show that we notice (does this remind you of the little boy in the waiting room described earlier?). The child will eventually be taught to work very hard not to notice, and rules about politeness and public behavior will become part of this child's impression management.

Building on the theater metaphor, Goffman points out that in our everyday performances we often rely on props to make ourselves more convincing. Social props are usually material objects (clothes, cars, houses, technology, lawns, to mention just a few). The marketplace sells us a great many props to bolster our cultural performances as we will discuss later. Some boys in my neighborhood like to race around on their four-wheeler all-terrain vehicles (ATVs). To critics, these vehicles tear up the earth, put out stinky exhaust, churn up mud in the winter and dust in the summer, create noise pollution, and statistically are connected with high rates of injury. But, for fans of ATVs, these props symbolize freedom and daring and allow their riders to impress each other with a masterful performance—in other words, they're having the time of their lives. These preferences, though, don't just depend on individual taste. They are strongly shaped by what we are socialized to value and the social groups or subcultures that reinforce our performances.

While props are usually material objects, Goffman points out that they can also be other people (who lend us credibility because we're seen "with" them). Props can even be facial expressions and body language. From a dramaturgical perspective, props can function in both positive and negative ways. Usually we think only of positive props—those that are intended to attract people to us—prestigious material goods, for example, in a materialistic society. But negative props are just as important. Unless you lead a totally sheltered life where others keep away undesirables for you, you will have to spend time in spaces where you might be approached by someone you would rather not interact with. Negative props include sunglasses, headphones, ear buds, talking on a cell phone (or at least pretending to), texting, reading a magazine in a waiting room, wearing a fake engagement or wedding ring in a bar—again, the list could be quite long. What's interesting is that the very props that we use to repel some people can be used to attract others like ourselves. Think of various subcultures and "scenes," like the punk aesthetic, for example, where hair, clothing, music and lifestyle are simultaneously an affirmation of a positive identity as well as a repellant meant to keep away those who don't share the same values. Socialization is at least as much about learning the rules of particular subcultures as it is about learning the general rules of society.

A classic sociological study demonstrating the importance of social learning in groups was Howard Becker's study of marijuana users (Becker 1953). His work challenged common assumptions about this behavior held by outsiders. These included the belief that smoking marijuana involved mostly a biophysical response, that only people with certain psychological traits engaged in it, and that it was immediately pleasurable and addictive. Becker documented how marijuana smokers had to be taught to find the experience pleasurable, since smoking per se is usually unpleasant on a first attempt, and marijuana smokers often don't experience a high when they first begin. Thus, it took effective coaching on the part of the group over time to produce an enjoyable experience. Notice how strongly this outcome depended on social cues and interaction.

Becker also wrote about the resocialization process experienced by other groups, including medical students and jazz musicians (based on his own participant-observation as a sociologist *and* a jazz musician). When you become a doctor, for example, your self begins to be radically altered in medical school. You learn to touch patients' bodies without embarrassing yourself or them. You learn to cut open cadavers without feeling nauseated or terrified, so that you can study how the body works (this is definitely a rite of passage in medical school!). You learn to function under conditions of extreme sleep deprivation. You learn that some patients will die no matter what you do. You might be the one who has to tell a patient's family that they have just lost a loved one. Like others developing a new self-concept (including jazz musicians), future doctors learn a new language (official medical terms as well as humorous and derogatory insider slang that help them get through difficult situations). They wear clothes that set them apart from others (a white coat, whose different lengths represent status in the medical hierarchy). Interestingly, medical schools have recognized that future doctors should know more sociology, so sociological questions on the MCAT (Medical College Admission Test) are becoming part of medical culture. While doctors are an example of just one subculture, what all have in common is a socialization process through which newcomers learn the rules (including lifestyle and values), so that they can become artful insiders. It doesn't matter whether the group is mainstream or deviant or whether the rules are written down or informal—a person's membership depends on successful socialization.

Goffman noted that just as stage actors perform from a shared script, there is a social script for everyday situations. This is similar to Mead's idea of the Me, although Goffman was more interested in how impression management varied from situation to situation than in any overarching social pattern (Mead's "generalized other"). The social script that we learn provides a set of shared rules, and when we perform from this script for our audience, we demonstrate that we are competent and in control of our performance. The script might be about anything—from expected gender roles to how we should behave in a dentist's office. Our performance is adjusted as we become more sophisticated in our understanding of the script and our own capabilities.

Obviously, the script will vary by culture and depend on whether we are in a highly formal situation or whether we are with friends, family, or other people who know us well. Taking this into account, Goffman offers the interesting concept of "front-stage" and "backstage" performance (if you've ever worked on a theater production, you'll certainly know the difference). Just as in a theater, where polished and flawless performances are presented front-stage while the often chaotic details of pulling together a performance are kept invisible backstage, Goffman suggests that we have front-stage and backstage performance areas in our lives. It's essential to know how to move from one to another and, more important, to keep them separate. Think of a situation like a job interview as an example of front-stage performance—here, we strive to give an impressive performance that will not hint at any less favorable or less competent aspects of our self. But back at home—or anywhere where we can be informal, let our guard down, and be spontaneous—we are in our backstage. A messy room or house, informal clothes, unsanitized language, uncombed hair, party-animal behavior, anorexia (the potential list is quite long)—all of these are revealed only to those who know us best and hidden from other audiences. Just as in a theater, only certain people are permitted backstage. If someone (especially the wrong someone) stumbles upon your backstage, the consequences can vary from the comic to the tragic. It may be parents coming for an unannounced visit to a college dorm; it may be someone who wasn't supposed to see someone else without makeup; it may be reporters exposing a politician who publicly supports abstinence but is having an extramarital affair with an assistant; it may be a professor catching a student cheating—you get the idea. In some situations, a bit of ridicule or gossip are the result. In others, the consequence might be the destruction of a career and the loss of public respect.

The rise of social media like Facebook, Instagram, and Snapchat raises interesting questions about front-stage and backstage. Problems have surfaced when participants post information that reveals too much private information, often because users see Facebook as a kind of comfortable backstage, without thinking of the other audiences that come into contact with it. Sadly, there have been growing incidents of pictures or videos posted on the Internet that are intended to cause harm by violating someone's privacy (backstage). Some of these have resulted in suicides. Commentators have argued that this is an example of how rules (i.e., a shared social script) for ethical social behavior haven't caught up with our technologies. This allows people to easily (and often thoughtlessly) inflict great harm by presenting information—and misinformation, as often happens in cyberbullying—to an enormous electronic audience. Notice how the damage done in these situations depends entirely on the assumption that backstage and front-stage should be kept separate. The cyberspace environment suggests that theories of socialization and dramaturgy must be extended to include this form of interaction since interactive media offer both fresh opportunities for honest and intimate communication as well as new potentials for deception and distortion.

New technologies that blur the lines between front-stage and backstage provide a good example of situations where the social script is unclear. We respond to these situations, Goffman says, through improvisation (again, like actors on a stage). For example, you might be visiting a country or region where you don't know the rules for interaction. Or—to use an example that came up in a sociology class—maybe your brother has had a sex change operation and is now your sister. How do you interact with her? Even if you have the best of intentions, you have no script. You must invent a new one that works. Some improvisations feel very personal and individual, but improvisation can involve changing relationships between entire groups. Recall the mutable self study that found generational differences in students' views of the self. In the twentieth century, movements for social change (e.g., the civil rights movement and the feminist movement) questioned established rules of society (racial segregation and discrimination and gender inequality, respectively) and created new ones. This often resulted in groups wanting to be named differently, and this changed some established rules for interaction. "Indians" became Native Americans or perhaps preferred tribal names. "Negroes" became blacks or African Americans. Spanish-speaking citizens became Chicanos, Hispanics, or Latinos. To pick a more recent movement, the word "queer," once (and to some people still) an insult, has been appropriated by a gender liberation movement so that it now contains a positive identity message, as reflected in the (still expanding) acronym LGBTQ (lesbian, gay, bisexual, transgender, queer). During times of change, not knowing what to call somebody (or an entire group of somebodies) can lead to awkward, improvisational interactions. Because improvisation carries a high risk of appearing incompetent, impression management strategies become even more important. At the same time, the backstage can become a refuge for those who do not want to change. Sociologist Joe Feagin uncovered such backstage areas when he conducted studies of white college students at a variety of institutions. He documented thousands of instances of backstage racism in all-white settings. Students, who were asked to keep journals as part of the research study, typically expressed surprise at the high number of racist remarks that they heard (and counted) in these settings. A sociological perspective helped them to notice something that they hadn't paid attention to before—a great example of making an invisible social structure visible.

A concept that goes along with impression management is Goffman's notion of "framing." Just as we might carefully pick out a picture frame to highlight certain colors in a painting, we symbolically frame or present our everyday actions by emphasizing some things and downplaying others. This framing behavior includes aligning actions—verbal and other strategies that we use to control impressions that we make on others. In fact, I notice this quite often in the classroom: a student may preface a remark by saying, "I don't know if this is what you're looking for, but . . ." Or, we might say to a friend, "I know this might sound crazy, but . . ." Here, we're signaling to our audience that we know that what we're about to say might sound a bit "off," but we're OK—we're aware of it. This protects us from negative judgments. We also might try to affect the audience's understanding of a past performance by explaining the circumstances ("I was so tired; I had just gotten back from a long trip"; etc.). Or we might offer a joke, laughing at ourselves to gain solidarity from the audience. In all of these instances, according to Goffman, we're hard at work on the process of framing the situation in our favor, polishing our social performance.

Not all aligning actions are verbal ones. Have you ever tripped over your own feet as you walked along? It's not unusual. The first reaction is often to turn around and stare incredulously at the ground as if *it* is somehow responsible for our clumsiness. A rock, perhaps, or a crack in the pavement? No. We're just awkward sometimes, but our aligning action redirects the blame. Or, maybe your body somehow makes a sound, in a relatively formal situation, that could be interpreted as crude, unpleasant, impolite, and certainly inappropriate. Maybe it sounds like what we politely call "passing gas," or, more informally "farting." Since our bodies are regulated by society, and competent performance includes mastery of our bodies according to social rules, we could be ridiculed. How can you help your audience to reinterpret the situation? If you are like many others, you might immediately

SOCIOLOGY AT WORK
WORK AND SOCIALIZATION/CULTURE: WORK DEVOTION
Arne L. Kalleberg

Some people live to work. We are all familiar with workaholics that bring their laptops to the beach or constantly check their smart phones 24/7, lest they lose contact with their offices or workplaces. Others work late into the night, day after day. For such people, work forms a large part of their identity and shapes how they view themselves. The most important things in their lives involve their jobs and work, and they try to fit their other activities around their work.

For others, work is simply a means to live. They find their greatest satisfaction in life in nonwork activities such as their families, hobbies, and other leisure activities such as sports or travel, or their communities or religion. They are able to "leave work at work" and to forget about it when they leave the workplace. Their identity is shaped mainly by what takes place outside of work.

Mary Blair-Loy (2003) uses the concept of "work devotion schema" to describe why women finance executives are willing to work long hours in demanding careers and be highly dedicated to their firms. Work devotion schemas are cultural models, such as the older Protestant work ethic that encouraged people to work hard. Work devotion schemas help people create their identities and to channel their efforts and passion to things outside themselves. The women that Blair-Loy studied are preoccupied with their work careers and their own career advancement, which provides meaning to their lives and opportunities for greater material rewards as well as interesting, challenging activities. These women spoke of being totally consumed by their work and of getting adrenaline rushes as they sought to achieve their goals. For these women, their personal goals and the company's goals were one: their loyalty and efforts on behalf of their companies were rewarded with promotions, greater learning opportunities, more challenging work, and greater material rewards.

The intense devotion these women gave to their work competed with their ability to invest their allegiance and passion in other activities, such as those associated with the family. Many of these women did not have children, which often represent sources of devotion that conflict with a single-minded commitment to work. When work devotion and family devotion schemas compete with each other, people often experience a work–family conflict between these two identities.

Work devotions can change over time, however. Many of the women interviewed experienced a decline in work as a central life interest over time. This was due to several factors. One was the increasing dominance of family devotion schema, as women got married or had children on which they wanted to focus more of their energies. Other women became disenchanted with their employers, who they perceived as breaking the implicit psychological contract by which they exchanged their effort and loyalty for opportunities of advancement and security. In some cases, employers reneged on their promises to promote the executives or even fired them.

Source
Blair-Loy, Mary. 2003. *Competing Devotions: Career and Family among Women Financial Executives.* Cambridge, MA: Harvard University Press.

make the sound again, only more loudly (the sound might have come from a squeaky chair or something else) so that the audience will *clearly* know what it was. Or maybe your cell phone is going off in a place where it's supposed to be turned off, but you act as if it's not your phone, looking around at everybody else, because there's really no way to tell. Performance certainly depends on audience and context. In a different situation, making rude body noises might be part of a backstage contest with friends. There, skilled performance and competence is the opposite of what it would be in a formal situation. The point is that in a Goffmanian universe, the performance never stops, and reading our audience well and framing our performance is an essential skill. In addition, Goffman offers us some laughs when he reveals our earnest maneuvers to look good to others.

What about the audience that witnesses these actions? Is it always hostile, just waiting for us to reveal the flaws in our performance so that they can ridicule or despise us? Interestingly, Goffman points out, the audience isn't as hostile as we might think. One of the best ways to see this is through a concept called "civil inattention," where strangers conspire not to notice something. Perhaps at a formal dinner someone commits a faux pas (like the previously mentioned rude sound or something else considered embarrassing). Unlike the child, who might giggle and point, adults will generally look away and act as if nothing has happened. There are several reasons for this. Sometimes we feel for the person who is experiencing some social awkwardness—it could easily have been us, and we feel empathy. But a more selfish reason, perhaps, is that sometimes it makes the social flow of interaction easier if we simply don't notice. That way we don't have to work to fix an awkward situation, and life proceeds more smoothly. So, like the actor, an audience has a variety of roles to play in a social situation, not all of them immediately obvious.

To conclude our discussion of Goffman, the self, as we see it represented in his work, is a constantly changing entity that strives to be a proficient actor, responding skillfully to a range of situations in order not to be discredited. We don't do this because we're neurotic egomaniacs. As Goffman (1963) pointed out in his book *Stigma: Notes on the Management of Spoiled Identity*, there's a high cost to being a social outsider, and most people avoid the pain of that situation by striving to seem as normal as possible. Goffman's research calls our attention to how much work we do as actors and audience, and how much effort it takes to accomplish social interaction and to master certain roles. Harold Garfinkel, whom we mentioned briefly earlier, developed a related strand of research known as ethnomethodology that documented down to the smallest detail how, on an everyday basis, we accomplish or "do" gender, for example (Garfinkel 1967). Some critics find Goffman's and Garfinkel's work to be trivial or perhaps not concerned enough with solving social problems in society. But symbolic interactionists, dramaturgists, and ethnomethodologists would all agree that these small interactions that take place on a micro level, often during very ordinary, everyday occasions, are what keep our sense of social order and "things being normal" in place. And that, they would say, is no small accomplishment and one that we need to pay attention to as sociologists.

THE SELF AS CONSUMER: CAPITALISM, CULTURE, AND GLOBALIZATION

On a trip through a Costa Rican rainforest several years ago, I watched a child explore the environment with a great sense of wonder and curiosity. Something that she said halted me in my tracks. She inhaled the sweet scent of orchids and other blooming flowers and observed, "This smells just like our laundry soap at home!" She was right—her laundry detergent at home probably contained chemical additives that made it smell fresh like flowers, like "nature" (this has been an effective marketing tool for quite a while). If she was lucky, her laundry soap smelled like flowers *and* was biodegradable, although the latter would be far less certain, in the United States, anyway. What caught my attention was a stunning reversal of the expected logical relationship with nature in this child's experience. Unlike the past, where children spent more time outdoors and in nature, this child came to recognize the scent of the flower through first experiencing the laundry detergent. In other words, she had never experienced the original thing (flowers) that the product was mimicking. So, to her, nature was imitating a consumer product, not the other way around. This was a fascinating example not only of what geographer Yi Fu Tuan calls the "interiorization" of experience, referring to how much time children and adults spend indoors in modern societies, but also the social construction of experience—and socialization—through a consumer product. Although we tend to dismiss it as irrelevant, we are indeed being "educated" all the time through the medium of advertising, and the more vulnerable the recipient (e.g., children), the stronger the impact. In her book *Born to Buy*, Juliet Schor (2004) documents how children in the United States "can recognize logos by eighteen months, and before reaching their second birthday, are asking for products by brand name" (19). She notes that by roughly age three, children "start to believe that brands communicate their personal qualities, for example, that they're cool or strong, or smart" (19). At the same time, children are playing less and shopping more, spending more time in an advertising-saturated environment that makes consumer culture appealing.

We can say, then, that socialization isn't only about interacting with one's friends, family, and acquaintances; it's also about what the self has come to be in a globalized world of consumption and advertising. Although some countries have a more privileged position at the core of the global capitalist system while others find themselves on the periphery (these terms come from sociologist Immanuel Wallerstein's "world systems" theory—a great example of a macro-level sociological theory), the experience of self as a consumer is becoming a globally shared phenomenon. It touches the smallest, most remote village along with large cosmopolitan cities. We often assume that advertising is trivial and doesn't affect us very much. But advertising is a multibillion dollar industry that works around the clock to make us feel that we have to look a certain way or buy more "stuff." Judging by studies of the impact of advertising on people's thinking and judging by what we actually buy (mountains and mountains of stuff), it must be working quite well. (For a short film that neatly and humorously sums this up, see Annie Leonard's [2007] *The Story of Stuff.*) A visitor to our planet (hypothetically speaking) would probably be stunned at the constant barrage of messages shouting at us that we should be eating something or driving something or taking a certain medication or using a new shampoo or finding a new way to lose weight. Of course, the messages don't just tell us to buy something; they tell us that if we buy it, people will really like us. And as sociologist and communications theorist Sut Jhally (2006) has pointed out, advertising has become as much of our environment as nature. So, the interesting question is, what happens to the self (your self, my self, many other selves) under these circumstances?

The circumstances that we're talking about are those found in capitalist societies, although as capitalism becomes a global system, one needn't live in a capitalist society to feel the effects. In the mid-nineteenth century, Karl Marx laid out a theory of capitalism as an economic and social system (this is a good example of a macro-level theory—focusing on large groups like economic classes). Like Adam Smith, he identified competition as a key element of the system. Unlike Adam Smith, who had a more benign view of competitive capitalism, Marx concluded that the logic of that system was inherently based on the misery of the many for the benefit of a few. For example, a high unemployment rate in a society is very good for a business owner/capitalist, because he or she can pay low wages to people who are desperate for the few jobs available. Because the key goal in capitalism is to make a profit, companies enhance their market position by cutting their production costs (like wages, health benefits, safety equipment) and maximizing their profits. Having studied the devastated lives of the working class in industrial London, Marx believed that workers had a chance to rise up and overthrow capitalism *if* they became conscious of their oppression and organized collectively. While there have certainly been efforts to overthrow capitalism since that time, it has remained quite resilient and powerful. Today the global political-economic system is dominated by capitalism and by those countries that are advantaged by its structure. So, an interesting question for social theorists is, how did a system that is admittedly oppressive to so many survive and even thrive into the twenty-first century? And sticking with our chapter's theme, how does this tie in with culture, socialization, and the self?

One sociological answer to these questions is suggested by the theorists of the so-called **Frankfurt School** (located initially in Germany, then in the United States, and eventually back in Germany). Adopting a neo-Marxist approach to analyzing society, they recognized the importance of economic relationships in our lives but also focused on the power of culture to socialize people and to hold a system of economic class privileges in place.

Theodor Adorno and Max Horkheimer (and related thinkers like Antonio Gramsci and György Lukács) looked beyond the economic power of capitalists and their *direct* control over workers in the workplace and focused more on how the *idea* of capitalism is spread throughout society by powerful social actors (i.e., the ruling class). Gramsci used the word *hegemony* to capture how the government itself, the educational system, the media, and other powerful interests support capitalism and exclude other options. Instead of military or police force being used, consumers are seduced by a system that sells them identity and symbolic power through advertising and other means. This is a softer form of coercion than a rifle but just as powerful, if not more so. Through hegemony, power relationships are more hidden and diffused throughout the entire society, so it is difficult to see and to challenge them. That is especially true when consumers are being distracted by "false choices," a favorite subject of the Frankfurt School.

One of Marx's key contributions was to call attention to the fact that economic systems are fundamentally *social*—they teach us what to expect from others and from ourselves, how we should spend our time, what we should value, and many other things that shape our imaginations and actions. This sounds very much like socialization, and in fact, that's why we're discussing it here. The Frankfurt School thinkers were especially interested in the rise of a "culture industry" that sells us everything from T-shirts to astrology readings to soap operas (and if they were writing today, they would probably say reality shows) and other consumer products that either keep us busy buying products or distract us from the need for real social change. We become so preoccupied with false choices (like what color the seats in your car should be) that we don't get to question whether that consumer item, or our relationship to it, is a good idea in the first place (is a car really the best way to get around in an era of finite renewable resources such as oil?). Does this affect our socialization? Rather dramatically.

One of the essentials of capitalism is the "social construction" of the self as a consumer. Consumption in and of itself need not be a problem—it depends on how it is carried out. But the kind of self that is useful in a capitalist system is a self that feels very insecure, very dissatisfied with him- or herself, very much in need of constantly trying to fill the void with new cutting-edge products and ego-enhancing items so that life can feel better. What would happen if a person said, "I think I have enough! No more shopping for me!" (Stop for a moment and think: What would your life be like if you said this? How would it feel different? What would your friends and family think?) Postmodern sociological theorist Zygmunt Bauman (1997) claims that such a person would become a dangerous deviant in a society that fuels itself on economic growth and competitive capitalism. The way things are set up, refusing to spend money on new products is subversive and suspect. Perhaps that explains former President George W. Bush's famous pronouncement in the wake of the 9/11 tragedy that people should go shopping. Stimulating the economy through buying new products was presented as an act of patriotism.

A particularly interesting theorist among the Frankfurt School is Herbert Marcuse. Marcuse used a blend of Marxism and Freudianism to analyze capitalist societies and the hold that they have on their members. For example, he took Freud's idea of "sublimation"—which refers to how people in societies are usually asked to restrain or rechannel powerful but often chaotic urges like sexuality—and Marx's idea that capitalist societies are repressive and created the concept of **repressive desublimation** (Marcuse [1964] 1991). Desublimation suggests that instead of curbing our basic drives, we are allowed to unleash them. Liberating, right? But the other half of the phrase suggests that this unleashing is repressive. Why? Because we are directed (even though it feels like pleasant seduction) to channel our creative energies into buying consumer products that keep the system of capitalism in place. So, in the case of sexuality, for example, advertisements encourage you to free yourself from past taboos and express yourself—to be beautiful, powerful, sexy, and creative—but only if you *buy* something. You never really move "out of the box" of products that were designed by somebody else to keep you spending money and being a consumer. The trick is, even though someone else is pulling your strings, you feel like you're creating yourself, exercising genuine agency instead of being constrained. Perhaps you're already beautiful and creative. Perhaps you don't want to support a competitive and consumerist society. In that case, you're not encouraged to desublimate!

Like Marcuse, symbolic interactionists would recognize that the experience of going shopping is quite pleasurable (well, not for everyone—it depends on who is doing the shopping, what is being bought, and where). The pleasure comes from fantasy elements, whether you're going directly to a store or taking advantage of 24-hour opportunities to shop on the Internet (where there are even fewer obstacles to compulsive behavior). A prospective consumer might act out "who I will be after I buy this product"—usually someone powerful, desirable, and loved. This role-playing process might remind you a little bit of the play stage that Mead wrote about. The difference is that in the play stage, the I–Me dialogue is laying a foundation for a self that will be restrained by the rules and needs of society rather than driven by impulsive wants. But according to theorists like Marcuse, capitalism stimulates constant dissatisfaction with what one already has (in that sense advertising is a rather powerful social mirror). This fuels an impulsive and unstable self often based on insecurity and even self-dislike. This self is "manufactured" along with the products themselves and can be endlessly seduced by the promise held out by the next consumer purchase. The identity needed to keep the markets running appears to be based almost exclusively on the impulsive I. This is amplified by some deep transformations in the advertising industry.

Social analysts of consumerism and advertising point out that both have been changed dramatically in the later part of the twentieth and early part of the twenty-first century. There is quite a difference, for example, between the macro-level social structure of **Fordism**—the assembly-line style of car production pioneered by Henry Ford, who wanted to produce a mass-market car that everyone could afford—and **post-Fordism**, a tendency in later capitalism to segment the consumer market to produce luxury or niche goods that target certain groups of likely consumers, including, increasingly, children. Post-Fordism depends on increasingly sophisticated advertising. Rather than having an (actor representing an) expert simply telling you why a product is good, contemporary ads rely on visual images and mimic the art of the short film to capture the attention of jaded consumers who have seen too many ads (Jhally 2006). Advertisements especially sell the idea that we're free to craft our identity by creatively selecting the right mix of constantly shifting products from an almost limitless marketplace (does this remind you, perhaps, of our earlier discussion of the mutable self?). We often assume that we like something "just because" we like it. But as sociologist Pierre Bourdieu (1979) has pointed out, there is a very active process of shaping taste and identity that goes on in any class-based society, and it's remarkably successful—so successful that we often don't know that it's happening.

Let's consider the example of coffee-drinking behavior in the United States. Do you, or most of your friends, make a habit of drinking coffee, especially the specialty coffees that establishments like Starbucks have put on the market? I wouldn't be surprised if the answer is "yes." But young people drinking coffee is a rather recent development, at least in the United States. An interesting study by anthropologist William Roseberry looks at how this came about. In the 1970s and 1980s, the coffee industry was in trouble. Young people were increasingly choosing soft drinks, and they were especially ignoring coffee. Coffee was seen as a boring nondescript beverage that older businessmen drank to get through the day. Or maybe it was something that you drank to pull an all-nighter in high school or college to finish an assigned paper (been there!). Roseberry studied, among other things, trade journals in the coffee industry and documented the strategies used to create a young consumer (they even gave the young market prototype a name: Joel). The solution was the rise of specialty coffees that could be sold as a luxury good, and, just as important, as a symbol of status and taste. We now know that "Joel" bought it (literally). So much so that when you buy a cup of coffee, it's not the boring drink of the 1950s and 1960s, but rather an emblem of taste and status and even cosmopolitan expertise (you know what all of those different drinks are—and the people who serve you are called "baristas"). This is a direct result of market strategizing several decades ago to resocialize you to imagine coffee as desirable—as something that tastes good, is worth paying a high price for, and announces something positive about your identity. Marcuse would find the specialty coffees to be a perfect illustration of "repressive desublimation." We can buy whatever we want to—so many flavors! But the choices are preordained and, in a way that is invisible to consumers, strategically created by the coffee industry to rope you in even as you feel you're practicing free choice.

With specialized organizations now studying your every purchase, analyzing demographic information about you, and selling this information to marketers, the art of seducing you just became more rational and sophisticated. We often forget that whenever we order something on the Internet or use search engines like Google, sophisticated computer technology takes note of our desires, interests, and social identities and then channels tailored messages our way, a form of "electronic profiling." Apart from the fact that we often already seek out people with opinions like our own, this is one of many reasons why the use of the Internet may narrow, instead of broaden, our horizons. Even the news that we get is likely to reinforce what we already believe (which helps to explain why the United States continues to have so many fervent climate change deniers). This makes it difficult to dialogue with those who are different from ourselves.

But wait a minute. Do we just take whatever the market hands to us and respond like robots to advertisements? Certainly not, although we probably do that more often than we realize. As mentioned earlier, social life and interaction are a constantly evolving process of structure and agency. Social structures constrain us, box us in, limit our freedom. And human agency replies to structure by resisting it, reshaping it, adapting to it, and sometimes trying to do away with it. For example, Starbucks began to sell a small amount of fair-trade coffee as a result of a consumer boycott, including on college campuses. The fair-trade label guarantees that small independent coffee growers, often in the periphery countries mentioned earlier, get a fair price for their coffee. This is a good example of how organizing for social change took place once people (students, in this case) became aware of an invisible social structure of inequality.

If we add a focus on globalization to our discussion about the self as consumer, we can learn some interesting lessons about how identity works in the contemporary world. A good example is the spread of the McDonald's franchise around the world. McDonald's—invented in the United States and the quintessential symbol of Westernization and fast food—has been hugely successful, so much so that sociologist George Ritzer wrote a very popular book called *The McDonaldization of Society* (Ritzer 2000). His book shows how the McDonald's model has influenced many aspects of society other than food—for example, people's expectations about receiving quick service and standardized products (whether that product is medical care or fried chicken). But successful as McDonald's has been in creating an international marketplace of new consumers, it has not been received with open arms everywhere. In Beijing, China, for example, it had to adapt to local culture and expectations even as it introduced new and unfamiliar elements (Watson 1997). Its appeal varies greatly between different generations. Young children, growing up in an environment saturated with fast-food advertising (and easily hooked on salt, fat, and sugar) often love going to McDonald's to eat and beg their parents to take them. Young adults may enjoy the social atmosphere and the symbolism of something exotic (in this case, something from the West) more than the food itself. Older generations are sometimes drawn by the chance to try something new that is associated with being a modern person in a global culture. More recently, McDonald's has lost market shares in China, a product of changing consumer tastes and complex negotiations with government authorities. So, even though McDonald's has made money by expanding its market in Asian countries, people consume (or don't consume) its products for complex and diverse reasons. The same can be said about the self in a global context—people don't just automatically or uncritically accept a Western identity, for example, although some are eager to do so. Although there are militant anti-Western movements, the more likely result is an evolving hybrid identity that accepts some elements of globalization but rejects others—in Mead's terms, a dialogue or process that is ongoing and sometimes unpredictable. In Zurcher's terms, a mutable self.

One thing is certain. As a global culture evolves, self and identity are being deeply affected. Where globalization takes hold, traditional views of life are often challenged by what sociologist Zygmunt Bauman (2003) calls "liquid modernity." From macro-level global institutions to micro-level interactions, deep changes in our social structure prompt a questioning of past identities and traditions. Sociologist Anthony Giddens (1990, 1992) describes transformations ranging from our most intimate interactions to shifting relationships between society and the natural environment. Many of these involve new experiences of time and space (e.g., the Internet) that represent a significant break with our past human experience. The frequent (although not inevitable) result is a self that is open to change, or "liquid." The risk is a loss of identity and sense of place, anxiety, and instability. The gain is a chance to reshape one's own identity and society more freely (although this may be an illusion, according to the Frankfurt School).

It is important to note that the liquid, mutable self, especially the version of it that depends on consumerism, is often a privileged self. For those who are barely making it from one day to the next because of oppressive social structures, self-creation may seem an unimaginable luxury. Of course, self-creation doesn't depend solely on money (nor does happiness, based on all of the available global indicators that we have). Self-creation, in a less benign sense, may also be forced on a person in dire economic need. Given the many persistent inequalities in the global system, it seems fitting to conclude this chapter with a brief look at the relationship between the self and movements for social change.

THE SELF AND SOCIAL MOVEMENTS

As a sociologist who studies social movements, I'm struck by how deeply they can reshape our sense of self. When a transformative social movement arises, it allows us to imagine something different, both about ourselves and about our society. Some movements, like the US civil rights movement that became visible between the 1940s and 1970s (although it actually began much earlier, and its work is still unfinished, as the Black Lives Matter movement so dramatically illustrates), have had a tremendous impact nationally and globally. Human rights movements in other countries have patterned themselves on the ideas and strategies of the US civil rights movement. Likewise, the US movement learned from Gandhi's movement in India—so you could say that this too is a kind of resocialization process, where groups working for social change around the globe learn from the successes and failures of other groups. Internet communication has helped to create truly transnational movements, like the global environmental justice movement, which battles disproportionate toxic dumping (including electronic waste from discarded computers) on minority communities. Many "selves" have been influenced by what is becoming a global process of reimagining social justice and human rights around the world, even though there are still deep disagreements about what some of these concepts mean across different cultures.

Social movements enter our lives in quite different ways. The civil rights movement had a presence associated with marches and demonstrations, acts of nonviolent resistance, and the symbolic power of a rhetoric demanding social justice and equality for all. It helped to resocialize not only several generations of activists but also members of the general public, many of whom were not born until after the movement. By contrast, the Occupy Wall Street movement that surfaced in 2011 had a looser organization and broader variety of tactics but was remarkably successful at revealing hidden social inequalities in US society. The Black Lives Matter movement has many commonalities with the earlier civil rights movement, but new technologies play an interesting mobilizing role, as people can more easily document incidents of injustice by taking pictures with their phones and quickly posting them online. Some movements resist change—like the women at the turn of the twentieth century in the United States who organized to *not* give themselves the right to vote or hate groups (mentioned earlier) that scapegoat racial, ethnic, and sexual minorities and violently resist the expansion of civil rights. I'm guessing that the person in front of me at a traffic light who had painted the words "Black Trucks Matter" on the back window of his black pickup truck was part of a backlash against a perceived expansion of minority rights, and he was wanting to make a statement. And then there are movements for social change that have a quiet presence, focusing more on lifestyle choices. Here is one that is making an impact: the slow food movement (I'll refer to it as the SFM).

The SFM is not often covered by mainstream media and exists somewhat under the radar. Yet more and more people are encountering it in some form. It began when Carlo Petrini, an Italian journalist (with a background in sociology), discovered that a McDonald's restaurant planned to open near the Piazza di Spagna in Rome. Petrini organized a protest against McDonald's, whose practices seemed an affront to valued Italian traditions. McDonald's symbolized the worst aspects of globalization—an incursion of unhealthy junk food, a hurried lifestyle, and the watering down of a unique cultural identity. The protest made an impact, the movement caught on, and it spread from Italy to other countries, including the United States. In the places where the SFM flourishes (especially where it has chapters, or convivia), it teaches both adults and children to ask questions like, where does my food come from? What and whom am I supporting when I buy a tomato in a "big box store" instead of a ripe tomato at a local farmers' market? Why does that local tomato taste so good? What are the environmental and cultural impacts of my food choices, locally and globally? How is my own identity linked to food? The SFM encourages support for small farmers and food artisans (e.g., producers of unique regional cheeses) who are getting squeezed out by globalization and standardization. It teaches people not to be passive consumers but rather to be co-producers, to exercise agency by becoming involved in new social relationships. This could involve getting to know the people who produce your food and learning to savor new flavors (not to mention finding out what to do with an heirloom purple tomato). You might learn new words like "terroir"—a French word that refers to how food takes on the taste of the soil and climate where it is grown—or "locavore," which refers to eating foods grown only within one hundred miles of one's household.

Of course, it's possible to use new words like terroir in an elitist way, to draw lines between yourself and others. The self as consumer has in fact been trained to do that. As Julie Guthman points out, expensive organic and artisanal foods can reinforce social inequality (Guthman 2003). Alternatively, the new words and knowledge can be used to build social change that will be more inclusive—to make good healthy food affordable for everybody, including inner-city children growing up in so-called food deserts, where fresh food literally isn't available. It can be used to lobby for global fair-trade practices that help small organic farmers around the world survive economic pressures of globalization. It can be used to help pass laws to label and monitor pesticides, antibiotics, hormones, and genetically modified organisms (GMOs) used in food products, so that parents can make more informed choices about what their children eat. The point is that social movements—whether they are as iconic as the civil rights movement or as subtle as the SFM—help us to imagine and to act on new possibilities. In other words, they continue to teach us about who we are. This, along with participation in new communities and social networks, can give us knowledge, confidence, and determination to work with others to shape the kind of self and societies that we want to have in the future.

Sociology, too, with its theories about culture, socialization, and the self offers tools that can lead to a better life. It can help you understand your self as an unfolding process in the context of modernization and globalization. It can give you perspective on what makes you unique as well as what you have in common with others. It can make you more aware of when and where you are free to act while increasing your understanding of the forces that might constrain you. It can help you see the invisible strings that connect you to people around the globe, all of whom are also making choices about identity and whose lives are connected to your choices, economically, ecologically, and culturally. It can assist you in working for social change (including altering what the Me voice is saying to you and to others). And as you can see from the work of Goffman, it can give you a few laughs along the way, coupled with fresh insights. Together with sociological theory, insight and humor are precious resources in a world where movements for a more just and sustainable society often face strong resistance. I'll conclude this chapter by inviting you back to its opening question, with every best wish for the future development of the dialogue of your self: who are you?

Lesson Take-Aways
- The "self" is created through a process of social interaction with many "agents of socialization" in an increasingly globalized environment.
- The theory of symbolic interactionism understands the self as a process emerging through social interaction.
- The theory of dramaturgy understands the self as an actor attempting to manage impressions, keeping "backstage" separate from "front-stage."
- Socialization in a capitalist society includes many subtle dimensions that tend to produce the "self as consumer."
- Social change movements have the potential to transform the self, society, and culture.

Discussion Questions
1. Do you remember experiencing Mead's play phase as a child? If so, who or what did you pretend to be? Why?
2. What are some examples of major resocialization experiences in your life?
3. To what extent do you experience the benefits of the liquid or mutable self in a globalized society? To what extent do you experience the negative side of such a self?

Sources
Bauman, Zygmunt. 1997. *Postmodernity and Its Discontents*. New York: New York University Press.

Bauman, Zygmunt. 2003. *Liquid Love*. Cambridge, UK: Polity.

Becker, Howard. 1953. "Becoming a Marihuana Smoker." *American Journal of Sociology* 59(3): 235–42.

Becker, Howard. 1986. *Doing Things Together*. Evanston, IL: Northwestern University Press.

Becker, Howard, Blanche Greer, Everett Hughes, Anselm L. Strauss, and Everett C. Hughes. 1976. *Boys in White: Student Culture in Medical School*. New Brunswick, NJ: Transaction.

Bourdieu, Pierre. 1979. *Distinction: A Social Critique of the Judgment of Taste*. Cambridge, MA: Harvard University Press.

Garfinkel, Harold. 1967. *Studies in Ethnomethodology*. Englewood Cliffs, NJ: Prentice-Hall.

Giddens, Anthony. 1990. *The Consequences of Modernity*. Palo Alto, CA: Stanford University Press.

Giddens, Anthony. 1992. *The Transformation of Intimacy: Sexuality, Love and Eroticism in Modern Societies*. Palo Alto, CA: Stanford University Press.

Goffman, Erving. 1959. *The Presentation of Self in Everyday Life.* Garden City, NY: Doubleday.

Goffman, Erving. 1963. *Stigma: Notes on the Management of Spoiled Identity.* New York: Simon and Schuster.

Guthman, Julie. 2003. "Fast Food/Organic Food: Reflexive Tastes and the making of 'Yuppie Chow.'" *Social & Cultural Geography* (4)1: 45–58.

Jhally, Sut. 2006. *The Spectacle of Accumulation: Essays in Media, Culture and Politics.* New York: Peter Lang.

Johnson, Allan G. 2000. *The Blackwell Dictionary of Sociology: A User's Guide to Sociological Language.* Malden, MA: Blackwell.

Kuhn, M. H. and McPartland, T.S. 1954. "An Empirical Investigation of Self-Attitudes." *American Sociological Review,* 19(1): 68–76.

Leonard, Annie. 2007. *The Story of Stuff* (Film). Berkeley, CA: Free Range Studios. http://storyofstuff.org/movies/story-of-stuff/

Marcuse, Herbert. [1964] 1991. *One-Dimensional Man.* Boston: Beacon.

Mead, George Herbert. 1934. *Mind, Self, and Society.* Chicago: University of Chicago Press.

Ritzer, George. 2000. *The McDonaldization of Society.* Thousand Oaks, CA: Pine Forge Press.

Roseberry, William. 1996. "The Rise of Yuppie Coffees and the Reimagination of Class in the United States." *American Anthropologist* 98(4): 762–75.

Schor, Juliet. 2004. *Born to Buy: The Commercialized Child and the New Consumer Culture.* New York: Scribner.

Swidler, Ann. 1986. "Culture in Action: Symbols and Strategies." *American Sociological Review* 51(2): 273–86.

Watson, James. 1997. *Golden Arches East: McDonald's in East Asia.* Palo Alto, CA: Stanford University Press.

Zurcher, Louis. 1977. *The Mutable Self: A Self-Concept for Social Change.* Thousand Oaks, CA: SAGE.

Related Websites

Racism Review: www.racismreview.com
Slow Food International: http://slowfood.com
Southern Poverty Law Center: http://splcenter.org

LESSON 3, PHOTO REFLECTION:

A food court somewhere in the United States on a Saturday afternoon.
Photo by Ken Gould.

Do you recognize the food court in this photo? We are not going to tell you where it is because it could be anywhere in America. You probably recognize the plastic furniture, and you are probably familiar with the choice of processed fast foods available. Is this in a shopping mall, a highway rest stop, or a college student union building? Is it in Massachusetts or Alabama, or somewhere else? It doesn't really matter. Once you are in this environment you understand what to do and what to expect. As corporations have taken control of more aspects of our social life, these generic corporate food courts have replaced mom-and-pop diners and other locally owned eateries. Nonfranchise restaurants used to offer local flavor, variety, and the unexpected (both delicious and disappointing). The food you ate would reflect the culture of the place you were—clam chowder in Massachusetts's maybe, hush puppies in Alabama perhaps. Food courts offer the comfort of no surprises and makes eating in one part of the country the same as eating in any other. This is what George Ritzer called the "McDonaldization" of society. If you were the photographer, what picture would you take to represent socialization and culture?

Is this a photo of a Department of Motor Vehicles office, a public aid office, a bank, or the student services counter at a public university? What do those places have in common?

4

Social Institutions

Naomi Braine

In daily language, people often use the word "institution" to refer to things that involve rigid bureaucracies and large buildings. Schools are considered institutions, for example, and so are prisons, corporations, and the US Senate. All of these have social power, shape our lives directly and indirectly, generally involve a lot of money and people, and feel too big to move or change in a meaningful way. This power and apparent unchangeability are part of what make us call something an institution; it's bigger than any individual and all too often rolls along uncaring of the lives and feelings of mere mortals.

Sociologists also consider corporations, schools, and the government to be examples of institutions, but sociology defines a **social institution** in ways that have nothing to do with administration or architecture. Social institutions are formal systems of shared behaviors, beliefs, and social norms that organize the major areas of social life; they are an important mechanism for what sociologists call "social cohesion," meaning that institutions bring people in a society together and create shared social worlds. In something closer to ordinary language, social institutions are the means by which a society creates and sustains a collective social life from day to day and year to year; they answer the question of "how do we _____ around here" (e.g., educate children, run a city, buy and sell things, etc.). Institutions provide the structures within which members of a society manage their lives at all levels, from the personal to the workplace to the government, and in doing that the institutions simultaneously maintain (or enforce) dominant understandings of "normal life." Some aspects of social institutions are institutions in the common-sense meaning of the term, while other aspects have become naturalized parts of daily life, experienced simply as "the way things are."

Traditionally, sociologists have identified five institutions as making up the core of social life, and these are sometimes called the primary social institutions: family, education, economy, government or politics, and religion (see Sidebar for definitions of each). These five exist in some form in all societies, although the precise form of each institution varies significantly across societies and historical periods. For example, education as a social institution includes not only the process of schooling from prekindergarten through the most advanced degrees—everything from school funding and educational policy to curriculum and administration to interaction in classrooms—but also those forms of education that happen outside of schools (e.g., internships, professional tutoring) and education-related organizations like school boards, advocacy groups, and organizations such as Teach for America. The family as a social institution is much larger than parents and children or even extended family ties (i.e., grandparents, cousins, aunts, and uncles). In addition to personal relationships, a wide range of family support services are part of family as an institution, particularly domestic supports such as child care or cleaning services and workplace policies like family leave. Some high schools and colleges have on-site day-care services, which can be seen simultaneously as a support service for families and part of the educational environment. As can be seen in these examples, understanding social institutions requires active use of the sociological imagination, in this case by thinking broadly about how a particular aspect of life is organized and all the different places it actually operates in our lives.

SIDEBAR: THE TRADITIONAL FIVE SOCIAL INSTITUTIONS

Family

Sociologists see the family as a set of relationships between two or more people related by birth, marriage, adoption, or long-standing ties of commitment and intimacy. The first three forms of relationship are all legally recognized in the United States as "family," while the last usually is not unless it is linked to one of the first three. Families provide certain elements of social organization, including socializing children, regulating sexual behavior and reproduction, distributing resources, and providing social support. In the United States, changing social norms about single parenthood and same-sex marriage have expanded the definition of "family" while enabling continuing regulation of social life.

Education

Sociologists understand education as the formal processes through which knowledge, skills, and values are systematically transmitted within the society, particularly but not exclusively from one generation to the next. Educational systems transmit shared values and beliefs and specific knowledge and skills and typically sort individuals on the basis of various characteristics. Educational systems also perform a variety of social control functions, particularly in relation to youth, and differential treatment of students (such as tracking) usually reinforces social inequalities.

Religion

Sociologists view religion as a social phenomenon that provides a system of shared beliefs and practices involving the supernatural and norms about the right way to live. Religious belief systems provide meaning for life,

Sidebar *continued*

reinforce social norms, strengthen social cohesion, and ritually manage certain kinds of life changes (e.g., marriage, death). Weber, a major sociological theorist, classified religions according to their approach to salvation: ascetic religions focus on self-mastery; mystical religions demand passive contemplation; other-worldly religions focus on a next life (e.g., heaven); and this-worldly religions focus on what happens on earth.

Economy

Sociologists define the economy as the methods through which a society produces, distributes, and consumes goods, services, and other resources. These processes lie at the core of a society, shaping work and occupations, the distribution of resources and opportunities, and many aspects of relationships between social groups. Economic organization determines the major features of a society and, in the modern era, of relationships among nations and global regions.

Politics/Government

Sociologists understand government and political institutions as the mechanisms that manage a society: the formal distribution of authority, the right to use force or violence (military and police), and the ability to engage in relationships with other societies and political units. The responsibilities of government include defining societal goals and ideals, maintaining group identity and norms, resolving internal conflicts, and protection from external enemies. All of these responsibilities have become considerably more complex and somewhat more shared across multiple national governments as a result of globalization, immigration, and the blurring of both cultural and economic boundaries. As will be discussed in the Macro sections of this chapter, corporations have become increasingly involved in areas traditionally allocated to governments.

In fact, exercising our sociological imagination suggests that, in the twenty-first century, the classic five seem too limited to encompass the core normative systems that organize life, particularly in Western societies but even in many developing countries. As societies change, sociologists may identify new institutions that become central to social life. In the contemporary world, it seems necessary to add media and health as these have become central to the social organization of both our daily lives and the larger society. The central role of media, from cable TV to the Internet to communications technology, may seem self-evident, as many of us cannot imagine (or have forgotten) lives that were not constructed through a constant succession of text messages, Google searches, tweets, or whatever applications have made this list obsolete and ridiculous by the time it is published never mind read.

The place of health in contemporary society may be less apparent and therefore more useful than media as a first, brief illustration of how sociologists think about institutions. We know that multiple forms of media lie at the center of our lives and the day-to-day operations of society, but on the surface health looks more narrow and limited to the activities of professionals, something that happens in doctors offices, hospitals, or pharmacies. Health sounds like a concern of the middle-aged and elderly, something parents worry about but that few people under 35 have to think about in relation to themselves. A slight step back, however, brings a larger domain into view that includes many day-to-day activities like food and eating, recreation, explanations for (or criticisms of) personal behavior, marketing strategies, clothing choices, and a wide range of technologies (e.g., Wii, exercise machines). Health has expanded and diffused over time from being primarily the domain of specialized professionals and those who are considered seriously ill to an individual responsibility that should be attended to in almost all areas of life. You are engaging with the social institution of health any time you think about whether the food you are eating is good for you, feel like you should go to the gym, or tell a friend to quit smoking.

The boundaries of social institutions are an area of research and theoretical debate. For example, an argument can be made for classifying science as a separate institution, independent of education or economy, because it has a distinct system of shared behaviors and norms, in the form of ethical and research frameworks that are shared across multiple disciplines. However, scientific work is embedded within systems of education, health care, and economic life to such a deep extent that it may not have an existence independent of these larger institutional structures. For example, at a material level, the connection between science and economic life has been embodied—or perhaps operationalized—in the requirement that scientists publicly disclose any financial conflicts of interest they may have in relation to their research, such as owning stock in a company that might profit from the research findings. The interesting sociological questions revolve around examining *in what ways* science is and is not an independent institution and what this illuminates about science, education, health care, and the economy.

INSTITUTIONS AT MULTIPLE LEVELS

Institutions operate at multiple levels, from the micro worlds of personal identity and social interaction through the meso level of work and organizations to macro questions of governance processes and economic systems. Sociologists use micro, meso, and macro as levels of analysis because they refer to examination of society at small, mid-range, and large scales of operation, respectively. We will go through a brief discussion of social norms and then ways to think about institutions at different levels of analysis, from the micro to the macro. Social norms are a thread running through social institutions at all levels, so it is useful to discuss them first and independent of any one level of analysis. Finally, we will explore in more detail two separate examples of social institutions. It is important to keep in mind that all institutions organize social life at multiple levels; for example, media technologies shape interactions among friends, teaching strategies in the classroom, the physical characteristics of classrooms and workplaces, rates of voting during elections, and political processes at national and international levels.

SOCIAL NORMS

From a common-sense perspective, institutions and social norms seem to occupy different realms, one formal and rigid and the other interpersonal and contextually variable. High school peer groups have different norms, for example, so how can social norms be an element of institutions? Social **norms** are one of those topics where sociologists use a term in a way that is both similar to and slightly different from day-to-day use. Societies have collectively understood norms—values, beliefs, and ways of behaving—that govern life and interaction across a wide range of social contexts, and violations of societal norms are immediately recognizable and often met with negative sanctions of some kind. Normatively governed ways of acting or interacting often become naturalized, simply perceived as the way things are, or at least how they should be. Social norms in this sense can be understood as the dominant patterns of action and interpretation in a society, which is a much broader framework than thinking in terms of attitudes, preferences, or social approval or disapproval. For example, members of different social networks may hold different attitudes toward cigarettes, but the policies that regulate smoking have become normal in US society and reflect the growing centrality of health as an organizing factor in social life. The legitimacy of regulating smoking represents a shift in societal norms; in the 1980s, it was considered normal for people to smoke in offices, cubicles, restaurants, and bars, despite general knowledge about the dangers of cigarettes. As this example shows, norms are powerful but not static and evolve in response to social action and societal change. The example of cigarette smoking also shows how social norms and norm-shift can operate simultaneously at the micro level of behavior and social interaction, the meso level of workplace rules, and the macro level of governmental policy.

Education provides rich material for thinking about the depth at which norms shape society and social interaction. For example, the teacher occupies the front of the classroom in virtually all schools from kindergarten through college, and student desks or chairs face forward. The arrangement of student seating may vary from circular to small groupings to rows facing forward, but a random scattering of seats facing in all directions would seem immediately odd to most students (and teachers) in US schools. Strategies for seat arrangement often signal different approaches to teaching, so students entering a classroom may adjust their expectations for teacher–student interactions based on seat arrangement. The cultural association between seat arrangements and classrooms is strong enough that any room with chairs and desks set up in rows facing one direction is likely to be perceived as a classroom unless there are clear indications to the contrary. These shared understandings about the relation between how furniture (desks and chairs) is arranged, intended uses of space, and expectations about patterns of social interaction between teachers and students reflect the power of social norms to organize social life. Again, norms operate across multiple levels of analysis, from student–teacher interaction (micro) to spatial organization and architecture (meso).

Societies are stratified and divided in systematic ways, and social norms often vary in certain ways by social context or location. For example, physical aggression, violence, or forcible control of another person's actions are generally forbidden between adults in the United States and most other countries. Certain occupational groups, most prominently the police, are permitted to engage in these actions under certain circumstances. While the right to use force when necessary is central to the normative definition of policing, studies that examine perceptions of when police use of force is necessary and how much is appropriate find that civilians and police often disagree (Johnson and Kuhns 2009; Dick 2005). A sociologist decided to study how new officers are trained on the job by systematically observing interaction among new and senior officers in squad cars; one of her findings was that new officers recently out of the police academy had to be systematically resocialized by experienced officers to perceive higher levels of force as normal (Hunt 1985). These different norms about use of force held by police officers and civilians and the professional **socialization** process for new officers direct our attention to how social status or role shapes perceptions in ways that are not neutral—in this case, about acceptable levels of violence by those who enforce laws and social order.

MICRO LEVEL: SOCIAL INTERACTION

At the micro level, social institutions shape patterns of interaction through creating the contexts, meanings, and interpretive frameworks within which we encounter each other. In the not-so-distant past, social interaction involved simultaneous contact, either face to face or through a telephone conversation. The recent emergence of new social media such as networking sites, Twitter, and text messaging have expanded the range of time and space within which interaction occurs, moving beyond simultaneous or face-to-face contexts to various forms of delayed contact in which participants interact across time and space through the medium of technology (Rettie 2009). Interviews with people who have Twitter followings found that their audiences are often fluid or unknown and that the Twitter user had to imagine an audience and construct a Twitter-self that could both attract and communicate authentically with the desired audience (Marwick and Boyd 2011). The emergence of a new social institution, like media, creates societal divides as older generations struggle to manage a new layer of social organization and norms that younger generations take for granted. The new interaction patterns, norms, and ways of creating meaning may be as large a barrier for older generations as the technology itself.

Thinking about how institutions shape interactions offers a new angle of vision on familiar contexts and activities. Most people expect teachers to interact somewhat differently with different students, but certain patterns of teacher–student interaction occur across a wide range of educational contexts and are so common that they elicit little notice. In the 1970s, two sociologists observed teaching and interaction in classrooms and found that, regardless of the size of the class, a few students take responsibility for the majority of participation, both asking and responding to questions, and their adoption of this role, combined with professors' unwillingness to call on students directly, enables the rest of the class to remain quiet (Karp and Yoels 1976). While much has changed since the 1970s, this particular pattern sounds familiar, and students can often identify who the designated participators are in a class. Classroom interaction is also shaped by larger social processes and prejudices. When data from 32 different studies of gender and classroom interaction were combined (a method called meta-analysis), the results indicated that teachers initiate more interactions overall with male students than with female students, although there was less of a gender difference for positive interactions specifically (Jones and Dindia 2004). When data on student conduct and discipline was collected from 43,000 public schools, it revealed that African-American boys are more likely to be punished, even for minor misbehavior, and classified as in need of special education than boys of other races and girls of any race (Gregory 1997). Teachers appear to have a different response to African-American boys than to white, Asian, or Latino boys even when they are behaving in relatively similar ways. These studies point to the ways that the nature of classroom interactions are shaped by education as an institution, including the ways it embodies systems of social stratification like race and gender and not simply by the characteristics of individual teachers or the dynamics of particular schools or even neighborhoods.

MESO LEVEL: WORK AND ORGANIZATIONS

It may seem self-evident to say that institutions affect the structure of work, especially given that common-sense definition of institution referenced at the beginning of the chapter. All social institutions operate at the level of work and organizations, although sometimes in ways that are not intuitively obvious. At the more obvious end, media technologies have had a significant impact on how work is conducted, with computers and digital communications integrated everywhere from factories to schools to corporate offices. For example, electronic textbooks, library websites with databases, and online classes are only small examples of how media has reshaped teaching (education as a form of work), the physical design of classrooms, and the organization of universities. It might be less obvious to say that the family, as a social institution, has significant effects on the social organization of work.

FOOD FOR THOUGHT
HOW THE STATE SHAPES WHAT YOU EAT
Justin Sean Myers

Have you ever given any thought to how the state shapes your eating patterns? Have you ever asked yourself, family, teachers, or administration why your school lunch was generally full of tater tots, French fries, chocolate milk, pizza, chicken nuggets, and hamburgers? Why your high school was lined with vending machines full of sugary snacks and bottled water? Why your school sold Taco Bell or McDonald's? Where on earth did that salad bar or tofu plate come from? Moreover, have you even asked why school lunch exists in the first place? Why doesn't everyone just bring a packed lunch from home or go off-campus to eat? The answers to these questions lie in the massive economic and political changes that transformed this country from an agrarian powerhouse to an industrial and now postindustrial titan.

In 2015 the school lunch program fed 31 million students a day and could be found in 99 percent of US public schools and 83 percent of private schools, making it the biggest youth nutrition program in the country. But the roots of the school lunch program are found in private initiative at the turn of the twentieth century and sought to address byproducts of immigration, industrialization, and urbanization. In many cities, low wages often required both parents to take work outside the home, and the loss of kitchen gardens meant many children could not go home to eat food for lunch, nor could they afford to buy food away from home, leading to high levels of hunger and malnutrition. Seeing this problem first hand, social reformers known as progressives began to popularize the idea that for students to learn and perform well in school required full bellies. Since education was perceived to be central to a functioning democracy as well as an engine of economic growth, it became necessary in the eyes of progressives to feed the youth whose families could not. This led to private and charitable interests setting up lunch programs for lower-class youth.

While more and more municipal and city agencies began to take over the responsibility of school lunch programs after 1900, the federal government did not get involved until the Great Depression, and even then the programs were temporary. This all changed in 1946 with the passage of the National School Lunch Act (NSLA). The NSLA created a publicly funded mandate for a national school lunch program based on arguments of political and economic necessity. During the World War II, many men were rejected from military conscription as unfit for duty because of childhood malnutrition. President Truman sought to correct this threat to the military might of the United States through the NSLA, thereby ensuring that youth were fed enough to counteract malnutrition. Despite this high-minded rhetoric, school lunch was in fact, first and foremost, a farmer income support program. The United States produces more corn, meat, and dairy than can be purchased on the domestic market, so new outlets have to be created to eliminate the surplus and keep market prices from collapsing. High school lunch is one of these programs; food stamps is another such program. High-fructose corn syrup and corn-based ethanol gasoline are two other solutions. Only secondarily does the school lunch program operate as a nutrition program combating hunger. The unhealthiness of school lunch is therefore rooted in these surplus-eliminating structures that deemphasize a nutrition-first program.

Food for Thought *continued*

This foundation was intensified through the privatization of food distribution at public schools. The constant attempt to trim public education budgets since the presidency of Ronald Reagan has pushed school districts to cut costs and increase revenues. This has lead in two directions: first, privatizing and outsourcing school food service management to for-profit companies, and, second, licensing exclusive access rights to food and beverage companies—vending machines, Taco Bell, McDonald's, and so on. These practices have either maintained or expanded unhealthy food options at schools and harmed a nutrition-first school food policy.

While the state was historically worried about malnutrition, this is no longer the case. Today, the rate of obesity, diabetes, and heart disease and their associated medical costs is what keeps public health officials, as well as Michelle Obama, up at night. Alongside of Michelle Obama's Let's Move! initiative, whose goal was to address childhood obesity through proper exercise and nutrition, the state is working towards "greening" the school lunch program. In 2010 Congress passed the Healthy, Hunger-Free Kids Act, which allows the US Department of Agriculture to create new nutrition standards for school breakfast and lunch. The new guidelines mandate reductions in fat, calories, and sodium and increases in vegetables, fruits, leafy greens, whole grains, lean protein, and water—all in the effort to create a healthy, stronger, and more affordable population. Yet, these changes have not been with conflict. Students claim they don't like the new bland-tasting food, parents have resisted the state telling their children what to eat, and school districts contend they are losing money and creating more food waste because students refuse to eat the food. Current findings dispute many of these claims though. Student lunches are healthier today, and participation rates have remained constant. In addition, more and more parents are demanding healthier lunches for their children. They don't want their children eating unhealthy fast food every day for lunch. These parents like the new lunch program.

The key takeaway from this short history of the school lunch program is that, in the eyes of the state, food is never just food. The transition from hamburgers to salads, tater tots to apples, and hot dogs to kale can be understood as more than just lunch. They are different solutions to particular health problems that are historically conditioned: the hamburger to fatten us up and the salad to slim us down.

Sources

Johnson, Donna B., Mary Podrabsky, Anita Rocha, and Jennifer J. Otten. 2016. "Effect of the Healthy Hunger-Free Kids Act on the Nutritional Quality of Meals Selected by Students and the School Lunch Participation Rates." *Journal of the American Medical Association* 170(1): e153918.

Levenstein, Harvey. 1988. *Revolution at the Table: The Transformation of the American Diet*. New York: Oxford University Press.

Levine, Susan. 2011. *School Lunch Politics: The Surprising History of America's Favorite Welfare Program*. Princeton, NJ: Princeton University Press.

Poppendieck, Janet. 1985. *Breadlines Knee Deep in Wheat: Food Assistance in the Great Depression*. Piscataway, NJ: Rutgers University Press.

Poppendieck, Janet. 2011. *Free for All: Fixing School Food in America*. Berkeley: University of California Press.

Families, however, require various forms of labor to function (e.g., child care, cooking, cleaning), and family responsibilities affect one's work schedules and priorities. In the last 40 years or so, changes in family structure have led to an expansion of employment areas such as child care, increased production of processed food, and the creation of flex time and maternity leave policies in professional workplaces.

The nature of the economy, at the most macro level, sets the terms for the structure of work and organizations at the meso level. For example, the division between nonprofit and for-profit organizations and corporations only make sense within a capitalist economic system, and in part because of this, the organizations called "nonprofits" in the United States are usually classified as nongovernmental organizations (NGOs) in other countries. The NGO category makes sense even in other developed capitalist countries such as Australia and much of Europe since, outside the United States, health care and social services are largely provided by the government; a health care service provider's relationship to the government is more relevant in most countries than its profit or market status. The conceptual distinction between nonprofits and NGOs illustrates connections between social institutions—in this case, health and economy; the structure of medical and social services delivery (government or private) affects whether organizations are primarily conceptualized in relation to the government (NGO) or corporations (nonprofit).

Each of these examples illustrates how a social institution operates at the level of work or organizations and requires thinking about the underlying processes that structure social life. This often means stepping back from some aspect of the social world—such as frozen food or the number of electronic outlets in a classroom—and trying to see it as if you came from another planet to identify the different social contexts it actually occupies. By definition, social institutions operate at all levels of analysis, from the most micro to the most macro, and the task of the sociologist is to investigate how. This process requires stepping back from what is common sense and shifting perspective to see things in new contexts; it also requires learning to think about what social processes take place in a particular context or level of analysis and how those processes reflect a given social institution.

MACRO LEVEL: GOVERNMENT, PROFIT, AND THE MANAGEMENT OF SOCIETY

The macro level is, essentially, the systemic level of societal management and organization; the policies, structures, and systems that provide the framework for the meso and, more distantly, micro levels. For example, an individual high school is a meso-level organization but the boards of education for New York City and the Los Angeles Unified School District are at the macro level of social institution of education. Governments share this level of social organization with large corporations and national or global nonprofits. In fact, at the macro level, governments, nonprofits, and for-profit corporations inhabit overlapping domains of interest, power, authority, and responsibility across multiple social institutions. In this section, we will look at three examples that are very different in some ways but illustrate related issues. We will start with a brief example in relation to health, move on to education, and finally consider the involvement of both the government and corporations in regard to prisons, which are part of the institution of governance. In combination, these three examples illuminate key aspects of the operation of social institutions at the macro level.

As already discussed, health is normatively defined in the United States as an individual responsibility, from eating and exercising to doctor's appointments to obtaining health insurance. In keeping with this social norm, health care in the United States is usually seen as part of the private sector, and most working age adults have to pay for private coverage from insurance companies (mostly for-profit corporations, with a few nonprofits). However, the largest single provider of health coverage is actually the federal government; Medicare, Medicaid, and the Veterans Administration are all government health programs and, combined, they make the government the largest single medical coverage provider. This statement may seem surprising, given the negative political discourse about (and often public perception of) government-funded health care in this country.

Political discourse needs to mobilize and interact with the norms at the core of social institutions, even when that conflicts with statistical data. This means that debates about health insurance have to negotiate—or interact with—societal norms about health care as a private, individual responsibility; government health-care programs violate that norm, and it's difficult for politicians to say that programs that violate such a strong norm are actually widely used (and popular). For example, in political discussions surrounding the passage of the Affordable Care Act, the possibility of Americans under 65 paying to be included in Medicare turned out to be more politically challenging than requiring Americans to purchase private insurance policies. We'll return to the Affordable Care Act and the macro level of health later in this chapter.

The institution of education provides a good illustration of the interaction of nonprofits, for-profit corporations, and the state at the macro level. The United States has experienced many waves of education reform, in which new ideas about teaching, learning, and school administration affect all levels of education from classroom interaction to government policies in areas such as how tax revenue can be spent (e.g., vouchers) and what counts as a public school (e.g., charter schools). Because government at local, state, and federal levels regulate schools in certain ways, education reforms and new types of schools must negotiate existing policy structures. In the United States, schools have traditionally been the responsibility of the state (public schools and state universities) and, secondarily, of private nonprofit schools and colleges (including the Ivy League universities) or religiously affiliated schools (particularly Catholic schools and universities). The majority of private schools and universities are still nonprofits, but the number of for-profit colleges has dramatically expanded over the past 20 to 30 years. At the K–12 level, charter schools combine public and private; they are taxpayer funded and formally part of a public school system but released from many of the regulations that govern public schools and largely run by nonprofit organizations and networks.

Charter schools and for-profit colleges and universities advertise themselves as innovative alternatives to traditional educational models, but research points to the importance of oversight in protecting vulnerable students. Overall, students at charter schools perform no better and sometimes significantly worse than students at regular public schools (Frankenberg, Siegal-Hawley, Wang, and Orfield 2012). Even more troubling, charter schools show significantly higher levels of racial segregation than regular public schools, including schools in the same city, and have not been held accountable to the civil rights statutes affecting public schools (Frankenberg et al. 2012). Similarly, for-profit colleges have more problems than nonprofit colleges and universities; graduation rates are less than half those of public colleges and only about one-third the rate of nonprofit colleges, yet students at for-profits generally carry two to three times as much debt (Education Trust 2010). However, students have limited options for complaint because for-profit colleges and universities often have students sign enrollment contracts that limit students' right to legal action if they feel they have been deceived or cheated by the gap between what they were promised and the education actually provided (Habash and Shireman 2016). The growing problems associated with for-profit higher education and concern about exploitation of vulnerable students has led to new government regulations about the use of various forms of student aid at for-profit colleges, including Pell grants, veterans benefits, and federally guaranteed student loans.

Another recent and disturbing trend in the movement of corporations into responsibilities traditionally held by government has been the **privatization** of prisons. The maintenance of social order and safety is one of the core elements of the social institution of governance, which includes police and prisons as well as courts and the military. From 1999 to 2010, there was an 80 percent increase in the number of federal and state prisoners held in private prisons, and in 2016, 12 percent of all federal prisoners were in private prisons (US Department of Justice 2016). A Department of Justice comparison of prisons managed by private corporations and those run by the Federal Bureau of Prisons consistently showed a higher level of a range of problems in private prisons, including significant human rights violations (US Department of Justice 2016). For example, in two of three private prisons investigated in depth, new inmates were housed in special housing units, which are highly restrictive and normally used as punitive disciplinary housing, until space became available in regular units (Department of Justice 2016). Privatization of prisons literally means that corporations are making a profit off of incarceration and therefore have a stake in maintaining high prison populations (Mason 2012). Private prisons initially claimed to be able to provide better services for less money, but cost containment has come at the expense of staffing, training, and services for inmates (Mason 2012), resulting in the problems described in the Department of Justice report.

Over the past 30 years, corporations have increasingly taken on societal functions that used to be primarily the domain of government or, secondarily, the nonprofit and/or religious systems. The evidence from for-profit colleges and universities and private prisons suggests that the pursuit of profit may have negative consequences in some areas, resulting in cost-cutting that brings significant harms to vulnerable people. The macro levels of social institutions manage the core structures and systems of a society, and questions of interest, profit, and motive become very important and can have far reaching consequences.

INSTITUTIONS IN DEPTH

So far, this chapter has defined social institutions and briefly explored different levels of analysis. The remainder of the chapter will focus on two very different social institutions, marriage/family and health, and examine each of these across multiple levels of analysis. These two examples provide very different lenses through which to look at the organization of social life. Health has emerged as a social phenomenon relatively recently and is often perceived or experienced as an institution primarily through the common-sense meaning of large bureaucratic entities (e.g., hospitals, insurance companies). In contrast, the family appears in some form across all societies and is experienced or perceived primarily at the micro level of individuals and small groups but is used by the state to organize society. In contemporary society, marriage is one of the central building blocks of our understanding of family, and we will focus specifically on marriage, rather than taking on the institution of family as a whole.

As we will see in the following discussion, each institution organizes social life at multiple levels of analysis, although with varying levels of visibility and awareness. One of the challenges of studying social institutions, as either a student reading a text or a sociologist doing research, is the tension between focusing on one piece of the institution at a time while trying to simultaneously hold as much of the big picture in mind as possible. In the following sections, marriage will be examined primarily at the micro and macro levels, while health will be explored at all levels in considerable depth. We will look at each level sequentially because it's not really possible to write clearly about them simultaneously, but each one makes up an element of a larger picture.

Marriage and the Family

The family is a complicated institution that affects many areas of life, but families in the United States have been normatively defined around a household consisting of a married heterosexual couple and their children. This social norm needs to be put in historical perspective; the nuclear family only came to be seen as the ideal after World War II; before that a range of other family forms were common with some differences between rural and urban areas (Coontz 1992). In the 1700s and 1800s, American families included multiple generations living together, many combinations of relatives (brothers, cousins, etc.) sharing a household, and households formed by migration in search of work. In the late twentieth and early twenty-first century, the married couple with children is again becoming less common (Cherlin 2005)—although it is still considered the ideal—in large part because marriage has become less important as an organizing force for adult life. In the 2010 census, only 20 percent of all households were married heterosexual couples with children at home (48 percent were married heterosexual couples overall), and 27 percent of households were adults living alone. Some of you will have noticed that this paragraph keeps specifying "heterosexual" in relation to marriage; in 2016, while same-sex marriage has been legalized by the federal government, there are only limited data on marriage that includes same-sex couples, and heterosexuality is still the dominant cultural ideal. The intersection of law and culture is part of what makes marriage a particularly interesting way in to thinking about social institutions.

We will focus on micro–macro linkages, looking at marriage and the state. However, the rituals and social processes associated with marriage have generated a huge commercial infrastructure that would provide rich material for meso-level analyses. The process of ending marriages has generated its own professional industry that would also shed light on marriage at the level of work and organizations.

Marriage and Family: Micro Level

It may seem slightly disorienting, even disturbing, to think of marriage as an institution. The decision to get married feels to most like a deeply personal, intimate act between two people who love each other and perhaps their immediate families. Each person in the couple may seek the advice of close friends before making the decision, but ultimately the decision to marry and the ongoing relationship that follows is understood in terms of the love and commitment shared by two people. In individual and interpersonal terms, most people experience marriage as a romantic event, embedded in the shared personal and social worlds of two people who hope to spend their lives together. A wedding may be logistically complicated, but it's not usually understood as a bureaucratic event.

However, as anyone who has gotten married knows, it requires getting a license from a state office. It also affects income tax rates and paperwork at both federal and state levels. These decidedly unromantic elements should lead a sociologist to wonder how many different contexts marriage actually occupies in addition to romantic love and personal commitment. The cultural construction of marriage as the ultimate expression of romantic love also sits alongside a more pragmatic understanding of divorce as a complicated legal process in which diverse institutional actors (e.g., lawyers, judges, real estate agents, social workers) play legitimate roles. As a guideline for social analysis, if the end of a social status or process requires significant institutional involvement, then other aspects of that status or process are also likely to be institutionally embedded, although perhaps less visibly.

Marriage and Family: Micro–Macro Interactions

The desire to get married may be anchored in a couple's feelings of love and mutual commitment in the context of family and (often) religion, but the state determines who has the option of getting married to whom. At the most basic level, marriage requires a couple and only a couple—one person cannot legally have more than one spouse in the United States, and a group of three or more people cannot have a collective relationship recognized as marriage. This reflects the dominant norms of Euro-American cultures but has never been universal across human societies. Some communities in the United States, particularly some Mormon groups, socially recognize marriage to multiple spouses, but these arrangements are either technically illegal or organized without use of state-sanctioned marriage. Despite this legal restriction, a recent popular TV program, *Big Love*, centered on a polygamous family. Marriage between first cousins is prohibited in about half of US states but permitted in the other half, although in some cases only if the couple is unable to have children due to age or documented infertility (National Conference of State Legislatures 2011). Limitations on cousin-marriage are justified by the increased potential for birth defects and genetically based problems in children with genetically related parents, which highlights the continuing centrality of childbearing to both normative and legal constructions of marriage. On the other hand, it also suggests that marriages between cousins of the same sex should not be legally problematic (if or when a case ends up in court).

Government regulation of marriage has often involved defining and regulating a range of social statuses or identities as well, which fits with the definition of social institutions as organizing core elements of social life. From that perspective, marriage can be seen as a way to regulate significant social ties between families and communities by defining socially appropriate kinds of partnerships. Historically in the United States, people of different races could not marry, and this was a significant way that social and legal boundaries between racial groups were defined and reinforced. This began under slavery, but antimiscegenation laws, as they are called, extended well beyond slavery geographically into free states and historically through 1967, when the Supreme Court finally overturned the remaining statutes (in the *Loving v. Virginia* ruling). Thinking sociologically and institutionally, antimiscegenation laws meant that race had to be legally defined and documented, adding a layer of judicial and legislative participation in marriage that had the larger social consequence of making racial identity a *legal* status long after the end of slavery (and outside the southern states).

More recently, marriage laws have been concerned with the legal definition of gender, since limiting marriage to heterosexual couples required a working definition of the boundaries of "man" and "woman." Before the Supreme Court decision in June, 2015 (*Obergefull v Hodges*), federal and most state laws limited marriage to heterosexual couples, defined as one man and one woman. In practice, this raised the question of when, where, and how gender was legally defined, which turns out not to be as simple as it might appear. For example, **transgendered** people, who do not identify with the sex assigned at birth, faced difficulties in getting married because the courts had little guidance on how to legally define gender (Herald 2009). The laws allowing transgender people to change the gender on a birth certificate vary from state to state; a person born in New York can change their birth certificate with a simple letter from a doctor while someone born in Missouri (no matter where they currently live) must provide extensive documentation of complete surgical change. This means two transgender people who live in the same city and have the same physical characteristics could have different legal genders depending on where in the United States they were born. While the *Obergefell* court case was not concerned with definitions of gender, the extension of marriage to same-sex couples removed the question of the legal definitions of male and female since those were only relevant to enforcing the boundaries of heterosexuality; now, no one has to "prove" his or her gender to get married.

Marriage and Family: Macro Level

Regardless of the gender of the partners involved, the symbolic weight of marriage obscures the extent to which it is also embedded in social welfare policies. At the most surface levels, marriage affects access to health insurance and a range of other employment-related benefits, to Social Security and other retirement benefits if a spouse dies, and to a green card or citizenship if relevant and simplifies a large number of parenting and inheritance issues. For low-income couples, marriage affects access to housing, emergency shelter, food stamps, Medicaid or other health insurance programs, and income support programs like Temporary Assistance to Needy Families. Married couples have the right to hospital (and prison) visitation and to make medical decisions for an incapacitated spouse and are protected from testifying against each other in criminal court. At the level of federal legislation, marriage provides 1,138 mutual benefits and responsibilities, and state legislation regulates a few hundred more (Marriage Equality Now). At the micro level, marriage may be a romantic personal commitment, but at the macro level it is clearly a mechanism for social organization that uses a normatively driven structure (romance and family) to accomplish a large number of policy objectives.

A brief look back at the political arguments over same-sex marriage can illuminate the multiple symbolic, pragmatic, and policy contexts that

SOCIOLOGY AT WORK
WORK AND SOCIAL INSTITUTIONS: WORK–FAMILY CONFLICT
Arne L. Kalleberg

Work and family are two of the most central institutions in a society. Virtually all men and a majority of women work for pay in the United States and other industrial societies, and most people also belong to families. Conflicts between the roles people play in these two important institutions arise when the demands they make on men and (especially) women are incompatible or contradictory.

Dan Clawson and Naomi Gerstl (2014) show how conflicts between work and family may be resolved in different ways depending on their gender and class. They studied four occupations in the health industry (physicians, nurses, nursing assistants, and emergency medical technicians [EMTs]). Members of these occupations differed in the amount of control they had over their work schedules in addition to their gender composition (physicians and EMTs were usually men, while nurses and nursing assistants were most often women), and these differences in control and gender affected the way they were able to manage their work and family lives.

Physicians had the most control over their work schedules and had high degrees of devotion to their jobs. While they worked the most hours of members of any of the four occupations, they were best able to resolve work–family conflicts because they generally had a spouse at home to take care of family matters (women physicians, by contrast, usually did not have this possibility and had to struggle to resolve work–family conflicts). Nurses also had considerable control over their work schedules. Rather than use this control to devote themselves to their work, however, nurses tended to use their leverage to obtain work schedules that enabled them to meet the needs of their families. That physicians used their schedule control to focus more on work while nurses used it for family purposes illustrates important differences in gender role expectations: males are generally expected to be the breadwinner in the family while women are assumed to be responsible for the family.

Nursing assistants had relatively little control over their work schedules and so had much more trouble resolving work–family conflict than physicians or nurses. A main way they were able to do this was by relying on relatives (other than a spouse) to help with their child-care responsibilities; they thus adopted a more inclusive view of the family than nurses or physicians since they were so dependent on their extended families. Nursing assistants also tended to have stressful home lives (in large part due to their relatively low salaries), so they tended to see their jobs as refuges from the stresses of family. Relatively few EMTs felt this way, however. Rather, EMTs saw family as a source of their greatest satisfaction rather than as a burden to be escaped. These men were very involved in their family lives and taking care of children.

These examples illustrate that work–family conflicts are not inevitable. How they are resolved depends a great deal of one's gender, which in turn shapes the expectations regarding one's work and family obligations, and class, which reflects the amount of control one has over work schedules and the resources available to manage family responsibilities.

Source:

Clawson, Dan and Naomi Gerstl. 2014. *Unequal Time: Gender, Class and Family in Employment Schedules.* New York: Russell Sage Foundation.

marriage occupies in our society. In the 1980s, partly in response to the AIDS epidemic, state and local laws began to recognize domestic partnerships as a way to extend employee benefits and some other protections (e.g., hospital visitation) to long-term gay and lesbian couples (Gossett 2009). Both the legislation and the legal struggles around it were largely based on policy technicalities, and arguments against domestic partnership based on marriage law or definitions of the family rarely succeeded (Gossett 2009). In contrast, political arguments against same-sex marriage invoked culturally normative understandings of heterosexuality as "natural" in contrast to constructions of homosexuality as variously unnatural, sinful, or hazardous to children (Fisher 2009). Over time, advocates for same-sex marriage shifted their own arguments away from the question of policy-related benefits and toward symbolic frames of equality and discrimination (Fisher 2009). The Supreme Court decision that legalized same-sex marriage argued for the importance of equal dignity and protection under the law in part on the grounds that marriage is "one of civilizations oldest institutions." In writing the text of the decision, Justice Kennedy explicitly invoked the ways marriage brings together intimate relationship, social recognition, and core elements of the organization of society.

In the next institutional example, we will add the meso level of analysis and do a more in-depth examination of how the institution operates at each level. We will also be looking at an aspect of society where the label "institution" is less disorienting than with marriage but where the micro-level aspects might feel surprising in regard to a social domain normally thought of only in regard to work, large organizations, and public policy.

Health

To think about health as a social institution, we have to start by stepping back from the obvious examples like doctor's appointments or community medical clinics to look for how health concerns or activities manifest in other areas of life. One place to see the pervasiveness of health as a form of social organization is to look at marketing; a wide range of products, from shoes to toys to food, are promoted at least in part by claims to improve or maintain health. Some shirts are now advertized as being treated with sunscreen to prevent skin cancer, there are shoes to improve your fitness (and how you look in shorts), and there's a line of processed frozen foods with the brand name Healthy Choice. Food marketing probably offers the most consistent example of this, but promoting or enabling health in some way has become a standard advertizing strategy either overtly, through direct claims to making consumers healthier, or covertly, though images of physical activity and models that radiate health. The impulse to characterize activities, preferences, and objects (e.g., clothing, shoes, food) in terms of health promotion has entered everyday conversation and even the stories we tell ourselves about what we are or should be doing.

Micro Level Health: Norms and Interactions

Within any society or social network, individuals account for, or explain, their choices and actions to themselves and others. These accounts have become one of the taken-for-granted ways that health organizes life at the micro level of individuals and small groups, as motivations and assumptions come to reflect the growing centrality of health concerns as an area of individual responsibility. For example, I have never liked onion rings, but over the past 10 years this longstanding personal preference has begun to elicit the response "How healthy of you" instead of the previous tendency toward "OK, there's more for me." This change in response patterns embodies the increasing centrality of health as a valued explanatory framework for personal action and for interpreting the actions of others, even when it does not reflect other explanations offered ("No thanks, I don't really like onion rings"); I put forth a neutral explanation and am offered a more normatively weighted one in return.

The question of accounts for action points to the overarching norm of health as personal responsibility. We are increasingly expected to manage and monitor our own health and bring our actions in line with the latest recommendations for diet and exercise. Weight has long been a focus for negotiations of status, and people considered overweight are at risk of job discrimination (Carr and Friedman 2005), but the language of criticism has expanded over time from questions of attractiveness or self-control to a concern with weight as a marker of health-related self-care. Patterns of norm-enforcement often reflect social stratification; women still face greater pressures to manage weight than men, despite the unquestioned evidence for weight-related health problems in men and the average longer life spans of women. In many areas, expectations for norm-compliance may be strongest in the middle of status hierarchies, as those at the top feel free to violate social rules and those at the bottom receive fewer rewards for compliance. The power of a social norm can be seen in patterns of violation as much as those of adherence, as rule-breakers and those around them manage the social implications of particular actions or practices. For example, parents who allow or participate in violations of health-related norms with their children, such as rewarding a child with bad food or too many sweets, may experience greater social disapproval than other adults, such as grandparents.

Meso-Level Health: Work and Organizations

The framework of health as an individual responsibility has, in our service economy, led to a proliferation of occupations and jobs designed to support the fulfillment of these responsibilities. A variety of support occupations serve those with sufficient disposable income to purchase assistance, and their availability may, paradoxically, increase expectations for personal health accountability overall by making it easier for some. Personal trainers work with those who have difficulty managing or adhering to exercise regimens, while exercise classes offer structure and guidance at a group level. A growing number of diet plans offer to deliver a week's worth of prepared food to participants' homes, circumventing the need to shop or cook and easing management of self as well as of time. It is worth noting here the overlap between fitness as health and fitness as sexual attractiveness, which allows products and services to speak to multiple motivations and populations. Access to such services obviously varies with income and neighborhood location, but their proliferation as an occupational niche derives from the growing centrality of health as a social institution. Other forms of personal assistance have also grown, like home health aides and elder care, but these are largely inside the medical care system and the services largely replace family labor.

Health care has become one of the larger domains of employment in modern societies, encompassing highly specialized professions, a range of service and administrative occupations, and large numbers of poorly paid aides and cleaning staff. Doctor's offices and hospitals bring together patients and their families, doctors, nurses, social workers, administrators, maintenance staff, and medical technologies of all kinds. Hospitalization is simultaneously a moment of stress, even an emergency, for the patient and his or her family and a routine day at work for the staff; this gap in social meanings suggests the power of social institutions to regulate action and interaction, since hospitals generally manage to effectively bridge these dramatic differences in experience. Two ethnographic studies of hospitals, one in the early 1980s (Strauss, Fagerhaugh, Suczek, and Wiener 1985) and the other in the mid-1990s (Heimer and Stevens 1997), examined the social organization of work, including the division of labor between occupations, use of technology, and interactions with patients. These two studies allow us to explore the hospital, a familiar element of the social institution of health, at the level of work and organizations; for someone whose only experience of a hospital comes from the emergency room, then thinking about hospitals as workplaces may provide a very new perspective.

Strauss and his colleagues describe a hospital as a set of interconnected work sites, situated within a larger societal health context. At the societal level, they identify an important tension that was relatively new in the late 1970s, when the study began, but has since become solidly established. Hospitals are typically understood as providing short-term care for immediate or acute health problems, like physical injury or a severe infection, but during the late twentieth century the main hospital patient population shifted from people with acute medical problems to those with chronic illnesses, like diabetes or cancer. This is in part an age divide, as young people still primarily use hospitals for transient problems, often through the emergency room, while the middle-aged and elderly are more likely to be chronic care patients. Chronic illnesses are conditions that a person may live with, and be treated for, over years and that usually get gradually worse. Common chronic illnesses in the United States include diabetes, cancers, hypertension, and multiple forms of heart disease. This shift from acute to chronic care results from societal-level changes in health and life expectancy, in part a consequence of things like improved antibiotics, vaccinations, and other medications. Someone who survives a heart attack usually then becomes a chronic heart disease patient and may return to the hospital repeatedly over the next 15 to 20 years. The increase in chronic disease patients has changed the nature of hospital work, making social interaction and interpersonal dynamics much more central than when most patients came and went quickly.

The last paragraph describes how changes in medical treatment (medications, antibiotics, treatment to survive heart attacks) affect the kind of conditions common among hospital patients (acute to chronic) that in turn makes social interaction a more central aspect of hospital work. It is also possible to make a connection between improved medical treatments and the diffusion of concern about health into many areas of life, as members of society learn to prevent, manage, and live with chronic illnesses that have a connection to day-to-day activities such as eating, exercise, stress management, and smoking cigarettes. This sequence provides a good example of why it is important to think about health as a social institution, an interconnected whole made up of multiple elements. A technical activity in one place (medical research) has an impact on all aspects of work in a separate but related place (the hospital) and affects day-to-day activities and social interactions throughout society by redefining ordinary things like meals and recreation as related to health and illness.

To return to Strauss et al.'s research and findings, they studied a *hospital,* an organizational entity, not the specifics of work done by every single occupational group within it. A study of surgeons would collect data on the practice of surgery, in addition to the social worlds within which it occurs, while a study of an organization places the social world itself at the center, addressing the holistic question of "How does this place operate?" instead of describing each type of work performed on site in detail. Strauss et al. describe five areas of work at a hospital: machine work, safety work, comfort work, sentimental work, and articulation work. Each area of these kinds of work is necessary to the running of a hospital and therefore an integral part of the social institution of health. Machine work includes the uses of technology in clinical practice, whether reading an X-ray or using a stethoscope, but it also includes the work of technicians, maintenance staff, and routine monitoring of various kinds. For example, a nurse at a central ward desk is constantly engaged in machine work as he or she enters data on a computer, listens to the patterns of beeps transmitted from different kinds of monitors in multiple rooms, periodically answers the phone, and ensures that no one's lunch ends up in the refrigerator reserved for medication and blood draws. Safety work includes everything from hand-washing to maintaining a sterile surgical environment to monitoring a wide range of clinical hazards, such as incorrect drug dosages or the risk of deteriorating heart function in a patient. Machine work and safety work are close to what we ordinarily think of as hospital work, but the other three areas define relationships, interaction, and interconnection as central to the work of hospitals.

Comfort and sentimental work primarily address the patient's subjective experience of illness and medical treatment. As the label indicates, comfort care addresses the many forms of discomfort patients experience, whether caused by a medical condition, a medical treatment, or the structure of hospital routine. Comfort care includes not only medication and supportive technologies or machines but also changing bed linens, providing blankets, and getting a new patient into a bed as quickly as possible. Where comfort care maintains some focus on the physical body as the site of medical work, sentimental care refers to the social and emotional work of direct contact with patients. Work on a human being requires communication and the management of interaction, especially when the human in question may be experiencing strong emotions as well as physical discomforts. The perception of hospitals, or individual providers, as dehumanizing, cold, uncaring, or lacking in bedside manner, reflect inadequate performance of sentimental work. Lastly, articulation work addresses the need for coordination, communication, and integration of the different forms of treatment and care provided to a patient. Articulation work may become most visible in its absence, when the pieces don't quite come together; successful articulation work transforms the separate efforts of individual medical workers into an integrated case or a rational trajectory of work.

Another study of hospitals can add to our understanding of social norms and the interactional complexities of medical care, the areas of work Strauss et al. define as sentimental care and articulation work. Heimer and Stevens examined interactions between parents of infants in intensive care units (ICUs) and the medical specialists who care for those babies. Medical specialists work within narrowly defined areas of expertise, with clear divisions of labor between specialty areas. Specialists often expect their communication with patients (or the parents of patients, in this case) to remain within their area of expertise, and other aspects of the patient's life are considered either irrelevant or the responsibility of a different kind of specialist. In practice, this means that patients and family members need to understand what aspect of their lives they can discuss with each category of professional and tailor their communication appropriately. Many parents of babies in the ICU do not understand how their lives map onto the different specialist domains and therefore talk about issues the specialist considers not her or his responsibility; parents and specialists have different normative understandings of appropriate communication and behavior in a medical appointment. To manage these conflicting norms, social workers have taken on the role of communication coaches and managers, instructing patients and family members in how to conform to the norms of the specialists and absorbing the interactional difficulties this may at times create. To relate this back to Strauss et al., the social workers are performing the sentimental work of managing communication and interaction and the articulation work of trying to fit together the different elements of patients' needs and professional expertise.

These two studies have taken us from a relatively abstract, big-picture discussion of social institutions into a closer and more detailed encounter with important elements of a particular institution. This reveals layers of interconnection with the micro, meso, and macro levels of analysis and between domains of social life that appear distant from each other. As already noted, improvements in medical care meant that hospitals had to shift their primary attention from acute medical problems to caring for people with chronic illnesses, and this made social interaction more central to hospital work. In the Heimer and Stevens study, the question of how social norms shape social interaction between patients and specialists becomes central to understanding potential problems in the delivery of highly specialized medical care and how managing this gets assigned to a particular occupation (social workers). Strauss et al. demonstrate that social interaction makes up a large part of the work in a hospital, and they do this by examining day-to-day activities of staff and patients. At the beginning of the chapter, social institutions were defined in part around the need to organize the activities and needs that constitute life in a particular society; we have been examining the multiple ways that concerns about health and the actual delivery of health care are organized at practical levels and the role of norms and social interactions within these processes. The discussion so far has addressed the micro and meso levels of analysis of health, and it's important to add the macro level.

Macro-Level Health: Government and Corporations

So far in this section on health, we have been considering ways that health and responsibility for health has been individualized and dispersed throughout multiple aspects of our lives. However, health insurance and the provision of health care are also a major aspect of the US economy, and most (though not all) insurance companies are for-profit corporations. The relationship between the federal government and the insurance industry is extremely complicated, involving some Medicaid and Medicare coverage (described earlier) and now the Affordable Care Act (aka Obamacare). Pharmaceutical companies may receive more media attention than insurance companies, but the government has a more direct relationship to the insurance industry, and the central role of private insurance drives the organization of health care in the United States.

Historically, the place of private insurance in the US health-care system comes from the relationship between employment and access to health care, which is unique to the United States in the economically developed world. In Canada, Australia, the United Kingdom, and all the countries of the European Union, health care is universally accessible to citizens and legal residents through a centralized funding system (the exact form varies across countries) and has no relationship to employment. In the United States, obtaining health insurance has been treated as an individual responsibility that is typically linked to a job, and people who are self-employed, work part time, or work at a job that does not offers health insurance as a "benefit" for employees must obtain insurance for themselves or pay for any medical care they receive entirely out of their own pockets. The exceptions to this, of course, are very low income people who qualify for Medicaid, citizens and legal residents over 65 who receive Medicare, and most military veterans. As noted earlier, these three groups that qualify for government-funded coverage are actually more than 50 percent of the United States population, but this is somewhat invisible because it violates the strong social norm of private insurance.

On the surface, the linkage of health insurance to employment implies that this lies entirely outside of government and primarily concerns businesses (including insurance companies) and the negotiations between employees and employers. This may have been true for the brief historical moment of 1950–1980, but for the past 30 years the government and insurance companies have had an increasingly close relationship. Under Medicaid and Medicare, the government used to directly pay doctors, clinics, and hospitals for services provided to individuals, and Medicare in particular has historically had low administrative costs (Potetz, Cubanski, and Neuman 2011). Starting in the 1980s and expanding rapidly in the 1990s, many states began to offer **managed care** programs as part of Medicaid, during a period when managed care programs were becoming increasingly common in private, employer-provided health insurance. In 2014, over half of all Medicaid beneficiaries received care through managed care organizations, and 39 states had contracts with insurance companies to provide services to Medicaid recipients (Paradise 2015). There has been a parallel trend in Medicare, although the cost of managed care has been consistently higher than traditional fee-for-service Medicare (Potetz et al. 2011). While it may seem unsurprising that private and public health coverage would be offered in similar forms, in practice this means federal and state governments pay private insurance companies to run Medicaid and Medicare managed care programs even though administrative costs are lower when run directly by the government. These managed care programs bring the government into an increasingly close relationship with insurance companies.

The Affordable Care Act (aka Obamacare) has had a fundamental impact on the relationship between government and insurance companies, in ways that go well beyond paying for services. A central element of the Affordable Care Act is the requirement that individuals have insurance coverage or pay a penalty for every year that they do not have coverage. The financial burden of this requirement gets mitigated through a system of federal subsidies and an option for states to expand Medicaid, but at its core this is a requirement that adults in the United States purchase private insurance. This requirement exists for auto insurance as well, but that only applies to people who own cars, not to every adult citizen or permanent resident of the United States. The Affordable Care Act includes a range of regulations for insurance companies as well, although market regulations and minimum standards for products are a more common role for government than requiring citizens to purchase a product.

The strategy of mandating that individuals obtain private policies stands in contrast to other developed countries that address the challenge of providing health care through systems of universal access with a single "payer" instead of multiple companies offering highly variable products. In comparison to other developed countries, the United States spends a higher proportion of its total economy on health care, including higher prices for prescription medications, and yet has higher rates of infant mortality and chronic disease and lower overall life expectancy (American Public Health Association 2016). The central role played by private companies, with the active participation of federal and state governments, has taken the United States in a different direction than other, comparable countries that have not organized health care through an open, commercial market.

As this examination of health and health care demonstrates, social norms organize health-related interactions and processes at all levels of analysis. Each level directs analytic attention to a particular set of social contexts and processes and particular kinds of research questions. Social interaction occurs in both friendship networks (micro) and hospital examining rooms (meso); the norm of health insurance as a personal responsibility has obscured the extent of government involvement in health coverage, while stigmatizing the single-payer model that operates in other economically advanced countries. The level of analysis affects the theoretical frameworks that guide research and analysis and how the interactions are situated within a larger social context (e.g., the neighborhood vs. a large organization). The two studies discussed in this section examine social interaction as an aspect of professional work in the meso-level context of large hospitals. A micro-level study might look at how interaction among friends can support or discourage health-promoting activities. Of course, the examples used throughout this chapter also demonstrate the ways in which levels of analysis overlap and show that individual action is shaped by social policy while social interaction lies at the core of effective operation in a hospital and even the highly technical environment of an ICU.

We have now explored two social institutions in depth. The last institution of health was primarily explored at the level of work but with some consideration of both the individual (micro) and government and corporate (macro) levels. Social norms and interaction were central to understanding how health, as a social institution, organized activity at both the micro and meso levels. The brief exploration of the macro level showed how the social norm of private insurance obscures the depth of government involvement with both health coverage and insurance companies. The institution of marriage was primarily explored in relation to how government policy sets the terms within which individuals organize an aspect of their lives that is normatively defined as purely personal and intimate. In both cases, a wide range of actions commonly understood in exclusively personal terms—what you eat, whether you take a walk or ride a bike regularly, and even who you decide to marry or whether you get married at all—are revealed to be organized and regulated at collective and societal levels.

CONCLUSION

The power of social institutions can be seen in the extent to which they are, in fact, invisible to us as we go about our daily lives; a strong social institution organizes a domain of life at such deep levels that it is seen as natural, simply the way things are or should be done. When a social institution becomes more visible as an institution, it is often because the elements of the institution no longer fit societal needs, which may help explain the anxiety around marriage and family expressed in a growing number of ways over the last 30 years. Economic and social changes mean that the family structure and related gender roles that were dominant in the 1950s and 1960s no longer fit contemporary social worlds in the United States, but cultural norms shift more slowly than daily life, especially for older generations, leading to the kinds of social and political tension visible around marriage and family structure in the early twenty-first century.

This chapter has provided a brief introduction to the social institutions that organize society at all levels. The question of norms lies at the core of all the examples provided, although the definition of norms used here is broader than that used in day-to-day life or in a psychology class. Norms in the sociological sense are attributes of human collectives and societies that shape how members of the collective interpret the world around them and how the society itself is structured at all levels. The existence of a norm does not imply universal agreement—the possibility of expanding Medicare to everyone (of all ages) was openly discussed in the 2016 presidential primaries—but even the process of disagreement must recognize and negotiate the existing normative system. In essence, a society consists of its core social institutions, which organize life at such deep levels that the whole becomes invisible as we live within its constituent parts.

Lesson Take-Aways

- Social institutions are formal systems of shared behaviors, beliefs, and social norms that organize the major areas of social life; they are the means by which a society creates and sustains a collective social life from day to day and year to year; they answer the question of "How do we _____ around here (educate children, run a city, buy and sell things, etc.)?"

- Institutions operate at multiple levels, from the micro worlds of personal identity and social interaction through the meso level of work and organizations to macro questions of governance processes and economic systems.

- The primary social institutions are family, education, economy, government or politics, and religion. These five exist in some form in all societies, although the precise form of each institution varies significantly across societies and historical periods. In the twenty-first century, it is interesting to think about whether new social institutions have emerged, such as health and media.

- Social norms are central to the function of social institutions. Norms in the sociological sense are attributes of human collectives and societies that shape how members of the collective interpret the world around them and how the society itself is structured at all levels.

Discussion Questions

1. Describe advertising that uses health claims as a marketing tool and discuss how you responded to those ads. Think about the interaction between fitness and attractiveness and health as both marketing devices and personal motivation.

2. List the different seating arrangements you have seen in classrooms and describe how your expectations for classroom interaction varied with each. What other things do you look for or pay attention to in the first one or two class meetings to guide your understandings about what the class will be like interactively? What makes you expect passive lecturing? What makes you think "Oh, I'm going to have to talk in this class"?

3. Describe the physical characteristics of the neighborhood you live in: Are there grocery stores? Parks? Usable sidewalks? Does it feel safe or dangerous to walk (and for whom)? How do the physical characteristics of your neighborhood affect your day-to-day life and the lives of the people you know in the area?

4. This chapter has given a few examples of ways that corporations are becoming increasingly involved in areas that used to be the responsibility of government. Do you think profit is a valuable motive in all areas of society? Are there certain aspects of a society where the profit motive might be destructive?

5. Legal definitions of the family in the United States don't recognize many of the relationships that increasingly sustain our lives as traditional family forms decline. Think about the people intimately involved in your life. How many of them are related by marriage, birth, or adoption (including siblings)? What kinds of relationships might be described as "longstanding ties of commitment and intimacy" but not fit the legal (and normative) definitions of family?

Sources

American Public Health Association. 2016, April 7. "National Public Health Week: Investing in the Healthiest Nation." https://www.apha.org/topics-and-issues/health-rankings

Carr, Deborah and Michael A. Friedman. 2005. "Is Obesity Stigmatizing? Body Weight, Perceived Discrimination and Psychological Well-Being in the United States." *Journal of Health and Social Behavior* 46(3): 244–59.

Cherlin, Andrew. 2005. "American Marriage in the Early 21st Century." *The Future of Children* 15(2): 33–55.

Coontz, Stephanie. 1992. *The Way We Never Were: American Families and the Nostalgia Trap.* New York: Basic Books.

US Department of Justice. 2016, August. *Review of the Federal Bureau of Prisons' Monitoring of Contract Prisons.* Washington, DC: US Department of Justice. https://oig.justice.gov/reports/2016/e1606.pdf

Dick, Penny. 2005. "Dirty Work Designations: How Police Officers Account for Their Use of Coercive Force." *Human Relations* 58(11): 1363–90.

Education Trust. 2010. *Subprime Opportunity: The Unfulfilled Promise of For-Profit Colleges and Universities.* Washington, DC: Education Trust. http://edtrust.org/wp-content/uploads/2013/10/Subprime_report_1.pdf

Fisher, Shauna. 2009. "It Takes (At Least) Two to Tango: Fighting with Words in the Conflict Over Same Sex Marriage." In Scott Barclay, Mary Bernstein, and Anna-Maria Marshall (eds.), *Queer Mobilizations: LGBT Activists Confront the Law,* 207–30. New York: New York University Press.

Frankenberg, Erica, Genevieve Siegal-Hawley, Jia Wang, and Gary Orfield. 2012. *Choice without Equity: Charter School Segregation and the Need for Civil Rights Standards.* Los Angeles: Civil Rights Project/Proyecto Derechos Civiles at UCLA.

Gossett, Charles W. 2009. "Pushing the Envelope: Dillon's Rule and Local Domestic-Partnership Ordinances." In Scott Barclay, Mary Bernstein, and Anna-Maria Marshall (eds.), *Queer Mobilizations: LGBT Activists Confront the Law,* 158–86. New York: New York University Press.

Gregory, J. F. 1997. "Three Strikes and They're Out: African American Boys and American Schools' Responses to Misbehavior." *International Journal of Adolescence and Youth* 7(1): 25–34.

Habash, Tariq and Robert Shireman. 2016. *How College Enrollment Contracts Limit Student Rights.* New York: The Century Foundation. https://tcf.org/content/report/how-college-enrollment-contracts-limit-students-rights/

Heimer, Carol A., and Mitchell L. Stevens. 1997. "Caring for the Organization: Social Workers as Frontline Risk Managers in Neonatal Intensive Care Units." *Work and Organizations* 24(2): 133–63.

Herald, Marybeth. 2009. "Explaining the Differences: Transgender Theories and Court Practice." In Scott Barclay, Mary Bernstein, and Anna-Maria Marshall (eds.), *Queer Mobilizations: LGBT Activists Confront the Law,* 187–204. New York: New York University Press.

Hunt, Jennifer. 1985. "Police Accounts of Normal Force." *Journal of Contemporary Ethnography* 13(4): 315–41.

Johnson, Devon and Joseph B. Kuhns. 2009. "Striking Out: Race and Support for Police Use of Force." *Justice Quarterly* 26(3): 592–623.

Jones, Susanne M. and Kathryn Dindia. 2004. "A Meta-Analytic Perspective on Sex Equity in the Classroom." *Review of Educational Research* 74(4): 443–71.

Karp, D. A. and W. C. Yoels. 1976. "The College Classroom: Some Observations on the Meaning of Student Participation." *Sociology and Social Research* 60(4): 421–39.

Marriage Equality USA. 2011, August. "The Practical." www.marriageequality.org/get-the-facts.

Marwick, Alice E. and Danah Boyd. 2011. "I Tweet Honestly, I Tweet Passionately: Twitter Users, Context Collapse, and the Imagined Audience." *New Media and Society* 13(1): 114–33.

Mason, Cody. 2012, January. *Too Good to be True: Private Prisons in America*. Washington, DC: The Sentencing Project. http://sentencingproject.org/wp-content/uploads/2016/01/Too-Good-to-be-True-Private-Prisons-in-America.pdf

National Conference of State Legislatures. 2011. State Laws in August.

Paradise, J. 2015, March 9. *Medicaid Moving Forward*. Menlo Park, CA: Kaiser Family Foundation. http://kff.org/health-reform/issue-brief/medicaid-moving-forward/

Potetz, L., J. Cubanski, and T. Neuman. 2011. *Medicare Spending and Financing: A Primer*. Menlo Park, CA: Kaiser Family Foundation. https://kaiserfamilyfoundation.files.wordpress.com/2013/01/7731-03.pdf

Rettie, Ruth. 2009. "Mobile Phone Communication: Extending Goffman to Mediated Interaction." *Sociology* 43(3): 421–38.

Strauss, Anselm L., Shizuko Fagerhaugh, Barbara Suczek, and Carolyn Wiener. 1985. *Social Organization of Medical Work*. Chicago: University of Chicago Press.

Related Websites

Legal Momentum: The Women's Legal Defense and Education Fund: www.legalmomentum.org/about

Institute for Policy Studies: www.ips-dc.org

Institute for Women's Policy Research: www.iwpr.org

Data Center, Research for Justice: www.datacenter.org

Drug Policy Alliance: www.drugpolicy.org

Urban Justice Center: www.urbanjustice.org

Make the Road: www.maketheroad.org

Community Voices Heard: www.cvhaction.org

LESSON 4, PHOTO REFLECTION:

Student services counter at an urban public college.
Photo by Ken Gould

Is this a photo of a Department of Motor Vehicles office, a public aid office, a bank, or the student services counter at a public university? The rows of chairs for waiting, the long counter, the service workers behind bullet-proof glass, and the screens displaying the next number to be served are nearly universal forms for the in-person processing of individuals by large bureaucratic organizations. Even if you don't know what organization is processing you for what, by looking at this photo you know what behaviors and roles are expected of you. Walking in the door you would probably know to take a number, take a seat in the rows of chairs, wait for your number to be called, walk up to the counter, and tell the person on the other side what you need. We chose this photo to represent the physical manifestation of the routinization of social life that social institutions provide. If you were the photographer, what picture would you take to represent social institutions?

PART 3

WHAT DIVIDES US?

Social relations are rife with dynamic tensions that generate both latent and overt conflicts between social groups. Very often, these tensions stem from cultural and institutional hierarchies of power and privilege. Inequalities between groups of people are reflected in established social norms, and struggles against inequalities therefore often require challenging the social norms that maintain structures of inequality. While there are many dimensions along which power inequalities in society are structured, the most prominent are those related to race, class, gender, and sexuality.

Institutional and cultural racism bestows privilege upon dominant racial groups and denies full citizenship and personhood to other racial groups. Struggles for racial equality involve struggles over the power to access and influence social institutions, to change social norms, and to alter fundamental elements of culture. As a social order that justified the slaughter of and expropriation of land from Native Americans on the basis of white racial superiority and the enslavement of Africans on the basis of white racial superiority, racial inequality was the social context within which the United States' institutions, culture, and social norms were formed. While our institutions, culture, and norms have changed over time, C. Wright Mills would argue that such a history impacts each of our biographies.

Social class, the relationship between owners and workers, and the outcomes of class divisions in terms of the unequal distribution of wealth and income are so central to the way that capitalist societies are organized that these divisions often appear naturalized. While we often view racial discrimination as unfair, we tend to view class inequalities as normal. Yet class inequality is socially constructed, and societies could be organized differently. Class inequality, as Marx pointed out, is a primary source of social tension and a primary driver of social change. Social class largely determines where you will live, what you will do for work and recreation, where you will go to school, the quality of that school, your long-term health, and your sense of agency within your society. Struggles over the control of production and the distribution of the costs and benefits of production permeate all aspects of social life.

Like social class, power hierarchies and inequalities based on gender and sexuality have also been largely naturalized in our society, although these have been more openly challenged in recent decades. Despite recent challenges, our social institutions reflect deep cultural commitments to gender and sexuality hierarchies that manifest in gender pay gaps, glass ceilings, the denial of basic rights to LGBTQ people, and an ongoing protection of rape culture at the highest levels of social power.

Each of these power hierarchies that divide us operate synergistically, meaning that people experience their social lives at the intersection of racial, class, gender, and sexuality power dynamics. Challenges to intersectional race, class, gender, and sexuality privilege have recently lead to cultural and institutional backlash, as powerful forces attempt to maintain their status and position. Despite the best hopes of the early sociological theorists like Marx, DuBois, and Perkins-Gilman, social conflicts at the intersection of race, class, and gender continue into the twenty-first century.

Which spaces foster interaction among races and which tend to be racially segregated?

5

Race and Intersectionality

Janine Kay Gwen Chi

WHY IS RACE IMPORTANT? WHY SHOULD WE CARE?

For many Americans, the topic of race can conjure up the images in the 1890s of Jim Crow whites-only water fountains, railcars, and bus stops. More recently, it can refer to photos of numerous young men and women at Black Lives Matter protests and rallies in cities and university campuses across the country. However, it can also evoke images of thousands of cheering supporters for the first African-American family in the White House on election night in 2008. How does one make sense of these conflicting images—one of racial segregation and exclusion and another of apparent overcoming of a racial divide at the highest political level only to simultaneously witness a deep racial divide within urban decay and economic decline?

Discussions of race become even more complex when considering the fact that as of 2010, Asians have surpassed Hispanics as the largest group of new immigrants to this country. Often touted to be the "model minority," Asian Americans, in most people's minds, have become symbols of the American dream; said to be able to overcome prejudice and hardship through individual hard work and quiet perseverance, many Asian Americans when compared to all US adults have experienced high levels of socio-economic mobility with 49 percent versus 28 percent possessing a college degree and a median annual household income of $66,000 versus $49,800 (Pew Research Center 2013). Ironically, due to their successes, they have been sometimes excluded from affirmative action programs and are even sometimes considered a hindrance to diversity initiatives.

To further complicate matters, what about the fact that the Census since 2000 allows for individuals to self-identify with one or more racial categories? A recent survey conducted by Pew Research Center estimates that, by taking into additional account the racial make-up of respondents' parents and grandparents, 6.9 percent of the country's adult population could be considered multiracial (Pew Research Center 2015). In addition, the Census Bureau estimates that there will be a 225 percent increase in the number of people identifying two or more races by 2060 and that while whites are currently the "majority" group, accounting for more than half of the country's total population, this group will likely be a majority-minority at 44 percent by 2060 (Colby and Ortman 2015). Given the rapidly changing demography in this country, is W. E. B. DuBois's ([1903] 1993, 19) famous declaration that "the problem of the twentieth century is the problem of the color line" still relevant today? Given recent election debates on the construction of a US–Mexico border "wall," numerous newspaper reports of police brutality against young black men and women, including the *Times* magazine cover of the 2015 Baltimore riots, and editorials on the plight of Syrian refugees and their struggles to assimilate into American society, are we misjudging the effects of economics and class and overemphasizing the role of racial politics?

Of course, most people today know better than to utter racial epithets in the company of others, and many individuals would easily and quickly disavow the occurrence of lynchings and other forms of hate crimes. In fact, many Americans consider the conversation on race to be dated and passé because they associate racism with the intentionality of individual persons. For example, you might have heard a parent telling a child on the neighborhood playground: "Be nice to everyone; don't judge people by the color of their skin." Recently, in response to the Black Lives Matter movement, this form of "color blindness" is manifested by the All Lives Matter countermovement. Many would rather stay within the confines of "not seeing" race and cling to the ideals of equal opportunity to avoid potentially uncomfortable and awkward conversations about racial inequality in this country. This colorblind approach to talking about race allows many postcivil rights era Americans to adhere to the core individualist ideals of the nation (Bonilla-Silva 2003). This approach is also characterized by a distinct absence of a discussion of racial inequality and systems of oppression; rather, it is characterized by a preference to talk about race in "happy," celebratory terms, usually in the form of nonwhites *"enriching* [emphasis added] the lives of whites" (Bell and Hartmann 2007, 16). The tendency to treat race as an inherent individual and personal trait allows people to ignore the systematic and structural ways in which race is deeply embedded in social institutions. In effect, people are willing to talk about race as long as it does not involve discussions of inequality, differences of power, and the privileges of whiteness.

There remains an important contradiction between the current ways in which we talk about race and the real structural inequalities involving race. As business leaders, Supreme Court justices, and politicians, including presidential candidates, extol the merits of diversity in the workplace and educational settings, debates and protests continue to surround numerous issues involving immigration law, crime and punishment, and the school-to-prison pipeline. Arizona's immigration law, Senate Bill 1070, which requires all immigrants in the state to carry their immigration documents, permits law enforcement officials "where reasonable suspicion exists" to ask about a person's immigration status, and "without warrant, may arrest a person" if the officer has probable cause to believe that the person has entered the United States illegally (Senate Bill 1010 §2). With the federal government estimating that Arizona has one of the fastest growing undocumented populations in the country (Hoefer, Rytina, and Baker 2008), commentators on the bill have raised possible issues of racial profiling of the large Hispanic population in the state. In fact, the pop cultural phrase "driving while black," or "DWB" in contemporary American vernacular, illustrates the manner in which race politics enters the most mundane of everyday activities. The recent national reporting surrounding the police shooting deaths of Michael Brown in Ferguson, Missouri, Philando Castille in Minneapolis, Minnesota, and the deaths of Freddie Gray in Baltimore, Maryland, and Eric Garner in Staten Island, New York during encounters with the police have brought to light the very real consequences of racial profiling and police brutality. Even the popular online marketplace site Airbnb, which offers rental accommodations in residences and homes of others as an alternative to hotels, has been found to discriminate against African Americans and other minorities, resulting in the recent Twitter hashtag #AirbnbWhileBlack. Researchers reported that Airbnb hosts were less likely to rent out their homes to guests with African American-sounding names than guests with white-sounding names despite the fact that hosts are only able to find replacement guests 35 percent of the time (Edelman, Luca, and Svirsky 2016). This finding provides empirical support for several anecdotal accounts and has recently led to alternative rental platforms like Noirbnb and Noirebnd, which are created for and by people of color.

If race is not solely relegated as a personal individual attribute, then the social reality of race becomes powerfully undeniable as a group experience. Racial discrepancies in wealth statistics, educational attainment, occupational structures, health measures, and general life chances exemplify how race pervades every aspect of our daily lives and are a testament to how race relations continue to be a central feature of contemporary American society (Brown et al. 2005; Chesler, Crowfoot, and Lewis 2005; Oliver and Shapiro 1995; Massey Charles, Lundy, and Fischer 2003). So if race continues to be a prevalent force in society, what is it? How did it come to be such a dominant force, and why does it continue to maintain its hold on our social reality?

RACE AS A SOCIOHISTORICAL CONSTRUCT

At a very basic level, the concept of race is used to physically and symbolically differentiate types of human bodies. The first, and foremost, lesson about the concept of race is that while it is often misrecognized as a "natural" category based on biology (phenotypes), there is no biological basis for distinguishing human groups along racial lines. Physical characteristics like hair color and texture, facial features, and skin tone are a function of long-term adaptive and evolutionary responses to the physical environment; such responses are not a function of an innate quality. In other words, despite popular inclinations to think otherwise, there does not exist a "race gene." Rather, race exists as a sociohistorical construct—a product of large sociopolitical processes and historical contexts; this fact explains how and why meanings of race have changed over time and space. For example, a close look at immigration patterns and citizenship laws in nineteenth-century America demonstrates how "whiteness" was constructed and that immigrant groups like the Italians and Irish have not always been considered white in this country; the "N-word" was often times used against the Irish in the early 1900s. In today's context, considering someone who is Irish or Italian to be nonwhite would be at best absurd, if not ridiculous. The reality is that between the 1840s and the 1920s in the United States, the rapid influx of immigrants from south-central Eastern (SCE) Europe created a crisis of citizenship that actually fractured the "white race" with debates over who was "truly fit for self-government" (Ignatiev 1995). The fact remains that although racial categories have become naturalized as if they were immutable and unchangeable, these categories are actually a product of social forces and institutions.

Another way to understand the sociohistorical construction of race is the fact that it is not simply an American phenomenon. A cursory look at comparative world history points to its significant racialization ever since the rise of the modern world system. From the advent of the slave trade and Western colonial exploits of the Americas, Africa ,and Asia during the fifteenth through the nineteenth centuries to the continuous process of global integration with postcolonialism and the collapse of the Iron Curtain in the twentieth century, national and cultural meanings of race have changed. For example, whereas one (or anyone with African descent) may be considered black in Chicago, Atlanta, or New York City, that same person may not be considered in the same way in Brazil; racial classifications in Brazil carry distinct class and economic distinctions along with immigration status. Recognizing the fluidity of racial categorizations, the Census Bureau has announced that they will stop using the term "race" in the 2020 census. With important social and political movements like the civil rights movement in America and the antiapartheid movement in South Africa, the content of the race concept has been challenged and yet, with recent instances of genocide in Rwanda and Dafur, it is clear that racial hierarchies remain substantially variegated across the world. As such, racial classifications are deeply connected to specific times and places, and the symbolic meanings of these racial categories are largely shaped by historical and geographical contexts.

So if race does not have a biological basis, then how did it gain such a strong foothold in our society? To fully understand how race became transfixed in our contemporary social reality, one must go back to the discovery of the New World and the associated rise of capitalism and nationalism as the primary features of the modern world. As a shared identity based on national affiliation rather than one based on family, trade, or religion began to take hold in the fifteenth and sixteenth centuries, the political landscape of Europe underwent massive reorganization. People began to see themselves as an "imagined community," as a "people" bounded together by a shared sociopolitical destiny with ideas of self-rule and freedom from tyranny (Anderson 1991). Simultaneously, there was a shift in the economic system from that of the medieval workshop to the capitalist factory in an attempt to increase profits and wealth accumulation. Europe's growing economic machine spurred the search for more material resources like rubber, sugar, cotton, and human labor, leading to the exploration and the discovery of new lands and the systematic **exploitation** of material resources and the securement of foreign lands and territories as colonies in the New World.

To legitimate this system of **colonialism** and domination, Europeans developed the ideology of a civilizing mission. This ideology was further secured by the rise of scientific knowledge and rational thought as the primary mode of explaining the world; the discovery of natural laws to explain natural phenomenon rather than superstition and myth led to great intellectual revolutions in philosophy, economics, political theory, and art. Colonizers created, used, and maintained systems of racial classifications that were seemingly naturalized by science and biology to support the colonial project of transforming indigenous populations into ruled subjects. This project utilized racialized distinctions that constituted a binary of "us" and "them" to legitimate the economic extraction of human labor and raw materials as well as the political domination of land and people. For example, the idea that African slaves were somehow less than human and therefore not deserving of self-government secured the system of slavery in the United States. Eighteenth-century India provides another example of how the British monarchy, motivated by mercantilist interests, established the East India Company to exercise political sovereignty over different territories under the Mughal Empire. Citing unruly social customs and corrupt and inept leadership, the British claimed to offer a "civilized" rule of law and "noble" system of governance that would "improve" the lives of the downtrodden natives. The opening stanza in Rudyard Kipling's famous poem "The White Man's Burden" (1899) characterizes the European stance toward colonial conquests—that it was justified because of the naturally inferior status of the colonized.

> Take up the White Man's burden
> Send forth the best ye breed
> Go bind your sons to exile
> To serve your captives' need;
> To wait in heavy harness,
> On fluttered folk and wild
> Your new-caught, sullen peoples,
> Half-devil and half-child.

The naturalization of race became further entrenched with the impact of social Darwinism in the late nineteenth and twentieth centuries. Known as "scientific racism," physical anthropologists, natural historians, and biologists in the sixteenth and seventeenth centuries sought to use the scientific method to prove that there was indeed a hierarchy of races and that this hierarchy was determined by biological differences between groups of people. Measurements of body parts ranging from cranial size to femur bone lengths were taken as scientists attempted to catalogue and categorize physical traits according to racial classifications. Physical differences in skin tone and eye color were taken to represent real and immutable racial categorizations. More important, these biological indicators of difference were used as explanations of inequality between groups; references to intellectual ability (IQ), athleticism, criminality, and even insanity were often made with respect to the innate biological differences, thus securing the permanence in the naturalized association between race and behavior.

Although modern day geneticists have now established that as a species human beings share 99.9 percent of the same genes as other human beings, ideas such as "blacks are better at basketball" continue to dominate popular discourse because of the fictitious idea that race is biologically determined. Herein lies the second lesson about the concept of race: systems of racial classification did not produce racism, but rather it was racist ideologies that led to the establishment of such systems to legitimate the unequal access to resources and systematic exploitation of different groups.

RACE AT THE CORE OF AMERICA AS A NATION

Although the discussion thus far portrays the topic of race as a powerfully divisive issue, it is important to understand how race can also serve as an effective unifying force. This is particularly the case when the concept of race is associated with two other concepts, ethnicity and nationality, which also refer to symbolic categories of representation. On a most basic level, ethnicity refers to a shared cultural heritage that is informed by historical and religious affiliations and confers a distinct social and linguistic identity. As such the US government uses the term "Hispanic" as an ethnicity rather than a racial category; Hispanic is defined as a person of "Spanish culture or origin regardless of race." In fact, the term "Latino" is often used interchangeably with the term Hispanic; Latino refers to someone with Latin American descent regardless of race while Hispanic typically refers to someone who speaks the Spanish language. In other words, a person from Spain could be considered Hispanic rather than Latino. In contrast, someone from Peru, who speaks Spanish, could be considered Hispanic or Latino. Given that there are multiple races in Latin America due to the transatlantic slave trade as well as centuries of immigration, Latinos (just as Hispanics) can be of any race; the former president of Peru, Alberto Fujimori, was of Japanese descent. Consequently, the Census Bureau uses the term "non-Hispanic whites" to refer to persons who are considered racially white and are not of Hispanic or Latino ethnicity or descent.

Nationality, in contrast, is largely connoted by citizenship and confers a political belonging to a specific geographical territory that is controlled by a government (Calhoun 1995). Typically, one considers his or her nationality in terms of his or her passport; depending on the country's citizenship laws, it is possible for someone to be a citizen of two or more countries. For example, it is possible for a US citizen to also be an Australian citizen. However, not all countries permit multiple citizenships; countries like Singapore and Japan do not recognize dual citizenship beyond the age of 21. Although nationality is often associated with place of origin, descent, and culture, it is important to remember that nationality is a status that is conferred by the state and carries with it sociopolitical rights and obligations. So, if one is Japanese-American (i.e., of Japanese ethnic ancestry), then one is a US citizen and not a Japanese citizen.

In general, the three concepts of race, ethnicity, and nationality inform each other, because all three influence how we understand our social surroundings and how we define ourselves. Another characteristic that these three concepts share in common is that they are situational and subject to change under different sociopolitical and economic circumstances. On the one hand, one may choose to highlight their ethnic heritage, say Irish during Saint Patrick's Day, or their nationality, American, if on a holiday abroad. On the other hand, that same person may identify themselves by their racial group, white, since most people of Irish descent would be classified as such by this country's standards. In this sense, ethnicity (being Irish) is racialized (being white), which is informed by nationality (being American). Therefore, much of how and what one chooses to highlight in terms of their ethnic, racial, or national identity is dependent on one's audience and situational context.

In many ways, the three concepts of ethnicity, race, and nationality are at the core of what divides us and what unites us. Whereas ethnicity can be deployed to distinguish culturally and sociohistorically specific identities within racial groups, nationality often relies on racial identities as a foundation to form a unique and distinct identity. For example, those that identify within the racial group, Asian American, often also identify with the specific ethnicities, such as being Chinese, Vietnamese, Laotian, or Thai. Each ethnic group has its own language, unique rituals and traditions, and different food specialties and preparations and possesses diverse sociohistorical experiences in this country. Interestingly, these different ethnic groups can also function as different national groups, especially if people in those groups identify primarily as immigrants and retain ties to their country of origin. For example, those who identify as Latino American can also identify with specific national countries of origin, such as Columbia, the Dominican Republic, or Brazil.

To further complicate matters, ethnic identities can also be racialized to form the basis of a national identity. Such was the case for over a hundred thousand Japanese Americans living on the West coast, who were forcibly relocated and confined in internment camps during World War II. Fearing that members of the Japanese-American community would betray the country and spy for the enemy, the American government racialized the group (of Japanese ethnic heritage) by treating them as if they were the "enemy from within" (as loyal subjects of the Japanese state). For much of American history, race has determined nationality and much of this relationship has had to do with immigration policies and practices. The third lesson on

FOOD FOR THOUGHT

INSTITUTIONAL RACISM AND THE PRODUCTION OF INEQUITIES IN FOOD ACCESS

Justin Sean Myers

Think about your typical trip to and from class. How easy is it to obtain fresh veggies and fruits as you walk, bike, drive, or take mass transit to school? Do you merely have to walk across the street? Is the grocery store just a few blocks away? Is the supermarket a quick five-minute drive? If you said yes to any of these questions, then count yourself privileged: you do not live in a *food desert*. Food deserts are low-income areas with limited access to fresh vegetables and fruits because grocery stores or super markets are out of reach (more than 1 mile in an urban area and more than 10 miles in rural areas).

According to the US Department of Agriculture, in 2010 18.3 million people lived in food deserts, and the majority of these people were located in urban areas. Due to the disproportionate concentration of blacks and Hispanics in low-income urban areas, food deserts are not race-neutral spaces. Food deserts are thoroughly racialized spaces. But the food desert concept only explains what is absent, not what actually exists in the community. The reality for many of these communities is that they are not food deserts so much as *food swamps*, "areas in which large relative amounts of energy-dense snack foods, inundate healthy food options" (Rose et al. 2009, 2). These urban communities are stocked full of bodegas, liquor stores, and fast-food restaurants that provide cheap foods high in fats, oils, sugars, and salts and lacking in vitamins and minerals. In addition, if a grocery store is to be found in these communities, the produce sold is generally of low quality, being damaged, spoiled, or past the sell-by date. Once you combine the limited access to fresh produce with easy access to cheap processed foods, constant junk food advertising, and limited incomes, what emerges is a path of least resistance toward the overconsumption of foods that should be eaten in moderation. Consequently, these communities suffer from the hunger–obesity paradox, having higher than average rates of malnutrition as well as obesity, diabetes, and heart disease.

How do we explain the existence of such food inequities? Do we presume that fast food predominates in these communities because the residents don't want to eat produce? Or do we associate poor food access with poverty, unemployment, and the processes of economic and political marginalization? Increasingly, food scholars are moving away from individual-level explanations toward underscoring the historical and structural factors that have produced inequities in food access. This shift in focus toward the structural roots of inequalities in food access is why some food scholars are using the term "food apartheid" instead of food desert or food swamp. These scholars underscore that the processes that produce food inequities are not natural nor are they the outcome of the personal eating habits of residents or the individual-level prejudice of politicians, bankers, or white suburbanites. They are the outcome of institutional racism and segregationist practices rooted in the actions of the state, corporations, and citizens.

Food for Thought *continued*

State and corporate actions include racialized practices that prevented investment in communities of color, including redlining, block-busting, urban renewal, and planned shrinkage, while at the same time shifting investment to the white suburbs through federal programs for highway construction and single-family home ownership. On top of state and corporate actions many white communities actively resisted the civil rights movement and racial integration in housing, education, and employment. These struggles against black and Hispanic entrance into white communities drew hard lines over where blacks and Hispanics could live and shop and reinforced ongoing state and corporate actions that confined communities of color primarily to urban areas devoid of good housing, employment, and education.

This economic disinvestment subsequently produced food access barriers for low-income communities of color as they pushed grocery stores to follow white flight to the suburbs. Food retailing is a very competitive industry with low-profit margins and profit is tied to volume sales, making a little on each sale but a lot of money through many sales. These industry dynamics have promoted a business model that seeks to reduce risks and increase long-term profit through large stores on cheap land, rapid turnover of product, and price premiums for upscale products; low-income urban areas don't fit this business model.

Given this historical and structural analysis of the roots of inequities in food access, solutions need to move beyond nutrition education or simply bringing a Walmart to low-income communities. Addressing poor food access nationally will require a substantial reinvestment in the education, employment, housing, and retail structures in low-income communities since, in the end, you can't afford good food without a good job.

Sources

Caruso, Christine C. 2014. "Searching for Food (Justice): Understanding Access in an Under-Served Food Environment in New York City." *Journal of Critical Thought and Praxis* 1(3): Article 8. http://lib.dr.iastate.edu/jctp/vol3/iss1/8

McClintock, Nathan. 2011. "From Industrial Garden to Food Desert: Demarcated Devaluation in the Flatlands of Oakland, California." Alison Hope Alkon and Julian Agyeman (eds.), *Cultivating Food Justice*, 89–120. Berkeley: University of California Press.

Rose, Donald, J. Nicholas Bodor, Chris M. Swalm, et al. 2009. *Deserts in New Orleans? Illustrations of Urban Food Access and Implications for Policy.* Paper presented at the University of Michigan National Poverty Center/USDA Economic Research Service Conference Understanding the Economic Concepts and Characteristics of Food Access, January 23, Washington, DC.

Treuhaft, Sarah and Allison Karpyn. 2010. *The Grocery Gap: Who Has Access to Healthy Food and Why It Matters.* Oakland, CA: Policy Link. http://www.policylink.org/site/c. lkIXLbMNJrE/b.5860321/k.A5BD/The_Grocery_Gap.htm

US Department of Agriculture. 2016. "Food Access Research Atlas: Documentation." http://www.ers.usda.gov/data-products/food-access-research-atlas/documentation. aspx

Winne, Mark. 2009. *Closing the Food Gap: Resetting the Table in the Land of Plenty.* Boston: Beacon Press.

race is that the formation of racial categories is at the center of many nation-building projects. An example of this is the historical formation of whiteness throughout the nineteenth and twentieth centuries. The debate on "Who is American?" centered on ideas about who was fit for self-government and exemplifies the convergence of race and citizenship (Jacobson 1999). Contrary to what the Statue of Liberty represents in American historical mythology, not everyone who came to the United States was considered free or considered to be even capable of living in a democracy; only those who were fit for self-government could claim to be American. In other words, the sociohistorical construction of a cohesive American national identity is tied to a civic story of **assimilation** of different immigrant (and racial) groups.

Here, it is important to remember that race is not an immutable construct, and many immigrant groups like the Irish and the Jews became white as they assimilated into American society (Ignatiev 1995; Brodkin 1998). During the 1790s, citizenship was reserved for free white persons and excluded not only persons of color but also all those who were nonfree. These included indentured Irish servants, many of whom would be considered white by today's standards. However, the increasing numbers of new immigrants from SCE Europe, who were blamed for the rise of urban slums, crime, and class competition, accelerated the debate on who was fit for self-government into a crisis about the overinclusiveness of whiteness. By the end of the nineteenth century, there was increasing hostility among native-born whites toward these new SCE European immigrants (Lieberson 1980). The establishment of new immigration laws in 1924 with national quotas and racial restrictions on citizenship resulted in the fracturing of whiteness and the development of a racial hierarchy paralleling definitions of who was American that went beyond that of the free and white. The racialized distinction between native-born whites and new SCE Europeans was very much integral to the negotiation of who was truly fit for self-government; although these new SCE European immigrants were phenotypically white, native-born whites argued that these immigrants did not possess what was necessary to live in a free and democratic society and thus did not qualify to be American. As such, citizenship laws became a useful way of defining those who belonged and those who did not.

So, if the new SCE European immigrants were not originally considered white, then how and why did this change? Ironically, it was the legalistic turn of events of permitting who was to be admitted into this country through the Immigration Act of 1924 that had the effect of not only defining who was an American but also framing race relations for the next century. The 1924 Immigration Act set national quotas for different groups entering the country limiting the numbers of incoming SCE European immigrants and actually accelerated their upward mobility by affecting the structure of the labor market and resulting occupational queues. Fewer members within each SCE European group meant less competition for employment between members of the group, which allowed members to move up the socio-economic ladder more quickly. Due to the racial and gendered hierarchies at the turn of the nineteenth century, the labor market had developed into different segments, with various groups dominating different occupations and sectors of the economy. This segmented labor market meant that there were a limited number of jobs available for certain occupations and sectors of the economy, while other segments would encounter more competition. The various segments were not only the result of economic changes but also due to racial and gender barriers to specific occupations.

Needless to say, the 1924 restriction of certain SCE European groups coupled with the rise of the black population in the North from the Great Migration of African Americans from the South, had significant effects on the labor market. For one thing, a larger supply of black workers meant that they could not command high wages since there were more within the group to compete with; similarly, a decrease in the supply of new European workers meant that the group could command higher wages than before. In other words, an influx of blacks entering the bottom of the occupation queue allowed the groups of new immigrants above them to move farther up the queue. This upward mobility was additionally facilitated by a decline in job competition among the new SCE European immigrants who had less of their own to compete with. Furthermore, larger numbers of blacks migrating to the North also made it difficult for blacks to develop unique market niches; the niches that did form could not sustain the same proportion of black population as they did in the case of other migrant groups. In his comparative study of black and white experiences in the late nineteenth and early twentieth centuries, Lieberson (1980, 280, 294) finds that even though new SCE European immigrants may have begun with similarly limited levels of education and capital as compared to southern-born blacks who were moving North, the rise of the black population in the North coinciding with the decline of new European immigration, affected the labor market in ways that explain why the new Europeans fared better than their free black counterparts. Faced with the opportunity for upward mobility, new Europeans began to assimilate into America and soon became unquestionably American.

However, unlike popular and mainstream assumptions about definitions of whiteness, the unification of whiteness as a singular race only became cemented during the 1940s. On the international front, the impact of World War II and geopolitical responses to Hitler's Germany transformed racial differences between whites into ethnic differences. Thus, Italians, Jews, and Irish became known as ethnic whites rather than nonwhites. This was coupled with the increasing assimilation of new Europeans into America, and distinctions between the white races became increasingly irrelevant. Of course, as America emerged on the postwar international political scene as a world leader, a sociopolitical program of democracy and the unleashing of a capitalist machine informed the answer to the question "Who is American?" America's previous answer—those who are "fit" for self-government—became increasingly untenable as America began to represent itself as the leader of the free world. Nationally speaking, the rise of the civil rights movement nationalized Jim Crow as *the* racial issue in political discourse and thus secured a binary between whites and non-whites to the definition of race relations in this country.

As this discussion thus far demonstrates, immigration policy serves to police the boundaries of both racial and national categories. When Congress passed the Immigration and Nationality Act in 1965, which abolished the national quotas and racial restrictions previously enacted, there was a legislative attempt to decouple race from citizenship. However, even though 1965 became a watershed moment for US immigration history, it could not erase previous centuries of the sociopolitical and economic associations between race and citizenship. The national image of an American continues to be constituted by race relations between whites and nonwhites. This is especially the case as we consider the number of times the term "foreigner" has been associated with Arabs or those who "look" Middle Eastern or who have an Arabic name. Or consider the number of times you have seen "Speak English" signs that are directed at Latino/a Americans and Chicano/as. The assumption is that these individuals are not likely to be American even if, according to the US Census Bureau, out of the 304 million people in the United States in 2006–2010, 5 million reported an Arab ancestry and that the Hispanic population is projected to grow from 17 percent of the total US population (55 million) in 2014 to 29 percent of the population (119 million) by 2060 (Asi and Beaulieu 2013; Colby and Ortman 2015). The fact of the matter is that we are more likely to assume that someone who is white is American than someone who is nonwhite.

While it is important to understand how the three symbolic categories of representation inform each other, it is equally important to differentiate between them. To be clear, while race has been erased as a historical experience for European immigrants, ethnicity has reemerged as the defining marker of cultural difference for many white Americans. Across the country, there are numerous annual festivals celebrating Polish, Irish, German, and Italian cultural heritages with traditional foods, authentic dress, and folk music. For nonwhite Americans, if not explicitly in political ways given the abolishment of race-based restrictions, race continues to define their citizenship in socioeconomic and cultural ways; nonwhite Americans continue to have to prove their worthiness of belonging by either demonstrating their membership through economic means via the middle class or by adhering to indicators of cultural membership via mastery of the English language and "sounding like an American."

DIFFERENCES BETWEEN RACISM, PREJUDICE, AND DISCRIMINATION

Now that we have established that there is no biological basis to racial classifications and that much of how we think about race as biology is a result of racist ideologies from periods of colonialism and Eurocentric ideals of citizenship and self-government, it is necessary to address some fallacies of racism and clarify what racism is exactly. A sociological approach to understanding racism distinguishes it from more personalized and individualistic accounts by focusing on group attitudes and behavior that is grounded in a particular social system. In simple terms, **racism** is an ideology that supports or rationalizes the belief that one racial group is innately superior or inferior to another. Racism is often associated with another concept—prejudice. **Prejudice** refers to a set of prejudgments that are based on generalizations (stereotypes) that people hold about other groups of people. Even though it is common to think that it is possible to relinquish all prejudices and abandon all stereotypes about others, prejudices serve as cognitive schemas—a way for us to make sense and interpret a vast amount of information. As such, it is impossible for us to suspend all of our prejudices, and relegating racism to a set of prejudices does little justice to the full range of institutional and systemic dynamics that maintain and perpetuate the effects of racism. Rather than treating racism as a function of individual ideas and prejudices, the sociological imagination allows us to view racism as intimately embedded within our everyday practices and social institutions like schools, governments, markets, and neighborhoods.

The tendency to conflate racism with the particular acts and thoughts of a racist individual suggests that racism is intentional and deliberate. The logic goes a little like this: if one is not intentional about their ideas or behavior, then they must not be racists. However, this can be a dangerous and problematic argument. If we can identify racists as a result of their intentionality, then we can also successfully separate ourselves as nonracists, and if we do not have the intention of racism, then this relieves us from responsibility for "their" intentions and resulting behavior. Consider the number of times you have told yourself when reading about a hate crime in the newspaper: "At least I would never behave this way, and I am not personally responsible for those people behaving this way." This personalistic conception of racism is dangerous because it suggests that racism is the fault of other individuals; it allows us to distance and disassociate ourselves with "those" racist individuals, excusing ourselves from responsibility for participating in, and even benefiting from, a racist system. Of course, intentionality is in no way a prerequisite for racism; the fourth lesson of this chapter is that much of contemporary racism is subtle, unintentional, well meaning, and implicit.

Racism, in today's context, takes place mostly in the form of discrimination, which refers to both the unequal treatment of persons as well as the disparate impact of decisions and procedures on producing and reinforcing racial disadvantage (Pager and Shepard 2008). It is important here to differentiate between types of discrimination: institutional and attitudinal. **Institutional discrimination** involves the systematic denial of opportunity, privileges, and rights. An example of this is the tendency of schools and universities to support curricula that highlight the contributions and accomplishments of European Americans while ignoring that of non-European Americans. In her study, Lewis (2001) discusses that even when multicultural education is introduced into school curricula, such as during black history month, the inclusions often revolve around trite displays of civil rights history and events. When the month is over, any visible trace of such displays are promptly removed. Another example of institutional discrimination is the practice of redlining, where the private banking and insurance industries can make it more difficult for people who live in minority neighborhoods to qualify for mortgage and home improvement loans. While the Fair Housing Act officially outlawed these practices in 1968, recent research suggests that new forms like banks' predatory lending and "retail redlining" where access to retail stores important for health are inequitably distributed across racially distinct areas remain persistent and alive (Kwate, Loh, White, and Saldana 2013).

In both of these examples, discrimination takes place regardless of the motives or intentions of the people carrying out the policies of the institutions at which they work. In either example, there can appear to be rational and objective reasons for such policies; in the case of school curricula, arguments are made about how it is impossible to include everything, and so something has to be left out. However, there is little to no opportunity to discuss the criteria for what gets included or left out in the curriculum. This is precisely how institutional discrimination works—by withholding resources and opportunities through a systematic manner, often through the establishment of policy, so that discrimination just becomes part of "the way things work" and becomes part of the normal and routinized procedure for the institution. This is in contrast to **attitudinal discrimination**, which can be overt and manifests in everyday interactions and practices. Most antiracism programs for children and teenagers focus on addressing the issues of attitudinal discrimination by focusing on overt prejudicial attitudes. In fact, much of news media attention on the topic of political correctness has to do with correcting attitudinal discrimination. For example, many high school diversity programs focus on appreciating difference as an appropriate attitudinal response and lessons on cultural awareness to combat ignorance.

While it is discriminatory attitudes that receive the most attention in media and popular discussions, of primary note for many sociologists is institutional discrimination. Institutional discrimination receives less attention from everyday conversations because it is often invisible and indirect. In the previous example of institutional discrimination in school curricula, non-European Americans are underrepresented in American history not because there is one single person or even a set of persons that decided that American history should focus only on the experiences of European Americans. Rather, this underrepresentation was the result of a systematic attempt to rewrite American history in school textbooks and curricula as one that celebrates democracy and **meritocracy** and highlights stories of individual success. To include a history of non-European Americans would necessitate a retelling of American history that would threaten the very core of deeply celebrated American ideals and an acknowledgement that many groups, particularly that of non-Europeans, did not receive the same privileges or advantages that many European groups experienced. It would have to include the forcible removal and killing of several different American Indian tribes, the systematic enslavement and repression of African slaves, the deliberate internment of Japanese Americans during the World War II, and the violent occupation of Texas, among others (Takaki 1994). It is obvious, then, why there is little vested interest in changing school curricula; as the practice of telling of American history as one of individual success and celebration continues and becomes institutionalized, it will be further embedded and more difficult to challenge and change.

Of course, attitudinal discrimination can also be covert as it is found in our habitual everyday practices. For example, there can be tendency to assume that the first language of a person of Asian descent is not English. Another example is when campus safety officers confront a group of black students about their presence in the student union with the assumption that they are not members of the student body. These examples illustrate the nature of our racialized dispositions as practical sense and everyday know-how when navigating our social reality. The song "Everyone's a Little Bit Racist" in the ever-popular musical Avenue Q is an example of how a well-meaning lesson on confronting one's prejudices can fall short if one assumes that racism operates on an individual level and is based on inappropriate or rude ideas about other people. While it is important to acknowledge one's own racist tendencies, it actually does little toward real social change because it fails to consider the ways in which social systems often operate—independent of one's intentions or, even sometimes, consciousness.

Given that racism is best understood as a systemic phenomenon, a common fallacy that people make is that racism is impossible to eradicate due to its pervasiveness. On the one hand, it is important to understand that racism is deeply embedded in much of social reality in this country. On the other hand, just because racism is engrained into the social institutions of which everyone belongs and participates in, it does not mean that the system cannot change or shift. Recall that the application of the sociological imagination reveals that our social system is a product of human agency and active social behavior—the relationship between history and biography (Mills 1959). Just as our behavior is a product of a particular social structure, our actions go toward reifying existing structures. In other words, eradicating racism is not impossible, but solutions cannot rest on not thinking mean thoughts about other people or individual modes of action. Instead, action and change must be directed at the very social system from which we all operate; systemic problems require systemic solutions.

The fifth lesson about race and racism is that discrimination involves the application of power and domination by those in possession of it in symbolic, economic, and political ways (Desmond and Emirbayer 2009). A common question among students in a class on sociology is, "Can a person of color be a racist?" The answer to this question depends on how we understand racism. If we are to follow the previous discussion, then we must consider the systematic and institutionalized nature of racism. Such a consideration suggests that, in this country, whites hold a certain amount of power and control a certain amount of resources that are not equally available to non-white groups. In this case, one must concede that a particular racial regime, or racial order, exists—one that has whites occupying and dominating positions of power (Bonilla-Silva 2015). It is precisely because of the need to recognize the manner in which people of color have been systematically disadvantaged that there has been significant criticism of the All Lives Matter countermovement. According to supporters of All Lives Matter, the focus on Black Lives Matter accentuates the focus on race and ignores the fact that all lives are the same and should matter equally. This colorblind approach is problematic as it ignores the fact that blacks experience social reality in different ways and invalidates the legitimate concerns that blacks have about an unequal system.

More important, this unequal division of power is often taken for granted and assumed to be the norm. Commonly referred to as "white privilege," this means that whites often do not have to consider what it means to be white in this country—or what it means to be a person of color for that matter (McIntosh 1988). For example, white people never have to worry that a security guard is going to stop them for stepping into an expensive clothing store or if the police are going to stop them, especially if they are driving a nice car. In fact, for many whites, persons of authority represent safety and security; this represents a stark difference from what blacks have experienced as evidenced by Black Lives Matter where the police often represent threats to safety and will require defensive behavior. While it may be the case that nonwhites can and do exhibit prejudicial attitudes toward whites as well as members of other nonwhite groups, the very reality of institutionalized racism implies that it is impossible for nonwhite groups to engage in a systematic denial of opportunity, privilege, and power to whites.

Unfortunately, people of color consistently report experiencing discrimination in the workplace, housing, and everyday social settings; in a 2001 survey, more than one-third of blacks and nearly 20 percent of Hispanics and Asians recounted that they had been passed over for a job or promotion because of their race or ethnicity (Schuman Steeh, Bobo, and Krysan 2001; Schiller 2004). In his interviews with black middle-class respondents, Feagin (1991, 10) found that there is a cumulative aspect to their experiences of public discrimination because such incidents are not isolated but rather there is a "lifelong series of such incidents." As a result, blacks have to develop a series of responses, one of which is a continual assessment of possible discriminatory situations and are a reflection of "the microworld by the macroworld of historical racial subordination" (115). The fact that whites have the ability or option of abstaining from having to identify their race as a function of their normality is a testament to the power of white privilege (McIntosh 1988; Frankenburg 1993). In fact, one of the most powerful and yet unspoken privileges of being white is that race or racism does not have to be a harsh reality that whites have to consider, confront, or even acknowledge as part of their own experience.

Now that we have clarified the differences between the concepts of race, racism, ethnicity, and nationality, we can discuss the various structural factors that affect the formation and nature of race relations. The following sections examine the major theoretical frameworks affecting race relations in a multilevel analysis; starting with a discussion of the research on interracial attitudes, we move to a meso-level analysis of interracial interactions in the context of labor markets and residential segregation, and finally conclude with an examination of macro-level theories of ethnic conflict and nationalism within an international context.

"MY BEST FRIEND IS BLACK": EXPLAINING INTERRACIAL ATTITUDES

"I'm not a racist; one of my best friends is black!" Consider how many times you have heard this among your friends, family members, and strangers. Even on popular television shows, the term "black best friend" is coined to refer to ways in which casts are made to appear racially diverse through a nonwhite character without storylines of their own but serve to support the main lead characters who are white. Applied as a key rhetorical device, the "my best friend is" strategy indicates the manner in which whites have developed and utilized strategies to conceal their racial prejudices (Bonilla-Silva 2002).

Of course, interracial attitudes have changed, particularly in the past four decades. Using a longitudinal study of American attitudes from 1972 to 2008 (General Social Survey; Wihbey 2014), Bobo, Charles, Krysan, and Simmons (2012) report that white Americans' attitudes have moved from overtly racist ideology, including revulsion against interracial marriages and beliefs about blacks being inherently inferior to broad support for equal treatment and large measures of racial tolerance. However, whites' support for government intervention in the form of affirmative action policies has remained largely tepid and limited, believing that blacks should be subject to the conditions of a free market. As such, contemporary negative stereotypes have become qualified, rather than categorical, and explanations for racial inequality have changed from a biological basis to one of culture.

In addition, researchers conclude that whites feel greater animus toward blacks than toward Hispanics and Asians. Whereas whites living in areas with higher percentages of blacks express more antiblack prejudice, larger percentages of Hispanics or Asians do not affect whites' prejudice toward those groups. Clearly, while white–black relations are embedded firmly into the country's history, relations between whites and Hispanics or Asians are more of a result of recent immigration history, albeit there are some exceptions including that of Mexicans in the southwestern United States and the Chinese on the West Coast in 1820 (Fussell 2014). As a result, white prejudice against Asians and Hispanics is consistently related to preferences for more restrictive and punitive immigration policies.

One of the most influential group-level approaches to explaining racial prejudice is Herbert Blumer's (1958, 2-4) theory on group position, also known as group threat theory, where "fundamentally racial feelings point to and depend on a positional arrangement of the racial groups". Moving the discussion of prejudice away from a set of feelings located within the individual, Blumer argued that an understanding of racial prejudice can be found in a collective process by which "racial groups form images of themselves and of others" and develop "a sense of social position" of each other. When there is a perceived challenge to this sense of group position, members of the group develop racial prejudice as a "defensive reaction to such challenging of the sense of group position." Blumer explains that the development of this sense of group position does not come about through the direct first-hand experiences of individuals, but rather through the characterization of the group as a whole in public arenas by those who hold prestigious and powerful positions. As such, racial prejudice is highly dependent on the prevailing social (and racial) order.

While Blumer's theory rests on the notion of a perceived collective threat, others have emphasized the real material collective threat to dominant group interests rather than the perceptions of group interests. Research indicates that whites support the principle of equality more than they do for race-targeted policies to achieve racial equality because such policies are particularly threatening to whites (Bobo 1983; Bobo and Kluegel 1993). Furthermore, Quillian (1995), in a cross-national study of anti-immigrant and racial attitudes in 12 countries of the European Economic Community, demonstrates that both the relative size of the subordinate group and economic situation of the particular country can influence people's perceptions of group position, and it is these perceptions that are related to prejudicial attitudes. These findings might suggest why some minority groups face more hostility from dominant groups than others. Not surprising, based on Blumer's theory, blacks living in neighborhoods where Latinos are more economically advantaged than blacks tend to hold more negative attitudes toward Latinos than blacks living in neighborhoods where they are economically advantaged to Latinos. Similarly, Asian entrepreneurship in low-income majority black neighborhoods accounts for black–Asian antagonism (Lee 2002), and while blacks may hold more pro-immigrant attitudes than whites, their sense of threat stems largely from economic competition. Perceived group threat also accounts for Latino's attitudes toward other immigrants, but it is mitigated by a host of other factors, including assimilation and proximity to other native-born Latinos and cultural affinity (Fussell 2014). In this line of research, prejudice is not conceptualized as a result of competition between individuals but rather as a group feeling that the dominant group is being threatened, which then leads to prejudicial attitudes toward the subordinate group.

In general, research by Schuman et al. (1997, 121) shows that white racial attitudes have consistently over the past five decades become increasingly accepting of the "principles of equal treatment and integration in most important areas of American life." What is interesting is that as whites are increasingly less likely to hold unfavorable stereotypes about blacks, they are also less likely to acknowledge the adverse effects of past and persistent discrimination against blacks and Hispanics, preferring the explanation that these groups do not work hard enough (Quillian 2005). This could explain why whites are overwhelmingly supportive of principles of equality and integration but far less supportive of government policies for implementation. For example, while a large majority of both whites (96 percent) and blacks (99 percent) in 1995 agreed that blacks and whites should go to the same schools, only about 25 percent and 57 percent, respectively, think that the federal government should be responsible for this happening (Schuman et al. 1997). Similar contradictions remained in 2008 when 28 percent of white respondents still supported an individual homeowner's right to discriminate on the basis of race when selling a home, and nearly one out of four educated northern whites adopt this position. Blacks were also likely to support discrimination by homeowners in selling to whomever they like but at levels well beneath those among whites. Accordingly, Bobo et al. (2012) conclude that blacks are more likely to endorse integrationist, nondiscriminatory views whereas whites are less in favor of governmental interventionist policies when it comes to racial integration.

Further, research on public opinion toward racial policies like affirmative action have shown that beliefs about the costs and benefits associated with the policy are not purely political calculations or a function of self-interest (Bobo 2000). Rather, such opinions are also informed by racial stereotyping and what scholars refer to as "symbolic racism" (Kinder and Sears 1981; Sears 1988). According to this perspective on racial attitudes, white American's reactions to racial policies are prompted by antiblack affect and beliefs about traditional American values like individualism, including "the belief that racial discrimination is largely a thing of the past, that blacks should just work harder to overcome their disadvantage, and that blacks are making excessive demands for special treatment and get too much attention from elites, so their gains are often undeserved" (Sears, Van Laar, Carrilo, and Kosterman 1997, 22). Thus, the sixth lesson of this chapter is that even while more whites are expressing tolerant attitudes toward blacks, whites are also more likely to uphold traditional values of individualism and less likely to acknowledge the structural impediments and disadvantages faced by blacks.

The good news is that survey research suggests that white respondents are less likely to support statements about blacks being less intelligent and hard-working than whites, and fewer white respondents verbally object to increasing levels of interracial mixing in neighborhoods and in marriage partners (Krysan 2000). Recent reports on attitudes toward interracial marriages find that Americans, in general, are becoming increasingly tolerant of members of their own family getting married to someone of a different race (Pew Research Center 2012). Based on data from the Census Bureau's American Community Survey (2008–2010), Pew's researchers determined that not only were attitudes toward interracial marriage becoming more

SOCIOLOGY AT WORK
WORK AND RACE: WHY BLACKS/AFRICAN AMERICANS ARE OFTEN DISADVANTAGED IN HIRING
Arne L. Kalleberg

It is a common belief in the United States that education is the great leveler and the road to opportunity in the world of work. Yet, there are big race differences in the quality of jobs that college-educated blacks and whites are able to obtain: racial differences are highest among the college-educated (as compared to those with less education), and black male college graduates earn about 75 percent of that earned by white male college graduates, while black women college graduates earn about 90 percent of the wages of white women college graduates.

The reasons for these racial gaps in earnings and jobs among college graduates have been the subject of considerable speculation. Some have argued that the gaps are due to differences in the quality of schools or the kinds of subjects and majors that are taken by blacks as opposed to whites. Others have maintained that employers discriminate against blacks, despite the existence of laws against it; for example, employers may believe that blacks have fewer "soft skills" than whites; soft skills are abilities and traits that are related to attitudes (such as work ethic) and personalities rather than to formal or technical knowledge.

One way of learning about racial differences in the earnings and jobs of college-educated persons is by means of an audit study. An audit study is a field experiment in which the researcher matches two individuals with nearly identical characteristics to see if the few ways in which they differ (e.g., in terms of their race/gender combination or type of college attended) are responsible for an outcome (such as being hired for a job). A recent example of such an audit study was by Michael Gaddis (2015), who created pairs of matched individuals that differed only in terms of their race/gender combination (he used common race/gender names—such as Lamar or DaQuan vs. Charlie or Ronny to signal whether the person was a black or white male, respectively, and Ebony or Shanice vs. Aubrey or Erica to denote black as opposed to white females) and the type of college they attended (elite private vs. less selective public university). He then sent out applications on behalf of each member of the pair to the same jobs. This strategy enabled him to assess the importance of race and perceived college quality in whether the applicant received a response from the employer to the job application.

He found that black applicants were much less likely than whites to receive a response from a job application. In addition, when blacks did receive a response, they were for jobs that paid less and involved less responsibility (e.g., were less likely to be managerial jobs) than those for whites. Moreover, blacks who were listed on the application as attending elite institutions (such as Harvard or Stanford) only did as well as whites that attended less selective universities (such as a less prestigious state college).

These results underscore the reality that in the United States a college education—even from an elite university—cannot overcome the impacts of racial discrimination in the labor market. Further, once black applicants do get positive responses from employers, they are usually for less desirable jobs than are those offered to whites.

Source

Gaddis, S. Michael. 2015. "Discrimination in the Credential Society: An Audit Study of Race and College Selectivity in the Labor Market" *Social Forces* 93(4): 1451–79.

---

tolerant, the percentages of interracial marriages among all married couples were also rapidly increasing from 3.2 percent in 1980 to 8.4 percent in 2010.

Of course, before one is convinced that white Americans are becoming less racist, these results must be considered in the context of changing social norms about what is appropriate to fill out on a survey; changes in racial attitudes may not necessarily reflect changes in actual behavior. In the case of increasing interracial marriages, a deeper analysis of pairings by race and ethnicity reveals underlying racial preferences in the friendship and marriage selection process. For example, in the same study recently done by Pew Research Center (2012), it is telling that less than one in ten whites (10 percent) married someone who is nonwhite whereas Asians and Hispanics have the highest level of intermarriage rates at 27.7 percent and 25.7 percent, respectively. Interracial marriage has a lot to do with contextual variables such as the size and composition of minority groups that affect the likelihood of interaction and contact. For example, research on friendships in schools find that the probability of interracial dyads being friends were lowest in the most diverse schools, and interracial friendships increase when opportunities for same-race friendships at school decline (Joyner and Kao 2000).

Similarly, as with mixed-race friendships, minority populations are most likely to out-marry because the pool of potential partners are largely made up of whites and other minority populations (Qian and Lichter 2011). However, as immigrant populations like Asians and Hispanics have grown, the marriage pool among US-born minority co-ethnics has grown, potentially reinforcing distinctive cultural and ancestral identities; research suggests that rates of Hispanic intermarriage with whites have declined for the first time during the 1990s with second generation Hispanics preferring to marry first- rather than third-generation Hispanics or whites (Lichter et al. 2011). Not only has the marriage pool been altered by a growth in the immigrant Hispanic population, it is also important to keep in mind the spatial redistribution of this population—moving away from metropolitan areas; many foreign-born Latinos have relocated to new suburban nonmetropolitan communities, significantly changing and affecting the ethnic make-up of rural America in a relatively short amount of time (Tienda and Fuentes 2014).

Bonilla-Silva (2003) points our attention to the ways in which racial prejudices are expressed within a contemporary color-blind ideology where racism is expressed in individual terms and no longer matters; in more recent work, he identifies the concept of a "racial grammar" as an organizational framework for racial interactions (Bonilla-Silva 2015). Using in-depth interview data collected from college students and respondents in the Detroit metropolitan area, Bonilla-Silva (2002) demonstrates the ways in which white respondents relied on "semantic moves" like "Yes and no, but . , ," or "I'm not black so I don't know . . ." to minimize the effects of discrimination and taking a racial view without opening themselves to the charge of racism. This study demonstrates the ways in which contemporary racist talk manifests itself, and while **color-blindness** maintains the appearance of avoiding racist terminology, it can be used to deny the continued relevance and presence of discrimination and racial inequality. This finding is further supported by Forman and Lewis' (2006) study of the shifting nature of white's racial attitudes through their response to the devastation in Hurricane Katrina. Identifying this relatively new and expanding form of racial prejudice, the authors demonstrate how racial apathy (not caring) and white ignorance (not knowing) of contemporary racial inequality are extensions of a color-blind discourse.

A word is due on the particular emphasis on the racial attitudes of whites toward blacks and the overwhelming absence of data on racial attitudes of nonwhite groups toward each other as well as to the white majority (Krysan 2000). Much of this lapse has to do with the way in which race and race relations have been defined in this country; one of the legacies of the civil rights movement coupled with changes in immigration practices and policies has led to a premium on interpreting race relations in terms of black–white relations. Meanwhile, Asian-American and Latino groups have largely been examined within an immigration framework, with a focus on their varying assimilation and acculturation experiences. Researchers and research subjects alike often conflate immigrants with Asians and Hispanics and natives with blacks and whites partly because of the way in which the concepts of race and ethnicity were measured (Fussell 2014). This tendency to focus on black–white interracial attitudes is also fueled by the social realities of racial segregation between blacks and whites and the overwhelming disparity between black and white wealth. Nonetheless, a significant gap remains in the literature on the racial attitudes of nonwhite groups.

WHERE WE LIVE AND RACE RELATIONS

One of the most widely cited and used measures of racial attitudes and preferences has been the study of residential patterns, specifically in the form of **residential segregation**, commonly known as "living on the wrong side of the tracks." In sociological terms, racial residential segregation refers to racially defined and separated settlements and remains a salient feature of contemporary American cities. Established to be the structural linchpin of racial inequality (Bobo 1989), residential segregation, especially between blacks and whites, appears to be unaffected by rising economic status (Massey and Denton 1993). Besides being associated with higher rates of infant and adult mortality for blacks, residential segregation has also been shown to affect lower rates of educational attainment and higher rates of unemployment for blacks and can even have negative effects on the educational attainment of second-generation immigrant communities (Acevedo-Garcia, Lochner, Osypuk, and Subramanian 2003; Portes and Rumbaut 2001).

While there has been an overall general decline in the level of residential segregation, experts agree that the rate of decline has been inconsistent across US cities, and black–white segregation remains very persistent in cities with large minority populations, such as Detroit and New York (Logan, Stults, and Farley 2004; Logan and Stults 2011). Furthermore, evidence from the recent housing foreclosure crisis in 2007 reveals not only that blacks and Latinos are more likely to experience foreclosure but also, due to predatory subprime lending and marketing practices, risky loans were more concentrated in minority neighborhoods (Bayer, Ferreira, and Ross 2013; Engel and McCoy 2011; Rugh and Massey 2010). In fact, a 2008 Federal Reserve Bulletin reported that among mortgage lenders who went bankrupt in 2007, black and Latino borrowers who received loans in 2006 were more likely to receive a subprime than a prime loan; white borrowers had an opposite experience— they were more likely to get a prime than a subprime loan from the same lenders (Avery, Brevoort, and Canner 2008). According to Hall, Crowder, and Spring (2015), the foreclosure crisis was very much "structured strongly along racial/ethnic lines" and, more important, "hardened racial/ethnic boundaries between neighborhoods and increased residential segregation beyond what it otherwise would have been" (544). Not only were foreclosures disproportionately concentrated in minority-populated and integrated neighborhoods, the crisis also further exacerbated residential segregation between blacks and whites and Latino and whites. In fact, Asians, Hispanics, and blacks are separated not only from whites but also from each other; different national-origin groups also live apart from each other, even those who share the same panethnicity like Asians and Latinos (Kim and White 2010; Parisi, Lichter, and Taquino 2011).

There are several common arguments about segregated communities. First, that such communities are separated because of class differences and economics rather than racial preferences. Second, that residential choices are a result of individual preferences. While research may not be able to firmly establish whether whites avoid living with blacks because of racial prejudice or if such preferences are motivated by a fear of the liabilities associated with integrated neighborhoods, such as crime and the decline in property values, the evidence is clear that much more than individual preference or choice goes into the selection of neighborhoods and housing (Charles 2003). Rather, it involves the ways in which race is integrated into a system that dictates the availability of mortgages and bank loans, the practices of real estate agents, and even the policies of the Federal Housing Authority. Specific practices include providing less information about housing units, less assistance with financing, and steering into less wealthy communities and neighborhoods with a higher proportion of minority residents. The seventh lesson on race and race relations is that the development of racially defined residential space is not a result of individual preference.

One of the clearest examples to demonstrate the prevailing influence of race on housing opportunities is a phenomenon known as redlining. This refers to the Federal Housing Authority's practice of using a red line to mark on a map neighborhoods and areas that were deemed less desirable. Banks and real estate companies would rely on a seemingly rational and bureaucratic system of appraisal of property values to inform and guide lending and purchasing housing options. These maps were largely based on assumptions of the community, rather than accurate assessments of individual household's abilities to satisfy lending criteria. Neighborhoods and districts that were redlined were typically ones that were populated by new migrant communities, tended to be in congested urban centers and, as such, failed to qualify for federal grants and bank financing. Although this federal practice was outlawed in 1968, it firmly secured the deterioration of many inner-city neighborhoods by withholding mortgage capital and home improvement loans and preventing these neighborhoods from attracting and retaining business investments and families who could purchase homes. Real estate agents and bank loan officers would rely on the information provided by these maps to determine which neighborhoods to steer potential buyers to as well as the feasibility of their requested loans.

A 1991 Federal Reserve study reported that commercial banks rejected black applicants for home mortgages two times as often as whites nationwide; the poorest white applicant was more likely to get a mortgage loan approved than a black applicant in the highest income bracket (Oliver and Shapiro 1995). These practices did not only apply to mortgage applications but also home improvement loans. Federal funds were redirected toward neighborhoods and communities where race was not an issue. As such, neighborhoods with older homes and larger communities of minorities often had lower property values, tended to have poorer school districts, and featured fewer favorable amenities, such as parks, shops and restaurants, and bank services. Consequently, this has a cyclical effect of discouraging purchases and private investments in these redlined neighborhoods while existing residents found their property quickly dwindling in value as their communities deteriorated and became increasingly abandoned.

While the argument that racial segregation has given way to class segregation is tempting, Douglas Massey and Nancy Denton (1993) in their book, *American Apartheid*, found that for black family incomes from less than $2,500 per year to those more than $50,000 per year, the experience of "black segregation does not vary by affluence" (85). Higher levels of income do not erase the effects of racial segregation, and high levels of segregation exist across all income groups for blacks. In fact, middle-class and affluent blacks live in suburban areas that are significantly less white and less affluent than their white counterparts (Alba, Logan, and Stults 2000). When it comes to housing for blacks, class is unable to overcome the effects of race.

It is important to note here that home ownership remains the largest single investment and asset for most Americans. Property taxes, which form the basis of most a school district's funding, can vary from suburb to suburb, some of which could be less than an hour away from each other. So if you live in a heavily minority-populated neighborhood that consists of relatively low property values, then chances are that you attend an overcrowded school with no arts or music education, little to no computer facilities, and dilapidated buildings. A recent *New York Times* article reported an example of this disparity by comparing two Connecticut school districts, Fairfield and Bridgeport, with dramatically different school resources—a result of funding inequities (Harris and Hussey 2016). Whereas in Fairfield, where students enter a "sandy-brick building buffered by an expansive, tree-lined lawn," students in Bridgeport have to use a school building with "crumbling walls, peeling paint, and classrooms that were sweltering." Such disparities, unfortunately, have become more common among schools across the country. Using longitudinal data from a representative sample of US individuals and families (Panel Study of Income Dynamics) along with census data, Lincoln Quillian (2014) determined that residential segregation "harms" the educational attainment of disadvantaged groups "without increasing the advantage of advantage groups" (421). Indeed, results indicate that as class and race segregation increases, poor and black students are less likely to graduate from high school whereas nonpoor and white students likelihood of high school graduation remains unchanged.

Moreover, and perhaps even more troubling, is the pervasiveness of the school-to-prison pipeline, where predominately black and Latino students in public schools are being suspended for disruptive behavior or minor infractions and funneled into the juvenile justice system, where many begin their encounter with mass incarceration. Reports indicate that compared to white students with the same offenses, black students are more likely to be suspended and to have encounters with police officers in schools (Losen and Gillespie 2012). Still, others prefer the metaphor of a web rather than pipeline to more appropriately represent the interconnected relationships between school policies, educators, immigration policies, and families (Pantoja 2013). Clearly, regardless of metaphoric framework, the early criminalization of young black and Latino students has a significant impact on their adult development and life chances. As a result of the cumulative effects of residential segregation, many black and Latino Americans have not been able to capitalize on the same advantages and opportunities provided to their white counterparts, and this demonstrates the pervasiveness of contemporary institutionalized racism.

Before we assume that residential segregation must be due to personal preference or individual choice—for example, that blacks are reluctant to live in largely white neighborhoods—we must consider the following research. In a Detroit Area Survey, when asked about various racial compositions in hypothetical neighborhoods, Massey and Denton (1993, 91-96) found that black respondents expressed preferences for integrated living, and "95% are willing to live in neighborhoods that are anywhere between 15% and 70% black" (91). This means that the common assumption that blacks just want to live with other blacks is simply incorrect. In addition, most white respondents indicated that a 50–50 threshold neighborhood would be unacceptable. In fact, the limits of racial tolerance for whites were reached when a neighborhood reached about one-third black. Clearly, there exists an inverse relationship between patterns of black and white demands for housing; when one or two black families enter a neighborhood, "white demand drops ever more steeply as black demand rises at an increasing rate." In other words, whites move out of a neighborhood at increasing rates when more blacks move in. So, perhaps, the reality for housing preferences between blacks and whites is such that it is whites who prefer to live with other whites. In a more recent study on the residential preferences of blacks, Krysan and Farley (2002) found that most African Americans are willing to move anywhere except into segregated neighborhoods and that "blacks are much more willing to live with white neighbors than whites are willing to live with African Americans" (960).

Given that waves of Hispanic and Asian immigration have transformed the demographic realities of many US cities, researchers Logan and Zhang (2010) have identified the presence of "global neighborhoods" that include all major racial/ethnic groups: whites, blacks, Hispanics, and Asians. However, results indicate that the more blacks, Hispanics, and Asians in a tract, the more likely whites will leave; in fact, racial heterogeneity is mainly found in black–Hispanic relationships. While most studies show that Hispanics are less segregated from whites than blacks, the complexity in multiethnic contexts makes interpretation difficult. Some researchers have argued that the growth of Asian and Hispanic populations is associated with lower levels of black–white segregation because the settlement of immigrant populations forms buffer zones. However, these studies are qualified by the fact that, taking into account English proficiency, generational status, and educational attainment reduce the spatial distance with whites, black Hispanics remain more segregated from whites than their lighter-skinned counterparts. So, while there is a presence of diversity in these global neighborhoods, it is still consistent with high levels of segregation, especially between blacks and whites.

Clear racial preferences in housing decisions are highlighted even more strongly in Camille Zubrinsky Charles's (2006) book *Won't You Be My Neighbor*, in which she examines how residential spaces shape people's racial attitudes in Los Angeles. Through a series of in-depth interviews with Los Angeles residents of different ethnic backgrounds, Charles finds that there is clear and consistent order of preference, with whites considered to be the most highly desired neighbors and blacks the least desirable. More interesting, this order of preference is also true for recent immigrants who technically have had little experience with America's race relations and history. That such racial preferences are taken on even by recent immigrants shows how dominant and pervasive the racial hierarchies are in this country and that the learning of racial attitudes exists far beyond the scope of parental socialization.

Of course, it would be a mistake to assume that either upwardly mobile blacks have moved out of all-black urban ghettos and integrated into white America or have remained locked in chronically impoverished gang-ridden neighborhoods. Not all minority neighborhoods are devastatingly poor, urban, and generally inhospitable to everyday suburban American life; simplification of the black experience misconstrues the ways in which race operates when it intersects with class. Conducting a three-year ethnographic study of a black middle-class neighborhood in Groveland, Illinois, Mary Pattillo-McCoy (1999) critiques existing research on urban poverty for neglecting to provide an account of the diversity within African-American communities and attempts to address this limitation by tracing the ecological contexts that affect a black middle-class experience. In her study, she finds that although by the typical income and occupational measures Groveland qualifies as a middle-class neighborhood, its spatial location as an "in-between" buffer zone between poor urban black and suburban white neighborhoods highlights the fact that black and white middle classes remain separate and unequal.

For many Groveland residents, their spatial proximity to nearby ghettos with dilapidated housing, substandard schools, and few businesses, presents an "extra challenge in managing the negative influences on black middle-class children" (Pattillo-McCoy 1999, 211-213). Pattillo-McCoy finds that local residents "utilize the existing relationships between the do-gooders and the law-breakers" to manage and arrive at a "quiet neighbor-hood." For example, local residents allow gang members to play dominoes at the community center if it means that members are not on the streets loitering.

Even among wealthier black middle-class communities, referred to as the "blue-chip black new middle class" by Karyn Lacy (2007), there is a complicated sense of identity—one that is distinct but fluid—where her subjects are "intent on nurturing and maintaining black identities, even as they ascend the class ladder" (220). Finding a distinction in the ways in which the elite black middle class and the core black middle class construct and maintain their racial and class identities, Lacy's ethnography of three Washington, DC suburbs, determines that residential location serves as an important mechanism by which class- or status-based boundaries are drawn. For example, residents of a more upper-middle-class black neighborhood distinguish themselves from the core black middle class by reproducing their status position like avoiding traditional schooling, preferring private schools or prestigious magnet programs within the public school system, and ensuring that their children have enriched cultural lives. In contrast, core middle-class residents focus on protecting what they have and do not necessarily believe in buying luxuries for their children, preferring to send their children to public schools. These differences suggest that middle-class blacks are not only concerned about dealing with racial discrimination in the public sphere, they are also invested to "nurturing a racial identity in their children," using "strategic assimilation" to balance being in the white world for work as well as black spaces for socialization (225).

This strategy of straddling two or multiple social worlds is one that is echoed in many studies of communities where analyses of race and class intersect (Anderson 2000; Small 2004; Lacy 2007; Venkatesh 2006). Whereas it is common to assume that impoverished communities lack order and social control, sociologists have long established this not to be the case. From the classic study of a Boston slum in William Whyte's (1943) *Street Corner Society* to a contemporary exploration of a Chicago ghetto in Sudhir Venkatesh's (2008) *Gang Leader for a Day*, sociologists have demonstrated that every community has its own organizational logic and structure. Residents of these marginalized communities find unique ways of establishing control and authority through informal means, and ideas of community are based on relationships of exchange prompted by situations of economic need and social instability. Unfortunately, scholars and policymakers alike often misinterpret these strategies as representations of the social ills and lack of morals that plague America's minority-populated neighborhoods.

For the black middle class in particular, having to reconcile the realities of a black urban underclass with the suburban expectations of a white middle class makes their experience of what it means to be mainstream American unique. It is clear that even while many blacks have experienced upward mobility, where they live continues to have a significant impact because of the repercussions that urban poverty have on middle-class blacks. Regardless of having made tremendous strides in upward social mobility, black Americans continue to be affected by urban poverty in ways that their white counterparts have not. This leads us to the eighth lesson on race: in some situations, especially for black Americans, class cannot overcome the intergenerational effects of race. So, just as it was for the characters Cameron and Christine Thayer (played by Terence Howard and Thandie Newton, respectively) in the movie *Crash* (2004), who are wealthy, educated, and accomplished professionals, being rich cannot erase the effects of being black.

"ARE THEY CRAZY? WHY ARE THEY KILLING EACH OTHER?": EXPLAINING INTERRACIAL AND ETHNIC CONFLICT

One of the most common questions about race relations is why conflict exists. Some of the related questions surround the issue of why prejudice, hostility and, in some cases, violence, occur. Answers to these questions range from a micro-level focus on attitudes to a more macro-level examination of migration patterns and citizenship policies. Recall that the sociological imagination prevents us from reducing individual behavior as a product of personality or mental state. Rather, the approach calls for a focus on the conditions, general mechanisms, and processes that generate or facilitate situations of conflict.

Again, a focus on the dynamics of a social structure does not mean that race or ethnicity is not real. Instead, it means that the meanings of race and ethnicity are so real that they can have life or death consequences (Ignatieff 1993). One only has to be reminded of incidents of ethnic violence in Nigeria, Chad, and Niger by the Boko Haram since 2009, between the Rakhine and the Rohingya in Myanmar in 2012, the ethnic Uzbeks in southern Kyrgzstan in 2010, and the recent 2016 resurgence of tensions in the Congo between the Nande and Hutu communities. Of course, media reports of such incidents tend to be chaotic, random, meaningless, and purely emotive with images depicting angry hordes of young men of color, armed, and menacing-looking. The ninth lesson in this chapter is that in contrast to popular interpretations, interracial and ethnic conflict is a product of rational and meaningful action rather than senselessness or irrationality.

A classic theory addressing the connection between racial attitude and prejudice with behavior is Gordon Allport's (1954) contact theory. Proponents of this theory suggest that if contact between blacks and whites were to increase, then racial attitudes would improve dramatically. In fact, much of the desegregation busing policies in the 1960s were premised on this idea that if whites were to have more contact with blacks, then there would be less interracial hostility. Unlike theories that are based on the premise that attitudes prompt behavior, Allport's theory suggests otherwise; it assumes that interracial contact affects racial attitudes rather than the reverse. According to Allport, prejudice is a function of competition and unequal statuses. If stronger bonds could be created through contact and cooperation between blacks and whites, then whites will exhibit lower levels of racial prejudice (Robinson 1980). Research suggests that while interracial friendship and neighborhood contacts did increase whites' desire for racial integration, those conditions do not necessarily guarantee that "whites will be more committed to engaging in social intercourse," and such contact may not always "affect racial attitudes, and even when it does, the effect is not always meaningful" (Sigelman and Welch 1993, 792). Therefore, even though there is some support for the hypothesis that interracial contact can foster certain attitudes more than the reverse, the issue of causal direction cannot be definitively determined without longitudinal data.

Whereas contact theory posits that interracial interaction affects attitudes, there is yet another theory that locates interracial and ethnic antagonism as a function of a split labor market. Proposed by Edna Bonacich in 1972, split labor market theory builds on the idea that competition and unequal statuses creates negative stereotypes between groups by focusing on the internal dynamics within the labor market where there is a large differential in the price of labor or wages for the same occupation. According to Bonacich, this wage differential is the result of the types of resources available to workers as well as the motives of the workers. Unlike many common explanations for differences in the price of labor, Bonacich does not attribute these differences to skill. Rather, the theory focuses on the structural location of the worker in affecting a difference in wage differentials; different sets of resources and motivations are allocated depending on where the worker is located in a society's social structure. For example, if a worker is seeking temporary work, she will have little incentive to join organizations of the settled population but will be more likely to accept lower wages. Of course, the willingness of a group to accept lower wages will pose a threat to permanent workers because temporary workers are perceived as undercutting their position.

Such was the situation in the United States during late 1880s when the Chinese were termed "Yellow Peril" and stereotyped to be opium addicts, gamblers, and sexual deviants. Posters depicted the "heathen Chinese" with their pigtails as cheap labor, threatening to steal jobs, money, and women of white men. The anti-Chinese movement reached its height as Chinese railroad workers posed a threat to white workers when the transcontinental railroad was completed and as a source of cheap low-skilled workers served to compete heavily with white laborers. As Bonacich's theory predicts, where there is a split labor market, a three-way conflict develops between business owners or employers, higher paid labor, and cheaper labor, and it is this competition between groups of workers that produces ethnic antagonism between the groups. The anti-Chinese movement eventually resulted in the Chinese Exclusion Act in 1882; it was the country's first significant law restricting immigration effectively stopping Chinese immigration for ten years and prohibiting Chinese from becoming US citizens. Accordingly, such antagonisms are a result of class conflict even if the conflict takes on the discourses and rhetoric of ethnicity and race.

Another more recent example of this is the vote by the United Kingdom to leave the European Union, an action known popularly as Brexit. Supporters of Brexit tended to be older working-class voters in skilled and unskilled labor, with little formal education; in contrast, voters for remaining in the European Union were of a younger age group, with formal education, and of middle-class professional and managerial occupations. Over the past two decades, British citizens, facing increasing competition in employment and increased migrant welfare payments as well as child benefits from neighboring European Union countries like Spain, Bulgaria, Poland, and Romania, have vocalized displeasure at "foreigners" or "non-Brits" settling in their communities and towns. It is, therefore, not surprising to see a surge in reported hate crimes and racist attacks in cities like London and Manchester and in small towns like Harlow in Essex. While some commentators argue that the Brexit vote has allowed xenophobic and prejudicial attitudes to be vocalized as Brexit supporters feel victorious in their campaign for a change in immigration policy, others argue that white supremacy groups are taking advantage of the Brexit vote to spread intolerance and hate-mongering. Regardless, it is clear that material competition is easily accompanied by ethnic antagonism and racial tension.

Studies of ethnic conflict can be different in terms of their methodology and use of data, ranging from large data sets through comparative studies with a small number of cases to single case studies; some studies utilize statistical analyses while others rely on qualitative interpretation. In fact, Brubaker (2004) suggests the phenomena of ethnic conflict is heterogeneous in that they usually span over a period of time and space and involve a composite number of different processes, mechanisms, and actions and that there is no reason to believe or expect that they can be explained through a single theoretical lens. Nonetheless, the point here is that regardless of the exact explanatory mechanism, accounts of ethnic conflict cannot be reduced to random acts of violence or attributed to "crazy people doing crazy things."

While common explanations of ethnic conflict tend to focus on two or more opposing groups, one of the more unexpected explanations for ethnic violence is found within groups rather than between them. Instead of locating the source of conflict as a function of intergroup dynamics, there are various intraethnic processes that can foster intergroup violence. One such mechanism involves the deliberate instigation or intensification of violent confrontations with outsiders by vulnerable incumbents who are seeking to deflect within-group challengers. Such strategies of provocation are likely to occur in newly democratizing but institutionally weak regimes (Synder 2000). Rather than having conflict as a result of opposing group interests, as a way of redefining the lines of conflict, it is actually intragroup competition that leads to violence against others. Such was one of the findings in a study of the role of intra-Serbian struggles during the collapse and breakup of Yugoslavia. In his study, Gagnon (2004, xvii) finds that ethnic violence was used by conservative elites in an effort to silence, marginalize, and demobilize the challengers to those elites; given that it was actually quite difficult for elites to play the ethnic card, elites had to resort to violent conflict to mobilize the population and "force a change in how people identified and what it meant to identify in particular ways." So, members of a group used violence to provoke other members of the same group, and it was that provocation that affected how people identified themselves and each other.

Rather than conceptualizing violence as a byproduct of larger conflicts as in the previous situation, another explanation for ethnic conflict is to view the violence as a result of a rational choice and reason. Fearon and Laitin (1996) identified that higher levels of violence occur in interethnic relations that are characterized by low levels of interaction and information whereas ethnic solidarity results from high levels of communication. Under conditions where the past behavior of members of an ethnic group are not known to members of another ethnic group, an ethnic incident can easily spiral into sustained violence if members of each group cannot identify the particular culprits and all or any members of the other group are punished. In situations where members of different ethnic groups are unfamiliar with each other, what is considered suspicious behavior can easily be ethnically or racially marked, and there is a heightened tendency for each group to want to maintain its position. Thus, due to the lack of information, violence becomes a rational means for group preservation and maintenance.

Still, other scholars have examined the culturally defined contexts that foster the role of ethnic elites in engendering ethnic insecurity through distorted narratives and representation (Atran 1990; Hansen 1996). The central issue here is that there are societal conditions that allow for the willful manipulation of information and propaganda to take hold and resonate with the general populace; messages about the "other group" are thus used by elites to engender fear and mobilize the population into violence. For example, messages about the Jews as cheats and subversive agents were used by Nazi Germany to create an atmosphere tolerant of violence against Jews. To be clear, no serious scholar of ethnic conflict would argue that violence stems directly from deep-seated cultural dispositions or propensities toward violence (Brubaker and Laitin 1998). Rather, their goal is to uncover the narratives, symbolic representations, rituals, myths, and commemorative practices that provide the basis by which intergroup fears and threats are made meaningful, real, and believed. One only needs to refer to the numerous protests, violent demonstrations and riots, and shootings regarding Denmark's newspaper *Jyllands-Posten*, Paris's magazine *Charlie Hebdo*, Sweden's cartoonist Lars Vilks, and a recent 2015 competition event in Texas featuring controversial cartoon images of Prophet Mohammad to see how religious and sacred iconography are often targeted through acts of desecration and disrespect to incite protests and provoke violence.

In addition to uncovering some of the mechanisms leading to ethnic conflict and violence, researchers have also focused on the importance of sociohistorical contexts in the formation of ethnic identities and formations of racial categories. This is especially salient in postcolonial societies in Africa and Asia, where many former Dutch, British, and French colonies were composed of socially and culturally discrete groups that practiced different customs and spoke different languages. These groups were integrated only through economic and political colonization. For example, when the British colonized India in the sixteenth century, it combined rule over 175 native princely and chiefly states into one under the central government of British India under the Viceroy. Similarly, in French West Africa, hundreds of tribal societies living in several different states were centralized under a federation of French colonial territories.

In an attempt to facilitate and maximize the extraction of resources in the form of raw materials such as timber, cotton, and labor as well as commodities like cloth and cigars, colonial governments would often create an ethnically segmented and sometimes segregated division of labor among these socially disparate groups. They would divide and separate the labor force across different ethnic groups even if these were socially disparate groups. Commonly known as "divide and conquer," this strategy successfully kept the colonized from banding together against the colonial masters by institutionalizing any perceived cultural and social differences into real material competition between groups. This form of indirect colonial rule was popular among the British in Asia from the late eighteenth through the nineteenth and early twentieth centuries. Local aristocracy were appointed to the colonial administrative structure and were allowed to keep some of their traditional cultural and religious authority while ceding political and economic rule to colonial advisors.

In Malaysia and Singapore, the majority of less educated and poor Malays were often relegated to small-scale farming occupations whereas migrant labor populations, such as the Chinese and Indians, were largely allocated to mining and rubber industries. This enabled the British to maintain a small, efficient, and effective administrative force. As leading scholar on ethnic conflict, Donald Horowitz (1985) argues, colonial policies strengthened group identities and comparisons between "advanced" groups on the one hand and "backward" groups on the other. In colonial Singapore, the racialization of the populations went as far as the creation of different racial and ethnic residential space and the establishment of ethnic neighborhoods like Little India and Chinatown. This strategy of keeping the different populations physically and socially segregated formed an internal colony where the colonial masters were able to remain in power as "neutral" keepers of authority and control (Hechter 1975).

What is most important here is that these colonial policies have had pervasive and long-lasting effects on the nation-building projects of many newly independent postcolonial states in Africa and Asia. Recall the second lesson in this chapter regarding the historical role of race politics in America's own nation-building project; this point is accentuated further when examining the processes of democratization and nationalism within a contemporary global context. The notion of "nation" is key here because it represents a collective and united reality for a country's "imagined community" of citizens (Anderson 1983). A national (as opposed to a citizen) is not only entitled to specific political rights and possesses social obligations but, more important, is imbued with ideas of cultural belonging. Inheriting the colonial policies and effects of an ethnically stratified society, recently independent states and new governments faced the arduous task of creating and establishing a cohesive collective national identity—one that would be more important than any other ethnic, religious, or social identities.

Of course, states have a vested interest in establishing a collective national identity because much of a state's legitimacy and the basis of its political authority derive from its ability to represent the people and the nation. Similarly, as much as the state needs to create a sense of loyalty among its nationals, the nation also relies on the state to form a coherent political representation in the interest of self-governance. Consider the role of a country's flag in its dual representation of both state and nation. Desecrating the American flag has become a popular way in which citizens express their political dissatisfaction with the federal government, as it was most recently in the 2011 Occupy Wall Street protest marches and sit-ins all across the country. It is also a popular method for people in other countries to express anti-American sentiments, particularly in the Middle East during the 2003 Iraq invasion as well as the continuous anti-American protests in Pakistan and Afghanistan in 2012. In the former situation, the flag represents the state whereas in the latter case, the flag represents the nation. As such, the nation and the state exists in a codependent relationship, but what remains key is the ongoing politicized negotiation of the racial and ethnic content of its national body.

While it may be tempting to think that globalization with all of its potential to facilitate economic and social exchange can decrease the relevance of race and ethnicity on a daily basis, the reality is that race and ethnicity have never been more salient in our lives as societies become increasing multicultural (Castles 2000). Any nation-building project invariably involves evoking the us-versus-them binary, but the task of creating a collective identity has been further complicated by migration patterns sped up through advances in technology and rapidly changing socio-economic structures in various parts of the world. As Stephen Castles and Mark Miller (2009) demonstrate in their authoritative text on the dynamics of international migration and its comparative effects on industrialized countries as well as the developing world, the increasing volume and changing nature of migration necessitates a reexamination of the relationships between ethnic and racial diversity and national identity and citizenship. With new forms of transnational labor urged on by rapid capital flow and new transient communities that are no longer fixed by rooted ideas of loyalty and belonging, racism and discrimination will take on new meanings as lines of exclusion and difference are redrawn.

The tenth and final, but not the least, important lesson in this chapter is that a study of race cannot really be determined by an investigation of its content; the question is not what is race but rather what does race mean for different groups at different times. The sociological imagination requires that we take seriously the fact that meanings of racial categories have changed over time and that any form of social difference will continue to be racialized whether it be in American society or elsewhere in the world. This chapter has attempted to demonstrate that the study of race is really a development of a critical perspective—one that intimately informs one's choices in life as well as influences how one interprets their own surroundings—and once you begin to develop this perspective, it is impossible to stop.

Lesson Take-Aways

- Race is a social fact, and manifests itself in different forms in all human societies.
- Although there is no biological basis for race, it has very real political and socio-economic consequences.
- While racism can be exhibited as an individual attitude, it is a function of privilege and unequal power structures.
- The meaning of race—what it means to be black or white—intersects with other social identifiers like gender; for instance, the racial experiences of black men are different from that of black women.
- Race relations are part of an ongoing national project on group membership, sociopolitical citizenship, and belonging.

Discussion Questions

1. Briefly describe and recount how and when you began noticing or realizing your race or ethnicity. In other words, what were the messages you received about your "place" in society as compared to other racial/ethnic groups—for example, as an African American male, a white Jewish female, or a Native American male? What social institutions contributed to these messages, and how have they affected your behavior?

2. Think about when, if at any point, you have attempted to transcend or reject your racial socialization. What did you do? If you have never done it, then reflect on why you never have. Be sure to consider the rewards and costs entailed even if you have not attempted to openly oppose your socialization. Compare and contrast the costs and benefits of your racial/ethnic socialization from someone else's in another racial/ethnic category. Consider how socialization processes affect social arrangements in American society and how they might differ in other societies.

3. What does the chapter suggest about the burden of race in American society? Are we all held accountable and do we all suffer—albeit in drastically different ways—from this burden? Since the concept of race is group-based and its effects are social, how can we, as individuals, make positive change in society?

Sources

Acevedo-Garcia, Dolores, Kimberly A. Lochner, Theresa L. Osypuk, and S. V. Subramanian. 2003. "Future Directions in Residential Segregation and Health Research: A Multilevel Approach." *American Journal of Public Health* 93: 215–21.

Alba, Richard D., John R. Logan, and Brian J. Stults. 2000. "The Changing Neighborhood Contexts of the Immigrant Metropolis." *Social Forces* 79(2): 587–621.

Allport, Gordon. 1954. *The Nature of Prejudice*. Boston: Beacon Press.

Atran, Scott. 1990. "Stones against the Iron Fist, Terror within the Nation: Alternating Structures of Violence and Cultural Identity in the Israeli–Palestinian Conflict." *Political Sociology* 18(4): 481–526.

Anderson, Benedict. 1991. *Imagined Community: Reflections on the Origin and Spread of Nationalism*. London: Verso Books.

Anderson, Elijah. 2000. *Code of the Street: Decency, Violence, and the Moral Life of the Inner City*. New York: Norton.

Asi, Maryam and Daniel Beaulieu. 2013. "Arab Households in the United States: 2006–2010." US Census Bureau Report No. ACSBR/10-20. https://www.census.gov/prod/2013pubs/acsbr10-20.pdf

Avery, Robert, Kenneth Brevoort, and Glenn Canner. 2008. "The 2007 HDMA Data." *Federal Reserve Bulletin* 94: 107–46.

Bayer, Patrick, Fernando Ferreira, and Stephen Ross. 2013. "The Vulnerability of Minority Homeowners in the Housing Boom and Bust." National Bureau of Economic Research Working Paper No. 19020.

Bell, Joyce M. and Douglas Hartmann. 2007. "Diversity in Everyday Discourse: The Cultural Ambiguities and Consequences of 'Happy Talk.'" *American Sociological Review* 72(6): 895–914.

Blumer, Herbert. 1958. "Race Prejudice as a Sense of Group Position." *The Pacific Sociological Review* 1(1): 3–7.

Bobo, Lawrence. 1983. "Whites' Opposition to Busing: Symbolic Racism or Realistic Group Conflict?" *Journal of Personality and Social Psychology* 45: 1196–1210.

Bobo, Lawrence. 1989. "Keeping the Linchpin in Place: Testing the Multiple Sources of Opposition to Residential Integration." *Revue Internationale de Psychologie Sociale* 2(3): 307–25.

Bobo, Lawrence. 2000. "Race and Beliefs about Affirmative Action: Assessing the Effects of Interests, Group Threat, Ideology and Racism." In David Sears, J. Sidanius, and Lawrence Bobo (eds.), *Racialized Politics: The Debate about Racism in America*, 137–64. Chicago: University of Chicago Press.

Bobo, Lawrence, Camille Z. Charles, Maria Krysan, and Alicia Simmons. 2012. "The *Real* Record on Racial Attitudes." In Peter V. Marsden (ed.), *Social Trends in American Life: Findings from the General Social Survey since 1972*, 38–83. Princeton: Princeton University Press.

Bobo, Lawrence and James R. Kluegel. 1993. "Opposition to Race-Targeting: Self-Interest, Stratification Ideology, or Racial Attitudes." *American Sociological Review* 58: 443–64.

Bonacich, Edna. 1972. "A Theory of Ethnic Antagonism: The Spilt Labor Market." *American Sociological Review* 37(5): 547–59.

Bonilla-Silva, Eduardo. 2002. "The Linguistics of Color Blind Racism: How to Talk Nasty about Blacks without Sounding 'Racist.'" *Critical Sociology* 28(1–2): 41–64.

Bonilla-Silva, Eduardo. 2003. *Racism without Racists: Colorblind Racism and the Persistence of Racial Inequality in the United States*. Lanham, MD: Rowman & Littlefield.

Bonilla-Silva, Eduardo. 2015. "More than Prejudice: Restatement, Reflection, and New Directions in Critical Race Theory." *Sociology of Race and Ethnicity*. 1(1): 75–89.

Brodkin, Karen. 1998. *How Jews Became White Folks: And What That Says about Race in America*. Piscataway, NJ: Rutgers University Press.

Brown, Michael, Martin Carnoy, Elliott Currie, et al. 2005. *Whitewashing Race: The Myth of a Color-Blind Society*. Berkeley: University of California Press.

Brubaker, Rogers. 1996. *Nationalism Reframed: Nationhood and the National Question in the New Europe*. Cambridge, UK: Cambridge University Press.

Brubaker, Rogers. 2004. *Ethnicity without Groups*. Cambridge, MA: Harvard University Press.

Brubaker, Rogers and David Laitin. 1998. "Ethnic and Nationalist Violence." *Annual Review of Sociology* 24: 423–52.

Calhoun, Craig. 1995. *Nationalism*. Minneapolis: University of Minnesota Press.

Castles, Stephen. 2000. *Ethnicity and Globalization: From Migrant Worker to Transnational Citizen*. Thousand Oaks, CA: SAGE.

Castles, Stephen and Mark Miller. 2009. *The Age of Migration: International Population Movements in the Modern World*. 4th ed. New York: Guilford Press.

Charles, Camille Zubrinsky. 2003. "The Dynamics of Racial Residential Segregation." *Annual Review of Sociology* 29: 167–207.

Charles, Camille Zubrinsky. 2006. *Won't You Be My Neighbor? Race, Class and Residence in Los Angeles.* New York: Russell Sage Foundation.

Chesler, Mark, James Crowfoot, and Amanda Lewis. 2005. *Challenging Racism in Higher Education: Promoting Justice.* Lanham, MD: Rowman & Littlefield.

Colby, Sandra L. and Jennifer M. Ortman. 2015. Projections of the Size and Composition of the U.S. Population: 2014 to 2060. US Census Report No. P25-1143. www.census.gov/content/dam/Census/library/publications/2015/demo/p25-1143.pdf

Desmond, Matthew and Mustafa Emirbayer. 2009. *Racial Domination, Racial Progress: The Sociology of Race in America.* New York: McGraw-Hill.

DuBois, W. E. B. [1903] 1993. *The Souls of Black Folk.* New York: Knopf.

Edelman, Benjamin, Michael Luca, and Dan Svirsky. 2016. "Racial Discrimination in the Sharing Economy: Evidence from a Field Experiment." Harvard Business School NOM Unit Working Paper No.16-069.

Engel, Kathleen, Patricia McCoy. 2011. *The Subprime Virus: Reckless Credit, Regulatory Failure, and Next Steps.* Oxford: Oxford University Press.

Feagin, Joe. 1991. "The Continuing Significance of Race: Antiblack Discrimination in Public Places." *American Sociological Review* 56(1): 101–16.

Fearon, James and David Laitin. 1996. "Explaining Interethnic Cooperation." *American Political Science Review* 90(4): 715–35.

Forman, Tyrone and Amanda Lewis. 2006. "Racial Apathy and Hurricane Katrina: The Social Anatomy of Prejudice in the Post-Civil Rights Era." *Du Bois Review* 3(1): 175–202.

Frankenburg, Ruth. 1993. *White Women, Race Matters: The Social Construction of Whiteness.* Minneapolis: University of Minnesota Press.

Fussell, Elizabeth. 2014. "Warmth of the Welcome: Attitudes toward Immigrants and Immigration Policy." *Annual Review of Sociology* 40: 479–98.

Gagnon, Valère Philip. 2004. *The Myth of Ethnic War: Serbia and Croatia in the 1990s.* Ithaca, NY: Cornell University Press.

Hall, Matthew, Kyle Crowder, and Amy Spring. 2015. "Neighborhood Foreclosures, Racial/Ethnic Transitions, and Residential Segregation." *American Sociological Review* 80(3): 526–49.

Hansen, Thomas B. 1996. "Recuperating Masculinity: Hindu Nationalism, Violence and the Exorcism of the Muslim 'Other.'" *Critical Anthropology* 16(2): 137–72.

Harris, Elizabeth, and Kristin Hussey. 2016. "In Connecticut, a Wealth Gap Divides Neighboring Schools." *New York Times.* September 11. https://www.nytimes.com/2016/09/12/nyregion/in-connecticut-a-wealth-gap-divides-neighboring-schools.html?_r=0

Hechter, Michael. 1975. *Internal Colonialism: The Celtic Fringe in British National Development.* Berkeley: University of California Press.

Hoefer, Michael, Nancy Rytina, and Bryan C. Baker, 2008. *Estimates of the Unauthorized Immigrant Population Residing in the United States: January 2007.* Washington, DC: Office of Immigration Statistics, Policy Directorate, US Department of Homeland Security.

Horowitz, Donald. 1985. *Ethnic Groups in Conflict.* Berkeley: University of California Press.

Ignatieff, Michael. 1993. *Blood and Belonging: Journeys into the New Nationalism.* London: BBC Books.

Ignatiev, Noel. 1995. *How the Irish Became White.* New York: Routledge.

Jacobson, Matthew Frye. 1999. *Whiteness of a Different Color: European Immigrants and the Alchemy of Race.* Cambridge, MA: Harvard University Press.

Joyner, Kara and Grace Kao. 2000. "School Racial Composition and Adolescent Racial Homophily." *Social Science Quarterly.* 81(3): 810–25.

Krysan, Maria. 2000. "Prejudice, Politics, and Public Opinion: Understanding the Sources of Racial Policy Attitudes." *Annual Review of Sociology* 26: 135–68.

Krysan, Maria and Reynolds Farley. 2002. "The Residential Preferences of Blacks: Do They Explain Persistent Segregation?" *Social Forces* 80(3): 937–80.

Krysan, Maria and Sarah Patton Moberg. 2016, August 25. "Trends in Racial Attitudes." University of Illinois Institute of Government and Public Affairs. www.igpa.uillinois.edu/programs/racial-attitudes/

Kwate, Naa Oyo, Ji Meng Loh, Kellee White, and Nelson Saldana. 2013. "Retail Redlining in New York City: Racialized Access to Day-to-Day Retail Resources." *Journal of Urban Health* 90(4): 632–52.

Lacy, Karyn R. 2007. *Blue-Chip Black: Race, Class, and Status in the New Black Middle Class.* Berkeley: University of California Press.

Lee, Jennifer. 2002. "From Civil Relations to Racial Conflict: Merchant–Customer Interactions in Urban America." *American Sociological Review* 67(1): 77–98.

Lee, Jennifer and Frank D. Bean. 2004. "America's Changing Color Lines: Race/Ethnicity, Immigration, and Multiracial Identification." *Annual Review of Sociology* 30: 221–42.

Lewis, Amanda. 2001. "There Is No 'Race' in the Schoolyard: Color-Blind Ideology in an (Almost) All-White School." *American Educational Research Journal* 38(4): 781–811.

Lewis, Amanda. 2003. *Race in the Schoolyard: Negotiating the Color Line in Classrooms and Communities.* Piscataway, NJ: Rutgers University Press.

Lichter, Daniel T., Julie H. Carmalt, and Zhenchao Qian. 2011. "Immigration and intermarriage among Hispanics: Crossing racial and generational boundaries." *Sociological Forum.* 26(2): 241-264.

Lieberson, Stanley. 1980. *A Piece of the Pie: Black and White Immigrants since 1880.* Berkeley: University of California Press.

Logan, John R. and Brian J. Stults. 2011. *The Persistence of Segregation in the Metropolis: New Findings from the 2010 Census.* Washington, DC: Census Brief prepared for Project US2010.

Logan, John R., Brian J. Stults, and Reynolds Farley. 2004. "Segregation of Minorities in the Metropolis: Two Decades of Change." *Demography* 41(1): 1–24.

Logan, John R. and Charles Zhang. 2010. "Global Neighborhoods: New Pathways to Diversity and Separation." *American Journal of Sociology* 115(4): 1069–1109.

Losen, Daniel and Jonathan Gillespie. 2012. Opportunities Suspended: The Disparate Impact of Disciplinary Exclusion from School. Los Angeles: The Civil Rights Project/Proyecto Derechos Civiles.

Massey, Douglas S., Camille Z. Charles, Garvey F. Lundy, and Mary Fischer. 2003. *The Source of the River: The Social Origins of Freshmen at America's Selective Colleges and Universities.* Princeton, NJ: Princeton University Press.

Massey, Douglas and Nancy Denton. 1993. *American Apartheid: Segregation and the Making of the Underclass.* Cambridge, MA: Harvard University Press.

McIntosh, Peggy. 1988. "White Privilege: Unpacking the Invisible Knapsack." Wellesley College Center for Research on Women Working Paper No. 189.

Mills, C. Wright. 1959. *The Sociological Imagination.* Oxford: Oxford University Press.

Oliver, Melvin L. and Thomas M. Shapiro. 1995. *Black Wealth/White Wealth: A New Perspective on Racial Inequality.* New York: Routledge.

Pager, Devah and Hannah Shepherd. 2008. "The Sociology of Discrimination: Racial Discrimination in Employment, Housing, Credit, and Consumer Markets." *Annual Review of Sociology* 34: 181–209.

Pantoja, Alicia. 2013. "Reframing the School-to-Prison Pipeline: The Experiences of Latin@ Youth and Families." *Association of Mexican American Educators Journal* 7(3): 17–31.

Parisi, Domenico, Daniel Lichter, and Michael Taquino. 2011. "Multi-Scale Residential Segregation: Black Exceptionalism and America's Changing Color Line." *Social Forces* 89(3): 829–52.

Pattillo-McCoy, Mary. 1999. *Black Picket Fences: Privilege and Peril among the Black Middle Class.* Chicago: University of Chicago Press.

Pew Research Center. 2012. *The Rise of Intermarriage: Rates, Characteristics Vary by Race and Gender.* Washington, DC: Pew Research Center. http://pewresearch.org/pubs/2197/intermarriage-race-ethnicity-asians-whites-hispanics-blacks

Pew Research Center. 2013. *The Rise of Asian Americans.* Updated ed. Washington, DC: Pew Research Center. http://www.pewsocialtrends.org/files/2013/04/Asian-Americans-new-full-report-04-2013.pdf

Pew Research Center. 2015. *Multiracial in America: Proud, Diverse and Growing in Numbers.* Washington, DC: Pew Research Center. http://www.pewsocialtrends.org/files/2015/06/2015-06-11_multiracial-in-america_final-updated.pdf

Portes, Alejandro and Rubén G. Rumbaut. 2001. *Legacies: The Story of the Immigrant Second Generation.* Berkeley: University of California Press.

Qian, Zhenchao and Daniel Lichter. 2011. "Changing Patterns of Interracial Marriage in a Multiracial Society." *Journal of Marriage and Family* 73(5): 1065–84.

Quillian, Lincoln. 1995. "Prejudice as a Response to Perceived Group Threat: Population Composition and Anti-Immigrant and Racial Prejudice in Europe." *American Sociological Review* 60(4): 586–611.

Quillian, Lincoln. 2005. "New Approaches to Understanding Racial Prejudice and Discrimination." *Annual Review of Sociology* 32: 299–328.

Quillian, Lincoln. 2014. "Does Segregation Create Winners and Losers? Residential Segregation and Inequality in Educational Attainment." *Social Problems* 61(3): 402–26.

Robinson, James Lee, Jr. 1980. "Physical Distance and Racial Attitudes: A Further Examination of the Contact Hypothesis." *Phylon* 41(4): 325–32.

Rugh, Jacob S. and Douglas S. Massey. 2010. "Racial Segregation and the American Foreclosure Crisis." *American Sociological Review.* 75(5): 629–51.

Schiller, Bradley. 2004. *The Economics of Poverty and Discrimination.* 9th ed. Upper Saddle River, NJ: Prentice-Hall.

Schuman, Howard, Charlotte Steeh, Lawrence Bobo, and Maria Krysan. 1997. *Racial Attitudes in America: Trends and Interpretations.* Rev. ed. Cambridge, MA: Harvard University Press.

Sears, David. 1988. "Symbolic Racism." In Phyllis Katz and Dalmas Taylor (eds.), *Eliminating Racism: Profiles in Controversy*, 53–84. New York: Plenum.

Sears, David O., Collette Van Laar, Mary Carrilo, and Rick Kosterman. 1997. "Is It Really Racism: The Origins of White Americans' Racism to Race-Targeted Policies." *Public Opinion Quarterly* 61(1): 16–53.

Sigelman, Lee and Susan Welch. 1993. "The Contact Hypothesis Revisited: Black–White Interaction and Positive Racial Attitudes." *Social Forces* 71(3): 781–95.

Small, Mario Luis. 2004. *Villa Victoria: The Transformation of Social Capital in a Boston Barrio*. Chicago: University of Chicago Press.

Synder, Jack. 2000. *From Voting to Violence: Democratization and Nationalist Conflict*. New York: Norton.

Takaki, Ronald. 1994. *A Different Mirror: A History of Multicultural America*. New York: Back Bay Books.

Tienda, Marta and Normal Fuentes. 2014. "Hispanics in Metropolitan America: New Realities and Old Debates." *Annual Review of Sociology* 40: 499–520.

Winant, Howard. 2000. "Race and Race Theory." *Annual Review of Sociology* 26: 26–85.

Whyte, William F. 1943. *Street Corner Society: The Social Structure of an Italian Slum*. Chicago: University of Chicago Press.

Venkatesh, Sudir Alladi. 2006. *Gang Leader for A Day*. New York: Penguin.

Venkatesh, Sudir Alladi. 2008. *Off the Books: The Underground Economy of the Urban Poor*. Cambridge, MA: Harvard University Press.

Related Websites

NPR: Talk of the Nation. Racial Screening, Nov. 30, 1999: www.npr.org/templates/story/story.php?storyId=1067265

NPR: School Money: The Cost of Opportunity. http://www.npr.org/series/473636949/schoolmoney

Understanding Prejudice: www.understandingprejudice.org/links/racnow.htm

Slave narratives: http://memory.loc.gov/ammem/snhtml/snhome.html

RACE—Are We So Different? A Project of the American Anthropological Association: www.understandingrace.org/home.html

Wihbey, John. 2014. "White Racial Attitudes Over Time: Data from the General Social Survey." August 14. http://journalistsresource.org/studies/society/race-society/white-racial-attitudes-over-time-data-general-social-survey

LESSON 5, PHOTO REFLECTION:

Children at play in an urban public park.
Photo by Ken Gould.

Race is a social construct. The visual cues of racial variety in this photo might represent an ideal to some or a nightmare to others, depending on whether they value racial diversity or homogeneity. Such moments and spaces of racial diversity are far more common in public spaces than they are in residential communities, but even public spaces often tend to illustrate racial homogeneity. When you are out and about, note those places where you see the most and least sharing of space across races and ethnicities. We chose this photo in part because racial identity and attitudes are learned by children at an early age. What do you think the children in this image might already think or believe about race? What might they be learning in that park? If you were the photographer, what picture would you take to represent race and intersectionality?

What can you tell about the social class of this setting?

6

Class and Intersectionality

Brian Obach

WHY CLASS MATTERS

Would you rather be wealthy or poor? This may seem like an absurd question because the answer is obvious for many of us. Of course, the answer you likely gave is that you would prefer to be rich. An easy follow-up to that question is, why would you prefer to be rich rather than poor? You can probably identify many things that you would like to do or have that require money. You can probably also identify many circumstances associated with poverty that you would like to avoid.

Sociologists have long recognized that one's economic condition is fundamentally important to defining how people live. The economic position in which one is situated and the opportunities associated with that position are what sociologists refer to as **class**. Given the significance of these economic factors, sociologists have sought to rigorously analyze class: how it should be defined, how it is structured in different societies, how it affects individuals, how it interacts with other social categories such as race and gender, and what, if any, problems there are with class systems.

It is practically impossible to identify aspects of life that are not affected by one's class. It greatly influences such fundamental matters as your access to education, the work that you do, the recreational activities you enjoy, the neighborhood in which you live, and many other aspects of your life. Your class position is directly associated with conditions that affect your health and survival, such as access to medical care and proper nutrition, whether you will fight in a war, and your vulnerability to crime. Thus, class is, in many ways, literally a matter of life and death.

Class, as a social category, can be somewhat more difficult to grasp than some of the other social categories that sociologists use to understand people's positions in society, such as race or gender. When someone has been made to endure some hardship due to their race or gender, as when one is the victim of discrimination, many react strongly in opposition to such injustice. For example, when we learn that polluting industries are more likely to be located in African-American neighborhoods than those inhabited by white people or that women are poorly paid relative to men for the same work, many view this as unfair.

Yet, by definition, people of lower classes are also made to suffer relative to more economically privileged groups. If every neighborhood were racially integrated, there would *still* be people living near hazardous industries and suffering from the toxic exposure. These people may not be racially distinct, but they would undoubtedly be distinct based on their class. Consider whether you have ever seen a factory spewing smoke in a wealthy neighborhood. Polluting industries are almost invariably situated in areas where poor people are made to live. If women were fully integrated into the economy and gender-based pay inequities were eliminated, there would *still* be people working at dead end jobs for low wages. While it is conceivable that we could correct the racial and gender disparities within the current economic system, unless the economy itself is fundamentally changed, this type of suffering would still plague people based upon their class position.

Of course, this in no way diminishes the importance of race or gender as social categories nor does it negate the injustice associated with discrimination or the mistreatment of people based on these characteristics. But, this does suggest that class, although seemingly more abstract or invisible than race or gender, represents a system of inequality that is pervasive within contemporary western societies. We do not want to see certain racial or ethnic groups disproportionately suffering from the effects of toxic exposure. But upon reflection, most would agree that we don't want *anyone* suffering from the effects of toxic exposure. We don't want to see women trapped in demeaning jobs working for low wages, but should *anyone* have to be in that situation? It is easy for many to recognize the significance of race and gender as social categories and the importance of eliminating racism and sexism. Far fewer see the importance of class as a defining social category, and fewer still suggest that the system that relegates people to different classes should be eliminated.

In part, some people may be more accepting of class inequality based on the notion that your class position is a result of your own actions (or, at least those of your parents). Perhaps the suffering associated with being in a lower-class position could be justified if one's class status was deserved or solely the product of one's own choosing. There are even some sociological theories that suggest that class inequality is functional for society, because it allows certain beneficial processes and tasks to be performed. Some go so far as to say that such inequalities are good or necessary to motivate lower-class people to work harder to avoid the suffering associated with poverty.

To the untrained eye, one's class status may appear to be irrelevant, invisible or possibly even deserved. But if we use what C. Wright Mills refers to as our "sociological imagination," we see that class is a fundamentally important social category and that it defines the lives of individuals in profound ways. Not unlike race or gender, one's class position is a product of forces that are in many ways beyond an individual's control. And just as racial or gender inequality raises questions about how to address injustice, sociologists are concerned about the way class inequalities may inhibit the opportunities available to individuals disadvantaged by their social class.

Sociological examination is necessary to uncover how the class system works and what could be done to address problems associated with this form of social inequality.

WHAT IS CLASS?

Class as Economic Gradations

In general, class is used to refer to one's social position in the economy. We hear people use terms to refer to class all the time, such as "rich," "poor," or "middle class," and you have probably used such terms yourself. People believe they have a basic understanding of the social phenomena they commonly talk about, but often these meanings are vague and contradictory when scrutinized. What counts as middle class? When you say that someone is poor, upon what are you basing that definition? What do you have to own or who do you have to be to be considered rich? Sociologists seek to develop clear definitions and measures as is necessary for a rigorous scientific approach to understanding society. However, beyond agreement about the very basic character of class as a position within the economic system, sociologists have offered differing interpretations about how to measure class and how it should be defined.

In popular discourse and in the work of many sociologists, class is thought of in terms of income or wealth. **Income** refers to the amount of money one makes on an annual basis, be it from wages, stock dividends, or interest on savings. **Wealth** refers to the total value of the things one owns, including material possessions, not only a car or house but also stocks, bonds, real estate, and money in the bank. Income and wealth are obviously related to one another, since those with a high income are likely to own things of value and those who have little income generally don't have many valuable possessions. But these are distinct ways of measuring aspects of class, and, theoretically, someone could be very wealthy but have a relatively small income. They could have inherited all their wealth at once and have it invested poorly such that they are not getting any substantial return on an annual basis. People could also have a high income but readily spend all of their money as they make it on exotic travels, expensive meals, or other consumable luxuries, leaving them with no accumulated wealth. But the point is that these are two concrete measures that some sociologists use as a basis for defining class, and in most cases, they are closely related.

We often hear reference to categories such as "lower class," "working class," "middle class," and "upper class." Sociologists may use measures of income or wealth to specify these distinctions. Dividing the population into quintiles is one way of distinguishing class based upon income or wealth. Using this measure, the top one-fifth of the income earners in the population are grouped together and the average level of income among them is calculated. The same is done for the next highest group, right down to the lowest fifth of the population.

Table 6–1 Mean Household Income Received by Each One-Fifth and the Top 5 Percent of the Population (2015)

Quintile	Average Income (US$)
Lowest fifth	12,457
Second	32,631
Third	56,832
Fourth	92,031
Highest fifth	202,036
Top 5%	350,870

Source: US Census Bureau (2016).

As Table 6–1 shows, there are vast inequalities when it comes to the distribution of income in the United States. The poorest households (those in the lowest quintile) on average live on just $12,457 a year. Bear in mind that this is the *average* income for the poorest 20 percent of the population. That means that many in this group earn even less. This compares with the average among the top income group (the richest 20 percent of the population), where the average annual income is over $202,000.

Class disparities in income pale in comparison to inequality measured in terms of wealth, as shown in Table 6–2. As you might imagine, those with low incomes spend almost everything they earn providing for their daily needs. The opportunity to save or invest is not possible given the basic cost of living. Conversely, those with higher incomes are able to save and invest. These investments enable them to accumulate still greater wealth, creating a vast gulf between those who have resources and those who do not. In this sense, the adage "the rich get richer and the poor get poorer" holds true. Without state intervention in the market through policies that provide opportunities for lower-income families, like public education, health care, Social Security, and other social welfare and worker protection programs, there is a tendency for wealth to become concentrated. As it stands, the top 20 percent of wealth holders in the United States control 84 percent of all the wealth in the country, while the poorest groups own almost nothing.

Perceptions of one's class status, or *subjective class identity*, do not necessarily correspond to these measures. In one survey, just 1 percent of the population identified themselves as upper class, and only 7 percent considered themselves to be lower class ("How Class Works" 2012). With a rate of poverty of over twice that figure, there are many people who do not identify

Table 6–2 Wealth Held by Each One-Fifth of the Population

Quintile	Percentage of Wealth Owned (%)
Lowest fifth	0.1
Second	0.2
Third	4
Fourth	11
Highest fifth	84

Source: Norton and Ariely (2011).

with their actual class status. Similarly, many very wealthy people appear to deny their upper-class position. This may be because other factors are taken into consideration when people think about class status. It also reflects the way that people in the United States may want to characterize themselves as "ordinary middle-class people" even when their economic situation is not ordinary. Think about how you identify your own class status. Do you consider yourself to be middle class? Does your wealth or income as reflected in the tables correspond to your subjective class identity?

Income and wealth vary considerably not only between people within one society but also between societies. In some societies, the average standard of living may be quite high, while in others, people live on relatively little. If we took all of the wealth created in 2008 in the United States and divided it among all Americans, each person would have $45,230. If we did the same thing in Turkey each person would have $10,031, and in the Philippines, each would have just $1,866. Obviously, analyzing class using measures based upon income or wealth will require different standards for different societies. A family with an annual income of $20,000 in the United States would be considered poor, and they may have a hard time making ends meet, while the same income in Mexico or China would make the family relatively well-off. The cost of housing, labor, and many goods in less economically developed countries is considerably lower than in the United States, allowing a family with a $20,000 income to live relatively well. Certain imported luxury goods may still be out of reach for such a family, since those items are traded on a world market, but it is important to recognize that when we use monetary measures, class must be understood in the context of the given society.

The distribution of people into different class categories also varies considerably between societies. Some are characterized by vast inequalities between rich and poor, while in other countries, everyone is grouped around the middle with few very rich or very poor individuals. Class measures based upon income make it easy to compare societies in terms of the distribution of wealth among the classes. A common measure of economic inequality is the Gini Index, which utilizes the distribution of family incomes within a country to generate a number that represents the overall level of inequality: the higher the Gini score, the greater the level of economic inequality in that society.

Table 6–3 shows selected countries and their Gini scores. Rich countries and poor countries are included among those in the list. Usually countries that are poorer overall tend to have higher levels of inequality. When comparing countries to one another based on something like inequality, it is most useful to compare countries with similar overall levels of wealth. When we do this, it is clear that in relation to other developed countries, the United States is outstanding in terms of the level of economic inequality. Compared to other wealthy nations such as Ireland, Japan, or Italy, the United States has very high levels of inequality. Even though a number of less developed countries top the list in terms of economic inequality, the United States has higher levels of inequality than even many less developed

Table 6–3 Distribution of Family Income in Select Countries, Gini Index

Country	Gini Index Score
Sweden	24.9
Netherland	25.1
Finland	26.8
Germany	27.0
Ireland	31.3
Ethiopia	33.0
India	33.6
Italy	31.9
Canada	32.1
France	30.1
Bangladesh	32.1
United Kingdom	32.4
Egypt	30.8
Tanzania	37.6
Poland	32.4
New Zealand	36.2
Indonesia	36.8
Japan	37.9
Ghana	42.3
Turkey	40.2
Venezuela	39.0
Argentina	45.8
China	46.9
Russia	42.0
Kenya	42.5
Thailand	48.4
Nicaragua	40.5
Nigeria	43.7
Malaysia	46.2
Iran	44.5
United States	**45**
Jamaica	45.5
Philippines	46.0
Costa Rica	50.3
Mexico	48.3
Dominican Republic	47.1
Zimbabwe	50.1
Panama	51.9
Chile	52.1
Guatemala	53.0
Brazil	51.9
Colombia	53.5
Haiti	60.8
South Africa	62.5
Namibia	59.7

Low scores indicate lower levels of income inequality.

Source: CIA World Factbook, https://www.cia.gov/library/Publications/the-world-factbook/rankorder/2172rank.html.

countries such as Nigeria, Venezuela, and China. Out of 134 countries, the United States ranked as the forty-third most unequal country in the world, and it is by far the most unequal of the developed nations (https://www.cia. gov/library/publications/resources/the-world-factbook/geos/us.html). Although wealthy countries tend to have lower levels of inequality compared to less developed countries, policies adopted in rich countries in recent years have led to growing inequality. This is especially so in the United States, which has witnessed dramatic growth in inequality in the last few decades. Later we will consider how economic and social policies relate to the level of economic inequality in the United States.

CLASS AS SOCIAL RELATIONS: MARX AND CLASS CONFLICT

While we can learn a lot just by comparing groups based upon levels of wealth or income, the concept of class is far more complicated than a simple hierarchy of categories with monetary cut-off points. Class does not just refer to your income but also to the kind of work that you do, your relationship to others in the economy, the prestige you hold, the political influence you command, and many other aspects of your life. This leads some sociologists to favor a different class perspective, one that is not based on monetary *gradations* but one that is based on social *relations*.

Karl Marx is the most prominent theorist to focus on class as a relational concept. Marx certainly recognized that having material goods was an important dimension of class, but his analysis emphasized the way in which those of the higher social class exploited and oppressed those below. To him, the fundamental determinant of class position was whether one was in control of the *means of production*, that is, the material equipment and resources necessary to make things that people want and need to survive. Factories, machinery, office buildings, computers—these are all used in association with the production of goods and services that people want and need. In a capitalist economic system, the dominant economic system in the world today, the means of production are controlled by private individuals or groups of individuals organized in the form of corporations. The business owners and investors who own and control the means of production, a class that Marx referred to as the "bourgeoisie," or the capitalist class, are in a position to further accumulate wealth by taking advantage of those who do not. The proletariat, or the working class, those who don't own the means to produce things and thus cannot provide for themselves, are vulnerable and dependent on those who control the means of production. They are forced to sell the only thing they have, their own labor, to those who control the resources that all humans need to survive (Marx and Engels [1848] 1998). In Marx's view, that is how we should understand "having a job." Vulnerable individuals who don't have the resources needed to survive are in a sense selling themselves to those privileged people who own the means of production and who control the resources that we all need.

We typically think of economic exchange as a voluntary, mutually benefi-cial arrangement. If you are selling your bike and I want to buy a bike, we agree on a price, make the exchange, and both leave happy. But Marx points out that the exchange of labor for wages is a very different kind of exchange. When you sell your labor, as you do whenever you have a job, you do not simply make the exchange and walk away (or ride away if you just bought a bike). When you sell your labor, you are entering into a social relationship and (unfortunately!) you have to be present to give your labor. That means that for a given period of time, someone is going to be telling you what to do. Generally people don't like to be told what to do, so most people probably wouldn't enter into such relationships unless they needed to.

Have you ever had a job? If you have, you probably entered this relation-ship with your employer because you needed money to survive or at least to get some things that you want or need. This places you at a great disadvan-tage relative to the employer who owns the business and controls wealth. Even though they may want to employ you so that they can run their busi-ness and make even more money, the fact that they have resources already suggests that they could probably survive just fine without you, especially if there are other available workers willing to take your place. So, according to Marx and other conflict theorists who have followed the Marxist tradition, class relations aren't simply a matter of who owns how much stuff, but they are relations of domination and subordination between people. It's not just that your employer owns more wealth than you do (a class system under-stood based just on economic *gradations*); their class position allows them to tell you and others in your class position what to do. It is a power relation-ship. If you seek to remain employed, you had better obey the commands of your employer. According to Marx, not being in control of your own labor is an affront to one's basic humanity. Some sociologists have studied the way that workers experience this subservience on the job. In her book, *Class Acts,* Rachel Sherman (2007) describes how workers at luxury hotels struggle to maintain their dignity while having to serve every whim of their elite cli-entele. To Marx, measures of wealth are important, but the most significant thing to understand about class is how it reflects *relations* between people of different classes, whether they own the means of production or if they are compelled to work for those who do.

Those social relations obviously have direct implications for how wealth will be distributed in society. The bourgeoisie uses their control over the means of production to get others to do work. In the process, workers create valuable usable goods or services that are eventually sold. The money from the sale is used to perpetuate the process—buying new raw materials, main-taining the means of production, and paying the workers. But the owners only give the workers a percentage of the value that the workers created. They keep the rest for themselves, in the form of something they call "profit." This is what Marx refers to as "exploitation," and it is a key characteristic of the class system from this theoretical perspective. It is also one that Marx found objectionable and unjust. The bourgeoisie, just by virtue of owning the means of production, are able to accumulate wealth. While it may appear to some that the owners are "giving jobs" to workers, Marx points out that this is an illusion created by the capitalist system. The workers are doing all of the work. They are the ones creating all the wealth, and the owners, in many instances, aren't doing anything productive at all. Their class position enables them to take advantage of those who do not own wealth and, in a sense, rob workers of the wealth they are creating through their labor. Because of this and the general tensions that arise when one group dominates another, Marx saw the bourgeoisie and the proletariat as locked in *class conflict.*

Marx believed that this class conflict would eventually come to a boiling point at which time the proletariat would overthrow the capitalist system and create a world in which the class system would be abolished once and for all. In the socialist society he envisioned, people would work together without the relations of exploitation and domination that characterize class systems. To some, that sounds idealistic, and it is certainly the case that the countries that claim to have adopted socialism failed in many respects. But those governments were flawed in many ways, and in other instances some elements of socialism have been effectively implemented. Many people throughout the world, borrowing from Marx's ideas, identify as socialists. We do not see perfect equality anywhere, but almost all governments have at least some programs and policies that seek to address class differences and that provide services to all citizens based on socialist principles. Can you think of any such policies in the United States?

FUNCTIONALIST THEORY: THE FUNCTIONS OF CLASS INEQUALITY

Most sociologists today, regardless of how they view capitalism or whether they consider themselves to be Marxists, tend to view class inequality as problematic. But this was not always the case, and for a while, the dominant theoretical perspective within the discipline was that class inequality was in some way necessary for social stability. Emile Durkheim is considered to be the father of functionalist theory. From this perspective, persistent and widespread characteristics of a society may be serving some purpose that allows the society to function. This is the case even if the social phenomena of interest appear to be harmful or problematic. Variations on Durkheim's perspective were common among sociologists through the early 1960s.

Durkheim was concerned about class inequality and social instability when he was alive during the nineteenth century. But others who modified his basic approach came to different conclusions. Structural functionalists who followed in the Durkheimian tradition offered an alternative view of class inequality. In 1945 Kingsley Davis and Wilbert Moore wrote an influential article examining class inequality from this perspective (Davis and Moore 1945). In their view, social inequality, or "stratification" as it is sometimes called, is necessary to ensure that essential roles in society are fulfilled. It was presumed that only some people had the talent to perform certain complicated and vital tasks. Performing these jobs well often requires long periods of education and the development of necessary skills. This time in preparation for these important tasks is generally not well compensated, thus these talented individuals are making a sacrifice as they prepare themselves for their future roles. Consider your position as a student. You are probably making less money (and accumulating more debt!) than some of your classmates who went on to get jobs right out of high school. But in the long term, you will likely end up making more money than them. According to some functionalists, that added income (and the inequality that inevitably results) is necessary to get qualified individuals to make this temporary sacrifice and then assume their important roles in society. Those who make the sacrifice will be rewarded not just with higher pay and the comforts that brings but also with less tangible benefits, such as ego satisfaction and more enjoyable diversions built into work life. After all, why go to school and study for many years without pay to become a lawyer or a corporate executive if, at the end of the day, you will get paid the same as a cashier or a ditch digger? This, Davis and Moore argued, serves as the source of social inequality. Thus, even if there may be some undesirable aspects of social inequality, some functionalists believe it is necessary for the overall functioning and well-being of society.

While the functionalist view of inequality is not widely held by sociologists today, many contemporary conservative media pundits and political leaders espouse views that reflect this perspective. They imply or state openly that the status held by rich and poor are in large part deserved. Those occupying the lower rungs of society could achieve higher status through hard work and ambition. From this perspective, if people remain poor, it must be because they are lazy or just content with their poverty. Likewise, those who occupy higher stations deserve their status for the significant contributions they make to society. It follows that measures to assist the poor are wasted efforts and utilizing public resources to aid them constitutes a punishment for wealthier people who pay taxes.

Many debates could be had about whether those in the upper class deserve the benefits they received from this system (i.e., whether they earned their initial wealth or inherited it, whether they work at actively running businesses or if they are just uninvolved investors, whether they possess unique talents or if they were simply born to the right parents, etc.). We even occasionally see claims reemerge about the innate capabilities or inabilities of certain groups based on race, ethnicity, or gender. If one's economic position is indeed a reflection of innate ability or character, it follows that those groups disproportionately represented among the poor are inferior in some way.

Most sociologists reject explanations of human behavior that rely upon biogenetic claims of innate superiority or inferiority. And as the following paragraphs discuss, the evidence suggests that one's class status and movement within the class hierarchy, as it stands, are not direct reflections of effort or ability, but rather they are in large part the product of the economic status of the family one is born into and structural forces that are beyond individual control. In light of this, at minimum, most sociologists would agree that policy reforms are needed to provide everyone with the opportunity to achieve their highest potential. But before turning to that, we'll consider other dimensions of the class system.

EDUCATION AND EMPLOYMENT

While wealth and income are the most commonly used quantitative measures of class status, sociologists have recognized that there are other aspects of economic life that are associated with class and that can be factored into class definitions. Education levels and types of employment are among the other factors that are often considered in association with class.

There is a clear relationship between education level, types of employment, and monetary measures like income and wealth, but the correlation is far from perfect. Some relatively less-educated workers may have high-paying unionized manufacturing jobs, yet they would probably still be considered working class based on their education level and the type of work that they do. Many such blue-collar positions may require very hard physical labor, but in terms of education, they could be done by people with no more than a high school degree. If the particular position requires skills, they may be acquired on the job or through an apprenticeship program. Besides requiring little formal education, such jobs can also be distinguished by the fact that those employed in such positions may have very little control over their work. These workers may take orders from supervisors all day or fill a position on an assembly line that requires repetitive procedures that must be done in accordance with the speed of the line.

Contrast this type of position with that of a college professor. Academic positions require years of education and, in most cases, entails earning a Ph.D. Yet some college professors earn less than some blue-collar manufacturing workers. In 2009, the average annual income for an assistant professor of sociology was under $56,000 (Spalter-Roth and Scelza 2009) while many unionized autoworkers earn over $60,000 ("UAW Losing Pay Edge" 2007). Of course, most manufacturing workers earn far less than that (especially if they are not unionized), and most college professors earn more, especially as they advance in their careers. But the point is that class cannot be considered strictly a matter of money, and we must examine these other dimensions of class status.

The work life of a college professor is obviously very different from that of an assembly line worker. While college professors may be required to teach certain classes, grade papers, attend meetings, and conduct research, how they teach their classes and what they do research on is largely up to them. Their work entails a great deal of autonomy and, at least in comparison to

FOOD FOR THOUGHT
THE RESTAURANT INDUSTRY: MAKING PROFIT OFF A SUBMINIMUM WAGE
Justin Sean Myers

In the United States we eat out a lot, not just at fast-food chains but also casual dining restaurants with table service. From the big chains to the smaller mom-and-pop-style restaurants, most of us eat at such establishments at least once a week, if not more. The perk? Not having to prepare our own meals at home with all the prep, cooking, and clean-up, not to mention the time spent grocery shopping. Eating out also allows us to try new dishes we don't know how to make and provides the privilege of having others wait on us while we spend time with family and friends. Beyond these reasons, who can say no to unlimited breadsticks, salad, and soup at Olive Garden for $6.99 or endless shrimp with salad and biscuits for $17.99 at Red Lobster? What about a salad, burger, and dessert for just $10 at Chili's? Don't forget at Applebee's an appetizer and two entrees is a mere $20! So much cheap food.

But as we interact with our wait staff and tabulate their tips so that we can pay our bill, do we ever think about the social costs of this cheap food? Who benefits from and who bears the burdens of cheap food? What are the working conditions of the wait staff serving us our food? Why do we even have to tip? If you start to investigate such questions, the answers you will find are not rosy. The base pay of many servers isn't even the regular minimum wage. Only seven states have the same minimum wage for tipped and non-tipped employees. In the other 43 states, tipped workers receive less than the minimum wage for non-tipped employees, with 17 states using the federal minimum tipped wage of only $2.13 per hour. How the tipped minimum wage works is simple. Your employer pays you the state legislated tipped minimum wage and if tips bring you up the state legislated non-tipped minimum wage, then everything is good. If your tips are below the state legislated non-tipped minimum wage, then your employer is legally obligated to make up the difference.

The tipped minimum wage first came into existence in 1966 and was pegged at 50 percent of the non-tipped minimum wage. While this may seem paltry, it was actually a gain for workers since prior to this the restaurant industry had fought to exclude servers from any minimum wage protections, which effectively left many servers to live solely off tips. Despite this win for servers, the real value of the tipped minimum wage has continued to decline under the pressure of the restaurant industry so that by 2010 the tipped minimum wage was worth only 29 percent of the non-tipped minimum wage. A key incident that facilitated this growing gap occurred in 1996 when President Bill Clinton was pushing congress to raise the minimum wage to reduce poverty and increase consumer-buying power. He was eventually successful in this effort, but he had to make a huge concession to the Republican-dominated Congress: exclude the tipped minimum wage from the increase and therefore keep it frozen at $2.13. Why did the Republican congress want this? Because the restaurant industry and its extremely powerful lobbying arm, the National Restaurant Association (NRA), wanted it to happen. This is understandable once you realize that the NRA's funding comes primarily from the big restaurant corporations, including McDonald's, YUM! Brands (Taco Bell, KFC, Pizza Hut, Long John Silver's), Darden (Olive Garden, Red Lobster, LongHorn

Food for Thought *continued*

Steakhouse, and Capital Grille), Applebee's, Chili's, Buffalo Wild Wings Grill & Bar, and IHOP, among others.

Through the decoupling of the tipped minimum wage from the non-tipped minimum wage, the restaurant industry has been able to essentially create a two-tiered wage structure where they are allowed to pay a subminimum wage and externalize the costs of their workforce onto customers and the general public, which has yielded increased and sometimes record profits for the major restaurant chains. The flipside is that servers, who are disproportionately women and minorities, have a poverty rate three times higher than the average worker and are twice as likely to need food stamps, principally because restaurant severs earn around $20,000 a year on average. Such a paltry hourly wage also underscores that in many states tips are not a luxury for servers but constitute the majority of their salary and are the difference between survival and destitution.

The ability of the restaurant industry to keep the federal tipped minimum wage at $2.13 and utilize tipping as a wage subsidy is a clear example of class power that benefits all restaurant owners but principally a few corporations, while keeping millions of workers in poverty. Through crafting employment regulations in a way where one section of the workforce is denied the same benefits as the rest, based purely on the power of lobbyists, we see that the poverty of workers and the wealth of corporations emerges from how corporations are able to shape labor market regulations in their favor and thereby deny many women and people of color an honest and hard-earned income.

Sources

Jamieson, Dave. 2012, June 2. "Minimum Wage for Restaurant Servers Remains Stagnant for 20 Years under Industry Lobbying." *The Huffington Post.* http://www.huffingtonpost.com/2012/06/02/minimum-wage-restaurant-workers_n_1515916.html

Restaurant Opportunities Centers United. 2015. *Ending Jim Crow in America's Restaurants: Racial and Gender Occupational Segregation in the Restaurant Industry.* New York: Restaurant Opportunities Centers United. http://laborcenter.berkeley.edu/pdf/2015/racial-gender-occupational-segregation.pdf

Restaurant Opportunities Centers United, et al. 2014. *The Other NRA: Unmasking the Agenda of the National Restaurant Association.* New York: Restaurant Opportunities Centers United. http://rocunited.org/wp-content/uploads/2014/04/TheOtherNRA_Report_FINAL2014.pdf

The Editorial Board. 2013. "Tips and Poverty." *New York Times,* September 14. http://www.nytimes.com/2013/09/15/opinion/sunday/tips-and-poverty.html

US Department of Labor. 2016. "Minimum Wages for Tipped Labor." *U.S. Department of Labor.* https://www.dol.gov/whd/state/tipped.htm

a manufacturing worker, relatively little in the way of taking orders from others. College professors also enjoy more prestige; rightly or wrongly, people often offer more respect and place greater value on the ideas and opinions of highly educated workers. Despite some income inconsistency, college professors would generally be viewed as having a higher class status than an assembly line worker. Some refer to the "professional class" to include the workers in these types of positions, along with others such as doctors, dentists, or lawyers. Education level and credentials are important defining features of this class position, but there are obvious correlations with income, autonomy, and prestige.

There is also the case of the small business owner. Being the owner of a large company or one who owns significant stock in corporations would clearly put one in the upper class, or in Marxist terms, it would make one a member of the bourgeoisie. But there are many smaller business owners who do not clearly fit in that class category. The owner of an independent book shop or a gas station may run the business all by themselves or employ only a small number of workers. They are owners, and they may have greater autonomy than some working-class people, but again, their incomes may not correspond to their higher class status.

Marx made some reference to the small business owner, or petit bourgeoisie, and the small professional class that existed during his time, although he centered much of his analysis on the bourgeoisie and the proletariat. But since his writings, these other groups have become much larger. Erik Olin Wright is a prominent sociologist who has sought to make sense of these various middle-class groups using Marxist concepts. Depending on their particular employment situation, Wright considers many middle-class workers to be in "contradictory locations" in the class system (Wright 1998). For example, a manager has some attributes of a capitalist in terms of their relations to the workers they oversee. Managers share an interest with capitalists in maximizing the work being carried out. At the same time, the manager is not an owner. Although they may receive reward for increasing productivity through the exploitation of workers, managers are themselves being exploited for the labor they contribute in managing production. The manager is doing actual work in supervising the other workers; only the capitalist owner is able to amass wealth without doing any work at all, and part of that wealth is derived from the efforts of the manager.

Highly paid entertainers and athletes, while very few in number, represent another complicated category. In a Marxist sense, they are workers, meaning that they expend effort within organizations owned by others. But their multimillion-dollar contracts would make it difficult to think of them as members of the working class. Bear in mind that there will always be odd cases that present challenges for sociologists seeking to create broad models that explain the general workings of society. While a few high-profile celebrities may be difficult to categorize, the vast majority of athletes and entertainers work very hard for little pay. For every superstar baseball player with a multimillion-dollar contract, there are hundreds struggling in the minor leagues making modest salaries during their short careers. And behind them all are team owners making far more in profits while never even swinging a bat. In that sense, the traditional Marxist view still works pretty well. In the meantime, Wright does a good job elaborating on Marx's ideas to make sense of the middle classes that were of little significance in Marx's time, but which now characterize a large segment of the economy.

Regardless of whether one is emphasizing income, education, job status, social relations or some other characteristic, it is necessary for sociologists to define the class categories they are using for their particular analysis as clearly as possible. We must use our sociological imaginations to make sense of a very complex social system and then use scientific methods to analyze what we observe.

CLASS CULTURE

Education level and employment type are important additional criteria to consider in any examination of class. Yet some have looked beyond the variables directly associated with the economy and work to consider the lifestyles, tastes, and habits of those of different classes. Have you ever been to a monster truck rally? How about the opera? Have you ever eaten caviar? How about Spam? Do you prefer abstract art, or do you find humor in pictures of dogs playing poker? These are among the distinctions that we commonly find among the tastes and habits of those of different classes.

You may have heard people say, in a complimentary way, that a person "has class" or that they are "cultured." What they are really saying is that the person to whom they are referring is demonstrating behavior that is associated with the upper class, that they are formal and polite, or that they are well-educated and knowledgeable. Of course, everyone is of one class or another, so really everyone "has class," and each class can be associated with certain practices and beliefs. But the common practices, values, and beliefs—that is, the culture associated with different classes—can be very distinct. What may be considered polite behavior within the culture of the upper class may be viewed as snobby or uptight from the perspective of those in a lower class. These cultural differences can be fascinating to consider in their own right, but some sociologists have identified how these cultural attributes help to perpetuate the class system.

French sociologist Pierre Bourdieu has examined the importance of **cultural capital**, those ways in which cultural practices reflect and reinforce class status (Bourdieu 1987). Being highly educated and having an advanced degree is one tangible way in which cultural capital is manifest. But there are more subtle forms of knowledge and behavior that also reflect class culture. Knowing about fine wine, being able to speak formal English or how to pronounce words in French, appreciating classical music, and being "well-traveled" are all elements of cultural capital possessed by many in the upper classes. Those who have been raised among people of a higher social class will likely learn all of these ways during their upbringing. This allows members of the upper class to maintain their class distinction even though others may accumulate similarly large amounts of wealth. Among the very wealthy, divisions are sometimes drawn between "new money"—people who do not have these cultural attributes—and more established families, dubbed "old money," who do.

The concept of cultural capital also suggests that education can serve as a means for class mobility even beyond obtaining a well-paying job. Having the right knowledge and cultural practices gives one entry into a social world that can prove to be advantageous in many ways. At the same time, individuals who lack these attributes may feel uncomfortable around those who behave in this way. "New money" individuals, despite being upper class based on their wealth, may find themselves marginalized or mocked by established wealthy families for their lack of knowledge or behavior deemed to be inappropriate.

The ways in which these cultural attributes relate to class are complex. Some of the cultural practices associated with the higher and lower classes are directly tied to wealth. Working-class people may not appreciate caviar and sipping fine wine at least in part because they simply can't afford it. Other cultural distinctions, such as a preference for NASCAR racing over horse racing, are more complex and require a careful historical analysis to fully reveal.

Some scholars have suggested that certain aspects of class culture can be directly associated with work life. For example, Fred Rose argues that working class people have different child-rearing approaches than parents of the professional class as a result of how they operate on their jobs (Rose 1999). As described before, part of what defines working-class employment is not having a great deal of control over your work. Working-class people, be they employed at a Walmart, an auto factory, or at a fast-food restaurant, are essentially told what to do all day. They must follow defined routines and obey instructions. According to Rose, this experience is transferred to how parents treat their children. Success for their children is defined by parents in the same way as success is defined for them at work. You succeed by following the rules and by doing what you are told, and children are disciplined accordingly with explicit rewards and punishments.

For professionals who have more autonomy on the job, success is found through creativity and innovation. The best lawyers and doctors are not the ones who approach every problem in the same way and simply address them by rote. They must be analytical and creative. Thus, parents who are of a professional-class position tend to give their children more autonomy and to encourage creativity. As these children are encouraged in this way, they acquire the cultural capital that will enable them to succeed in professional careers thus reproducing the class system.

Cultural distinctions between classes can be found in every society, but the particular cultural attributes of the upper and lower classes are in many ways specific to the society being analyzed. Styles of music, taste in food, and preferred visual aesthetics are all going to vary from one society to the next, and that which is considered polite and culturally refined by the upper class in one society may be considered crude in another.

There is one economic class that is increasingly homogenous internationally, and that is the very wealthy. Many very wealthy people from all countries have ties with one another through business dealings, expensive recreational activities, and exclusive social networks. Some charge that members of this international "superclass" have more in common with one another than with the people of their respective countries and that they use their privileged positions to perpetuate the global economic system that most benefits them (Rothkopf 2009). This leads us to consideration of the relationship between class, the state, and political power.

CLASS, THE STATE, AND POLITICAL POWER

According to Karl Marx, members of the same economic categories share the same fate and have common concerns that he refers to as "class interests." These interests can manifest themselves in the political behavior of groups and individuals in subtle (and sometimes not so subtle) ways. For example, the owners of businesses to some degree have a shared interest in opposing government regulation of the workplace. Strict rules about worker health and safety are likely to lead to greater costs of doing business, and this can in turn threaten profits. In one case during the 1990s labor unions and other workers' rights organizations were pressing for regulations that would protect workers from repetitive motion injuries. Hundreds of thousands of workers are injured annually carrying out repetitive tasks, whether they are typing at a keyboard or butchering animals in a meat packing plant. Businesses roundly opposed expanding regulation into this area of workplace injury, fearing that it would be very costly to reorganize work in ways that would protect workers from this kind of harm. This is an example of what Marx would consider class conflict: that which would benefit the working class would harm the interests of business owners leading to a political clash.

Class conflict often plays out in the electoral arena. Vermont Senator Bernie Sanders, a self-described socialist, made direct class appeals during his run for the Democratic Party nomination for president in 2016. He drew support from many who were struggling economically, including college students who are burdened by tremendous debt due to rising tuition and declining public funding for higher education. Sanders railed against growing class inequality and made raising taxes on the wealthy and on corporations a centerpiece of his campaign. This kind of explicit class appeal is relatively rare in American politics, but class interests underlie much political conflict.

One might expect that political ideology and behavior would correspond with these broad class interests. At the organizational level, this is true to a degree. In the United States, labor unions, representing working people, have long been champions of policies designed to protect the interests of the working class. They have lent support to social welfare programs, public education, worker health and safety legislation, and the regulation of big business. Organizations representing big business tend to oppose regulation, favor lower taxation, and generally support free markets (except when government programs channel public money to their businesses, such as the defense or prison industries). There are some exceptions to these patterns. Labor unions have at times supported policies that were of benefit to their particular members, but harmful to other members of the broader working class. Similarly, there are also those rare business leaders who throw their weight behind causes that would benefit workers, even though it seemingly violates their class interests. But for the most part, organizations created to represent businesses or working-class people will operate in ways that advance the material interests of their class.

Yet, on the micro level, the relationship between class and political ideology is more complex. Many working-class individuals hold political views that would seem to contradict their class interests. They may oppose "big government" and the regulations and social welfare programs that are designed to protect their interests as workers and consumers. Some analysts were surprised to find many working-class people, white males in particular, supporting the Republican presidential campaign of billionaire businessman Donald Trump. Trump offered few in the way of policies that would improve their economic lot and the historical record shows that worker interests are better served by policies typically offered by Democrats. Marxists would say that such workers lack "class consciousness." They are unaware of what is truly in their interest as members of the working class. In a sense, one could argue that these voters have been fooled by the capitalist class. They have been tricked into directing their legitimate economic grievances at immigrants or racial minorities instead of at the corporations that have profited immensely by increasingly exploiting the working class. By endorsing policies and voting for candidates who are not supportive of workers' interests, such workers are advancing the interests of the capitalists who exploit them.

Political theorists of the liberal tradition would not characterize this political behavior in this manner. From this perspective, if a worker opposes worker health and safety regulation or some other policy supposedly designed to protect them, they must have good reason to do so based upon their understanding of their own best interest. They may believe, rightly or wrongly, that such policies would increase costs to employers to such a point that it would result in businesses closing and laying off workers. This is the kind of argument that business leaders make, and some workers may find it convincing. In that sense, it may be in workers' interest to side with business owners in opposition to such policies to avoid job loss. Some Marxists would still consider this problematic in that such workers are pursuing their short-term individual self-interest, rather than uniting as a class to oppose the system that exploits them and makes them vulnerable to this sort of blackmail. To Marxists, workers who willingly vote against their own class interests demonstrate the overwhelming power of the capitalist class to maintain the class system and to secure support even from those who are harmed by it.

Others have found that political ideology is wrapped up in more than the material interests associated with social class. Regional differences, religious beliefs, racial identity, age, and other variables all shape the political views that individuals adopt. For example, many white working-class people oppose social welfare programs based on the stereotyped image of racial minorities taking advantage of the system (in fact, most welfare recipients are white, and very little fraud has ever been detected within the social welfare system). Many poor people with strong religious convictions support candidates who oppose aid to the poor because those candidates may also oppose abortion, which some voters prioritize over any economic interest. Again, some Marxists and other critics would argue that social issues such as abortion, gay rights, and gun control are simply being used by strategists in the capitalist class to divide working-class people and divert attention from their real class interests. Alternatively, class may simply not figure as prominently in the lives or in the minds of people as Marxists believe.

One thing is clear from any analysis of class and its relation to politics, and that is that the upper classes command disproportionate control over the political system. Lower-income people are less likely to vote or to otherwise be engaged in political efforts to advance their interests. In contrast, the wealthy tend to vote regularly, and they are more actively engaged in a wide range of political efforts, including the contribution of funds to political campaigns. Candidates running for office are heavily dependent on this financial support, and the vast majority of these funds are contributed by wealthy individuals and business interests. Research has demonstrated that these contributions have a clear, measurable impact on the actions of elected officials in terms of the policies they create (Task Force on Inequality and American Democracy 2004). While labor unions representing the interests of working people also pool funds and support candidates for office, the Center for Responsive Politics reports that business interests outspend labor by a ratio of almost 17 to 1 (Center for Responsive Politics 2017).

Elite-owned or funded media and research organizations also ensure that policy is always shaped and presented in ways that do not fundamentally challenge the status quo and the interests of the wealthy who are best served by the existing system. In fact, most major office holders are themselves among the economic elite. The majority of US senators have a net worth of over $1 million. C. Wright Mills refers to those who occupy these positions of economic and political leadership as the **power elite** (Mills 1956). He argues that they, together with leaders in the military, exercise a great deal of direct control over society and that fundamental policy decisions, be it a decision to make war on an oil rich nation or to cut social welfare spending, are always made with the goal of maintaining their status and control.

This direct control over the state does not necessarily mean that political leaders will not, at times, enact policies that benefit the working and middle classes. There is some degree of democratic accountability, and on occasion workers have united in ways that enabled them to score major political victories. In addition, some elected officials may simply be of a political ideology whereby they seek to aid those of other classes. But candidates who directly challenge the class system are unlikely to receive much needed support from economic elites and business interests. The Bernie Sanders campaign was notable in that almost all of the campaign money he raised came from small donors, working- and middle-class people who could not afford a $1,000 fund-raising dinner but who could kick in $25 to support their candidate. Yet, in the end, Sanders was defeated and lost the presidential nomination to Hillary Clinton, a candidate who was less confrontational with economic elites and who received considerable financial support from corporations and the wealthy. This reflects the way in which economic power can be translated into state power. Critics of the class structure argue that at the macro level the interests of the ruling class are always paramount within the capitalist system. Regardless of political party control or the actions of some elected officials, reforms will always be limited, and the state will always protect the long-term interests of the capitalist class (Domhoff 2001).

POVERTY

One group that has received a great deal of attention from sociologists is that composed of the most economically disadvantaged members of society. Some sociologists have referred to them as the "underclass." Given the class structure in the United States, there has always been a segment of the population that struggles just to get by. They often lack steady employment, and the most destitute among this group may find themselves without shelter or even the food necessary for proper nutrition and health. It may seem surprising that this can happen to anyone in the wealthiest nation in the history of the world, but the United States actually has more poor people than many countries that are less economically advanced. We will consider how this relates to public policy, but first, let's consider who the poor are.

As with other social categories, how we define poverty or the poor is open to interpretation. An important distinction to make right from the start is that between "absolute" and "relative" poverty. **Absolute poverty** is a measure that is based on access to some necessary set of material goods, especially adequate food and shelter, but some also include access to basic services such as health care, education, and other services widely considered to be fundamental human rights. People who do not have regular access to these necessities are considered to be living in absolute poverty. They would be considered to be poor no matter where they live.

Absolute poverty is common throughout the less-economically developed parts of the world. According to the World Bank, in 2012 almost 900 million people, or 12.7 percent of the global population, were living in extreme poverty. By the World Bank definition, people are living in extreme poverty when they are surviving on less than $1.90 per day (World Bank 2016). Globally, almost 800 million people suffer from hunger. That's roughly one out of every nine people on the planet (FAO, IFAD and WFP. 2015). Sadly, poverty is very widespread in the world today.

Relative poverty is a measure that considers economic well-being within the context of a given society. In countries where the standard of living and the cost of living are high, people are still considered to be poor even if they are well above the standards that define poverty in other parts of the world. It would be virtually impossible to survive in the United States on less than $2 per day. Thus, someone who is making over fifteen times that amount is still considered to be poor in the United States. Given the cost of living within the United States, someone with an income that small is still likely to lack access to adequate shelter and nutrition. Some conservative critics argue that relative poverty measures skew our perceptions about the plight of the poor, making their condition seem worse than it is. They point out that many of those considered to be poor in the United States today still possess things like refrigerators and televisions, goods that are out of reach of poor people in many other countries. Yet even though such consumer goods are fairly cheap and readily available to many in the United States, poor Americans may still be severely lacking in access to more costly and essential goods and services such as health care, education, quality housing, and adequate nutrition.

The "poverty line" is the term used to refer to the annual income level below which people are considered to be officially poor within a given country. In 2014 in the United States a family of four with two children was considered officially poor if they had an income of $24,230 or less. A single individual living on his or her own was considered to be poor if he or she had an income of less than $12,316. In 2014 14.8 percent or 46.7 million people in the United States were living in poverty (US Census Bureau 2015). In recent years, the number of people in poverty is higher than it has been since the US Census Bureau began tracking the figures in the 1950s.

Who are the poor? When you think of an impoverished person, what image comes to mind? The stereotype image of someone in poverty is the homeless panhandler on the street, typically a male, and oftentimes showing signs of mental illness or drug and alcohol dependence. For many people, this is their most recognizable encounter with poverty. This image perpetuates the belief that poverty is caused by individual personal or psychological inadequacies. Sociologists recognize that poverty is a *structural* issue rooted in the economic system and the policies designed to address its failings. While there are certainly homeless poor people who have mental health problems or who are addicted to drugs (often *resulting* from poverty and not its cause), the true face of poverty is far more diverse and complex.

Single mothers with children are those most likely to be living in poverty in the United States. About one-third of single females with children live in poverty. Overall, over one in five children live in poverty in the United

States. In what has been referred to as the **feminization of poverty**, women in general are more likely to be in the lower classes and to be poor. In 2014 15.3 percent of females ages 18 to 64 lived in poverty relative to 11.6 percent of men (US Census Bureau 2015). Employment discrimination, changes in social welfare policy, and the rise in the number of women raising children without the support of a partner are all factors that contribute to female poverty.

Another common misconception about the poor is that they are always unemployed. In fact, many people living in poverty have jobs; they just do not earn enough to rise out of poverty. Often those in poverty lack the skills and education that would qualify them for better-paying employment. There is also often a geographic mismatch between where jobs are available and where impoverished people reside. Whether they are living in an isolated rural area or in the middle of a blighted urban community, impoverished people often lack job opportunities in the area accessible to them. As a result, if poor people are able to secure employment at all, it is often low-wage work that provides little opportunity for advancement. These limitations are often overlooked by those who believe that anyone could have a job if they wanted one and if they were ambitious enough. One may see "help wanted" signs at the fast-food restaurant in a suburban community and believe that an unemployed or homeless person should just take that job. But given a lack of transportation, skills, and even the right "cultural capital," these opportunities are not truly available to the poor. If this is coupled with the need to care for children, as is the case for single parents living in poverty, securing stable, long-term employment is virtually impossible. The costs of childcare quickly exceed the earning power of parents who lack skills and social support.

Despite all these limitations, most poor people struggle desperately to pull themselves out of poverty. They may rely upon family members or friends to watch their children while they endure a long commute using public transportation to get to a job that pays minimum wage. Yet for people living under these conditions, what are minor inconveniences for most people readily become major crises that can dash hopes for upward mobility. A late bus or a relative who gets sick and can't watch the children means missed work and that can easily result in job loss. Thus, many poor people find themselves in and out of work and unable to gain an economic foothold for a better, more secure life.

Poverty does not afflict all groups equally. In 2014 the rate of poverty for non-Hispanic whites was 10.1 percent while the poverty rate for blacks and Hispanics was 26.2 and 23.6, respectively (US Census Bureau 2015). The reasons for these racial disparities are many, from official policies that systematically excluded racial and ethnic minorities from employment and educational opportunities in the past to persistent institutionalized discrimination today.

Sociologist William Julius Wilson has focused research on the black urban underclass (Wilson 1987). While overt racism has historically served to perpetuate poverty among African Americans, Wilson argues that race is no longer the most important explanatory factor. He examines the shifting nature and location of employment to explain why there are large pockets of poverty within many urban African-American communities. Essentially what he finds is that the "ghetto poor" have been abandoned in urban areas devoid of economic opportunity. While city-based manufacturing industries once provided opportunities for black workers, some of whom began to make economic headway during the 1960s and early 1970s, the decline of manufacturing employment generally and the relocation of these industries out of the urban core left no substantial economic base to support these communities. Relatively wealthier individuals, including not only many white workers, but also some from the growing black middle class, were able to leave these areas to follow employment opportunities elsewhere. Although Wilson sees class issues as paramount, other sociologists, such as Massey and Denton, emphasize the persistent effects of racial discrimination, especially when it comes to housing (1998). Segregation based on race has certainly played a large role in the economic plight of low-income black people. Today, as wealthy people return to some urban areas, those who had been abandon and left in poverty find themselves being pushed out of neighborhoods they had resided in for years as the newcomers drive up housing prices, a process known as "gentrification." These patterns of economic inequality and segregation demonstrate the complex interactions of race and class.

As with other class issues, sociological theorists have offered different interpretations of the structural causes of poverty. Marx saw the presence of desperately poor people as a means by which the bourgeoisie could strike fear in the working class and maintain low wages. The presence of impoverished people makes clear, even to low-wage workers, that there is something worse than being exploited by a capitalist, and that is *not* being exploited by a capitalist. Thus, from a Marxist perspective, the "reserve army of the unemployed" is a necessary component of maintaining the capitalist system and securing the interests of the ruling class.

Sociologist Herbert Gans offers a functionalist account of poverty in which he describes the many benefits that the impoverished class provides to other members of society and to the social order as a whole (Gans 1971). He notes that poor people create employment opportunities for several types of workers, from police officers to social service providers. The poor provide more privileged groups with the opportunity to busy themselves and feel a sense of personal satisfaction though charitable giving. The poor also serve as scapegoats for social ills and can be held up as deviants to reinforce norms of hard work and ambition that thereby strengthen the social order. You can probably imagine other ways in which poverty could be justified from a functionalist perspective. While clearly problematic in many ways, functionalist theory suggests that persistent social phenomena like poverty must directly or indirectly be serving some positive functions.

SOCIOLOGY AT WORK
WORK AND CLASS: WHY DO CEOS GET PAID SO MUCH MORE THAN WORKERS?
Arne L. Kalleberg

Apple Computer is one of the most successful companies in the world. It has changed how we listen to music, watch movies, make telephone calls and communicate with each other, and read magazine and books. After the 2011 death of its legendary founder, Steve Jobs, Tim Cook became Apple's chief executive officer (CEO). For his first year as CEO, Apple's Board of Directors gave Cook a compensation package worth $378 million (Lowenstein 2012). By contrast, the salespersons and technicians in the Apple stores earn salaries in the range of $36,000 to $40,000, according to a story in the *New York Times* (Segal 2012).

This gap between the earnings of CEOs and workers is exceptionally large, but the fact that CEOs in the United States earn much more money than ordinary workers in their companies is not. And the gap is growing: in 1965, the average direct compensation of CEOs was about 20 times that of the average production worker. In 2015, the ratio was about 276 (Mishel and Schieder 2016). So, if you were an average production worker earning $50,000 per year in 2015, the head of your company earned an average of $13.8 million!

What explains this great inequality in earnings between CEOs and ordinary workers? It is not due to differences between these two groups in their education or in how hard they work. CEOs and workers are often highly educated, and both groups work hard. These differences also don't result from the need to provide CEOs with adequate incentives to run companies, since these gaps in earnings are much greater in the United States than in other countries.

Rather, these gaps in earnings reflect class differences in the United States: CEOs and other top managers exert control over the company and its resources; they control the capital or economic assets belonging to the company and the means of production used by the company to create products and services. As a consequence of this control, CEOs have a great deal to say about how the company's profits are distributed among the various individuals and groups that make it up. CEOs also often have considerable influence over their boards of directors, which determine their economic compensation. Workers, on the other hand, do not control organizational resources. While some workers have more power than others due to their membership in unions or other occupational associations—or because they have more education, experience, and other assets—their ability to obtain a significant share of the company's profits is generally very limited. Workers' power has also shrunk in the past three decades due in large part to the decline in unions; this reduction in workers' power is reflected in the growing share of income going to CEOs and other top managers as opposed to workers.

Sources
Lowenstein, Roger. 2012. "Is Any CEO Worth $189,000 per Hour?" *Bloomberg Businessweek*, February 20–26.

Mishel, Lawrence and Jessica Schieder. 2016, August 3. "Economic Snapshot: CEOs Make 276 Times More Than Typical Workers." Economic Policy Institute. http://www.epi.org/publication/ceos-make-276-times-more-than-typical-workers/

Segal, David. 2012. "Apple's Retail Army, Long on Loyalty but Short on Pay." *New York Times*, June 24. http://www.nytimes.com/2012/06/24/business/apple-store-workers-loyal-but-short-on-pay.html

Regardless of one's theoretical perspective, most sociologists tend to view poverty as undesirable and seek ways to alleviate it. Even Gans, despite his functionalist account, was very sympathetic to the plight of the poor and envisioned ways in which poverty might be overcome. Yet poverty remains a vexing problem in capitalist economies, and the structure of the system provides little hope that it can be addressed without significant reform. However, real reforms stand little chance of being implemented given the relationship between economic and political power. Those who wield power in government have little incentive to address the needs of those who rarely vote and who lack the resources to contribute substantial sums to their campaign funds. While policies designed to address these issues are occasionally offered, the dominant message within the culture is that individuals should simply pull themselves out of poverty. Next we'll consider the prospects for movement within the class system.

SOCIAL MOBILITY

Do you believe that one's ability to advance in life is affected by whether that individual was born wealthy or impoverished? Although it is common in our culture to believe that everyone can advance if they work hard and "pull themselves up by their bootstraps," most of us recognize that the situation into which one is born will have an effect on how hard it will be for that person to become wealthy or the likelihood that he or she will live a life of poverty. Certain barriers inhibit the ability of some to improve their condition while others, due to the privileged economic circumstances under which they were born, have many opportunities readily available to them.

Sociologists have long been interested in the extent to which **social mobility**, the ability to move up (or down) in the class structure, is possible within a given economic system. After all, if social mobility is not difficult, then those who are economically deprived could simply rise out of poverty if they so choose, and there would be little need for policies designed to address the issue. Some functionalist analysis rests upon the idea that even innately talented people must be able to access training and develop the skills necessary to fulfill their function helping to maintain society. Before considering social mobility in contemporary American society, let's assess the prospects for such movement in other types of social and economic systems.

Slavery was a system in which humans were considered the property of other individuals. In some societies slaves had certain rights, but for the most part they were locked into a life of servitude to the slave owning elites. In feudal systems, such as those in much of Europe during the Middle Ages, most people fell into one of two basic social categories. There was a relatively small group of elite land-owning aristocrats, and there were the peasants who worked the land and paid tribute as part of their obligation to the feudal lords. In both slave-based and feudal systems there were others who occupied intermediate locations in the social hierarchy, such as small merchants or crafts people. These systems provided very little opportunity for social mobility. Under certain circumstances, slaves could win their freedom or members of a lower status could make their way into the aristocracy, but for the most part individuals were locked into their social position that greatly defined their life and limited their economic opportunities.

The caste system, historically found in parts of India, represents another form of rigid status hierarchy. In this system, one's caste status is hereditary; individuals are born into a caste from which they cannot move in their lifetime (although based on some Hindu beliefs, it is possible for one to be reincarnated into a different caste). Historically, members of each caste had designated roles to play in society. The "untouchables," the members of the lowest caste, were limited to certain occupations, usually involving the most onerous and dirty tasks. Higher caste positions included roles for farmers, artisans, scholars, and leaders. In recent decades, these rigid caste distinctions have weakened, but the traditional caste system is one in which social mobility was very limited.

Capitalist economies, the class system that we have been considering, allow for considerably more social mobility than some of these other systems. According to the classical sociological theorist, Max Weber, economic groups should *only* be considered "classes" in the context of a market system. While Marx uses the concept to understand the relationships between groups in different economic contexts, Weber thinks of it only in terms of market economies because of the emphasis that he places on the opportunities available to different groups within the market system. He defined groups of people who share similar opportunities within the system as being of the same class. Yet, like Marx, he recognized that the ownership of property and wealth was a key determinant of one's opportunities within the market system. There are certainly other factors, and Weber, like many sociologists after him, was interested in the particular opportunities and limitations faced by different groups within the economy. As we will see, opportunities for social mobility in the United States, while greater than that found in some other systems, are far below the ideals espoused within American culture.

We commonly hear stories about individuals who were born poor who, through hard work and the strength of their character, achieve economic success. It is a common theme for popular movies and books. When an individual of humble beginnings "works his way to the top," his life story is repeatedly emphasized. But how often do we hear the more common cases of privileged people retaining their privilege? Can you imagine hearing a prominent politician or business leader being introduced with the words "Mr. Drumpf was born rich and he's still rich today"? And we certainly hear very little about those who were born poor and remain so.

Rags-to-riches cases do exist, and we should not diminish the hard work associated with such accomplishments. But as sociologists we seek to avoid the misconception of the "self-made man" (or woman). Even in instances when disadvantaged individuals achieve great success, upon close examination we often find that they were also the beneficiaries of government programs or were given significant support by a more privileged friend or relative. As sociologists we know not to base our understanding of society on individual stories or experiences, whether they are real or mythological. We need to carefully examine the broader patterns that characterize the class system as a whole.

Those cases in which individuals born into poverty achieve wealth later in life would be examples of upward mobility. Perhaps you or some of your classmates come from a working-class or even a poor family. The type of job you are likely to get after obtaining a college degree will probably place you somewhere in the middle class. To the extent that social mobility occurs, these small steps are much more common than the rags-to-riches leaps. Of course, social mobility can also work the other way. When someone loses her job, she may slip down in the class system.

This provides an opportunity to consider how macro-level economic changes can impact organizations and even individuals on the micro level. Consider the case of Cynthia Norton, a 52-year-old administrative assistant in Jacksonville, Florida (Rampell 2010). Norton had worked for decades as a secretary for a number of different firms, and her skills and hard work placed her in jobs that enabled her to live a middle-class lifestyle. However, she lost her job working for an insurance company when the world economy went into recession, a downturn in the economy that occurs as a regular part of the business cycle in capitalist systems. Many workers lose their jobs during economic recessions. In 2009, the unemployment rate, the percentage of unemployed people actively seeking work, was over 10 percent. Many workers are rehired when the economy enters the recovery phase of the business cycle, but the longer-term shifts in the economy can have devastating consequences for some workers.

In Norton's case, the skills upon which she built her career are no longer in demand as much as they once were. Technology has already eliminated many of the tasks that secretaries used to perform. Few take dictation from their supervisors or know how to write shorthand. Computers allow executives to send their own e-mail and to maintain their own schedules. Records are stored as computer files, and there is little need to hire clerks to alphabetize documents in manila folders. Such improvements in efficiency help to build the economy overall, but workers are often the collateral damage of an ever-changing market system.

Cynthia Norton tried to adapt to those changes by borrowing money to enroll in a medical assistant program. Yet without any experience, Norton was not competitive in this field and could not land a paying job. Instead, she was forced to take a part-time job as a cashier at Walmart, making a fraction of what she once earned. Norton provides a look at downward social mobility, and it is unlikely that she will ever recover.

Norton's case is a classic example of what sociologist C. Wright Mills referred to as the relationship between "private troubles" and "public issues" (Mills 1959). To the untrained eye, Cynthia Norton is an individual experiencing personal problems with her employment situation. Many of us may experience our own problems in the same way. We might blame ourselves and imagine different choices we could have made at various junctures in our lives. But if we use our sociological imaginations, we can see that her case is not a matter of individual failing; it is tied to the broader institutions that characterize our society. She did not cause the recession nor did she elect to live in a capitalist system. She was born into a preexisting economic order and the class system itself allocates people into the positions they occupy. Character and hard work play a role as to who ends up where, but luck and the structure of the economy itself have a very large role in determining the fate of everyone in the system. The 2008 recession made this vividly clear to millions of workers. Many lost jobs and were unable to find employment, sometimes for years. When jobs did become available, many found that they had lost ground financially. No amount of ambition on the part of any worker can alter the fundamental structural changes that occur in the economy.

Just as there are different ways to measure class, there are several ways in which we can examine social mobility. In the examples previously described, where an individual moves up or down economically, we refer to that as **intragenerational mobility**. That is, someone can experience social mobility herself within her own lifetime. It is also possible to measure social mobility over generations. An immigrant who lacks skills who comes to the United States hoping to improve her economic standing may find her opportunities fairly limited. She may remain poor or not move above the working-class status that she held in her country of origin. But if her children can make use of educational opportunities in their new and more prosperous country, we may see **intergenerational mobility**—that is, a change in class status that occurs over generations.

There is a great deal of emphasis placed on inter-and intragenerational mobility due to the importance ascribed to the individual and the family in Western culture. However, a good deal of the social mobility that we have seen historically is best considered **structural mobility**. In many cases, movement in terms of economic class can best be understood by looking at the changing economic structure of the society, not at the strategies used by individuals to improve their economic condition. For example, in the years following World War II there was dramatic economic growth in the United States. Manufacturing employment was booming as American workers were called upon to supply a devastated Europe and to feed a growing consumer culture at home. Workers who lacked skills and who previously may have been living on the economic margins were able to get well-paid, unionized manufacturing jobs. A middle-class lifestyle became available to many people as a result of these economic changes. At the same time, there was significant growth in the demand for managers and professionals, thus creating lucrative career opportunities and improved class standing for those who were able to obtain higher education.

Thus, the vast changes in class status that occurred for so many people during those years can best be understood by looking at the broader changes that were occurring in the American economy. This period of economic growth and significant upward structural mobility reinforced the cultural belief that opportunity is always available to anyone who seeks it. It allowed many people to embrace the myth that the improvement in their living standards was solely the product of their own hard work. Individual choices and behaviors always play a role, but broader structural forces may determine whether the strategies that individuals adopt to improve their condition will pay off or leave them perpetually struggling. As a college student, you are following a path that will likely pay off financially. On the whole, those with college degrees tend to earn more than those without. But going to college today does not necessarily provide you with the same advantages it did in other periods under different economic conditions. Student loan debt, wage stagnation, union decline, and other changes in the economy will affect the extent to which your individual choices regarding education and career path will provide for social mobility. Individual choices do matter, but they must be examined within the context of the larger structural forces that shape our lives. The prosperous decades following World War II may prove to be an anomoly in economic history. The latter part of the twentieth century and the beginning of the twenty-first century have provided more difficult economic times for many, and we may be witnessing a structural shift that will leave more people facing economic stagnation despite their individual efforts.

One of the structural features of great importance today is the extent to which our economy is integrated with the rest of the world. Economic globalization has affected the status of many American workers. New technologies and the migration of factories to other countries have substantially reduced manufacturing employment in the United States. Opportunities for less-educated workers to achieve a middle-class standard of living have diminished. Manufacturing jobs have been replaced with service industry employment, which tends to be nonunion and low-paying. While some service jobs require skills and provide workers with a middle- or professional-class status, many more require few skills. Workers at retail stores like Walmart or at fast-food restaurants, while similar to autoworkers in terms of their skills and formal education, are not paid nearly as much.

Some service industry workers have sought to form unions to improve their economic standing. It was the unionization of blue-collar workers in the United States that built the middle class and reduced class inequality. Even given the economic growth that occurred following World War II, labor unions ensured that the great wealth being created during that period was shared with the workers who created it and not simply claimed by corporate executives and investors as is increasingly the case today. Wealth could be redistributed as it was in the postwar period if workers, especially those in the service sector, are able to form unions or otherwise organize to build power. Productivity has been on the rise and the economy is recovering. More wealth is being generated, but how that wealth gets distributed depends on the power of different groups to advance their interests. As Charles Derber writes in *Corporation Nation*, right now there is a great power imbalance:

corporations and the wealthy have used their position to shape economic policy and law in ways that advantage themselves at the expense of workers (Derber 1998). That includes policies and employment practices that have greatly weakened labor unions, the primary vehicles that workers have used to advance their interests. Union membership is just a fraction of what it was in the mid-twentieth century when workers were able to use their power to claim a share of the wealth being produced.

In the face of the disadvantages now encoded in law, some worker advocates have shifted strategies. Rather than focus on union formation alone, some service sector workers, in particular those in the fast-food industry, have advocated for a rise in the minimum wage up to $15 an hour (see http://www.fightfor15.org). They have achieved success in some cities, and they have used protest to bring pressure to bear on leading fast-food chains. Without strong unions or government policies that ensure opportunities for economic advancement, wealth tends to become concentrated in the hands of a relative few. Today we are witnessing a growth in economic inequality as the changing economy reallocates workers and wealth within the class structure. It is not clear if organized worker resistance will yield reforms that could reverse these trends or if inequality will grow to greater extremes.

Like the class structure itself, social mobility differs between different countries. It was long believed that the United States provided the highest levels of social mobility. The comparatively high rates of social inequality in the United States were not seen as overly troubling given the ease with which ambitious individuals could achieve the American dream and work their way up the economic ladder. But the data do not support the reality of this cultural ideal. Recent studies have shown that income mobility in the United States is less than that of similar economically advanced nations such as Canada, Great Britain, and Sweden. In part, the lack of social mobility in the United States can be attributed to the higher rates of social inequality found in this country. Social mobility around the middle classes is more common. The child of working-class parents may obtain a college degree and enter the professional class. Yet little mobility is seen among those who are very rich and very poor, and given the levels of inequality in the United States, the overall degree of mobility is lower (Beller and Hout 2006).

It is easy to see not just how the class system reproduces itself, but how many people are unlikely to move very far from their class position, even over the course of generations. People born into very wealthy families have all of the advantages that will make it easier for them to be wealthy themselves. Their parents can afford to send them to the best private schools and colleges. Given the system of education funding whereby schools receive funds through local property taxes, even the public schools in a wealthy community are likely to provide a very high-quality education. With a college degree from a prestigious institution, these individuals will be advantaged in the labor market. If they don't automatically assume a high-ranking position in the family business, they will still have all the network ties that their wealthy, well-connected parents and classmates can provide in terms of finding a good-paying job, not to mention the cultural capital that they can use to impress prospective employers. Graduating from college debt-free, thanks to help from their parents, these well-educated, well-connected, well-paid workers can immediately invest in a house and start accumulating wealth just like their parents before them.

In contrast, we can see how those born in poverty are likely to remain there and to even pass on this legacy of disadvantage to their children. The children of the poor attend schools that reflect the property values and economic conditions of their own communities. Too often the buildings are in disrepair, educational materials are outdated or nonexistent, and under-paid teachers are unable to provide a high-quality education to the children crowded into their classrooms (Kozol 1991). The problems that plague poor communities like health issues, violence, and despair will be present in the schools, further diminishing the experience of those who attend. If some children overcome the odds and manage to graduate, it is unlikely that their diploma from a poor-performing school will impress college admissions committees. And given the quality of education that one is able to get at such institutions, college exam scores may not stand up well against those of children from more advantaged backgrounds. Some may attend community college, transfer to a four-year school, graduate, and enter the workforce. If they are lucky, they'll find a decent-paying job, perhaps as a civil servant or in a low-level management position with a private firm, then start paying off student loans while struggling to make rent and car payments. With careful financial management, they may one day be able to purchase a home of their own and formally enter the middle class. But many others will remain trapped in the cycle of poverty. If little is being learned at school, many will not continue through graduation. Lacking education, skills, money, the right cultural capital, and job opportunities, these young people will essentially remain trapped in the impoverished communities in which they were born, perhaps passing on this inheritance to the next generation.

CLASS AND POLICY

The United States was founded on the ideal of equality, and many find persistent and rising levels of social inequality to be troubling. Class inequalities in the United States are vast and growing. The notion that individuals can simply pull themselves up by their own bootstraps is as far-fetched as, well, pulling yourself up by your own bootstraps. The class into which you are born has a significant impact on opportunities available to you. This will work well for you if you won the "birth lottery" and entered the world into economically comfortable circumstances. But many sincerely subscribe to the ideal of equal opportunity for all, and to overcome the random disadvantages of birth, policies are needed to address class inequality.

In the United States, educational opportunity has long been seen as the most important policy dimension of social mobility. Yet as previously described, the funding system for public education inhibits the ability of students from poor areas from obtaining a quality education. Given their disadvantaged family backgrounds, these children need more help than their wealthier counterparts, yet they receive less. Those who are able to graduate from high school are often finding that the costs to attend college has grown out of reach. Significant reform in public school funding is essential if lower-class children are to be given a fair opportunity to advance, public colleges must be well-funded and made affordable, and aid programs (not just student loans that saddle new graduates with massive debt) need to be expanded.

Improved schools alone will not solve the problem of unequal opportunity. Those living in poverty face a myriad of challenges at home and in their neighborhoods that inhibit economic success even when quality education is available. Social welfare programs can also help to rectify some of the unjustness of the class system. In the United States, welfare assistance is meager and punitive. Major reforms enacted in 1996 have failed to reduce poverty. The new system was designed to facilitate a transition to work, but the educational aid and child-care support offered through the Temporary Aid to Needy Families program is not adequate to provide real upward mobility. Part of the reason that other industrialized nations have less social inequality and higher rates of social mobility is because their welfare programs are truly designed to provide disadvantaged people with opportunity.

There are several successful social welfare programs that have helped to alleviate poverty and inequality in the United States including Social Security, Medicare, and unemployment insurance. Social Security alone helped to reduce poverty among the elderly from over 35 percent in 1959 to less than 10 percent in 1999 (Anzik and Weaver 2001). Almost every other economically advanced country has more expansive programs that serve to reduce inequality and provide economically disadvantaged people with greater opportunity. The United States is alone in not having a national health-care system, a public provision that alleviates many of the most challenging problems faced by the poor. The Affordable Care Act, commonly referred to as Obamacare, has addressed some of the shortcomings of the US health-care system, but millions of American remain uninsured or otherwise lacking access to quality health care. Health crises are responsible for more personal bankruptcies than any other factor. Those already facing poverty are handicapped by health-care issues, but even those with insurance and decent incomes can face financial ruin when they experience health problems. Subsidized child-care programs are another means by which other countries have reduced inequality and expanded economic opportunity for the parents of children. Without child-care support, very few single parents living in poverty are able to work their way out of this economic trap.

As Dan Clawson writes in *The Next Upsurge*, strengthening labor unions is another means by which class inequality can be reduced (Clawson 2003). An employer assault on unions, economic globalization, the decline of manufacturing employment, and weak labor laws that provide workers with few protections have all contributed to the drop in unionization. With that decline we have seen a corresponding stagnation of wages for working people and growing inequality as the wealthy claim a greater share of the wealth being produced. Clawson argues that new forms of worker resistance are emerging and that unions in alliance with community organizations, student groups, and others can challenge corporate domination and growing class inequality.

CONCLUSION

Class is among the most important social categories for understanding the conditions under which people live their lives and the opportunities available to them. As with all social phenomena, class must be recognized as a social system. While individuals occupy social class locations and have some degree of control over their own economic situation, the class structure itself determines the positions that are available and the opportunities for individuals to move from one position to another. It is simply erroneous to say that individuals are in full control of their own economic destiny.

Sociologists have analyzed the ways that the class system functions and how class status confers advantages and disadvantages on those who occupy different positions. The class system in the United States is characterized by high levels of social inequality and limited opportunity for social mobility. To the extent that these qualities conflict with ideals regarding equality and opportunity, policy changes are needed to address these shortcomings. Sociological analysis allows us to not only understand how social systems operate, but it also provides insight into how social problems, including injustices associated with the class system, can be addressed.

Lesson Take-Aways

- People's position in the economy, their class status, has a dramatic effect on how they live their lives and the opportunities available to them.

- Class status is commonly measured using quantitative indicators like income level or personal wealth, but it can also be examined in relational terms like worker and owner.

- Sociologists have analyzed class in different ways with some emphasizing the problems of class inequality and associated conflicts and others examining how class may play a positive role in society.

- The United States has particularly high levels of economic inequality compared to most developed countries.

- Class intersects with race and gender, with white people and males tending to enjoy higher average class status relative to other racial and ethnic groups and women being more likely to live in poverty.

- Social mobility, the ability to change one's class status, is relatively low in the United States with those in extreme poverty facing particularly difficult challenges when seeking to improve their class standing.

Discussion Questions

1. What are the most important factors in determining whether people will be wealthy or poor? Are opportunities for upward social mobility equally available to all? If not, what policies could provide for more equal opportunity?
2. In what ways do your tastes and habits reflect your class status? Do you think that your preferences in music and food, your hobbies, and other aspects of your lifestyle result from your economic position?
3. Should we be concerned about the rising levels of inequality in the United States? If so, why should we care, and what should be done about it?

Sources

Anzik, Michael and David Weaver. 2001. "Reducing Poverty among Elderly Women." Social Security Administration Office of Research Evaluation and Statistics Working Paper No. 87. www.ssa.gov/policy/docs/workingpapers/wp87.pdf

Beller, Emily and Michael Hout. 2006. "Intergenerational Social Mobility: The United States in a Comparative Perspective." *Opportunity in America* 16(2). https://www.princeton.edu/futureofchildren/publications/docs/16_02_02.pdf

Bourdieu, Pierre. 1987. *Distinction: A Social Critique of the Judgment of Taste.* Cambridge, MA: Harvard University Press.

Center for Responsible Politics. 2017. "Business-Labor-Ideology Split in PAC & Individual Donations to Candidates, Parties, Super PACs and Outside Spending Groups." www.opensecrets.org/overview/blio.php.

Clawson, Dan. 2003. *The Next Upsurge: Labor and the New Social Movements.* Ithaca, NY: ILR.

Davis, Kingsley and Wilbert E. Moore. 1945. "Some Principles of Stratification." *American Sociological Review* 10(2): 242–49.

Derber, Charles. 1998. *Corporation Nation: How Corporations Are Taking Over Our Lives and What We Can Do about It.* New York: St. Martin's.

Davis, Alyssa and Lawrence Mishel. 2014. "CEO Pay Continues to Rise as Typical Workers Are Paid Less." Economic Policy Institute Issue Brief 380. http://www.epi.org/publication/ceo-pay-continues-to-rise/

Domhoff, William. 2001. *Who Rules America? Power and Politics.* New York: McGraw Hill.

FAO, IFAD and WFP. 2015. *The State of Food Insecurity in the World 2015. Meeting the 2015 international hunger targets: taking stock of uneven progress.* Rome, FAO.

Gans, Herbert J. 1971. "The Uses of Poverty: The Poor Pay All." *Social Policy* 2(2): 20–24.

"How Class Works." 2012. *New York Times.* www.nytimes.com/packages/html/national/20050515_CLASS_GRAPHIC.

Kozol, Jonathan. 1991. *Savage Inequalities: Children in America's Schools*. New York: Crown.

Marx, Karl and Friedrich Engels. 1998 [1848]. *The Communist Manifesto*. London: Merlin.

Massey, Douglas and Nancy Denton. 1998. *American Apartheid*. Harvard University Press: Cambridge.

Mills, C. Wright. 1956. *The Power Elite*. Oxford: Oxford University Press.

Mills, C. Wright. 1959. *The Sociological Imagination*. New York: Oxford University Press.

Norton, Michael I. and Dan Ariely 2011. "Building a Better America— One Wealth Quintile at a Time." *Perspectives on Psychological Science* 6(1): 9–12.

Rampell, Catherine. 2010. "In Job Market Shift Some Workers Are Left Behind." *New York Times*, May 13. http://www.nytimes.com/2010/05/13/business/economy/13obsolete.html

Rose, Fred. 1999. *Coalitions across the Class Divide*. Ithaca, NY: Cornell University Press.

Rothkopf, David. 2009. *Superclass: The Global Power Elite and the World They Are Making*. New York: FSG.

Sherman, Rachel. 2007. *Class Acts: Service and Inequality in Luxury Hotels*. Berkeley: University of California Press.

Spalter-Roth, Roberta and Janene Scelza. 2009. *Sociology Faculty Salaries AY 2008–2009: Better Than Other Social Sciences, but Not Above Inflation*. Washington DC: American Sociological Association. http://www.asanet.org/research-and-publications/research-sociology/research-briefs/sociology-faculty-salaries-ay-200809-better-other-social-sciences-not-above-inflation

Task Force on Inequality and American Democracy. 2004. *American Democracy in an Age of Rising Inequality*. Washington DC: American Political Science Association.

"UAW Losing Pay Edge: Foreign Automakers' Bonuses Boost Wages in US Plants as Detroit Car Companies Struggle." 2007. *Detroit Free Press*, February 1.

US Census Bureau. 2016. *Historical Income Tables: Income Inequality*. Washington DC: US Census Bureau. www.census.gov/hhes/www/income/data/historical/inequality/index.html.

US Census Bureau. 2015. Income and Poverty in the United States: 2014. Washington DC: US Census Bureau. http://www.census.gov/library/publications/2015/demo/p60-252.html

US Department of Health and Human Services. 2012. *Frequently Asked Questions Related to Poverty Guidelines and Poverty*. Washington, DC: Office of the Assistant Secretary of Planning and Evaluation. http://aspe.hhs.gov/poverty/faq.shtml#developed

Wilson, William Julius. 1987. *The Truly Disadvantaged*. University of Chicago Press: Chicago.

The World Factbook 2017. Washington, DC: Central Intelligence Agency, 2017. https://www.cia.gov/library/publications/the-world-factbook/index.html

Wright, Erik Olin. 1998. *The Debate on Classes*. Verso: London.

Related Websites

US Census Bureau, Income: www.census.gov/hhes/www/income/income.html

Economic Policy Institute, Jobs, Wages and Living Standards: www.epi.org/issues/category/wages_and_living_standards

AFL-CIO, Executive Pay Watch: www.aflcio.org/corporatewatch/paywatch

Inequality.org: http://inequality.org

Stanford Center for the Study of Poverty and Inequality: www.stanford.edu/group/scspi/

University of Texas Inequality Project: http://utip.gov.utexas.edu

Institute on Race and Poverty: www.irpumn.org

University of Michigan Program on Poverty and Social Welfare Policy: www.fordschool.umich.edu/research/poverty

United Nations Development Program, Human Development Reports: http://hdr.undp.org/en

Who Rules America? http://sociology.ucsc.edu/whorulesamerica

LESSON 6, PHOTO REFLECTION:

Storefront of an upscale handbag store in an upscale mall in an upper middle-class suburb in the Midwest.
Photo by Tammy Lewis.

Consuming products is one way we signal our class status to others. Most Americans couldn't buy a bag at this store, but there are plenty of cheaper knock-off versions that people buy to display their taste and status. Where you shop—at a Walmart or H&M or Anthropologie—is related to your social class. You may have noticed this if you have ever been in a store where you didn't fit in because it didn't match the social class markers that you were displaying with your clothes and accessories. Taste is also a class marker. Consider the foods you like, your hobbies, and the sports you play (or don't play). Though we often consider these to be based on personal preferences, taste also has a class-based component. We chose this photo to provoke discussion about how social class markers pervade daily life. If you were the photographer, what picture would you take to represent class and intersectionality?

Little league baseball players dream of one day playing in the majors. What do little league softball players dream of?

7

Gender, Sexuality, and Intersectionality

Nancy A. Naples

D o you ever find yourself looking off into the distance and seeing someone who has not yet come into view and wonder if the person is a girl
or boy, woman or man? As they come into view and you still can't
decide their gender, does that make you uncomfortable or anxious? Have
you ever been in a bathroom and thought that perhaps the person who
walked in after you might not belong there? Or perhaps you have had an
experience where someone challenged you in this setting? If so, do you ever
wonder why it seems to matter so much? What happens to people who do
not fit the norm of what a girl or boy, woman or man should look like? Why
is gender considered a binary and not a more fluid social identity? And how
do we form our gender and sexual identities?

Gender and sexuality structure our lives from our earliest experiences.
When a woman shares that she is pregnant, the first question often asked
is "Is it a girl or a boy?" Gifts given at the baby shower are also coded by
gender. If the parents choose not to know the gender before the birth, friends
and relatives try to avoid the pink or blue choices for clothing and related
items. You need only walk into a toy or children's clothing store to see how
much ideas about femininity and masculinity organize what we think is
appropriate for girls and what is appropriate for boys. Boys or girls who
are drawn to modes of dress or activities that are defined as gender inappropriate in today's society are often teased and even bullied. In many instances, they are accused of being gay or lesbian as a way of shaming them
about their choices. Yet why is homosexuality still such a discredited form
of sexual expression even though there are many signs of wider societal acceptance as evident in the national legalization of same-sex marriage in the
United States in 2015? Sociologists of gender and sexuality are interested in
understanding these messages and how they contribute to everyday experiences of those who express different gender identities or diverse sexual
desires. They also are interested in how these experiences differ by race,
class, culture of origin, and physical and mental ability. This intersectional
approach avoids pitting one social category against the other as we engage
in social interactions.

Feminist sociologists are also interested in how gender and sexuality
structure cultural practices and social institutions—not only the family and
economy but also religious and political institutions. For example, do you

ever wonder why so few women are elected to the US Congress or why the majority of CEOs are men? In 2016, only 20 women (out of a total of 100 senators) served in the US Senate. Only 74 women out of 435 Representatives served in the House. Sadly, this low percentage of women was the highest percentage to date (Center for Women and Politics 2016). In 2015, women gained some ground in the office of governor: six of the US state's governors were women in 2015, and only two were women of color. Hillary Clinton's historic campaign for president of the United States marks almost one hundred years since women first gained the vote. Sociologist Raewyn Connell explains that if we examine the gender of those who inhabit different organizations, we can see that most are "masculine" institutions. The majority of those holding the top positions in government, business, medicine, science, and religious institutions are men, and the norms within these organizations privilege workers who have little to no responsibility for caretaking. Since women tend to have the greater responsibility for caring for children and sick family members, they are further disadvantaged in advancing in occupations that require long hours. Furthermore, those working in occupations that employ a majority of women tend to earn lower wages than those working in predominantly male occupations when controlling for or holding level of education steady. The presumption of heterosexuality, or **heteronormativity**, has also shaped employment opportunities. Title VII of the Civil Rights Act of 1964 prohibited discrimination on the basis of sex, race, color, religion, or national origin. Sex in this context referred to what we now understand as gender. Twenty-two states have statutes that prohibit employment discrimination based on sexual orientation, but no federal mandate exists that would cover all LGBT (lesbian, gay, bisexual, transsexual) workers. Until 2011 you could be dishonorably discharged for being gay or lesbian if you served in the military. Even today, gay and lesbian athletes and entertainers hesitate to reveal their sexual identities for fear of negative press coverage and backlash against them.

Clearly there have been changes over the last few decades, but not as much has changed over time as we would expect given that women got the vote in national elections in the United States in 1920. What contributes to the continuity as well as changes in the gender balance of men and women in positions of power? How do gender and sexuality continue to shape different jobs, preferences, and attitudes? What is the role of the family, education, and the media in influencing gender and sexual identities? And, more generally, what is the relationship between gender and sexuality? This chapter describes the different explanations identified by scholars who apply a sociological imagination to these questions and foregrounds two different approaches: social constructionism and social structural analysis. I conclude with a discussion of strategies for social change that would contribute to gender equity, **sexual citizenship** and social justice. In the next section, I consider the competing and changing definitions of sex and gender.

SHIFTING CONCEPTUALIZATIONS OF SEX AND GENDER

Until the mid-twentieth century, academic understandings of differences between men and women were primarily tied to explanations that essentialized both the biological and psychological differences between them. There was little recognition of multiple genders. Sociologists writing in the mid-1900s adopted an essentialized version of differences between men and women when they analyzed a division of labor between them. In an approach called "role theory," researchers assumed that women's social role was to perform the expressive functions in a society and men were assigned the instrumental roles. In this structural functional view, men and women needed to perform these different functions in the family and in other social institutions to maintain society equilibrium.

This normative division between instrumental functions and expressive functions persisted into the 1970s when feminist sociologists challenged this approach. They argued that the social construction of sex differences justified women's subordinate status and relegation to the private sphere and called for a distinction between sex and gender. **Sex** was defined as the biological differences between men and women including hormonal and reproductive differences. **Gender** was conceptualized as the consequences of social constructions of femininity and masculinity and processes of socialization, cultural practices, and societal expectations that were built into all institutions from the family to work, politics, and law. Feminist anthropologist Gayle Rubin (1975) introduced the term "the sex/gender system" to emphasize the relationship between the body we are born with and the gender process by which gender is socially constructed to impose a division between femaleness and maleness. Rubin stressed that these socially constructed differences are not natural or necessary but are social taboos that inhibit our ability to easily transcend them.

Before 1960 the term "gender" was rarely used in the psychological and social science literature. Psychologists Charlene Muehlenhard and Zoe Peterson (2011) reported on their search of pre-1960 literature and found 6,756 uses of the term "sex" and only 32 uses of the term "gender." When the term "gender" was first used, it was adopted as an alternative to the term "sex" or to refer to sexuality. Psychologist John Money who was one of the first researchers to study intersex infants born with ambiguous genitalia. He also distinguished between sex and gender. As Muehlenhard and Peterson (2011, 792) explain, Money "distinguished among individuals': (a) anatomical and physiological makeup . . . (b) childhood socialization . . . (c) psychological characteristics"—namely, gender role and orientation. Money, Hampson, and Hampson (1955) defined gender role as including "general mannerisms, deportment and demeanor; play preferences and recreational interests . . . and evidence of erotic practices" (302; cited in Muehlenhard and Peterson 2011, 792). They conclude that current usage of sex and gender includes a range of applications.

Sex and gender continue to be used interchangeably by some scholars, while others researchers reserve "sex" for reference to sexual behavior. Still others use the term "sex" only to refer to physical differences in hormones, chromosomes, and reproductive anatomy. **Gender** can be defined as maleness and femaleness or related to individuals' social traits and characteristics. Some scholars use gender to refer to societal expectations and stereotypes attributed to men and women. Most recently, feminist scholars who adopt a social constructionist approach define gender as "performance of a socially expected role or doing gender" (Muehlenhard and Peterson 2011, 799). As noted, in this chapter, I explore two different theoretical approaches to understanding gender and sexuality: social constructionism and social structural theory.

CULTURE, MEDIA, CONSUMPTION, AND GENDER SOCIALIZATION

We learn our social roles first in the family by watching how our mothers and fathers divide emotional and instrumental functions in the home. A child's understanding of gender and sexuality expands as he or she enters school and interacts with other institutions such as the media, sports, and religious institutions. Learning one's gender role and appropriate forms of sexual desire includes understanding dominant norms or beliefs. Beliefs about appropriate gender behavior are incorporated into law, medicine, religion, sports, media, and education as well as early childhood socialization.

You can walk into any toy store to see what society expects of girls and boys and what these gendered messages convey to them as they learn about their social roles. One side of the store is comprised of pink aisles filled with dolls, play kitchens, and sewing kits, while on the other side of the store shelves are filled with brown and green toys that include trucks, cars, soldiers, toy guns, and kits designed to teach boys how to build different kinds of machines. Sociologist Christine Williams (2006) spent six weeks working in a toy store to explore the gender, race, and class dynamics in one of the most gendered organizations in US society. Williams's study clearly demonstrates how children and their parents are targeted by corporations as gendered consumers whose range of choices are predetermined by culturally dominant notions of appropriate gender. Toy stores are not the only places where consumers come to reproduce gendered expectations in their children; it is also a workplace where the dynamics of race, class, and gender are further reproduced every day. Williams's study reveals that the gendering of toys is further contextualized by the gendered, racialized, and class interactions between the customers and employees. She describes the way in which the workers, especially the male workers, negotiated their roles in the store. For example, customers directed their attention to the Asian-American male worker to help them with electronics, while the white male worker distanced himself from the awkwardness of selling Barbie dolls to little girls and their mothers. This finding relates to constructions of Asian men as feminized and therefore constructed more closely to women than to the dominant image of white male (Park 2013). This construction is woven through immigration law as well as US cultural imaginary and media (Eng 2001).

Corporate America also reproduces gender and sexuality in the production of television shows and movies. One of the most successful media franchises that has expanded to include theme parks and ocean cruises is the Disney corporation. The stories that children are introduced to and the TV and movies they watch further reinforce their ideas of appropriate gender behavior and heteronormativity. The nine Disney princess films have given rise to over 25,000 products. But what are the messages girls and boys receive from these films and products? Family studies scholars Dawn England, Lara Descartes, and Melissa Collier-Meek (2011) examined these messages by coding the different characteristics and behaviors of the characters in the films released until 2009. Using a quantitative analysis of the coded data, they concluded that there have been changes over time in the move toward more egalitarian gender roles, although gender stereotypes persist in the representation of the princes and princesses.

Scholars have also analyzed Disney films to explore how messages about gender, race, and cultural background are shaping children's interpretation of girls and boys and men and women's roles in society. In a study of the film *Sleeping Beauty*, sociologist of education Lasisi Ajayi (2011) demonstrates how third-grade students from different racial and cultural backgrounds interpreted the film through their different social identities. For her study, Ajayi used the students' drawings, their written discussion of their drawings, and observations of the learning environment and teacher–student interactions. She concluded that teachers who are using a film like *Sleeping Beauty* in their classroom must consider, among other things, "(a) What does the black color 'mean' in classrooms with African Americans? [the witch in the video is dressed in black]; (b) Why does Sleeping Beauty represent women as witches while on the other hand portray a man [Phillips] as a prince and savior?" (408).

The activity of differentiating between girls and boys, women and men is especially evident in the playground. Sociologist Barrie Thorne (1997) was interested in why and how girls and boys begin to form separate playgroups in the playground. She examined the role of peers in the gender socialization process and the gendered organization of classrooms and playgrounds. Thorne observed children in a study of kindergarten and second, fourth, and fifth graders at an elementary school in the United States to examine the gendered organization of classrooms and playgrounds. She chronicles the gender play in games such as "chase-and-kiss" and "cooties" among other activities. Rather than understand gender socialization through a focus on individual children, she demonstrates that gender socialization is a social group process. Teachers contribute to this process by organizing children in gender-differentiated groups for different classroom activities.

One of the main topics in the sociology of gender and sexuality focuses on examining how cultural understandings shape the beliefs of what a heterosexual feminine body or masculine body should look and act like (Lorber and Moore 2006). Feminist sociologists have paid a great deal of attention to the dominant standards of femininity and masculinity as they apply to evaluations of appropriate body size and shape for women and men, stigma attached to those who do not adhere to these standards, and the ways in which early childhood socialization and media serve to enforce these norms. Cultural ideals related to body type are also very clearly racialized constructions that can be especially problematic for girls who are not phenotypically white (Collins 2003). In their famous study of African-American girls and their preference for white dolls, psychologists Kenneth Clark and Mamie Clark (1940) conducted research with African-American girls in Washington, DC, who were enrolled in segregated schools. They showed them several different dolls with different skin colors and asked them which dolls they preferred. Other than skin color, the dolls were identical. When compared to African-American girls in New York City, the girls in the segregated schools tended to choose the white doll over the black doll. The Clarks argued that this finding was a consequence of internalization of racism that resulted from the stigma of segregation and discrimination. The findings from their research was used to support the Supreme Court ruling *Brown v. Board of Education*, which argued against segregation of schools based on the premise that "separate is not equal." Seventy years later, sixteen-year old filmmaker Kiri Davis (2005) asked twenty-one boys and girls which doll they thought was prettier, and 70 percent said the white doll. The findings from this study with such a small sample cannot be generalized to all African-American girls, but it does show that segregation and dominant ideology about ideals of gender continue to shape their views of beauty, which is internalized to their detriment.

Sociological analyses emphasize how socialization processes draw on culturally dominant notions of gender and sexuality to reinforce masculinity, femininity, and heterosexuality. For example, drawing on data from a cross-cultural study of paths toward manhood, anthropologist David Gilmore (1990) demonstrates how culturally produced scripts or ideas about manhood contribute to constructing what is determined by a society to be appropriate expressions of manhood in different cultures. Sociologist Michael Kimmel (2000) analyzes the rules associated with appropriate masculinity in the United States that include accumulating multiple sexual partners, rejection of caretaking behaviors, and sexuality without emotional bonding or sensuality. Kimmel argues that these messages lead to an exaggeration of masculinity, or **hypermasculinity**, which has negative social consequences including aggressive behaviors and violence against women. A major component of these sexual scripts is hatred toward men who display any characteristics or behaviors associated with a culturally defined femininity.

Sociologists of gender and sexuality have identified messages given to boys in the United States that are designed to enforce a heterosexual masculinity. These messages, it should be noted, are based on rules that are white and Eurocentric (in other words, there are different types of masculinities promoted in different cultures and among different economic classes). Some of these messages are:

a. No sissy stuff; avoid all behaviors that even remotely suggest the feminine.
b. Be a big wheel: success and status confer masculinity.
c. Be a sturdy oak: reliability and dependability are defined as emotional and affective distance.
d. Give 'em hell: exude an aura of manly aggression—go for it; take risks. (David and Brannon 1976, cited in Levine 1998).

If a boy does not adhere to these rules, he may be attacked verbally and physically. The form of masculinity that is expressed through these rules is a heterosexual one. When boys violate these rules, they are often called "sissies" or other negative terms used to denigrate homosexuals. The rules for girls include maintaining so-called ladylike behavior and cautions against expressing their views forcefully or dominating cross-gender interactions. However, girls have greater leeway to perform male-identified activities. To be called a "tomboy" does not carry the connotations of "sissy." Sociologists of gender argue that since masculinity is privileged in a patriarchal society and femininity is devalued, there is greater stigma attached to rejecting male privilege.

In her fascinating study of masculinity, sociologist C. J. Pascoe (2007) examines how young men negotiate their gender identities and respond to institutional messages about appropriate gender behavior and sexuality. She conducted fieldwork at a high school in a working-class suburb in California. In addition to spending 18 months observing in the school and the broader community, Pascoe interviewed 50 students plus faculty and administrators. Her study revealed how masculinity and heterosexuality is organized and institutionalized and reinforced by adolescents who maintain the boundaries of acceptable heterosexual masculinity by homophobic slurs like "Dude, you're a fag."

Adolescent girls were also policed by their peers, especially those who challenged feminine gender norms. Teachers and school administrators participated in the process of **compulsory heterosexuality** that forms the centerpiece for a socially accepted masculinity. The teachers and administrators ignored the taunts and rewarded hypermasculine behavior, including aggressive actions by the boys. Racialization processes also shaped the treatment of minority students. Although African-American boys did not utilize the "fag discourse" as much as the white boys, they were punished more severely by teachers and school administrators when they did engage in it.

In his study of *Guyland: The Perilous World Where Boys Become Men*, sociologist Michael Kimmel (2008) interviewed four hundred predominantly white, middle-class men between the ages of 16 and 26. He concludes that many of the men had difficulty committing to their romantic partners and utilized a guy code that emphasizes the importance of sexual conquests, sports, and violence. What explains these findings? Are men biologically wired to need greater sexual encounters, to be more violent, and have trouble forming deep, long-lasting emotional attachments than women? Are women biologically wired to be more caring and emotionally expressive than men? Or, do the gendered messages and structure of society contribute to these differences?

THEORIES OF EARLY GENDER AND SEXUAL IDENTITY FORMATION

Until the 1970s, sociologists approached the study of gender and sexuality through the theoretical lens of **structural functionalism**. Structural-functional theory argued that to maintain social equilibrium in a society, institutions needed to provide a structure to ensure that both expressive functions (e.g., caring for children, the sick, the elderly) and instrumental functions (e.g., growing food, building shelters, and producing other necessary goods) will be performed by different social actors. Those who adhere to this approach argue that all societies must create institutions that organize family; economic, political, and religious practices; and social relations to ensure that the different functions are systematically performed from one generation to another.

Structural-functional theory is considered a social structural theory since it is attentive to macro-level analyses of social structures as they relate to the organization of gender and sexuality. There are four main theories that are posited as contributing to the development of gender differentiation at the micro level of everyday life. They are psychoanalytic theory, social learning theory, cognitive development theory, and **social construction**. Each of these approaches emphasize a different process of gender development and gender differentiation. Sigmund Freud, who is credited for the development of **psychoanalytic theory**, argued for the significance of internal psychological patterns that occurred during the first two or three years of life. His approach argues that individuals have an innate predisposition to identify with their same-sex parent. However, Freud's approach fails to account for external social demands that shape young children's identify formation.

The second theory, **social learning theory**, examines how individuals learn what behaviors are appropriate for their defined gender and sexual identity. This approach includes an emphasis on how rewards and punishments used by significant others in their lives reinforce children's understanding of socially accepted gendered behaviors. Unlike Freud, social learning theorists believe that children are born malleable, with no predetermined innate script or tendency regarding how to perform gender in a socially appropriate way. The limit of this approach is that it does not leave room for the ways that children might resist, differently interpret, and determine their own gender identity formation and performances.

The third approach, **cognitive development theory**, takes into account children's agency in the learning process. Those who adhere to this approach argue that children are born with certain psychological needs, and their need is for cognitive order more generally rather for a specific form of gendered behavior or identity. Referring back to the opening of the chapter, this approach would explain our need to know the gender of the stranger in the distance as a consequence of our desire for cognitive order. However, this approach does not address the social pressures that are placed on children as they come to understand and form their own gender identities and practices. What is the role of social context in shaping gender identity and gender difference?

In contrast to these three psychological and social psychological approaches, sociologists of gender and sexuality are especially interested in understanding how the local social context in which children grow up can explain gender differentiation or sexual differences. One influential contribution to this effort was a study by feminist sociologist Nancy Chodorow (1978) called *The Reproduction of Mothering*. Starting from Freud's argument of the importance of a process of identification in establishing gender identity, Chodorow developed a theory of gender identity formation to explain why women appear to be more relational in their social identities when contrasted with men. Chodorow argued that it is important to examine the division of labor between mothers and fathers. Mothers tend to do the majority of the caretaking in the home, while men tend to be assigned activities that take them outside the home. Even when mothers and fathers both work outside the home, studies show that women perform more household labor and child care than men. Of course, there are many exceptions to this pattern, but, on the whole, women continue to do more household labor and child care than men. According to Chodorow, since women are the primary nurturers of young children, girls form a close bond or connection with their mothers that, in turn, contributes to their social development as more relational than men. However, since fathers are often more removed from daily caretaking, boys form their identities by constructing them against women's identities.

This so-called **object relations theory** of gender identity formation posits that since fathers are less likely to be performing daily child care, the boy must learn about what it means to be a boy or a man by collecting abstract images or elements of masculinity that have less to do with a personal identification with his father as a known individual. In contrast, because their mothers are more likely to be caring for them on a daily basis, girls can develop their feminine identity in close connection and continuity with their mother as their primary caretaker. Chodorow concludes that boys' need to distance themselves from their close connection to their mother to form their masculine identity may contribute to their tendency toward aggression and problems with intimacy. Unfortunately, Chodorow explains, this gender identification process may contribute to boys' hostility to girls and women. In their effort to distance themselves from activities and behaviors associated with girls, boys may develop antagonism toward femininity more generally. This negativity could also be expressed in harassment toward boys who appear to be feminine in some ways, such as in their mannerisms, lack of interest or ability in sports, and even in their interest in playing with girls.

In response to Chodorow's analysis, poet and social critic Adrienne Rich (1994) raises the question of why women would choose to romantically attach to men given men's negative views and treatment of women. Rich posits that if the bond between mothers and daughters is so strong, the decision to leave her for a man must be a consequence of cultural pressure that insists on compulsory heterosexuality, which could explain women's rejection of these emotional ties to form intimate relationships with men. Compulsory heterosexuality is defined as societal pressure and cultural presumption that heterosexuality is the preferred, if not the only, acceptable sexuality. The culture is therefore set up to promote and reward heterosexuality through family arrangements, law, religion, and the media. A stark example of the presumption of heterosexuality is found in fairy tales where the prince and princess live happily ever after. No other alternative view is presented for a happy future.

Chodorow's work prompted other scholars to further investigate whether women grow up to be more oriented to care giving than men, and, if so, is that due to the division of caretaking in the home, rather than to an innate psychological process that is contoured by the identity of the caregiver. Feminist philosopher Sara Ruddick (1989) argues that women's development of an "ethic of care" derives from their social role, which contributes to research findings that women are more oriented to peace and caring for the planet than men.

But what happens in families that do not follow the traditional two-parent heterosexual model? It should be noted here that Chodorow's model suggests that if there are changes in the division of labor around nurturing and child care, perhaps there would be a change in gender identity formation. Chodorow's and Ruddick's arguments are based on a normative or traditional social division of labor between husband and wife. Critics argue that they neglect the diversity of family forms, household arrangements for care, and race, class, and cultural differences. Furthermore, their theories do not help explain the growing number of children who do not identify with one gender or the other or the gender that matches the one assigned at birth. Chodorow's approach emphasizes the importance of early gender identity formation in children younger than six years old. Other feminist sociologists focus on how children understand, experience, and perform gender and sexuality throughout their childhood and into adulthood.

This later approach takes two different forms. One focuses on the content of messages in a child's everyday life that includes examining the gender organization of play, dress, hairstyle and body displays, and depictions of gender in the media and other cultural texts. The second focuses on the interactions that contribute to and reinforce the performance of gender and sexuality. I offer a more detailed discussion of the theoretical approach, the social construction of gender, since it is currently one of the most dominant approaches in sociology and best illustrates the power of the sociological imagination to reveal hidden processes that are often taken for granted in our daily lives.

FOOD FOR THOUGHT
SELLING GENDER THROUGH HAMBURGERS: CARL'S JR., AND THE BEAUTY MYTH

Justin Sean Myers

If you watched Super Bowl XLIX between the New England Patriots and the Seattle Seahawks you probably still remember the interception of Seahawks quarterback Russell Wilson by Patriot's rookie Malcolm Butler in the end zone with twenty-six seconds left in the game, a feat that sealed the win for the Patriots. However, the Super Bowl isn't just about football; it is also about the commercials—with a 30-second spot going for $4.5 million, there is a lot of money to be made. And given the high ratings of the Super Bowl, many companies are willing to spend millions to create and market their latest products. In this vein, Super Bowl XLIX was the unveiling of the newest Carl's Jr. hamburger, this time featuring Charlotte McKinney, most well known for being a Guess Jeans model.

In the advertisement, Charlotte McKinney walks through a farmers' market while appearing to be naked as men fall all over themselves to gawk and ogle her naked body, particularly her "big boobs," to use her own words. As she walks through the market, her naked body is artfully covered through well-placed tomatoes, cantaloupes, ice blocks, and water sprays while her voiceover, in a sultry tone, proudly proclaims, "I love going all natural. It just makes me feel better. Nothing between me and my 100 percent all natural, juicy, grass fed beef." At the end of the commercial she steps into the open, reveals that she is in a bikini, and promptly bites into the new All Natural Burger as a male voiceover actors claims that the new Carl's Jr. burger is the first fast-food burger that is "all natural with no antibiotics, no added hormones, and no steroids."

The double entendres and the nudity in the advertisement play into the concept of the burger as all natural and reinforce the sexual objectification of women, but in claiming that Charlotte McKinney's body is all natural, the advertisement isn't just selling sex and sexuality but it is also reinforcing what Naomi Wolf (1990) calls "the beauty myth." The beauty myth tells society that "the quality called 'beauty' objectively and universally exists. Women must want to embody it and men must want to possess women who embody it" (Wolf 1990, 12). In short, a women's social worth is based on her attractiveness to and for men. In this case, the commercial presents Charlotte McKinney's body as "natural" when in fact it is a social construction based on a society that values the traits of whiteness (thin with light skin and blond hair) as well as voluptuous mammary glands (yes, they exist first and foremost to provide life to children). If you peruse all the Carl's Jr. commercials on YouTube, you will find that the models all contain the same attributes: they are tall and thin with blond hair and tanned skin, generally have large breasts and are wearing very little clothing. These are the women college males pin up in their dorm room and college women may aspire to look like through excessive exercise, disordered eating, and plastic surgery. When Carl's Jr. creates such commercials, they aren't just selling hamburgers or women as sex objects, they are attempting to naturalize one female body as the only body of social worth and esteem.

Food for Thought *continued*

Beyond perpetuating the beauty myth, the commercial also reinforces conventional gender roles through reproducing the process of compulsory heterosexuality, where women are socialized to be sexually accessible to males and men are socialized into sexual conquest, a running theme in hamburger commercials since at least the 1990s. But rather than blaming Charlotte McKinney for her performance in the commercial, we could reflect on how the commercial represents the Faustian bargain that many women are forced to make in a society that treats women as sex objects and holds out the lure that if you can achieve the ideal female body, you can exchange it for power, prestige, and wealth. Often when women do engage in this bargain, they are slut-shamed, called gold diggers, and stigmatized for using their sexuality to extract benefits in a society where the alternative might be working the counter at McDonald's, being paid minimum wage in child care, or going into tons of debt for a college degree that might not pay off in the long run.

For women, it is a catch-22. Choices that include working at McDonald's or making a lot of money being a sex object in a Carl's Jr. ad are limiting. What would a world look like if women didn't have to choose between low-wage work and being a sexual object? Moreover, what would a world look like if there was no beauty myth, women's social worth wasn't tied to their attractiveness, and all bodies were considered beautiful?

Sources

Buerkle, C. Wesley. 2011. "Meterosexuality Can Stuff It: Beef Consumption as (Heteromasculine) Fortification." In Psyche Williams-Forson and Carole Counihan (eds.), *Taking Food Public: Redefining Foodways in a Changing World*, 251–64. New York: Routledge.

Pascoe, C. J. 2012. *Dude, You're a Fag: Masculinity and Sexuality in High School.* Berkeley: University of California Press.

Wolf, Naomi. 1990. *The Beauty Myth.* New York: Chatto & Windus.

SOCIAL CONSTRUCTION: DOING GENDER AND SEXUALITY IN EVERYDAY LIFE

The social construction of gender and sexuality includes powerful processes that contribute to a belief among many that girls and boys, women and men are essentially different from one another. This process reinforces gender and sexual differences and includes strong messages that if you do not dress or act as expected for your assigned gender that includes the presumption of heterosexuality, there are negative consequences. It also constructs different expectations and stereotypes for women and men from different racial, class, and cultural backgrounds. Sociologists began to identify the content of stereotypes associated with female and male. They recognized how these beliefs were opposites. For example, femininity was associated with terms like "irrationality," "passivity," "subjectivity," and the "private sphere." Masculinity was linked to "rationality," "activity," "objectivity," and the "public sphere."

Learning about gender and sexuality through our everyday activities, social interactions, and engagement with various cultural representations is but one aspect of how gender and sexuality is produced in everyday life. Feminist sociologists argue that we perform gender and sexuality every day in every interaction and social activity (West and Fenstermaker 1993; Fenstermaker and West 2002; Kimmel 2007). This approach follows from two interrelated theoretical perspectives under the umbrella term of social construction. These approaches are known, respectively, as **dramaturgical theory** and **ethnomethodology**. These ideas were introduced in a general sense in Chapter 3. The scholars who took the lead in carving out these related approaches and applying them to gender are Irving Goffman (1976) and Harold Garfinkel (1967).

In his book *The Presentation of Self in Everyday Life*, Goffman (1959) sets out a framework that includes attention to how the body serves as a sign or a mode of communication. He uses the term "performance" to refer to the activities including how body language influences the way observers respond to us or interpret our presentation of self. He compares the performance of gender or any other social identity to a drama where there is the setting or background that includes scenery and props (clothing can be considered props in this framework). We put on a performance of what we believe to be most salient or most relevant in each setting. However, in addition to the front-stage performance, Goffman also notes that there is a backstage where, when someone unknowingly enters into that arena, they may find stark discrepancies between the front- and backstage personas. This analysis applies to gender in the sense that we must decide which aspects of our gendered identity are appropriate in different situations. We will dress and act according to the messages we want to convey in each context. The type of clothing we choose will reflect our understanding of what is expected of us as mothers, workers, students, or girlfriends and boyfriends.

Garfinkle was less interested in the presentation of self and more focused on how people learn about and reproduce the unspoken rules of everyday life. He wanted to understand how people make sense of their world, communicate their understanding to other people, and consequently co-construct the social world. In his famous study of Agnes, a trans woman who had to convince a panel of doctors of her legitimate right to a sex change operation, Garfinkle explains how Agnes (who was born male and raised as a boy) learned how to perform a female identity and to persuasively argue that her desire to become a woman was based on some inherent biological tendencies over which she had no control. In his analysis of transcripts from her meetings with the doctors and from interviews with her, Garfinkle discovered that, in fact, Agnes had been taking her mother's hormones for several years before making her appeal to the doctors. Agnes learned what the medical professionals needed to hear and see before they would grant her request. Her self-conscious performance succeeded in convincing the doctors to approve the sex change operation. She presented herself to the doctors as "naturally" female by the way she dressed, spoke, and interacted with them.

Garfinkel (1967) explained that Agnes "treated her femininity independent of" genitalia (135). She explained that although she did have male genitalia, Agnes believed that her "male genitals were a trick of fate, a personal misfortune, an accident" (131). This construction was part of her overall effort to pass as "a natural, normal woman" (122). Her success in passing as a natural woman, which was a performance aided by her use of her mother's prescribed hormones, resulted in the doctors' granting her request for a sex change operation. It is difficult to assess whether the doctors' decision would have been the same without Agnes's use of steroids; however, it is clear that Agnes did need to perform femininity to overcome the fact that she did have fully developed male genitalia.

Scholars who adopt an ethnomethodological approach do not view gender as a role or a set of specific characteristics. In contrast, they view gender as produced through interactions that include the social construction of gendered meanings that can vary across time, culture, and space. Gendered meanings are further shaped by language, which was one of the first arenas to become a target for social change by feminist scholars. Feminist sociologists argued that the use of terms like "men" to cover all human beings or to refer to specific occupations as was the case with "firemen" and "policemen" constructed these occupations as inappropriate for women. As women were making claims for inclusion in different occupations and in society more generally, they recognized the important way that language shaped societal expectations of men and women as well as how people internalized these expectations through language and cultural images. Researchers also identified many other cultural processes and institutions that shaped the constructions of femininity and masculinity, which in turn are communicated to children throughout their childhood and into adulthood. Parents, teachers, and peers exert pressure on young people to learn and adhere to appropriate gender identities in dress, play activities, and social interactions.

However, there are some male and female bodies that do not conform to their biologically defined gender. Holly Devor calls these bodies **gender blending** since their bodies can be read as either male or female, or androgynous, that is, neither male or female. Illustrations include women who are tall and who have a large build. Length of hair is also another feature that, at least in the United States, can be associated with gender. However, even without these bodily clues, many times all a girl or woman needs to do is show presumed masculine characteristics such as being assertive or physically active to be taken as male. These girls might be called "tom boys" or, in some cases, defined as males by strangers who they encounter in their everyday lives. Different styles of dress can also trigger ambiguous presentation of gender. In her study of gender blending, Devor finds that despite the fact that the women in her study defined themselves as female, they were often mistaken for male. Some were stopped when they tried to use women's bathrooms or were called "mister" by salespersons and servers in restaurants. This caused emotional distress for some of the women in her study. Others found that being defined as male provided them with more freedom of movement, especially at night, since they did not have to fear street harassment or other risks that women face in public places. Referring back to the opening discussion, if a gender-blending woman is seen from the distance, she is likely to be taken as male since, according to Devor, male is the presumed category when a gender determination is being made.

ANALYZING AND EXPLAINING GENDERED AND SEXUAL VIOLENCE

Sociologists of gender and sexuality have long been interested in documenting and analyzing the many ways that women, minority men, and sexually nonconforming men face violence against them. Studies of domestic violence were noticeably missing in early sociological literature on the family. In contrast, feminist sociologists recognized the ways that power inequalities in marital relations contribute to women's risk of violence in the family. Women and sexual minorities are also targets of sexual harassment at work and in public spaces.

According to the Centers for Disease Control (CDC; DeNavas-Walt, Proctor, and Smith 2010), one in five women in the United States has been sexually assaulted and nearly one in two has experienced sexual violence other than rape in their lifetimes. Similarly, one in three have experienced domestic violence in the form of physical or sexual abuse. These rates go up drastically to 35.5 percent in households with incomes at or below $15,000 (CDC 2005b). Rates also vary widely by racial and ethnic category. For example, 38.8 percent of women in multiracial non-Hispanic households, while a smaller percentage (28.1 percent) of women in white non-Hispanic households are likely to experience domestic violence. Of course, this is still an unexceptionally high number. In Native American and Alaska native households the rate rises to 45.3 percent. Each year, intimate partner violence results in an estimated two million injuries to women (CDC 2005a). In 2007, researchers from the Bureau of Justice Statistics (Catalano Smith, Snyder, and Rand 2009) found that 45 percent of all female homicide victims were killed by an intimate partner.

One explanation for the extent to which women are the target of violence that is offered by feminist sociologists relates to what is termed "rape culture" (Boswell and Spade 1996). **Rape culture** is defined as the general acceptance of male aggression in the context of women's subordination, which is exacerbated by male dominant or male-only institutions such as the military, certain team sports, and fraternities. In her study of fraternities and gang rape, after documenting the large number of cases of gang rape on campuses, Peggy Reeves Sanday (2007) explains that it is important to examine the broader "sexual culture" that includes boys' fears of being perceived as effeminate and general acceptance of "boys will be boys" to support male aggression (Weiss 2009). As a consequence of this dynamic, children who do not present a normative or socially expected gender identity face harassment on the playground and in other social settings. The social construction of gender and sexuality have material consequences for gender and sexual nonconforming youth who experience bullying and harassment to a much greater extent than other youth. The heteronormative imperative and local bullying contributes to the fact that the rate of suicide attempts is four times greater for lesbian, gay, and bisexual youth than for heterosexual youth (CDC 2016). In 2015, there were 16 hate-related homicides of trans and gender nonconforming people (67 percent of all LGBTQ); 13 of those were trans women of color. Twenty-two percent of the survivors of hate crimes identified as trans. Continuing a multiyear trend, transgender and gender nonconforming people, particularly trans women of color, made up a majority of the homicides reported (National Coalition of Anti-Violence Programs 2015).

Immigrant women also face interpersonal and structural violence that has different features when contrasted with other survivors of violence as Roberta Villalón (2010) demonstrates in her rich intersectional analysis of the challenges immigrant women face as they negotiate violence against them and its effect on the possibilities for citizenship. Villalón explains that due to their immigrant and underprivileged economic status, Latina immigrants are vulnerable to family violence and have few avenues to escape from it. Her multimethodological approach includes participant observation in an immigrant rights organization, interviews with attorneys and other relevant actors, and archival research. As a result, Villalón was able to uncover the myriad of ways that staff attempt to support Latina immigrants Villalón's rights and how the women negotiate the relevant laws and social policies as well as the obstacles they face as undocumented immigrants. However, the staff inadvertently made judgments regarding which immigrant women are deserving of assistance and which legal cases should be pursued. Villalón examines the effect on the women's lives as well as the advocacy work of nonprofit organizations at the local level to understand how social policy reproduces inequalities and leaves immigrant women vulnerable to further abuse. Villalón's study illustrates the importance of examining structures that shape gender and sexuality. For example, feminist scholars who take a social structural approach examine the roles of global capitalism and militarism in increasing risks of violence against women (see, for example, Enloe 2000). Factors they consider are the development of coercive sexual labor in military zones and gendered constructions of violence in armed conflict, the use of rape as a tool of war, and the international crisis of sex trafficking and forced marriage, which have been targeted by international human rights groups.

Much of the literature on gendered and sexual violence focuses on the problems faced by women in the home, in public spaces, and in the economy, but a great deal of contemporary scholarship also attends to the ways in which women and others who are marginalized in today's society respond to and fight against patterns of violence and the reproduction of inequality.

GENDER, SEXUALITY, AND POLITICAL ACTIVISM

Despite the belief that women were traditionally less involved in politics than men, gender scholars have documented women's extensive political history as social reformers and community activists promoting social support and social justice for poor women (Gittell and Shtob 1980).[1] Of course, women were in the forefront of the push for suffrage in the United States and elsewhere. Middle-class reformers of the early 1890s, such as Jane Addams, Florence Kelley, and Mary Church Terrell, argued for "new spaces for citizen participation" and gender equality in politics and other institutions (Sarvasy 1994, 55). As these women reformers engaged in the war against vice and other social ills, their understanding of the structural factors contributing to poverty grew. This is especially evident when we look at the political work of women like Jane Addams and Florence Kelley, who helped organize the settlement house movement in the United States (Elshtain 2001; Gittell and Shtob 1980).

Until the 1980s, women's community work and other political activism, when noticed at all by academics, was understood primarily as a natural extension of their caretaking roles and as part of a *maternalist politics* in which women's engagement in the public sphere was justified through their identities as mothers. Women's community work has often been framed as **maternalism** or social housekeeping—a political claims-making strategy that served as a justification for white middle- and upper-income social reformers to transcend the ideological barrier between women's "proper place" in the home and the so-called public sphere. Historians Seth Koven and Sonya Michel (1993) define maternalism as "ideologies and discourses that exalted women's capacity to mother and applied to society as a whole the values they attached to the role: care, nurturance, and morality" (4). Many women draw upon their gender identities to describe their activism but do not adhere to a traditional gender division of labor ideology nor did they believe that all women could unite on the basis of their mothering status. Race and class formed powerful dimensions of mothering as well as political analyses. Through the lens of maternalist politics, the specificity of low-income, working-class, and nonwhite women's activism is rendered invisible.

Traditional conceptualizations of "politics" did not fit the ways in which the community workers viewed their community-based political activities. A great deal of scholarly attention was paid to the work of middle-class women reformers, and academics were slow to acknowledge the significant role that working-class women played in the labor movement and other campaigns for social justice and economic security and against violence and abuse in families and in other settings. Sociologists of gender emphasize the significance of women's activism in the civil rights and welfare rights movements as well as in voluntary associations that took up political issues (Robnett 1990; West 1981). Many of these women activists were motivated by some of

---

[1] Portions of this section are excerpted from Naples (2011, 268–70).

the same concerns that shaped the urban reformers of previous decades, but their activism reflects the growing empowerment of women from diverse racial and class backgrounds. Through their community-based struggles, working-class women "challenge deeply rooted patriarchal and heterosexist traditions, confront the limits of democracy in the United States, and, in some instances, experience sharp disapproval from other members in their communities" (Naples 1998, 1).

While many women did draw on their gender and maternal identities to describe their activism, they did not believe that all women could unite on the basis of their mothering status. Marilyn Gittell and Teresa Shtob (1980) challenge the view of women's activism as seen exclusively through a maternalism lens. Furthermore, they note the politicizing effect of women's participation, even when originally motivated by their social roles as mothers and community caretakers. Most of these women began their activism when political parties tended to be composed primarily of men who were unlikely to support women candidates. As a consequence, many women who entered electoral politics began their political careers as community activists working with parent–teacher or neighborhood associations (Gittell and Naples 1982). Race and class form powerful dimensions that further shape women's political analyses and political strategies. For example, while women working with women's organizations often define their issues as woman-specific, such as challenging sex discrimination in the workforce or fighting for reproductive rights, women of color as community activists typically focus attention on the entire community and stress education, housing, and child care, or "what needed to be done" (Naples 1998, also see Collins 2008).

Sociologists of gender have also explored the relationship between local organizing and transnational processes such as militarism. For example, Yoko Fukumura and Martha Matsuoka (2002) detail women's resistance to US militarism in Okinawa, Japan, and explain the complex role the US military plays in supporting global trade, destroying the local environment, and placing residents of the Pacific region in jeopardy. The nongovernmental organization, Okinawa Women Act Against Military Violence (OWAAMV), has been effective in its struggle against the US military presence in Okinawa, but OWAAMV activists are concerned that once the military sites become available for local development, another battle over control of the development process will ensue. Political scientist Cynthia Enloe (2000) points out that activists in communities surrounding US military bases in other parts of the world are also fighting an increase in sexual violence and exploitation that accompanies these installations. Here we can see the intersection of gender, race, class, and colonialism as women from third-world or non-Western countries are more likely to be affected than women in Western countries.

An intersectional approach is also valuable in understanding the activism of LGBT people of color. Some studies indicate that "membership in stigmatized groups generally leads to greater levels of activism on the behalf of that group" (Swank and Fahs 2012, 661). However, in their survey of lesbian and

SOCIOLOGY AT WORK
WORK AND GENDER: THE GENDER PAY GAP
Arne L. Kalleberg

A persistent fact about gender and work is that women earn less than men, even in the same occupation. The gender gap has closed somewhat in recent years, from full-time working women earning on average only about 65 percent per year what full-time men earned in the mid-1950s to about 80 percent today (Blau and Kahn, 2016).

What accounts for this persistent gender gap in earnings? Social scientists have offered a variety of explanations, many of which have now been discredited. These include women are less educated than men (this is no longer true as women now receive more education than men); women don't want to pursue high-paying careers (not true, as many women do); and women are less likely than men to belong to unions (there is not much difference by gender in union membership).

Sociologists have shown that the single largest cause of the gender wage gap—accounting for over half over it—is the fact that men and women work in different kinds of jobs. Women are disproportionately likely to work in certain kinds of occupations—such as nurses, elementary school teachers, administrative assistants, flight attendants, and waitresses—and these occupations tend to pay less than occupations in which men typically work—such as engineering, law, and medicine.

But women earn less than men even when working jobs that require similar amounts of education, skills, and responsibility. For example, the average earnings of information technology managers (which are mostly men) are about 27 percent higher than the earnings of human resources managers (mostly women). And janitors (who are mostly men) earn 22 percent more than maids and housecleaners (mainly women). Sociologists have also found that when women start moving into formerly male dominated occupations, the jobs pay less. For example, the gender composition of the field of recreation went from mostly male to mostly female from 1950 to 2000, and hourly wages declined by 57 percent. And, when women became designers in large numbers, the wages of this occupation fell by 34 percent. By contrast, when men take over an occupation (as in computer programming; a relatively unskilled job at the time, it was done mainly by women), wages for that occupation tend to increase (Miller 2016).

It seems, then, that the kinds of work that women do are considered less valuable than the work that men do. Some of this might be due to outright discrimination against women. And some of it might be due to differences in the preferences that women have (e.g., to be nurses as opposed to physicians since nurses have more flexible schedules). But the gender gap is also due to culturally ingrained biases as to the appropriate activities for men and women. For example, women are commonly expected to be caregivers within the family, taking care of children, husbands, and parents. Thus, when women work in occupations that involve caregiving, like nursing or elementary school teaching, they are often viewed as having jobs that do not require much skill (and so don't need to be paid very highly). Social factors, then, are central for explaining differences in how men and women are treated at work.

Sociology at Work *continued*

Sources

Blau, Francine D. and Lawrence M. Kahn. 2016. *The Gender Wage Gap: Extent, Trends, and Explanations*. IZA Discussion Paper No. 9656, Institute for the Study of Labor, Bonn, Germany.

Miller, Claire Cain. 2016. "As Women Take Over a Male-Dominated Field, the Pay Drops." *New York Times*, March 18.

---

gay male activism in the United States, Eric Swank and Breanne Fahs found that whites were overrepresented in the more general protests and petition-signing associated with the national movement. However, lesbians and gay men of color have organized their own organizations to protest racialized, gender, and homophobic violence and discrimination and to advocate for the needs and rights of their communities. For example, Asamblea Gay Unida Impactando Latinos A Superarse [AGUILAS], one of the first Latino LGBT advocacy organization, was first organized in 1992 to advocate on behalf of Latina/o lesbians and gay men and the Gay Asian Pacific Alliance (2016) describes its vision as achieving "a nationally influential API [Asian/Pacific Islander] LGBTQ community that provides and amplifies our collective voices to promote equality and positive social perception."

Trans activists are using the Internet and intersectional activist strategies to promote the rights of trans people. For example, the Remembering our Dead project builds solidarity for trans victims of violence (Rawson 2014). The Transgender, Gender Variant and Intersex Justice Project, run by trans and gender nonconforming people of color helps empower trans prisoners and former prisoners (Currah 2008). They explain that "because of the profound and complex impact the prison industrial complex has had on the disabled, poor communities, communities of color and TGI [transgender, gender variant, and intersex] communities, TGIJP operates at the intersections of race, gender, sex, class, sexual orientation, intersexuality, and ability, among others" (TGIJP 2007; quoted in Currah 2008, 98).

GENDER, SEXUALITY, AND EMPLOYMENT

Feminist sociologists, who focus on social structure rather than individual identities and social interaction, explore how gender and sexuality structure women's employment opportunities using quantitative data. Until recently, potential employers frequently questioned women's attachment to the labor force due to an expectation that all women would become wives and mothers. Since women were expected to provide the major role as caretakers in the family, male workers with children were assumed to have a greater attachment to the workforce. These employers argued that if women were only in the workforce temporarily, why waste time in training them or hiring them for jobs that would require long hours or out-of-town travel. Even when we examine relatively new fields such as information technology (IT), the gender differences persist. At the peak of the IT boom in 2008, the number of women in the field remained significantly below men's, under 1 million women compared to over 3.75 million men were employed in mathematical and computer sciences that year (see Figures 7–1 and 7–2; Alegria 2012).

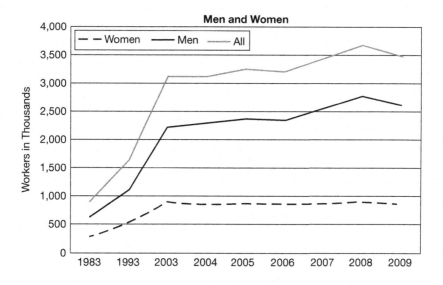

Figure 7–1 Workers 16 and Over Employed in Mathematical and Computer Science, Selected Years, 1983–2009 Annual Averages.

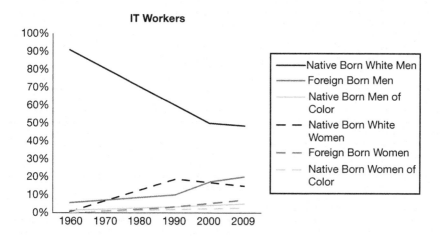

Figure 7–2 IT Workers with at Least a Bachelor's Degree by Demographic Group, 1960–2009.

US-born women of color are further disadvantaged in the IT field, comprising only 2 percent of the total workforce in 2009 compared to native-born white women who were approximately 10 percent of the workforce and native-born white men who made up about 50 percent of the workforce. Furthermore, women of different racial-ethnic and class backgrounds have very different opportunities to earn a living wage and to be living in poverty. For example, women of color are more likely to be living in poverty than are white women. When we examine poverty rates for women of different racial-ethnic backgrounds, especially those who are single mothers, we find that a disproportionate percentage of African-American and Hispanic women are living in poverty when compared to white women. The Census Bureau report for March 2016 reveals that while only 9 percent of the white population in the United States was living in poverty, 24 percent of blacks, 21 percent of Hispanics, and 14 percent from Asian-American or those from other racial-ethnic backgrounds were living in poverty (Kaiser Family Foundation 2016).

In her study *Complex Inequality: Gender, Class and Race in the New Economy,* sociologist Leslie McCall (2001) demonstrates that both economic factors, such as the economic basis of a local economy, and social factors, such as gender differences in education, shape women's economic opportunities and wages. These factors intersect to explain why women are more disadvantaged by the decline in the value of the minimum wage. Her quantitative approach utilizes a variety of economic and demographic data to examine the economic variation in different regions of the United States. McCall found that women living in Dallas, Detroit, Miami, and St. Louis have different patterns of inequality when compared to men and to other women due to the different kinds of industries and employment opportunities. She explains how the differences relate to the greater amount of high-tech manufacturing in St. Louis, the large immigrant workforce in Miami, the postindustrial economy in Dallas, and the continued dependence on industrial employment in Detroit. These lead to different wage structures, and, due to gender differences in jobs, she finds different work opportunities for men and women. In other words, McCall argues, to understand differences in wages between men and women and between men and women of different races, it is necessary to understand the complexity of different job markets. Differences cannot be explained solely by a comparison of men's and women's wages without paying attention to the structure of the job market in different parts of the country.

While women have made inroads into many occupations that have been the purview of men, such as law, medicine, biological sciences, and firefighting, occupational segregation between the jobs women do and the jobs men do persists as well as the wage gap between what men and women earn. Hegewisch and Ellis (2015) in a study for the Institute for Women's Policy Research (IWPR) report that in 2014 "the median gender earnings ratio for all full-time weekly workers was 82.5 percent, reflecting median weekly earnings for all female full-time workers of $719, compared with $871 per week for men" (1). Hegewisch and Ellis also find that "without exception, women's median earnings are lower than mens' in the 20 most common male occupations for which data are available" (3). They also note that "four of ten [women] (39 percent) work in female-dominated occupations and slightly more than four of ten men (43.3 percent) work in male-dominated occupations" (1).

In another IWPR report, Hegewisch, Williams, and Henderson (2011) explain "that the gender earnings gap is as much due to pay differences within occupations as it is due to differences in pay between occupations" (6). Not surprisingly, "occupations which employ more men tend to provide higher earnings, particularly in high-earnings occupations" (6). They note:

> Closing the gender wage gap also requires effective enforcement of labor and effective enforcement of labor and equal employment opportunity regulations so that women may choose the occupations they would like to work in, free of discrimination and harassment; it requires the enforcement of equal pay laws so that women and men can be sure they are paid fairly for their skills, experience and performance and not on the bases of their sex, age, race or ethnic background; and it requires better career advice so that potential earnings are part of the available information used when people choose their careers. (6)

In 2014 IWPR researchers concluded:

> To improve women's earnings and reduce the gender gap, women and their families need enhanced efforts to ensure non-discriminatory hiring and pay practices, better training and career counseling, and improved work-family supports. Such public policies as raising the minimum wage, which increase wages in the lowest-paid jobs, are especially important for women, particularly women of color. (Hegewisch and Hudiburg 2014, 5)

Workplace discrimination and harassment based on gender and sexuality are intersecting practices that enforce both normative or dominant ideas of gender behavior, dress and appearance and normative performance of heterosexuality. For example, in their study of lesbian, gay, bisexual and queer workplace harassment, Verónica Rabelo and Lilia Cortin (2014) found that "gender harassment . . . rarely occurred absent heterosexist harassment, and vice versa" (378). As remedies, they argue for "broadening judicial interpretations of Title VII [of the Civil Rights Act], passing new legislation (e.g., the Employment Non-Discrimination Act, or ENDA), and strengthening organizational supports and policies that protect against sexuality-based abuses" (378).

INEQUALITY REGIMES IN ORGANIZATIONS

Feminist sociologists point out that the social structure of organizations are responsible for much of the gender, race, and, of course, class inequalities in the United States and other countries. Sociologist Joan Acker examines what she terms "inequality regimes" and explores the practices and meanings that systematically create and maintain disparities between workers at different levels of power and control within organizations. One of Acker's (2006) studies examined the inequality regime in six Swedish bank branches. She noted that the branch with a majority of women in positions of power organized work in a more collective fashion and shared power more equally than the branches with a majority of men in power. In her US-based research, she observed how segregation by gender and race also varied across organizations and occupational category. However, even though there is evidence that occupations are less segregated than in the past and more women and minorities are found in previously male dominated fields such as medicine, women and racial minorities are more likely to be found in the low-paying jobs within this profession. This is also the case in the fields of law, engineering, and science.

Wage differences within organizations also vary. In organizations with more elaborated hierarchical structures, like large corporations, top executives, who are disproportionately white and male, can make upward of 185 times the average employee. Furthermore, professional women of all racial-ethnic backgrounds and men of color are overrepresented in public sector jobs where they are often paid less than some of their counterparts in the private sector. In the current economy where there is an increase in service sector jobs, which are less likely to be unionized and tend to employ a greater proportion of minorities and white women, the pay scale is typically lower than in other sectors. The growth in the service sector is tied to global economic restructuring that includes decrease in state support for public assistance, loss of union jobs, movement of jobs out of industrialized countries, and decrease of regulations on corporations.

Poorer and less industrialized countries are asked to restructure their economies in exchange for loans from international groups such as the World Bank and US Agency for International Development. These practices have been especially difficult for women in all parts of the world. For example, poor women, who are disproportionately women of color, shoulder a disproportionate burden of the economic and social dislocation resulting from economic restructuring. Consolidation of land for corporate agriculture and the shift in food production from sustainable produce to export items, such as coffee, means that women are unable to have access to land to grow their own food and do not have the money to buy food to feed their families. In industrialized countries like the United States, loss of social services and state support for low-income families means that women have an increased burden in caring for elderly or sick relatives and a harder time finding accessible and affordable child care to maintain full time employment.

Sociologists of gender and sexuality highlight the fact that globalization, the increased speed of financial, migration, and cultural processes across the globe, is a result of particular actions taken by identifiable actors, most of whom are white heterosexual men from European backgrounds. While it is accurate to point out that most of those in positions of power are men from these backgrounds, sociologists who study inequality regimes in institutions point out that, regardless of your gender, race, or class background, to be successful in most of the dominant political and economic institutions, one has to adopt a **masculinist** approach.

Rather than view globalization as a process that occurs at a distance from the everyday lives and activities of particular actors, sociologists demonstrate that global economic and political change is manifest in the daily lives and struggles of women and other members of communities in different parts of the world in ways that are often hidden from view in analyses of globalization. Instead, discussions of globalization typically begin from the perspective of multinational corporations, transnational organizations, and international political institutions. Sociologists of gender argue that the structural conditions that contribute to the impoverishment of women and children around the world can be understood as a form of **structural violence** (Farmer 2005). Poverty and lack of access to health care, food, safe and affordable housing, and water can be explained through the lens of structural violence when we examine the government and economic structures that leave some people in poverty while rewarding others. For example, the gap between the poor and the wealthy in the United States could be understood as an illustration of structural violence in that a change in tax structure could address or correct the differences through greater taxes on the wealthy. Since 1972, we have seen a deepening of class and racial inequality in this country. By way of illustration, "the top 0.01 percent of earners paid over 70 percent of their income in federal taxes in 1960" (Piketty and Saez 2007, 22), but they paid only 19.53 percent in 2012 (Dungan 2015). Meanwhile, the "average federal tax rates for the middle class have remained roughly constant over time" (Piketty and Saez 2007, 22). In addition, corporate income tax has declined as a percent of the gross domestic product from 3.85 percent in the 1965 to 2.19 percent in 2015 (OECD 2016). The Pew Research Center (Kochhar and Fry 2014) reports that "the current gap between blacks and whites has reached its highest point since 1989." The median wealth (assets minus debts) of black households was $11,000 in 2013, the median wealth of Hispanic households was $13,700, and the median wealth of white households was $141,900. In this current economy, "the top 1 percent of the population holds at least 20 percent of the wealth" and "the very top 1 percent of Americans earns an average of $27 million a year per person, while the bottom 99 percent of Americans earns an average of $31,000 a year" (DeVega 2011).

One of the most frightening statistics that I came across in preparing this lesson comes from the Pew Research Center. They report that due to preexisting racial inequalities and compounded by the disproportionate number of racial minorities targeted for empty mortgages and junk loans, as of 2013 "the wealth of white households was 13 times the median wealth of black households . . . [and] the wealth of white households is now more than 10 times the wealth of Hispanic households" (Kochhar and Fry 2014).

When we examine the data by gender differences, we find that women are more likely to be living in poverty across all racial and ethnic groups (Tucker and Lowell 2016). In 2015, 22.7 percent of Native American women, 23.1 percent of African American women, 20.9 percent of Hispanic women,

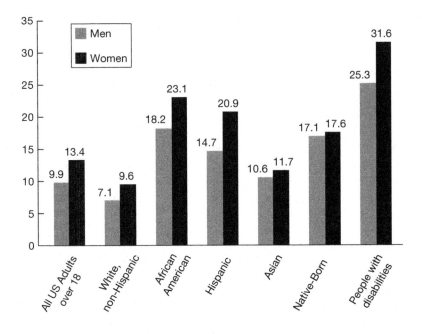

Figure 7-3 Percentage of Men and Women in Poverty by Race/Ethnicity and Disability, 2015.

Source: Census Bureau, reported in Tucker and Lowell 2016

11.7 percent of Asian women, and 9.6 percent of white women are poor, compared to 7.1 percent of white men (see Figure 7–3). Ability also contributed to differences in poverty rate. Almost 32 percent of women with disabilities and 25 percent of men with disabilities lived in poverty in 2015 (Tucker and Lowell 2016).

INTERSECTIONAL ANALYSES OF GENDER AND SEXUALITY

As this chapter highlights, the differences found in the poverty rate of men and women across different racial-ethnic groups and ability demonstrates the importance of intersectional analysis, namely, how gender, race, and class simultaneously structure the differences in women's lives. By way of illustration, ask yourself: What's more important to you? Your gender? Your race or ethnicity? Your age? Where you were born? Your religion? Your sexuality? If you cannot answer this question easily, you will be thinking intersectionally. The idea of intersectionality was developed in the field of women's studies as scholars and activists tried to account for the complexity and diversity of women's lives.

Early scholarship in the field of women's studies took what is called an additive approach that treated gender, race, and sexuality as autonomous dimensions that needed to be accounted for separately. As research developed to examine women's lives and compare their experiences across race, class, and sexuality, scholars began to understand that each of these aspects of social and personal life were intertwined. It was impossible to determine which was more important or more relevant in different social situations. More recently, feminist scholars have discussed these features as co-created or co-constructed. In other words, it is impossible to separate them, one from the other, in any meaningful way.

One of the goals of intersectional studies is to uncover the ways in which different institutions are constructed along the intersecting dimensions of gender, race, class, and sexuality (Naples 2009). In other words, institutions as well as individual identities intersect. For example, sociologist Alison Griffith and Dorothy Smith (1990) reveal how often unspoken within the daily practices of teachers and administrators are the expectations that much of the learning process depends upon mothers' work in the homes (supervising homework, assisting in school projects), in the schools (serving as volunteers in the classroom or for school trips), and in the community (fundraising and organizing school-community events). Smith (1991) uses the term "relations of ruling" to capture the ways in which these different institutional arrangements intersect to shape everyday life.

CONCLUSION

Gender and sexual norms and expectations become internalized by individuals through the process of socialization beginning in the family and then extend to all other areas of social life. We first learn our social roles in the family by watching the division of labor and the expectations of our parents. Children gain insight into how gender and sexuality are organized in society as they receive gifts for their birthdays or accompany their parents to the mall. They also observe how gender organizes employment as they note that most firefighters are male and most nurses are women.

While the social constructionist approach remains central to sociological analyses, it has been criticized for lack of attention to the ways that gender and sexuality are institutionally structured. In other words, despite our agency in constructing, interpreting, and performing gender and sexuality, there are powerful structures in place that inhibit our success in communicating and establishing our desired goal in everyday interactions or that shape our decisions or choices in many ways that are invisible to us. Sociologists of gender and sexuality who take a social structural approach focus on how gender and sexuality structure social institutions and examine how they structure gender and sexual relations, societal expectations, and differences in income and employment opportunities, among other factors that go beyond individual experiences or expressions of gender and sexuality. Gender and sexual identities and experiences are also shaped by other structural factures such as race, class, citizenship status, ability, age, and religion. This calls for an intersectional approach that does not fragment our lives into separate compartments and calls for the simultaneous analysis of race, class, gender, sexuality among other factors.

Women, gender nonconforming people, and sexual minorities have been making claims for inclusion and social transformation for many decades. Women have achieved some inroads in politics, employment, and gender relations but many challenges remain, especially in the areas of income inequality, sexual harassment, and other forms of gender and homophobic violence. Claims for expansion of sexual citizenship by sexual minorities include challenges to heteronormatively, heterosexism, and equal access to immigration, same-sex marriage, and freedom from employment discrimination, bullying, and violence. LGBT people of color experience greater negative impacts than white LGBT people in the areas of law enforcement, welfare and family policy, and safe schools initiatives that call for increases in police surveillance of schools and disciplinary consequences. However, Sean Cahill (2010) argues, "It also offers opportunities for strengthening alliances among communities with common interests in significant policy change" (205).

Calls for intersectional understanding of gender were first expressed by feminists of color, who critiqued approaches to gender that addressed women's concerns without attending to the ways that race, class, and sexuality contributed to different experiences among women. Early challenges to feminist analyses of women's lives include the approach taken by welfare rights activist Jonnie Tillmon, who organized ANC Anonymous, the welfare rights group in Los Angeles. In 1972 Jonnie Tillmon famously stated:

> *I'm a woman. I'm a black woman. I'm a poor woman. I'm a fat woman. I'm a middle-aged woman. And I'm on welfare. In this country, if you're any one of those things, you count less as a person. If you're all those things, you just don't count, except as a statistic. I am a statistic. (Tillmon 2002)*

Tillmon was reflecting the concern held by many African-American women activists and others involved in different social justice movements that black women are valued less by society then white women, that poor women are valued less than wealthier women, that young women are valued less than older women, and that fat women are valued less than women who are slender. Taken together, Tillmon argued, women who embody all of the less valued attributes "just don't count." The Combahee River Collective added another dimension; namely, that of sexuality. The collective was formed by a group of black lesbian feminists who also felt that their lives were not represented by women's movement activists who were fighting for women's equal rights but who did not consider the different political concerns and challenges of women who were not white, middle-class, and heterosexual.

Fortunately, times have changed from the early 1970s when Tillmon made her statement with the development of enhanced solidarity and cross-issue and cross-race and class organizing. The following quote from the Combahee River Collective (1982: 18) captures a key insight of intersectional analysis:

> *The major source of difficulty in our political work is that we are . . .*
> *trying . . . to address a whole range of oppressions. . . . We are dispossessed*
> *psychologically and on every other level, and yet we feel the necessity to*
> *struggle to change the condition of all Black women. . . . If Black women were*
> *free, it would mean that everyone else would have to be free since our freedom*
> *would necessitate the destruction of all the systems of oppression.*

As you can tell by now, the notion of intersectionality has origins in the women's movement; however, it has become one of the key concepts in the academic fields of sociology and women's, gender and sexuality studies.

Author's note: My thanks to Barbara Gurr for her contributions to the section on violence against women and to Malaena Taylor and Cristina Khan for research assistance.

Lesson Take-Aways

- Learning one's gender role and appropriate forms of sexual desire includes understanding dominant norms or beliefs about gender and sexuality.

- Those who do not present a normative or socially expected gender or sexual identity face discrimination, harassment, or even violence against them in different social and institutional settings.

- Individual experiences and life chances vary depending on the ways in which gender and sexuality intersect with race, ethnicity, national origin, ability, religion, and other social factors.

- Until the mid-twentieth century, academic understanding of differences between men and women were primarily tied to explanations that essentialized or naturalized the biological and psychological differences between them.

- Contemporary sociologists more frequently focus on the social construction of gender and sexuality in everyday life and in social institutions as well as how social institutions structure gender and sexual relations, societal expectations, and differences in income and employment opportunities, among other factors.

Discussion Questions

1. What are some of the messages given to boys and girls that contribute to gender differences? How do these messages contribute to compulsory heterosexuality?
2. What is the difference between a biologically determinist approach to gender and sexual differences and a social constructionist approach? What is the difference between a social learning approach and a cognitive developmental approach to gender and sexuality?
3. Why do feminist and queer sociologists argue for an intersectional approach to understanding gender and sexuality?

Sources

Acker, Joan. 2006. "Inequality Regimes: Gender, Class, and Race in Organizations." *Gender & Society* 20(4): 441–64.

Ajayi, Lasisi, 2011. "A Multiliteracies Pedagogy: Exploring Semiotic Possibilities of a Disney Video in a Third Grade Diverse Classroom." *Urban Review* 43(3): 396–413.

Alegria, Sharla. 2012, February. *An Analysis of Broadening in Two Science Fields.* Paper presented at the Eastern Sociological Society, New York, New York.

Boswell, A. Ayres and Joan Z. Spade. 1996. "Fraternities and Collegiate Rape Culture: Why Are Some Fraternities More Dangerous Places for Women?" *Gender and Society* 10(2): 133–47.

Catalano, Shannan, Erica Smith, Howard Snyder, and Michael Rand. 2009. *Female Victims of Violence.* Bureau of Justice Statistics Selected Findings. NCJ No. 228356. http://www.bjs.gov/content/pub/pdf/fvv.pdf

Cahill, Sean. 2010. "Black Sexual Citizenship: Understanding the Impact of Political Issues on Those at the Margins of Race, Sexuality, Gender, and Class." In Juan Battle and Sandra L. Barnes (eds.), *Black Sexualities,* 190–212. New Brunswick, NJ: Rutgers University Press,

Center for American Women and Politics. 2016. "Current Numbers." http://www.cawp.rutgers.edu/current-numbers

Centers for Disease Control. 2005a. "Adverse Health Conditions and Health Risk Behaviors Associated with Intimate Partner Violence—United States 2005." *MMWR* 57(5): 113–7. www.cdc.gov/mmwr/preview/mmwrhtml/mm5705a1.htm.

Centers for Disease Control. 2005b. *Behavioral Risk Factor Surveillance System Survey: Summary Data Report.* Atlanta, GA: CDC. http://ftp.cdc.gov/pub/data/brfss/2005summarydataqualityreport.pdf

Centers for Disease Control. 2010. *National Intimate Partner and Sexual Violence Survey.* Atlanta, GA: CDC. http://www.cdc.gov/violenceprevention/pdf/nisvs_report2010-a.pdf

Centers for Disease Control. 2016. "Sexual Identity, Sex of Sexual Contacts, and Health-Risk Behaviors among Students in Grades 9–12: Youth Risk Behavior Surveillance." MMWR 65(9). https://www.cdc.gov/mmwr/volumes/65/ss/pdfs/ss6509.pdf

Chodorow, Nancy. 1978. *The Reproduction of Mothering.* Berkeley: University of California Press.

Clark, Kenneth B. and Mamie Phipps Clark. 1940. "Skin Color as a Factor in Racial Identification of Negro Preschool Children." *Journal of Social Psychology, S.P.S.S.I. Bulletin* 11(1): 159–69.

Collins, Patricia Hill. 2003. "Color, Hair Texture, and Standards of Beauty." In Estelle Disch (ed.), *Reconstructing Gender: A Multicultural Anthology,* 127–31. New York: McGraw-Hill.

Collins, Patricia Hill. 2008. *Black Feminist Thought:* Knowledge, Consciousness, and the Politics of Empowerment. New York: Routledge.

Combahee River Collective. 1982. "A Black Feminist Statement." In Gloria T. Hull, Patricia Bell Scott, and Barbar Smith (eds.) All the Women are White, All the Blacks are Men, But Some of Us Are Brave, 13-22. Old Westbury, NY: The Feminist Press.

Connell, Raewyn 1995. *Masculinities.* Cambridge: Polity Press.

Crenshaw, Kimberlé Williams. 1991. "Mapping the Margins: Intersectionality, Identity Politics, and Violence Against Women of Color." *Stanford Law Review* 43(6): 1241–99.

Currah, Paisley. 2008. "Stepping Back, Looking Outward: Situating Transgender Activism and Transgender Studies—Kris Hayashi, Matt Richardson, and Susan Stryker Frame the Movement." *Sexuality Research & Social Policy* 5(1): 93–105.

David, Deborah, and Robert Brannon. 1976. *The Forty-Nine Percent Majority: The Male Sex Role.* New York: Random House.

Davis, Kiri. 2005. *A Girl Like Me* (video). Brooklyn: Reel Works Teen Film-Making.

DeNavas-Walt, Carmen, Bernadette D. Proctor, and Jessica C. Smith. 2010. "Figure 4: Number in Poverty and Poverty Rate: 1959–2010." In *Income, Poverty, and Health Insurance Coverage in the United States: 2010.* Washington, DC: US Census Bureau. http://www.census.gov/prod/2011pubs/p60-239.pdf

DeVega, Chauncey. 2011. "Tea Party and the Right: Debt Ceiling Holy War: Why Do Conservatives Have Unshakable Faith in Ideas that are Totally, Demonstrably False?" Alternet, July 18. http://www.alternet.org/story/151673/debt_ceiling_holy_war%3A_why_do_conservatives_have_unshakable_faith_in_ideas_that_are_totally,_demonstrably_false

Devor, Holly. 1989. *Gender Blending; Confronting the Limits of Duality.* Bloomington: Indiana University Press.

Dungan, Adrian. 2015. "Individual Income Tax Shares, 2012." *Statistics of Income Bulletin.* Spring. https://www.irs.gov/pub/irs-soi/soi-a-ints-id1506.pdf

Elshtain, J. B. (ed.). 2001. *The Jane Addams Reader.* New York: Basic Books.

Eng, David L., 2001. *Racial Castration: Racial Castration: Managing Masculinity in Asian America.* Durham, NC: Duke University Press.

England, Dawn, Lara Descartes, and Melissa Collier-Meek. 2011. "Gender Role Portrayal and the Disney Princesses." *Sex Roles* 64 (7–8): 555–67.

Enloe, Cynthia. 2000. *Maneuvers: The International Politics of Militarizing Women's Lives.* Berkeley: University of California Press.

Farmer, Paul. 2005 *Pathologies of Power: Health, Human Rights, and the New War on the Poor.* Berkeley: University of California Press.

Farmer, Paul, Margaret Connors, and Janie Simmons (eds.). 2007. *Women, Poverty and AIDS: Sex, Drugs and Structural Violence.* Monroe, ME: Common Courage.

Fausto-Sterling, Anne. 2000. "The Five Sexes, Revisited." *Sciences* 40(4): 18–23.

Fenstermaker, Sarah and Candace West (eds.). 2002. *Doing Gender, Doing Difference: Inequality, Power and Institutional Change.* New York: Routledge.

Fukumura, Yoko and Martha Matsuoka. 2002. "Redefining Security: Okinawa Women's Resistance to US Militarism." In Nancy A. Naples and Manisha Desai (eds.), *Women's Activism and Globalization: Linking Local Struggles and Transnational Politics,* 63–70. New York: Routledge.

Garfinkel, Harold. 1967. *Studies in Ethnomethodology.* Cambridge, MA: Blackwell.

Gay Asian Pacific Alliance. 2016. "Vision." http://gapafoundation.org/about/ http://gapafoundation.org/about/

Gilmore, David. 1990. *Manhood in the Making: Cultural Concepts of Masculinity.* New Haven, CT: Yale University Press.

Gittell, Marilyn and Naples, Nancy A. (1982). "Activist Women: Conflicting Ideologies." *Social Policy* 13(4): 25–27.

Gittell, Marilyn and Nancy A. Naples. 2011. "Activist Women: Conflicting Ideologies." In Kathe Newman and Ross Gittell (eds.), *Activist Scholar: Selected Works of Marilyn Gittell*, 295–300. Thousand Oaks, CA: SAGE.

Gittell, Marilyn and Teresa Shtob. 1980. "Changing Women's Roles in Political Volunteerism and Reform in the City." *Signs: Journal of Women in Culture and Society* 5(3): S67–S78.

Goffman, Erving. 1959. *The Presentation of Self in Everyday Life*. New York: Anchor Books.

Goffman, Erving. 1976. "Gender Display." *Studies in the Anthropology of Visual Communication* 3: 69–77.

Griffith, Alison I. and Dorothy E. Smith. 1990. "What Did You Do in School Today? Mothering, Schooling, and Social Class." In G. Miller and James A. Hostein (eds.), *Perspectives on Social Problems*. Vol. 2, 3–24. Greenwich, CT: JAI.

Harding, Sandra. 1991. *Whose Science? Whose Knowledge? Thinking from Women's Lives*. Ithaca, NY: Cornell University Press.

Hegewisch, Ariane and Emily Ellis. 2015. *The Gender Wage Gap by Occupation 2014 and by Race and Ethnicity*. Institution for Womens Policy Research No. C431. http://www.iwpr.org/publications/pubs/the-gender-wage-gap-by-occupation-2014-and-by-race-and-ethnicity

Hegewisch, Ariane and Stephanie Keller Hudiburg. 2014. *The Gender Wage Gap by Occupation 2013 and by Race and Ethnicity*. Institute for Women's Policy Research No. 414. http://www.iwpr.org/publications/pubs/the-gender-wage-gap-by-occupation-and-by-race-and-ethnicity-2013

Hegewisch, Ariane, Claudia Williams, and Amber Henderson. 2011. *The Gender Wage Gap by Occupation*. Institute for Women's Policy Research No. C350a. http://www.iwpr.org/publications/pubs/the-gender-wage-gap-by-occupation-updated-april-2011

Kaiser Family Foundation. 2016. "Poverty Rates for Race/Ethnicity." *Based on the Census Bureau's March 2016 Current Population Survey (CPS: Annual Social and Economic Supplements)*. www.statehealthfacts.org/comparebar.jsp?ind=14&cat=1.

Kimmel, Michael S. 2000. *The Gendered Society*. New York: Oxford University Press.

Kimmel, Michael. 2007. *The Sexual Self: The Construction of Sexual Scripts*. Nashville: Vanderbilt University Press.

Kimmel, Michael. 2008. *Guyland: The Perilous World Where Boys Become Men*. New York: Harper.

Kochhar, Rakesh and Richard Fry. 2014. "Wealth Inequality Has Widened along Racial, Ethnic Lines Since End of Great Recession." *FactTank*, December 12. http://www.pewresearch.org/fact-tank/2014/12/12/racial-wealth-gaps-great-recession/

Koven, Seth, and Sonya Michel (eds.). 1993. *Mothers of a New World: Maternalist Politics and the Origins of Welfare States*. New York: Routledge.

Levine, Martin P. 1998. *Gay Macho: The Life and Death of the Homosexual Clone*. New York: New York University Press.

Lorber, Judith and Lisa Jean Moore. 2006. *Gendered Bodies: Feminist Perspectives*. New York: Oxford University Press.

McCall, Leslie. 2001. *Complex Inequality: Gender, Class and Race in the New Economy.* New York: Routledge.

Money, John, and J. G. Hampson, and J. . Hampson. 1955. "An Examination of Some General Sexual Concepts: The Evidence of Human Hermaphroditism." *Johns Hopkins Hospital Bulletin* 97: 301–19.

Muehlenhard, Charlene L. and Zoe D. Peterson. 2011. "Distinguishing between Sex and Gender: History, Current Conceptualizations, and Implications." *Sex Roles* 64(11–12): 791–803.

Naples, Nancy A. 2009. "Teaching Intersectionality Intersectionally." *International Feminist Journal of Politics* 11(4): 566–77.

Naples, Nancy A. 1998. *Grassroots Warriors: Activist Mothering, Community Work and the War on Poverty.* New York: Routledge.

Organisation for Economic Co-operation and Development. 2016. "Revenue Statistics 2015." https://data.oecd.org/tax/tax-on-corporate-profits.htm

Park, Michael. 2013. "Asian American Masculinity Eclipsed: A Legal and Historical Perspective of Emasculation Through U.S. Immigration Practices." *Modern American* 8(1): 5–17.

Pascoe, C. J. 2007. *Dude, You're a Fag: Masculinity and Sexuality in High School.* Berkeley: University of California Press.

Piketty, Thomas and Immanuel Saez. 2007. "How Progressive is the US Federal Tax System: A Historical and International Perspective." *Journal of Economic Perspectives* 21(1): 3–24.

Rabelo, Verónica and Lilia M. Cortina. 2014. "Two Sides of the Same Coin: Gender Harassment and Heterosexist Harassment in LGBQ Work Lives." *Law and Human Behavior* 38(4): 378–91.

Rawson, K. J. 2014. "Transgender Worldmaking in Cyberspace: Historical Activism in the Internet." *QED: A Journal of GLBTQ Worldmaking* 1(2): 38–60.

Rich, Adrienne. 1994. "Compulsory Heterosexuality and Lesbian Existence." *Blood, Bread, and Poetry.* New York: Norton.

Robnett, Belinda. 2000. *How Long? How Long? African-American Women in the Struggle for Civil Rights.* New York: Oxford University Press.

Rubin, Gayle S. 1975. "The Traffic in Women: Notes on the 'Political Economy' of Sex." In Rayna R. Reiter (ed.), *Toward an Anthropology of Women,* 157–210. New York: Monthly Review.

Ruddick, Sara. 1989. *Maternal Thinking: Towards a Politics of Peace.* Boston: Beacon.

Sanday, Peggy Reeves. 2007. *Fraternity Gang Rape: Sex, Brotherhood, and Privilege on Campus.* New York: New York University Press.

Sarvasy, Wendy. 1994. "From Man and Philanthropic Service to Feminist Social Citizenship." *Social Politics* 1(3): 249–55.

Smith, Dorothy E. 1990. *The Conceptual Practices of Power: A Feminist Sociology of Knowledge.* Boston: Northeastern University Press.

Smith, Dorothy E. and Alison I. Griffith. 1990. "Coordinating the Uncoordinated: Mothering, Schooling, and the Family Wage." In Gale Miller and James A. Holstein (eds.), *Perspectives on Social Problems.* Vol. 2, 25–43. Greenwich, CT.: JAI.

Swank, Eric and Breanne Fahs. 2012. "An Intersectional Analysis of Gender and Race for Sexual Minorities Who Engage in Gay and Lesbian Rights Activism." *Sex Roles* 68: 660–74.

Thorne, Barrie. 1997. *Gender Play: Girls and Boys in School.* New Brunswick, NJ: Rutgers University Press.

Tillmon, Jonnie. 2002. "Welfare Is a Women's Issue (1972)." *Ms. Magazine.* http://www.msmagazine.com/spring2002/tillmon.asp

Tucker, Jasmine and Caitlin Lowell. 2016. *Income Security and Education National Snapshot: Poverty Among Women and Families, 2015.* National Women's Law Center. https://nwlc.org/wp-content/uploads/2016/09/Poverty-Snapshot-Factsheet-2016.pdf

U.S. Census Bureau. 2009. *Current Population Survey, 2008 Annual Social and Economic Supplement.* Washington, DC: US Census Bureau.

Villalón, Roberta. 2010. *Violence against Latina Immigrants: Citizenship, Inequality, and Community.* New York: New York University Press.

Waters, Emily Chai Jindasurat, and Cecilia Wolfe. 2015. *Lesbian, Gay, Bisexual, Transgender, Queer, and HIV-Infected Hate Violence in 2015.* 2016 release ed. New York: National Coalition of Anti-Violence Programs. http://www.avp.org/storage/documents/ncavp_hvreport_2015_final.pdf

Weiss, Karen. 2009. "'Boys Will Be Boys' and other Gendered Accounts." *Violence Against Women* 15(7): 810–39.

West, Guida. 1981. *The National Welfare Rights Movement: The Social Protest of Poor Women.* New York: Praeger.

West, Candace and Sarah Fenstermaker. 1993. "Power, Inequality, and the Accomplishment of Gender: An Ethnomethodological View." In Paula England (ed.), *Theory on Gender: Feminism on Theory,* 131–58. New York: de Gruyter.

West, Candace and Don Zimmerman 1987. "Doing Gender." *Gender & Society* 1(2): 125–51.

Williams, Christine. 2006. *Inside Toyland: Working, Shopping, and Social Inequality.* Berkeley: University of California Press.

Related Websites

Asamblea Gay Unida Impactando Latinos A Superarse [AGUILAS], Lesbian and gay Latina/o organization committed to advocacy: sfaguilas.org

Center for Women and Politics, Rutgers University: www.cawp.rutgers.edu

Clayman Institute for Gender Research, Stanford University: http://gender.stanford.edu

Convention on the Elimination of All Forms of Discrimination against Women, United Nations, Division for Advancement of Women, Department of Economic and Social Affairs: www.un.org/womenwatch/daw/cedaw

Gay Asian Pacific Alliance: http://gapafoundation.org

International Center for Research on Women: www.icrw.org

Intersex Society of North America: http://isna.org

National Women's Studies Association: www.nwsa.org

Kinsey Institute for Research on Sex, Gender and Reproduction, Indiana University: www.kinseyinstitute.org

Society for the Psychological Study of Men and Masculinity, American Psychological Association: www.division51.net

Sociologists for Women in Society: www.socwomen.org

LESSON 7, PHOTO REFLECTION:

Little league softball player.
Photo by Ken Gould.

Sports are sex-segregated. With very few exceptions, same-sex teams play other same-sex teams, of the same sex, in same-sex leagues. Title IX created more opportunities for women in sports but did little to erode sex segregation and has not resulted in anything close to parity in professional sports opportunities for women. Sports are gendered, and sports participation in most cases requires more complex gender performances for women than for men. We chose this photo because it speaks to the gendered nature of the intersection of biography (one girl's sports ambition) and history (the gender-differentiated opportunities for sports careers). While boys who play baseball can hope to become major league ballplayers, girls play softball and can't hope to become major league ballplayers without dramatic social change. If you were the photographer, what picture would you take to represent gender and intersectionality?

PART 4

HOW DO SOCIETIES CHANGE?

While our social institutions, culture, and socialization processes all serve to maintain the continuity of our society over time, there is no denying that our society, and all societies, change over time. The United States' and global society are noticeably different from when you were born, let alone from when your parents were born or when their parents were born. Social change is both enabled and constrained by the structure of the social institutions, the culture, and the social norms inherited from the past. The economy of the present creates opportunities and constraints for the economies of the future. The way we govern in the present provides pathways and barriers for the way we will govern in the future. Karl Marx said in *The Eighteenth Brumaire of Louis Napoleon* (1852), "Men make their own history, but they do not make it as they please; they do not make it under self-selected circumstances, but under circumstances existing already, given and transmitted from the past." We have agency in influencing the direction of social change, but we do that from the starting point of the social world that was constructed without our influence or consent. Note that the fact that we would not use the term "men" as a general term to refer to all people in the twenty-first century is a cultural marker for a set of social changes in gender norms that have occurred since Marx wrote that passage.

One major set of social changes that have been generated over the past half-century are those associated with globalization. Human society is increasingly globally organized, and changes at local, regional, and national levels both reflect and impact changes at the global scale. We live in a world linked by global communication technologies, with increasingly global social norms, and an economy that operates at a global scale. We also face global scale problems such as climate change, the sixth mass extinction, and those associated with the mass migration of human populations. We live in an era of globalization because people, acting in and upon social institutions, made decisions that promoted a particular set of social changes.

Sociologists are both subject to social change and are agents of social change. The simple act of generating new knowledge and understanding of how social systems operate changes society by providing a new level of societal self-reflection and social awareness. Of course, the more widely disseminated new sociological insights are, the greater the impact they are likely to have. Public sociology is an effort on the part of sociologists to generate social change by making sociological knowledge available to wider publics. The hope is that by understanding what unites us, what divides us, and how societies change, people will be empowered to direct social change in ways that enhance social justice, the expansion of human rights, the attainment of greater social equity, the preservation of the earth upon which we depend, and the improvement of human quality of life. For public sociologists, the whole point of doing sociology is to make the world a better place. That is, to make social change.

This book is the property of Oxford University Press.

What might motivate you to take part in collective action for social change?

8

Forces of Social Change

Jason Konefal

ocieties change. The United States today compared with just 20 years
ago, let alone 50 years ago, is quite different. Today, more people live in
urban areas than ever before. People are living longer. The number of
people getting college degrees is at an all-time high. Whereas people used to
be farmers or work in manufacturing, today the majority of people work in
the service sector. There is greater racial, ethnic, and gender equality in the
United States today than ever before. New technologies such as cell phones,
computers, and the Internet have changed how we work and live. Clearly, the
society of today is different from the society of yesterday. And the society of
tomorrow will be different from today's society.

Social change is usually thought of as a good thing. Indeed, many of the
previously mentioned changes have been positive in that they have led to improvements in the quality of life for people. However, sociologists argue that
social change is more complex and varied. On the one hand, the benefits of
social change may not be equally distributed in that some may benefit more
than others. For example, since 1980 economic policies have led to greater
class inequality in the United States. Thus, while wealthier Americans have
benefited from such policies, the majority of the population has benefited
very little if at all. On the other hand, social change may be negative. Take the
case of nuclear weapons. The invention of nuclear weapons can be viewed
as a negative development in that it has created the possibility for society's
annihilation.

In fact, viewing social change as positive or negative oversimplifies the
possibilities, as it often has both positive and negative effects. Genetic technologies are an excellent example of how new technologies have both benefits and drawbacks. Genetic technologies offer the promise to reengineer
plants and animals and thus may make it more possible to feed the world.
However, such technologies also may create new environmental problems,
have unknown health effects, and extend corporate control of food. In addition, whether social change is positive or negative is often in the eye of the
beholder. Returning to the previous economic example, for a small handful,
the economic developments of the last several decades are clearly a positive
form of social change, whereas for the majority of others they are not.

The sociological imagination impels sociologists to examine the social
and historical contexts that affect people's everyday lives. In this chapter,

the sociological imagination is used to help understand social change. Social change is the process through which culture, institutions, social structure, and how people interact are transformed. Specifically, this chapter addresses the following big sociological questions: (1) Why do societies change, and (2) how do societies change? These questions have been central to sociology since its founding. And, as you will see in the following discussion, sociologists do not always agree in answering these important questions.

How do sociologists study social change? By examining the actors involved and the processes by which social change takes place. To do this, sociologists use multiple methods and a variety of data. Qualitative, quantitative, and historical methods are all used to study social change. Data may come from interviews, observation, surveys, historical documents, and the media. For example, some sociologists examine historical documents to better understand earlier examples of social change, like the Industrial Revolution. Other sociologists conduct interviews with people today and partake in participant-observation to understand current processes of social change.

Why should you care about social change and how it takes place? Quite simply, because it affects you! If you are not white, male, and wealthy, you are, in part, reading this book thanks to changes that took place in US society over the last 100 years. In other words, many of us have the opportunities we do today because of the efforts of previous generations. For example, social movements, such as the civil rights movement and feminist movement, have played integral roles in increasing racial and gender equality in the United States. Sometimes the effects of social change are felt directly and immediately. For instance, when the economy goes into a recession there is a loss of jobs. This affects the day-to-day lives of many people. In other cases, the effects may not be felt directly or until some future date. Whereas changes in public policies may not impact you now, they may affect your ability to get a job, buy a house, afford health care, and retire in the future. Lastly, there is one more important reason why you should care about social change and the way it takes place. Understanding how societies change is potentially empowering in that it demonstrates that actions by people can make a difference and that different orderings of society are possible.

The remaining portions of this lesson are organized as follows. First, two general sociological models of social change are presented. They are the evolutionary and dialectical models. Second, key insights from structural, interaction, and poststructural theories that pertain to social change are discussed. Third, those actors that bring about social change are examined. They include the state, corporations, experts, and social movements. Fourth, using nested analysis, examples of social change in action are provided. Lastly, discussion questions and lesson take-aways are presented that encourage you to consider the ideas and information provided in this lesson and social change generally.

TWO UNDERSTANDINGS OF SOCIAL CHANGE

There are two general models of social change in sociology. The first position conceptualizes social change as an evolutionary process. From this perspective, social change is understood as a continual process of adaptation to changes taking place in society and the environment. The second model of social change is the dialectical model. In this model, social change is the outcome of conflict between different actors and its resolution. Whereas social change functions to maintain the stability of society in the evolutionary model, in the dialectical model social change can either be adaptive or transformative. The main tenets of each of these models are briefly sketched out in the following sections.

Evolutionary Model

The **evolutionary model of social change** has its roots in the work of Emile Durkheim. At the core of Durkheim's sociology was the idea that society was a social organism. Just like the parts of bodies contribute to the healthiness of the body, Durkheim theorized that the parts of society contributed to the stability of society. For example, culture functions to provide people with common values, the economy to meet needs, and the government to provide security. Congruent with his understanding of society as a social organism, Durkheim conceptualized social change as an evolutionary process.

Durkheim most clearly developed a theory of social change in his work on the growing division of labor in society. In *The Division of Labor in Society,* Durkheim ([1893] 1984) theorized the increasing specialization of society as a response to changes in the social environment. Specifically, he presented specialization as beginning with population growth, which produced urbanization, which led to increased competition for jobs. Thus, specialization enabled society to accommodate changes resulting from population growth. In short, for Durkheim, the growing complexity of the division of labor was the result of society adapting to changes in its social environment. In this way, Durkheim theorized social change as a mechanism for the maintenance of social stability.

Durkheim's ideas became the basis of structural functional theory, which emerged in the United States in the 1950s. In brief, structural functionalism posited that the parts of society functioned to maintain the stability of society. For example, families functioned to ensure reproduction; the economy to provide people with incomes and the goods that they needed; and education to provide people with knowledge and skills. Similar to Durkheim, for functionalists, social change was understood as a process of society adapting to changing conditions. On the one hand, society changed to eliminate things that were dysfunctional (i.e., things that undermined the stability of society), such as racial inequality. On the other hand, society changed to accommodate new needs, such as increasing ethnic and religious diversity. Thus, for functionalists, the twin processes of "differentiation" and "integration" characterized social change. That is, new institutions were developed to accommodate new needs, and over time such new institutions would become integrated to the general values of the larger society. The outcome was the "adaptive upgrading" of society (Parsons 1971).

Take the example of racial inequality in the United States. Functionalists understood mid-twentieth century racial inequality as a problem of integration. The formation of civil rights groups represented the development of new institutions to meet the needs of African Americans. Racial equality was then a question of generalizing US values of equality to African Americans. For this to occur, the subsystems of society (e.g., political, economic, and social) would have to be brought into alignment with US cultural values. Among other things, this meant that such subsystems should be based on achieved and not ascribed characteristics. Put differently, racial equality entailed the extension of the rights of white citizens to African Americans. From a functionalist perspective, this was accomplished through getting rid of formal segregation in the military, education, and economy, among other places.

In sum, the functionalist model postulates that social change is an evolutionary process that is characterized by differentiation and inclusion. Thus, for functionalists, social change is a process of integration as opposed to transformation. The result is that social change functions to maintain the stability of society. Furthermore, social change is understood as a process of adaptive upgrading in that it leads to higher levels of development. Hence, social change entails a movement from "primitive" to "modern" societies.

While it provided a number of useful insights, structural-functional theory has been widely critiqued and is no longer a prominent theory in sociology. As to its conceptualization of social change, three primary shortcomings have been identified. First, where are the actors? In the evolutionary model of social change, there is little role for people, groups, governments, corporations, and others. That is, functional theory does not account for **agency** (i.e., the ability for people to act). Second, the functionalist model of social change is normative in that it presupposes social change as positive. In other words, there is little room for analysis of the uneven impacts of social change and the ways that social change may have negative impacts for society. Lastly, the evolutionary model fails to examine changes that do not integrate but transform. For example, there is no space in functionalist theory for such social movements as women and gay rights, economic justice, radical environmentalism, and white supremacy, which seek to transform society. Nevertheless, understanding functionalist theory and its model of evolutionary change is important because they continue to influence understandings of social change as well as public policy. In part, this is because the evolutionary model tends to justify the status quo, and thus it legitimates the current order of society.

Dialectical Model

The roots of critical understanding of social change are located in the theories of Karl Marx. Marx understood society as characterized by contradictions,

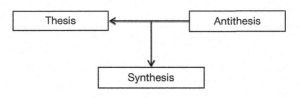

Figure 8–1 Dialectical Model of Social Change.

and it was in the working out of contradictions that society changed. Most notably, he theorized that the competitive forces in capitalism impelled owners to exploit workers. Over time, the result would be an increasingly small number of owners who controlled most of society's wealth, and a large number of workers who had very little. Marx theorized that a point would come where the workers would band together (i.e., form unions) to challenge both the owners and the larger system of capitalism. If successful, the outcome would be social change in the direction of a more egalitarian society (Marx and Engels [1848] 1998).

In contrast to the functionalist model previously discussed, Marx developed a **dialectical model of social change** (see Figure 8–1). A dialectical model of social change consists of three parts. The first is the thesis, which is the existing structure and relations in society. The second is the antithesis, which is an oppositional force that emerges to contest the thesis. The third component is the synthesis, which is the outcome of the conflict between the thesis and antithesis. The synthesis becomes the new thesis once the conflict is settled. A key insight of the dialectical model is that the synthesis is a combination of thesis and antithesis. In other words, neither side tends to get everything it wants.

Applying the dialectical model to the case of racial equality in mid-twentieth century America, the thesis would be the institutionalized system of racial inequality in the South. The antithesis would be the civil rights movement. The synthesis would be the elimination of formal racial inequality but the continuation of many informal forms of racial discrimination. Thus, in contrast to the evolutionary model of social change, the outcome is not integration but a transformation of society. Put differently, social change does not just involve the assimilation of marginalized groups into the dominant culture but also changes the dominant culture and structure of society. Therefore, racial equality entails not just the inclusion of African Americans as equals but also the inclusion of aspects of African-American culture in the dominant culture and institutional restructuring to eliminate discriminatory practices.

In addition to conceptualizing social change as transformative, the dialectical model differs from the functionalist model in three additional ways. First, the dialectical model focuses attention on the process of social change. In other words, change does not just happen; it needs to be brought about by people and groups. In the case of the elimination of formal racial segrega-tion in the United States, social change happened because large numbers of people organized and took action, such as marches, sit-ins, speeches, voter registration drives, and boycotts. As civil rights groups faced resistance, the dialectical model also draws attention to how social change is often charac-terized by conflict, as it tends to entail changes in power relations and the distribution of resources. Second, the dialectal model has no normative com-ponent to it. Unlike the evolutionary model, social change is not assumed to be better than the previous ordering of society in the dialectical model. Third, the dialectical model does not conceptualize social change as deter-ministic. That is, there is no preset pattern by which society develops. Rather, social change is an emergent phenomenon, which is dependent on relations between actors.

THEORETICAL INSIGHTS

While the previous models of social change are squarely situated in spe-cific theoretical traditions, other sociological theories offer insights into the merits of each model as well as social change more generally. The following sections briefly review three sets of sociological theories as they pertain to social change: structural, interaction, and poststructural theories. Structural theories focus attention on how the structure of society influences social change. Interaction theories highlight the ways that people interacting can either maintain or change society and the importance of collective under-standing. Lastly, poststructural theories draw attention to the ways that knowledge and its production affect social change.

Structural Theories

Structural theories are macro theories in that they focus on how the structure of society and institutions enable and constrain people and their actions. The roots of such theories date back to Marx ([1852] 2000), who observed that "men make their own history, but they do not make it just as they please" (329). Marx simply meant that the structure of society affects people's options. For him, what was most important was a person's position in the economy. That is, whether they were workers or owners. For example, for workers, their ability to act was constrained by their position as wage-laborers. As wage-laborers, Marx theorized that workers only got paid enough to reproduce themselves, worked under alienating conditions, and were nearly powerless in the workplace. Consequently, without banding together, they had little power over their day-to-day lives or their work.

Writing not long after Marx, Max Weber extended many of Marx's in-sights to noneconomic domains. Specifically, he theorized that the in-creasing tendency of society to be organized in a rules-based manner (i.e., formal rationality) was creating an "iron cage" (Weber [1905] 2010). In other words, society was becoming rationally ordered to the extent that there was increasingly less space for such things as creativity and originality. Recently, Ritzer (2010) has extended Weber's arguments with the idea of "McDonaldization." Ritzer argues that society is coming to resemble McDonalds in that it is more and more organized according to the criteria of efficiency, predictability, and quantification. For example, this is increasingly taking place in education with the growth of standardized curricula and testing. The effect is the dehumanization and depersonification of society. According to Ritzer, the outcome is a society where possibilities for social change are increasingly constrained, as there is little incentive for critical thought or creativity.

Interaction Theories

At the core of micro-level interactionist theories, such as symbolic interaction and ethnomethodology, is the notion that humans, through interacting, construct and maintain society (Blumer 1969; Garfinkel 1967). In other words, society is an outcome of interaction and only continues to exist as long as people continue to perform their roles. However, in many instances, people's performance and interactions are scripted. As such, they are performing the roles designated to them by society and its institutions. For example, Judith Butler (1990) argues that people tend to "do gender" in that for most men and women gender is a scripted performance in that they are simply adhering to predetermined gender roles. Consequently, most people do not question or even think about what it means to be masculine and feminine; they just do it. Thus, people's day-to-day interactions often function to maintain the status quo.

While they theorize that much of life is scripted, interactionist theories also focus attention on the power that people have to change society. If society is a performance that is maintained through interaction, this implies that people have the capability to change society. In other words, if people stopped following norms, this would lead to a breakdown in the current rules of society and the potential emergence of new rules. For example, in the American South prior to the passage of civil rights legislation, norms included African Americans riding at the back of the bus and eating at separate lunch counters. Crucial to the end of such segregation practices were people breaking the rules by not sitting and eating in their designated spots. Thus, interaction theories highlight the importance of **deviance** to social change. A person who is deviant is simply someone who breaks a norm. In intentionally or unintentionally breaking norms, people often are challenging a certain aspect of society and people's understanding of society. In doing so, they not only create opportunities for social change but also often face resistance, as the current debate about transgender people and bathroom choice illustrates.

Poststructural Theories

Poststructural social theories extend the purview of sociology to include knowledge and language. Specifically, poststructural sociologists are interested in questions of how we know what we know, how knowledge is legitimated, and the ways that knowledge affects human action. Michel Foucault (1995) observed that power and knowledge are linked. On the one hand, actors who have power largely control knowledge and its production. On the other hand, actors who have knowledge tend to have more power. Thus, laypeople are often excluded from scientific and technical decision-making, as they are considered unqualified. At the same time, experts tend to be privileged in such processes because of their specialized knowledge.

For social change, the implications of Foucault's argument are twofold. First, knowledge and power give some actors privileged positions. Thus, marginalized groups who want to contest some aspect of society must either find ways to legitimate their knowledge or rely on experts to legitimate their position. Second, if current knowledge is utilized to formulate alternatives, then the kinds of changes that are achievable are limited. According to Foucault, this is because in using established knowledge they are using the ideas of the powerful, which function to maintain the status quo. Thus, from a poststructural perspective, individuals or groups that challenge the order of society are contesting not just power relations but also the knowledge on which those power relations rest.

SOCIAL CHANGE: THE ACTORS

In examining society, sociologists focus on the actors and the practices that they use to try and change society. While many actors affect social change, sociologists have identified four primary actors as drivers of social change. They are the state, corporations, social movements, and experts. The role each actor plays in social change is examined in the following sections.

State

The state, or government, is a key actor in social change. The most notable way that the state affects social change is through enacting laws. Historically, states have passed many laws that have resulted in social change. For example, the passage of the National Labor Relations Act in 1935 legalized **collective bargaining** by workers in the United States. This resulted in changes in the workplace, between workers and owners, and in the lives of many workers. The state can also affect social change through how they decide to implement and enforce certain policies. For instance, the state can support workers against hostile owners in their right to collectively bargain, or they can do nothing. Similarly, at times, the state has actively enforced environmental laws and, at other times, has looked the other way. Lastly, the state may undertake actions that lead to social change, such as war.

Sociologists have shown that a key function of the state is for it to repro-duce itself or maintain its authority. To do this, the state needs to fulfill two primary functions: accumulation and legitimation (Habermas 1973). Accu-mulation means that the state needs to create conditions that foster economic growth. In other words, a primary function of states is to implement policies and construct infrastructure that facilitate economic growth. Legitimation refers to the need for the state to ensure it has the general support of the people. For the state, this entails ensuring its citizens' benefit from economic growth, protecting basic rights, providing services (e.g., education), and reg-ulating culture, among other things. In short, the legitimation function of the state entails ensuring the public good.

Sociologists have pointed out that these two functions—accumulation and legitimation—are often in conflict in contemporary society. That is, fostering accumulation often entails actions that may undermine a state's legitima-tion, and vice versa. For example, beginning with the New Deal in the 1930s up until the late 1970s, the United States had what is referred to as a social welfare state. In a social welfare state, the government plays an active role in ensuring the public good. Consequently, it is during this era that consider-able legislation favorable to workers, civil rights legislation, and environ-mental laws were passed. While this legislation reflected the interests of a majority of Americans and thus functioned to legitimate the state, much of it also impinged on accumulation. For instance, both labor and environmental laws are often blamed for increasing the cost of doing business in the United States. As such, they are often portrayed as a driving force behind companies moving operations overseas. There has also been a concerted effort over the last 30 years by corporations to shift the state back toward policies that are more business-friendly. Hence, there has been a shift by the US government away from social welfare policies toward neoliberal policies, which promote less government intervention in society. Among other things, this has led to deepening class inequality and social polarization and a consequent revival of class-based politics in the United States. The most visible example is the Occupy Movement and its slogan of "the 99 percent versus 1 percent," which called attention to how the state has prioritized accumulation over the public good. Thus, while the state often enacts laws and undertakes actions to pre-serve its authority, other actors are influential as to the content of such laws and actions.

Corporations

Today, the economy is one of the most important institutions in the United States and globally. Corporations are the most powerful economic actors, as they have significant resources and often operate across the world. For ex-ample, the top 10 US companies—all of which have operations in multiple countries—had revenues of over $2 trillion in 2015 (see Table 8–1). In addition, examining the profitability of these companies, it becomes clear that they have tremendous resources at their disposal, more than most other actors

FOOD FOR THOUGHT
THE FIGHT FOR $15: ORGANIZING FOR A LIVING WAGE
Justin Sean Myers

In 2014 1.3 million people earned the federal minimum wage of $7.25 and 20.7 million people earned less than $10.10 an hour. Many of them work in the restaurant and food service industries, which is the single biggest industry relying on low-wage employment. No matter whether you earn the minimum wage or a near minimum wage, it is a poverty-level wage. If you earn $7.25 an hour and work 40 hours a week all year round with no time off, your take home pay before taxes is $15,080. If you earned $10.10 an hour your income was $21,008. As a result, people working at the bottom rung of the economic ladder suffer from social, economic, and physiological burdens that no one should face, including the inability to pay rent, own and maintain a working automobile, and put food on the table. They don't have enough money to save for a rainy day let alone for vacation or retirement. Many of them are so poor they qualify for public housing, food stamps, and subsidized utility bills. Such a life tends to contribute to sleep deprivation, high levels of stress and anxiety, and higher rates of ill-health and premature death than more affluent people.

In short, you can't talk about poverty and inequality in the United States today without discussing the inability of the minimum wage and near-minimum wage to feed a family. While the minimum wage has never been a living wage, it's economic worth used to be much higher. The real value of the minimum wage peaked in 1968 when it stood at 99 percent of the poverty level for a family of two adults and two children. Since then the real value of the minimum wage has declined significantly and hovered around 60 percent of the poverty level, largely as a result of conservatives, corporations, and business lobbies fighting to keep wages low to keep profits up. These bleak conditions are not inevitable though, as has been evident with the mobilization and organization of low-wage workers and the emergence of the Fight for $15 (http://fightfor15.org/).

On November 29, 2012 fast-food workers across New York City staged a one-day strike to fight for better working conditions, higher wages, and the right to form and join unions. This event would be the first of a rolling series of walkouts and one-day strikes that continues to this day and has reshaped the national dialogue around how to combat poverty not through cheap goods from China or cutting taxes on the wealthy but through raising the minimum wage. The November event was repeated on July 29, 2013 and September 4, 2014 with thousands of workers engaging in walk outs to protest low wages. The September event was significant because it signaled a change in tactics for the movement, as employees didn't just walk out but engaged in more active forms of civil disobedience, including stopping automobile traffic and sitting on sidewalks. Alongside these actions, organizations affiliated with the movement, including the Service Employees International Union, had been pushing politicians at the municipal and state level to support legislation that would increase the minimum wage to $15. The focus was on raising the wage through direct action and legislation rather than unionization because legally many fast-food workers are considered employees of individual franchise owners rather than the corporate chains, which would necessitate organizing each restaurant one-by-one rather than a single companywide mobilization for unionization, which was not seen as an effective use of resources or politically viable. However, this all changed in August of 2014 when the National Labor Relations Board stated that employment and wage violations that occurred at McDonald's franchise locations were the responsibility of both franchise operators as well as McDonald's. This legal ruling sets a precedent that empowers the Fight for $15 and potentially opens the door to broader unionization attempts.

Since 2014 the movement has only grown in numbers, visibility, and power. That year marked the first time the movement expanded beyond fast-food workers to include child-care workers, airport workers, adjunct professors, Walmart workers, and home care assistants, among other low-wage workers. It was also the year that the City of Seattle passed legislation for a $15 minimum wage. Then, in 2015, the movement was given national exposure and support through the presidential campaign of Senator Bernie Sanders, who actively called for a $15 minimum wage and spoke about the Fight for $15 at his rallies. This visibility was followed in May 2016 with California and New York passing bills that will raise the minimum wage to $15 by 2021. This legislation will increase the salaries of more than one in three workers in both states, around 8.8 million people, by at least $4,000 a year. Many workers will see an increase closer to $10,000 a year. For these workers, this increase will not be enough to put them in the middle class, but it will be enough to enable them to quit their second or third job and generally lift them out of poverty.

The Fight for $15's success displays the tangible gains that can be achieved through a combination of direct action, coalition building, national media exposure, a political climate open to addressing inequality, strategic support by municipal and state politicians, and the benefits of national publicity via presidential campaigns. Since 2012, when the first strike occurred, 51 states and cities have raised their minimum wage rates and the struggle continues with a push to raise the federal minimum wage to $15. Beyond these immediate economic gains, the long-term effects of the movement lies in its ability to shift the national debate as well as public policy away from supply-side economics toward demand-side economics through emphasizing that a high-wage model is better at facilitating economic growth and more equitably distributing the benefits of that economic growth than the current low-wage/high-debt model.

Sources

Desilver, Drew. 2015. "5 Facts about the Minimum Wage." *FactTank*, August 5. http://www.pewresearch.org/fact-tank/2015/07/23/5-facts-about-the-minimum-wage/

Liu, Yvonne Yen and Dominique Apollon. 2011. *The Color of Food*. New York: Applied Research Center. http://arc.org/downloads/food_justice_021611_F.pdf

National Employment Law Project. 2016. *Fight for $15 Impact Report*. New York: National Employment Law Project. http://nelp.org/content/uploads/NELP-Fact-Sheet-Fight-for-15-Impact-Report.pdf

Tung, Irene, Yannet Lathrop, and Paul Sonn. 2015. *The Growing Movement for $15*. New York: National Employment Law Project. http://www.nelp.org/content/uploads/Growing-Movement-for-15-Dollars.pdf

Table 8–1 Ten Largest US Companies by Revenue, 2015

COMPANY	Revenues ($ millions)	Profit ($ millions)
Walmart	482,130	14,694
Exxon-Mobil	246,204	16,150
Apple	233,715	53,394
Berkshire Hathaway	210,821	24,083
McKesson	181,241	1,476
United Health Group	157,107	5,813
CVS	153,290	5,237
General Motors	152,356	9,687
Ford	149,558	7,373
AT&T	146,801	13,345

Source: www.fortune.com/fortune500.

and even many governments. Corporations use these resources to increase their profitability and, in doing so, often drive social change. Thus, whereas corporations are primarily concerned with the economy, their actions often affect other parts of society as well.

Corporations can bring about social change in a myriad of ways. On the one hand, corporations have developed a plethora of products and services that have changed society. For example, information technologies, such as smartphones, and social media, such as Facebook, Twitter, and Snapchat, have changed how people interact. Medical technologies have changed the process of aging. Changes in food products have affected eating and have had numerous implications, which include increasing rates of obesity. On the other hand, corporations have developed new production practices, which have resulted in social change. Perhaps most notable is the advent of mass production techniques, such as the assembly line and today the use of robots, which significantly affect how people work and live. In terms of work, mass production led to a general deskilling and the creation of alienating work experiences and today, with robots and automation, the loss of jobs altogether. However, such production practices have also enabled the production of more products at cheaper costs. This has made it possible for a greater portion of people to afford many kinds of goods.

In capitalist economies, sociologists and economists agree that the primary objective of corporations is to make money. This means that most actions undertaken by corporations are designed to increase their profitability. In many instances, such actions may lead to social change that benefits society. As previously noted, the drive to increase profitability has resulted in innovations that lower the costs of goods and new kinds of products that increase the quality of life. However, corporate practices can also lead to social change that undermines the public good or is harmful to a part of society.

Beginning with Marx, sociologists have noted the conflictual relationship between labor and business. That is, corporations tend to increase profitability through increased exploitation of workers. Among other things, this has led to significant gaps in pay between managers and workers and efforts by corporations to limit worker benefits and has contributed to the growth in class inequality in the United States over the past three decades. For example, for large corporations, CEO compensation has increased from 42 times the average worker pay in 1980 to approximately 303 times in 2014 (AFL-CIO 2011; Mishel and Davis 2015). Thus, while good for corporate profitability, workplace innovations and corporate restructuring (e.g., moving manufacturing operations to other countries) have largely not benefited American workers, whose wages have been mostly stagnant for the past three decades. Similarly, sociologists have noted that the drive by corporations to increase profitability tends to lead to increased environmental degradation (Schnaiberg and Gould 1994). In short, while corporations have been and continue to be important drivers of social change, they are driven by a narrow objective: making money.

Corporations have sought to exert their influence on society in a variety of ways. First, they seek to influence electoral politics and government policy through financing campaigns and lobbying. As the amount spent on lobbying indicates (see Tables 8–2 and 8–3), corporations clearly devote a significant amount of resources to influencing the state. Furthermore, with the 2010 Supreme Court ruling in the *Citizens United* case, corporate funding of electoral politics is now at an all-time high.

Second, corporations have established their own interest groups to promote their interests. The most prominent of which is the Chamber of Commerce, which promotes business interests generally. In addition, corporations have created sector-specific interests groups, such as the National Petroleum Council and the Pharmaceutical Research and Manufacturers of America. Third, corporations often provide funding to interests groups and think tanks that advocate for specific issues. For instance, over the past two decades a diverse array of corporations have provided funding to organizations opposed to the idea of global climate change. ExxonMobil alone has provided funding to over one hundred organizations that deny human-caused global climate change (Monbiot 2007). Fourth, some corporations

Table 8–2 Lobbying Spending by Industry from 1998–2016: Top Five

Industry	$ Spent on Lobbying
Pharmaceuticals/Health Products	3,395,880,031
Insurance	2,348,468,087
Electric Utilities	2,129,376,100
Business Associations	1,946,673,849
Electronics Mfg & Equip	1,940,503,766

Source: Center for Responsive Politics, www.opensecrets.com.

Table 8-3 Lobbying Spending by Company from 1998–2016: Top Five

Company	$ Spent on Lobbying
General Electric	342,000,000
Blue Cross/Blue Shield	283,584,849
Northup Grumman	238,252,213
Boeing	235,153,310
Exxon Mobil	226,102,742

Source: Center for Responsive Politics, www.opensecrets.com.

have established their own interests groups or think tanks. One form this has taken has been the creation of "Astroturf" organizations. This is the creation of what appear to be spontaneous grassroots organizations or disinterested think tanks. This strategy has been widely used by corporations to counter the environmental movement. For example, research shows that the "wise use" movement, which emerged in the American West in the 1980s and advocated for the opening of public lands to development, was largely created and funded by corporations (Beder 1997). Lastly, corporations often enroll or hire experts to advocate on behalf of them.

Social Movements

Social movements are a leading driver of social change in the world today. Typically, they emerge when concerns are not being addressed by the state. A social movement is defined by three characteristics (Diani 1992). First, it consists of networks of individuals and organizations. A social movement can vary in size from very large, such as the US environmental movement, which consists of a large number of organizations, to quite small. An example of a smaller social movement would be the white supremacy movement. Second, the organizations in the movement are involved in a conflict regarding part of society and thus want to change some aspect of society. The kinds of conflicts social movements can be engaged in can be political, economic, social, and cultural. Third, the individuals and organizations that are part of a social movement have a **shared identity**. This means that they are linked together by a common understanding of the problem or injustice, its causes, and the kinds of changes necessary. The process by which social movements define the problem and its solution is what researchers refer to as "framing" (Benford and Snow 2000).

Today, there are a plethora of social movements that address nearly every social issue and problem. This includes, economic, political, social, and cultural focused movements. A long-running concern of social movements has been economic issues, most notably the distribution of resources. Economic-oriented social movements tend to be class-based in that they represent the poor and working classes and tend to advocate for changes in the distribution of resources. Today, with increases in economic inequality in the United

States and economic survival remaining a paramount issue for many people in less industrialized countries, economic-oriented social movements continue to be widely found. In the United States, a recent movement focused on class issues was the Occupy Movement, which began as a spontaneous movement with a single protest in New York City on September 17, 2011 and spread to more than 1,400 US cities by the end of that fall. Under the banner of the "99 percent," the movement was a response to variety of class-based issues, including wage stagnation, corporate greed, crony capitalism, lack of job opportunities, and crippling personal debt.

A second kind of social movement with a long history is movements focused on political rights and democratization. There have been and continue to be social movements by oppressed groups for control over their political rights. For example, during the colonial period, in many colonized nations, social movements played a key role in decolonization. More recently, there was the Arab Spring movement in a number of Arab countries. These were massive popular uprisings calling for democratization, which led to dictators in Egypt, Tunisia, and Yemen being forced to relinquish power. In addition, within democratic countries, political rights and democratization continue to be important issues. In the United States today, there are a variety of movements focused on issues of campaign finance and voting practices (e.g., voter requirements, redistricting, voting machines).

Following World War II, social movements concerned with social issues, culture, and minority rights began to emerge. Some of the more prominent examples of such movements include the civil rights movement, women's movement, gay rights movement, and environmental movement. Today, cultural issues and rights, such as gay, gun, and reproductive rights, are among the most controversial, debated, and contested issues in the United States. Consequently, there are numerous social movements organized around such issues, both in favor and against changes in such rights. Lastly, an increasing number of contemporary movements are multifaceted in that they simultaneously focus on a combination of economic, cultural, political, or environmental issues. The economic justice movement, which emerged in the 1990s in responses to globalization, exemplifies such a movement in that its aim is a world that is more economically just, environmental sustainable, democratic, and multicultural.

Two organizational models have developed among social movements: professional and participation. Each model tends to use different practices to frame problems and their solutions, mobilize people, and undertake actions. In addition, to accomplish these tasks, social movements need resources, most notably money, people's time, and expertise. Thus, a key task of social movements is procuring resources, which also varies between the two models (McCarthy and Zald 1977). In the professional model, social movement organizations are managed by professional staff, which consists of paid employees. Such organizations tend to procure resources through donations, membership dues, and foundation funding. Professional organizations tend to have passive memberships in that members are not involved in day-to-day activities or movement actions. In some instances, professional organizations will have no memberships. Social movements organizations that focus on national or global issues tend to be organized according to the professional model. Examples of professional social movement organizations include large unions like the American Federation of Labor and Congress of Industrial Organizations (AFL-CIO), and many large environmental groups, such as the World Wild Fund for Nature and the Environmental Defense Fund.

The second model is the participant model. In this model, organizations are primarily made-up of volunteers who donate their time. While participant-modeled organizations often engage in fundraising, it tends to include more personalized activities, such as door-to-door canvassing. The participant model tends to apply more to local and grassroots groups. In addition, whereas professional organizations tend to rely on money to fund paid staff, for local and grassroots organizations, people's time is often a more important resource. Examples of participant modeled groups include the Occupy Movement and most college-based advocacy organizations, such as campus environmental organizations, chapters of United Students against Sweatshops, and lesbian, and gay, bisexual, transgender, and queer (LGBTQ) student organizations.

It needs to be noted that these models are ideal types in that many social movement organizations encompass characteristics of both the professional and participant models. On the one hand, large global or national professional organizations may have local chapters that are primarily participant-based. On the other hand, local groups may have small paid staff and use direct mailings to raise funds.

Social movement organizations use three kinds of tactics to achieve their goals: **routine politics, contentious politics**, and **market politics**. Routine politics is the use of legitimate political practices, such as voting and lobbying. In using routine politics, social movement organizations are trying to pressure the state to enact legislation. Historically, routine politics has been a key strategy used by social movements in the United States and today, most social movements continue to devote significant resources to such strategies. Contentious politics refers to the use of tactics that are not sanctioned by the state. Such tactics includes forms of civil disobedience (e.g., marches, sit-ins, and blockades), advertising, monkey-wrenching (e.g., property destruction), and violent actions (e.g., armed conflict and bombings). Typically, social movements turn to contentious politics when routine politics is closed off to them or they are unsuccessful in the use of routine politics. The use of contentious tactics by social movements has been quite common. For example, a central strategy of the civil rights movement was civil disobedience, while the Occupy Movement used "encampments" in which they reclaimed public spaces.

The third tactic used by social movements is market politics. Market politics is where social movement organizations use the marketplace to try to pressure corporations. While social movements have used market politics, such as boycotts, for quite some time, its use has become more common in the past decade. In addition to the use of boycotts, social movements are now using "buycotts" (i.e., promoting the purchase of certain products), pressuring larger buyers to carry or not carry certain products or implement certain standards, the creation of private labels (e.g., fair trade and sustainable), and the targeting of branded companies, such as Nike.

Most movements use some combination of the three tactics. For example, the antiabortion, or pro-life, movement uses routine politics in that it pressures government to pass legislation limiting abortions. It engages in contentious politics in that it holds protests in front of abortion clinics. Lastly, it has also utilized violent tactics in that some of its activists have bombed abortion clinics and shot doctors that provide abortions. Social movements will pick and choose from the repertoire of possible tactics and strategically use those that they think gives them the best chance of achieving their goals. In addition, with time, movement organizations may shift their choice of tactics depending on a variety of factors. Specifically, the opportunities approach in social movement research examines how external factors, such as the structure and practices of the political system and economy, influence the choice of strategies by movement organizations (McAdam 1999).

Experts

Experts have been important actors in social change. An expert is someone who possesses specialized knowledge that the ordinary person does not have. Some of the more prominent experts in contemporary society include scientists, religious leaders, and professionals, such as doctors and lawyers. Experts change society in two ways. First, experts, particularly scientists, often develop new ideas as to how the parts of society should function. For instance, new economic theories by economists have led to changes in the structure and practices of economies. Similarly, new findings by scientists often lead to new understandings of society, which may lead to social change. For example, the publication of *Silent Spring* in 1962 by Rachel Carson (2002) is commonly considered one of the formative events of the US environmental movement. Carson was a zoologist by training who was long interested in issues of nature and conservation. In *Silent Spring*, Carson linked DDT, which at the time was a pesticide widely used in agriculture and to control insects more generally, to disease and death in animals and possible human health complications. Despite a strong countercampaign by industry, *Silent Spring* raised public awareness regarding chemical use and helped to expand environmentalism from a handful of organizations to a full-fledged movement.

Second, during controversies, experts are often called upon to provide input. On the one hand, as they have specialized knowledge, it is assumed that they can provide information that may help resolve controversies. On the other hand, experts are often viewed as disinterested observers. As such, they are viewed as having the ability to objectively evaluate a controversy, unlike those who are involved. Consequently, experts are often called before Congress to testify and commonly serve as key witnesses in judicial hearings.

The result is that experts often have more input in decision-making, and thus they play an influential role in social change.

SOCIAL CHANGE IN ACTION

This section examines social change in action. That is, it presents examples of social change and how it comes about. Using nested analysis, social change is examined at different sociospatial scales beginning with the local and working through the global. As will become clear in the following discussion, nested analysis of social change is somewhat difficult, because social change often simultaneously involves actions at multiple levels. Thus, while each section focuses on a particular sociospatial scale, it is important to note that complementary processes are often occurring at other scales.

THE INDIVIDUAL LEVEL

Individuals are important actors in social change. As interactionist theories note, individuals have the ability to change society through their actions. However, for sociologists, while individuals are integral to social change, they do not change society by themselves. Rather, it is the role that individuals play in groups and organizations and how individuals may influence groups and organizations that is of interest to sociologists. For example, while politicians can affect social change, they primarily can do this because of the institution that they are part of, namely the state. To illustrate how individuals can affect social change, the options that individuals have when faced with injustices or when they want to support specific causes are examined. Two options in particular are highlighted. First, people can participate in a social movement. Second, in some instances, people can express their views through their consumption habits. Each of these is subsequently discussed.

Individuals and Social Movements

People are a vital component of social movements. Ultimately, the power of social movements rests on their ability to get people to act. People can play two roles in movements: leaders and participants. In some instances, such as the Occupy Wall Street Movement and Black Lives Matter, movements are largely leaderless and decision-making is diffused and collective. However, in most movements leaders are quite important: "They inspire commitment, mobilize resources, create and recognize opportunities, devise strategies, frame demands, and influence outcomes" (Morris and Staggenborg 2004, 171). Key to the early success of the farm workers movement was Caesar Chavez's charismatic character and his consequent ability to mobilize farm workers. Similarly, a key contribution of Martin Luther King Jr. was his ability to powerfully articulate the experiences, feelings, and injustices of African Americans. In addition to such public faces, social movements also tend to have behind the scene leaders. One example is emotional leaders, which are integral in providing day-to-day support to movement participants (Robnett 1997).

The other role of individuals in social movements is that of participants. While leaders are crucial, everyday individuals also play vital roles in social movements, particularly those movements where the participant model is more common. In participant organizations, such as local and grassroots organizations, it is typically volunteers who keep the organization running day to day and undertake movement actions (e.g., protests, marches, gathering petition signatures). For national- or global-focused movements, individual participation is also important. In particular, movement organizations need to be able to mobilize supporters to partake in actions. Thus, participation by individuals is crucial to the success of social movements.

Lastly, it needs to be noted that for people, participation in a social movement can be a transformative experience in itself. William Gamson (1992) observes "participation in social movements frequently involves an enlargement of personal identity for participants and offers fulfillment and realization of self" (56). In short, participation in a movement is often transformative, liberating, and empowering. In the following section on local action, this is seen in the example of Lois Gibbs, who was transformed from a housewife to political activist as a result of her participation in trying to get herself and her neighbors relocated from a toxic environment. In this way, even if they are not successful in achieving their immediate objectives, social movements can generate forces of social change through creating an empowered citizenry.

Social Change and Shopping

Today, walk into almost any supermarket in America and you will find organic milk prominently featured in the dairy section. Not all that long ago this would not be the case. What happened? How did organic milk go from almost nonexistent to among the best-selling organic foods in just over a decade? DuPuis (2000) notes that "consumer demand for organic milk arose without the significant social and political organizing that created the organic food system over the last few decades" (286). In short, it appears that organic milk is the outcome of consumer demand. More explicitly, organic milk is in nearly every supermarket because individuals, reacting to the perceived riskiness of conventional milk, demanded it. The implication is that individuals are capable of producing social change through their shopping practices.

However, can we really shop our way to social change? Currently, there is significant debate in sociology regarding the power of consumption to change society. On the one hand, some sociologist see consumption as a

SOCIOLOGY AT WORK
WORK AND SOCIAL CHANGE: FROM MANUFACTURING TO SERVICES
Arne L. Kalleberg

International Business Machines Company (IBM) is one of the largest corporations based in the United States. Founded in the nineteenth century, IBM is best known for manufacturing and selling mainframe computers, electric typewriters, and personal computers. In the early 1990s, however, IBM shifted from a hardware company to a software company; it now makes most of its profits from selling software and computer services. Similarly, General Electric Company (GE)—founded by Thomas Alva Edison, the inventor of the light bulb and many other things—used to manufacture a wide range of products from engines to medical equipment. Now it earns most of its profits from financial and other services.

These shifts in IBM's and GE's corporate strategies reflects a fundamental social change in the evolution of work in modern societies, the shift from manufacturing to service industries. In 1960, almost a third (28 percent) of the US labor force worked in manufacturing; in 2010, manufacturing employed only about 10 percent of the labor force ("The iPhone Economy" 2012). The biggest private company in the United States in 1960 was General Motors, which manufactured automobiles and employed nearly 600,000 workers. In 2010, the biggest private US-based company was Walmart, the retail giant that employed over two million workers. The second largest company in 2010 was Kelly Services, the temporary help agency.

Manufacturing industries involve making tangible things of various kinds, both durable goods, such as automobiles and refrigerators, and nondurable (or consumable) goods, such as food. By contrast, service industries create a wide variety of things that are done in return for payment, such as educational experiences, musical concerts, medical care, and tax advice. Nations that are dominated by manufacturing industries are called "industrial" countries, while those dominated by service industries are referred to as "postindustrial" societies. Technological advances such as automation make it possible for companies to produce goods more efficiently and with fewer workers, which leads to a decline in the percentage of people who work in manufacturing industries. For example, there are fewer automobile workers now because robots play an increasingly important role in putting together cars on the assembly line.

The shift from an industrial, or manufacturing-dominated, to a postindustrial society, or service-dominated, economy has important implications for the kinds of jobs that people have in these societies. Blue-collar workers who work with machines dominate manufacturing industries; such occupations typically do not require college degrees, as the skills they need are often learned in vocational schools or on-the-job. Service industries, by contrast, involve *both* very highly skilled workers (those in professional occupations such as teachers, lawyers, and doctors, who have a lot of education and knowledge) as well as low-skilled workers (those who work in retail stores such as Walmart or as temporary workers in clerical jobs). This distinction between high- and low-skilled jobs in service economies underscores the importance of education as a way of obtaining good jobs and avoiding bad jobs.

Sources
"The iPhone Economy." 2012. *New York Times*, January 21.

powerful practice by which people can express their preferences and values. Proponents of **political consumerism** argue that consumption is "an organizing relation" in that it potentially can be used to change society (Micheletti 2004). If one examines the increasing array of products with social and ethical attributes, such as fair trade, organic, sustainable, sweatshop-free, and local, among many others, it appears that consumers are affecting the market and how things are produced. In addition, to aid consumers in making ethical choices, a variety of apps and websites are now available that provide ethical and environmental product ratings, such as the GoodGuide (www .goodguide.com).

On the other hand, some sociologists view the ability of individuals to change society through consumption as quite limited. There are two general concerns. First, there is the question of the power of consumers compared to corporations. In other words, consumers, who tend to be relatively unorganized, are often viewed as less powerful than corporations, which have more resources. For example, DuPuis (2000) notes that organic milk is also so prevalent because producers and retailers realized it was profitable. In other words, did organic milk emerge because consumers demanded it or because corporations viewed it as profitable?

Second, some sociologists have begun to question the kinds of social change that may result from political consumerism. In *Shopping Our Way to Safety*, Andrew Szasz (2007) observes:

> A person who, say, drinks bottled water or uses natural deodorant or buys only clothing made of natural fiber is not trying to change anything. All they are doing is trying to barricade themselves, individually, from toxic threat, trying to shield themselves from it. Act jointly with others? Try to change things? Make history? No, no.(4)

In other words, Szasz argues that consumption is not a collective activity, and while it may lead to more options, it does not produce social change. Using the example of unsafe drinking water, Szasz argues that people can either organize and partake in collective action to reform the public water system or buy bottled water. The former, Szasz contends, leads to social change as the public water system is reformed, and thus all users benefit. The latter does not lead to social change, as the substandard public water system remains and those that cannot afford bottled water have to continue to rely on it. Put differently, people can make water into what Mill's referred to as a "public issue" by organizing collectively or treat it as a "personal trouble" by responding individually. The latter, Szasz contends, potentially may produce socially regressive forms of social change in that access to public goods such as clean water may become increasingly a class-based commodity. And, as the recent case of lead-contaminated water in Flint, Michigan, a predominantly poor African-American community, indicates, access to safe drinking water is not guaranteed for poor communities in America today.

THE LOCAL LEVEL

The local level is where the effects of injustice or problems are often first felt. Hence, demands for social change often emanate from the local or community level. One of the richest areas of local action in recent decades has been community-based environmentalism. Industrial and agriculture processes have created significant pollution. The question of what do with such pollution has been and continues to be a vexing question for America. At the same time, a lack of environmental laws and weak enforcement have often allowed for disposal practices that degrade the environment and threaten human health. This is evident in that many communities continue to have air quality that does not consistently meet government regulations and water systems with elevated levels of contaminants. The pollution of many communities and the lack of government protection from such pollution spurred the emergence of community-based environmentalism across much of the United States beginning in the 1970s. The case of Love Canal is presented to illustrate how community activism works and how it can drive social change.

At first glance, Love Canal was a typical middle-class suburban neighborhood of approximately five hundred families that was located near Niagara Falls in western New York. However, it was built on a site previously owned by Hooker Chemicals, which had dumped more than 21,000 tons of chemical waste into the ground decades earlier. In 1952, Hooker covered the waste canal and sold the site to the town of Niagara Falls for $1. Soon thereafter a neighborhood was constructed on and around the site. The 99th Street elementary school was constructed almost directly over the waste canal where Hooker had disposed the bulk of their chemicals.

In the 1960s and 1970s, residents began to notice a black oily substance seeping into their basements, strong chemical odors, yards where grass and plants did not grow well, and what seemed to be an abnormal number of children with birth defects (Cable and Benson 1993). However, it was not until a previously nonpolitically active stay-at-home mom, Lois Gibbs, became alarmed enough to start asking questions, mobilizing neighbors, and confronting politicians that something happened (Gibbs 2011). Her son Michael had just started attending kindergarten at the 99th school when a series of articles was published in the Niagara Falls *Gazette* on how the school and neighborhood had been built on a site where potentially toxic chemicals were previously disposed. In fact, it was later discovered by residents of Love Canal that the original building plans of the school had to be modified when the contractors ran into chemicals while digging the foundation. These articles "panicked" Gibbs, as her son had started having seizures and his white blood cell count had fallen since starting school. She requested that her son be allowed to transfer schools at the start of the next school year, but the superintendent denied the request. Angry, she decided to go door to door in the area with a petition to allow parents to send their children to other schools. Reflecting back, she recalls being nervous, thinking to herself, "What am I doing here? I must be crazy. People are going to think I am" (Gibbs 2011, 30). Rather, she discovered that many of the people had similar concerns about the school and the neighborhood, and many related their own personal experiences of health problems.

An important event for the formation of a social movement response to the contamination of Love Canal was the recommendation by the New York State government that pregnant women and children under the age of two move out of the area. This led to significant outrage by many citizens, as the state did not commit to helping people relocate, and if the neighborhood was not safe for pregnant women and infants, how could it be safe for anyone else. In response, Gibbs and other concerned citizens decided to form the Love Canal Homeowners Association. At its initial meeting, which had over 550 people sign on as members, four goals were identified: (1) evacuation and relocation of all residents, (2) protecting property values, (3) properly fixing the canal, (4) and testing to determine the degree of pollution. The Homeowners Association quickly became the leading advocate for relocation and cleaning up Love Canal.

Receiving little cooperation from the state or federal government—and often hostility—the Homeowners Association undertook a variety of actions to achieve its goals. Aided by an independent scientist, residents collected their own data on contamination and its health effects in the area. While initially rejected because it was "put together by a bunch of housewives with an interest in the outcome" (Gibbs, 2011, 105), future data supported their findings. To raise public awareness and pressure public officials, the homeowners used symbolic and contentious tactics, including picketing the closed-off Hooker site, protests at public official visits to the area, speaking tours, and public demonstrations. One particularly effective example was the 1980 Democratic presidential election in which the Homeowners Association sent a busload of members to New York City as the "Love Canal Boat People." Referencing the Carter administration's aid to Cuban refugees, their signs and slogans stated: "President Carter, hear our plea—Set the Love Canal people free!" (Gibbs, 2011, 191).

Another particularly powerful action by the Homeowners Association was the spontaneous kidnapping of two Environmental Protection Agency officials. On May 19, 1980, the White House announced that it was not going to relocate the residents of Love Canal. Hundreds of residents began gathering in front of the Homeowners Association building in frustration and anger. With the group teetering on the edge of violence, Gibbs and the Homeowners Association held two Environmental Protection Agency officials hostage for the course of the day, until threatened by an FBI raid. The homeowners' persistence and effort paid off when on October 1, 1980—nearly four years after Gibbs first went door to door—President Carter signed a bill to evacuate all families from Love Canal. Over the next few years, over 1,500 families were relocated and a 350-acre area was closed off.

The case of Love Canal indicates several general characteristics of social change at the local level. First, social change that contests established processes often has to begin with everyday people. That is, everyday people have to initiate the process of identifying the problem and its causes and undertaking actions. For example, typically people cannot wait for scientists to tell them that environments are contaminated and that this is negatively impacting their health, because this may never happen. Rather, they have to first deduce this from their everyday experiences and then enroll experts to support their position. Second, the previous examples indicate that people cannot always count on the state to protect them. Consequently, community-based environmentalism has devoted considerable effort to just trying to get the state to enforce laws. Lastly, Love Canal and other instances of local action fostered the development of a national and global environmental health and justice movement. In other words, local actions can give rise to larger movements and more general concerns.

THE NATIONAL LEVEL: BLACK LIVES MATTER

While the United States has a long history of civil rights mobilization and activism, today there is a new wave of mobilization and activism around issues of racial discrimination. Spurred by violence against African Americans and facilitated by social media, a new movement for racial equality and justice has emerged: Black Lives Matter (BLM). The origins of BLM can be traced to the evening of George Zimmerman's acquittal for the shooting of Trayvon Martin in the Summer 2013. At the time of the decision, Alice Garza, a community activist in Oakland, California, was sitting in a bar. When the decision was announced, she recalls:

> Everything went quiet, everything and everyone. And then people started to leave en masse. . . . Seeing these black people leaving the bar, and it was like we couldn't look at each other. We were carrying this burden around with us every day: of racism and white supremacy. It was a verdict that said: black people are not safe in America. (Day 2015)

Following the decision, Garza posted a message on Facebook that ended with "Black people. I love you. I love us. Our lives matter" (Day 2015). Soon thereafter, Garza's friend Patrisse Cullors forwarded the message to friends and fellow activists with the hashtag: #BlackLivesMatter. Garza, Cullors, and a third activist, Opal Tometi, then established a series of social media sites for BLM and encouraged people to share their stories.

On August 9, 2014, approximately a year later, Michael Brown was shot dead by a police officer in Ferguson, Missouri. This was followed by a series of shootings and violent incidents against African Americans; most prominently, the police shooting of Tamir Rice (November 2014) and Walter Scott (April 2015), and the death of Freddie Gray (April 2015). Unlike shootings that predated Trayvon Martin's death, these incidents drew public attention, in part because of the BLM activists' use of social media. Using Facebook, Twitter, and Instagram, among other social media apps, BLM activists were able to publicize these incidents not only locally but nationally. Thus, in addition to sparking local protest, they were also able to demonstrate that violence against African Americans is a national problem.

Historically, national movements, such as the civil rights movement, required large institutional structures to coordinate multiple and ongoing actions and events. For example, in its effort to get rid of racial segregation in the American South, the civil rights movement needed offices and staff across the South. In addition, social movements in the United States have often been dependent on newspaper and television (i.e., old media) coverage to publicize their cause and spread information about their actions to the general population.

Today, movements do not need large institutional structures and media coverage to the extent that they did previously. BLM, as well as other recent movements, such as the Occupy Wall Street and Arab Spring movements, are using new forms of social media to bypass large organizational structures and the old media. With the advent of social media, a plethora of new opportunities has opened up for social movements. Stephen (2015) observes:

> If you're a civil rights activist in 2015 and you need to get some news out, your first move is to choose a platform. If you want to post a video of a protest or a violent arrest, you put it up on Vine, Instagram, or Periscope. If you want to avoid trolls or snooping authorities and you need to coordinate some kind of action, you might chat privately with other activists on GroupMe. If you want to rapidly mobilize a bunch of people you know and you don't want the whole world clued in, you use SMS or WhatsApp. If you want to mobilize a ton of people you might not know and you do want the whole world to talk about it: Twitter.

Activists in the BLM movement are using social media in two ways. First, they are using it to disperse information to the general population. In doing so, BLM activists are able to avoid the biases of traditional media both in terms of what they cover and how they cover it. We see this with uploaded cellphone footage of police violence, including Walter Scott getting shot repeatedly in the back by a police officer (https://vimeo.com/124336782) and Eric Garner in a chokehold repeatedly saying, "I can't breathe" (https://www.youtube.com/watch?v=JpGxagKOkv8). In the words of writer Darryl Pinckney (2016), "social media have removed the filters that used to protect white America from what it didn't want to see."

Second, social media has become an innovative tool used by activists to communicate and organize. For example, following the shooting of Brown, DeRay McKesson, a civil rights activists and part of BLM, said he realized that "we didn't need institutions to do it [movement building]" (Stephen 2015). Thus, what has emerged with BLM as well as other recent movements is a new organizational form that is much less bureaucratic than earlier social movements. Rather than having a hierarchical structure with established organizations and leaders, BLM more closely resembles a network. In other words, it consists of lots of autonomous groups and individuals that are connected, sometimes strongly and sometimes weakly, by a common cause (e.g., racial inequality and injustice). In the words of one BLM activist, the structure of the BLM movement is "decentralized but coordinated. There are no top–down mandates" (Stephen 2015).

Some commentators argue that BLM as well as Arab Spring and Occupy Wall Street signify a new form of social change—what they refer to as "horizontalism" (Mason 2013). These movements are characterized by strong democracy in that all members have a say in the movement. For example, in BLM there is "no Martin Luther King Jr. or Malcolm X, no single charismatic voice that claims to speak for many" (Day 2015). Such movements also seek to be strongly inclusive in that they embrace and incorporate diversity (e.g., gender, sexuality, and religious) into their aims and objectives.

Although horizontal social movements have the potential to build inclusive coalitions and democratize social change, it needs to be underscored that this new form of networked activism also faces significant challenges. On the one hand, the decentralized and democratic character of such movements may result in a splintering of the movement into disparate causes and priorities or individuals or groups appropriating the name of the movement for their own cause. The latter is seen in the emergence of the slogan and hashtag "All Lives Matter," which, from the perspective of BLM activists, undercuts their core claim that black lives have not mattered as much as white lives (Victor 2016). On the other hand, as the end of the Occupy Wall Street and Arab Spring movements illustrate, implementing the next step after the initial set of protests can be difficult. Neither movement has had much success in continuing to advocate for social change after their initial bursts of fury and mobilization.

Similar to the Occupy Wall Street and Arab Spring movements that preceded it, the BLM movement now faces the question of how it should move forward. Specifically, the movement faces the challenge of maintaining its horizontal network, and, at the same time, building durable organizations that can maintain the movement over time. Although it is still too early to assess the movement-building efforts of BLM, there are some initial indications that the movement has given rise to a new set of civil rights activist organizations. For example, there are now 27 BLM chapters in the United States (www.blacklivesmatter.com). While part of a national coalition, each chapter is autonomous and chooses its owns aims and actions. The BLM movement has also spurred the development of new activists organizations focused on specific racial issues, such as Mapping Police Violence, Black Youth Project 100, and the Dream Defenders (Day 2015).

While the fate of the BLM movement and the kinds of changes that may occur in the United States as a result of it are still very much unfolding, the effects of the movement already can be seen. It has been empowering to African Americans and black communities throughout the United States in that it has given them a platform and tools to share black vulnerability and injustice both internally as well as with Americans generally (Stephen 2015). It has brought race and policing issues into the public spotlight once again, and in doing so, it has seriously challenged the notion of color-blindness in America. It has helped to spawn investigations by the US Department of Justice into policing practices in several cities, including Ferguson and Baltimore. Consequently, reforms in policing practices are being implemented in those cities. Lastly, it has contributed to symbolic changes, such as the removal of the Confederate flag from the South Carolina capital and a vote by the Houston School Council to rename several schools named after Confederate leaders. In sum, with BLM and other recent movements, we maybe witnessing the emergence of a new form of social movement and social change.

THE GLOBAL LEVEL: CONSERVING RAINFORESTS

Increasingly, we live in a globalized world. For social change, a globalized world means that things that happen in one location, can affect people in other locations. For instance, while a small number of industrialized nations have emitted the overwhelming majority of carbon into the environment, climate change threatens people across the world. Globalization also means that people in one part of the world can influence events and practices in another part of the world. For example, today people and organizations concerned with environmental degradation, human rights, and gender equality are often not only concerned with these issues in their home countries but also across the world.

Governments, corporations, and experts have long been active in parts of the world besides their home countries. Governments have long sought to affect the policies and practices of other countries through war, colonization, foreign aid, and supranational political organizations (e.g., the United Nations and World Bank). Corporations have long operated internationally, and today nearly every major corporation is multinational in that it has operations in multiple countries. Since the beginning of modern science, experts have disseminated their findings internationally and have long advised foreign countries. More recently, the increase of global problems and global concerns has given rise to transnational social movements. One prominent form that global social movements have taken is transnational advocacy networks (TANs). Keck and Sikkink (1998) define a TAN as characterized by "the centrality of valued or principled ideas, the belief that people can make a difference, the creative use of information, and the employment of nongovernmental actors of sophisticated political strategies" (2).

One early prominent example of transnational activism is concern with tropical deforestation. Beginning in the 1970s, a small network of scientists and environmentalists began to be alarmed by tropical deforestation and called attention to it. Whereas tropical deforestation was not a concern as of the late 1960s, by 1974 leading environmental organizations were calling tropical rainforests "the most important nature conservation programme of the decade" (Keck and Sikkink 1998, 134). Beginning in the 1980s, a TAN began to coalesce around tropical deforestation when additional environmental and development organizations as well as local actors from the Amazon region joined the initial collection of scientists and environmental organizations. The formation of a TAN both diversified the actors involved in fighting against tropical deforestation as well as the kinds of strategies and tactics being used.

The initial efforts of tropical forest advocates in the 1970s focused on gathering data and providing information to policymaker in the hope that more rational forest policy plans would be enacted. In the 1980s, recognizing that the Brazilian government was unlikely to stem deforestation without external pressure, the TAN expanded their repertoire of approaches. First, deforestation was linked to development and movement organizations began to pressure the **World Bank** to take environmental considerations into their project planning. Campaigns directly targeting the bank and efforts to pressure the primary funders of the World Bank (i.e., industrialized countries) were used. For example, movement organizations lobbied the US Congress to attach environmental stipulations to its funding of the World Bank. One outcome of such actions was the creation of an environmental department in the World Bank that would evaluate the environmental impacts of World Bank-sponsored projects.

A second strategy of the tropical deforestation TAN was to politicize tropical deforestation. Movement actors used media campaigns and symbolic actions to draw the public's attention to tropical deforestation. A stirring image from television and magazine covers in the 1980s was huge swaths of the Amazon rainforest—the earth's "garden of Eden"—either burning or completely deforested. Movement organizations also sought to connect rainforest deforestation to people's everyday practices and particular corporations in the United States and Europe. The "hamburger connection" is an example of such a strategy. In this case, the consumption of beef, particularly hamburgers in fast-food restaurants, was framed as a driving force behind the clearing of the Amazon rainforest.

A third, and particularly important, aspect of the tropical deforestation TAN was the development of alliances with the rubber tappers and indigenous groups in the Amazon who were losing their livelihoods as a result of deforestation. One of the leaders of the rubber tappers was Chico Mendes. Beginning in the mid-1970s, Mendes and his fellow rubber tappers began to fight against the clearing of the Amazon and the loss of their livelihood through *empates,* or stand-offs. In an interview years later, Mendes reflects on the first empate in 1976:

> *I remember very well that day in 1976, when three rubber tappers came racing into town in great consternation because a hundred-man crew guarded by gunmen had started to clear their area of trees. For the first time*

ever we got together seventy men and women. We marched to the forest and joined hands to stop them from clearing (Hecht and Cockburn, 1989, 169).

The inclusion of the rubber tappers helped to legitimate the tropical deforestation TAN by countering the claim that "rainforest destruction was simply a concern of privileged northerners" (Keck and Sikkink 1998, 141). In other words, the plight of the rubber tappers put a human face on deforestation in that it connected environmental degradation and the loss of people's livelihoods. In December 1988, worldwide attention was focused on the Amazon and deforestation when a cattle rancher assassinated Chico Mendes.

Lastly, frustrated with the lack of progress in trying to get regulations enacted, the tropical deforestation TAN began to use market-based approaches in the late 1980s. Specifically, movement organizations began to pressure retailers that sold large quantities of tropical hardwoods. For example, they would try to expose Home Depot's role in tropical deforestation by filling their parking lots with inflatable chainsaws (Bartley 2003). These market campaigns created incentives for large retailers, such as Home Depot, to seek sustainable sources of tropical timber. Thus, in part, such campaigns made possible partnerships between environmentalists, retailers, and timber companies, which led to the establishment of the Forest Stewardship Council. The Forest Stewardship Council is an independent organization that was founded in 1993 that develops standards for sustainable forestry, which forests can be certified as complying with. Today market-based approaches have become a leading strategy for trying to conserve the Amazon and other tropical forests.

The tropical deforestation TAN has had mixed results. Tropical deforestation continues at fairly significant rates in the Amazon as well as in tropical forests in other parts of the world. However, the tropical deforestation TAN has led to institutional changes in development policies, the development of extractive and nature preserves, and the formation of private governance mechanisms to regulate forestry practices. Thus, while substantive changes have been limited, institutional changes have taken place, which may lead to greater conservation of tropical forests in the future. Lastly, the tropical deforestation TAN indicates that global social change requires cooperation among a diverse set of actors from local to global; entails building coalitions among groups with different framings of the problem, its causes, and its solutions; and is influenced by the political practices of many nations and organizations.

DISCUSSION

Societies are always changing. The key questions for sociologists are, who drives social change, how do societies change, and what are the implications of social change? Building on the ideas, concepts, and examples presented in the reading, a set of questions are presented at the end of the chapter to stimulate your further thinking on social change.

In sociology, there are two historical models of social change: the evolutionary and dialectic model. In the evolutionary model, social change is conceptualized as a process of adaptation that functions to maintain the stability of society. In contrast, the dialectical model views social change as a process characterized by conflict, negotiation, and compromise among different groups. Does one model more accurately theorize social change? Do both models tell us something about social change? Can social change sometimes correspond to the evolutionary model, and other times the dialectical model?

The theoretical frameworks of sociology may also help in thinking about how social change takes place. For example, structural theories highlight the ways that the structure of society affects the ability for people and groups to act. As Marx originally argued, does the structure of society and a person's position in it affect their ability to change society? If Ritzer is correct and the world is becoming increasingly McDonaldized, what are the implications for social change? Applying interaction theories to social change, can small actions in our everyday lives make a difference? For instance, can deviant acts, such as biking and walking instead of driving, growing your own food, and breaking gender and sexuality norms make a difference? Lastly, poststructural theories point to the role that knowledge and language play in social change. Important questions raised by such theories include, do we need new ideas to stimulate social change? What are the consequences of increased corporate control over the media for social change? Is the Internet a tool that social movement groups can use to communicate and spread alternative forms of knowledge? How does growing corporate funding of universities affect knowledge and, hence, social change?

A key insight of sociology is that it tends to take groups or organizations to bring about social change. However, such groups require the participation and support of people. Why do people become involved in a social movement? Under what circumstances do they partake in dangerous activities, such as civil disobedience? Sociologists have identified four actors as key drivers of social change: the state, corporations, social movements, and experts. While all play key roles in social change, are certain actors more important than others in bringing about change? Similarly, are some actors able to influence social change more so than others? If yes, why? What might enable some actors to have more influence than others?

In the last section, social change in action, actual examples of how social change takes place were presented. The three examples—Love Canal, BLM, and tropical deforestation—illustrate that social change is often a contested and lengthy process. However, they also demonstrate that people, if they mobilize and take action, can bring about change. In all three cases, every day people and social movement organizations challenge powerful actors in society—states and corporations—and are able to change society to different degrees.

Lesson Take-Aways

- Social change is a complex process that involves multiple actors, is often contested, and has winners and losers.

- Social change is both a personal issue in that it affects individuals in specific ways and a public issue in that it affects large groups of people and the structure of society.

- Today, social change tends to be technologically mediated and multi-scaled in that it produces both local and global changes.

- Social change takes place on an unlevel playing field. Marginalized groups often have fewer resources and less power. For such groups, collective action and social change for necessary for social change that improves their lives.

Discussion Questions

1. Think about your life. Consider your social location: class, race, ethnicity, religion, gender, and sexuality. Think about the things you use: technology, clothes, food, and transportation. Ask yourself: How much control over these do you have? If you wanted to make changes in who you are and what you use can you? Why or why not?
2. Why are so many young American adults not politically active or involved in social movements? What is necessary to get more people involved in social issues and social change?
3. How do you view social change? Do you agree with the evolutionary model, the dialectical model, or both? Who do you see as influencing social change the most: the state, corporations, social movements, or experts? Why?

Sources

AFL-CIO. 2011. "Executive Paywatch." www.aflcio.org/corporatewatch/paywatch.

Bartley, Tim. 2003. "Certifying Forests and Factories: States, Social Movements, and the Rise of Private Regulation in the Apparel and Forest Product Fields." *Politics and Society* 31(3): 433–64.

Beder, Sharon. 1997. Global Spin: *The Corporate Assault on Environmentalism.* Totnes, UK: Green Books.

Benford, Robert D. and David A. Snow. 2000. "Framing Processes and Social Movements: An Overview and Assessment." *Annual Review of Sociology* 26: 611–39.

Blumer, Herbert. 1969. *Symbolic Interaction: Perspective and Method.* Englewood Cliffs, NJ: Prentice-Hall.

Butler, Judith. 1990. *Gender Trouble: Feminism and the Subversion of Identity.* New York: Routledge.

Cable, Sherry and Michael Benson. 1993. "Acting Locally: Environmental Injustice and the Emergence of Grass-Roots Environmental Organizations." *Social Problems* 40(4): 464–77.

Carson, Rachel. [1962] 2002. *Silent Spring.* New York: Houghton Mifflin.

Day, Elizabeth. 2015. "#BlackLivesMatter: The Birth of a New Civil Rights Movement." *The Guardian,* July 19.

Diani, Mario. 1992. "The Concept of Social Movement." *Sociological Review* 40(1): 1–25.

DuPuis, Melanie E. 2000. "Not in My Body: rBGH and the Rise of Organic Milk." *Agriculture and Human Values* 17(3): 285–95.

Durkheim, Emile. [1893] 1984. *The Division of Labor in Society.* Translated by W. D. Halls. New York: Free Press.

Foucault, Michel. 1995. *Discipline and Punish: The Birth of the Prison.* Translated by A. Sheridan. New York: Vintage Books.

Gamson, William A. 1992. "The Social Psychology of Collective Action." In Aldon D. Morris and Carol M. Mueller (eds.), *Frontiers in Social Movement Theory,* 53–76. New Haven, CT: Yale University Press.

Garfinkel, Harold. 1967. *Studies in Ethnomethodology.* Englewood Cliffs, NJ: Prentice-Hall.

Gibbs, Lois Marie. 2011. *Love Canal and the Birth of the Environmental Health Movement.* Washington, DC: Island Press.

Habermas, Jurgen. 1973. *Legitimation Crisis.* Boston: Beacon Press.

Hecht, Susanna and Alexander Cockburn. 1989. *The Fate of the Forest: Developers, Destroyers and Defenders of the Amazon.* New York: Verso.

Keck, Margaret E. and Kathryn Sikkink. 1998. *Activists Beyond Borders.* Ithaca: Cornell University Press.

Mason, Paul. 2013. "From Arab Spring to Global Revolution." *The Guardian,* February 5.

Marx, Karl. 2000 [1852]. "The Eighteenth Brumaire of Louis Bonaparte." In D. McLellan (ed.), *Karl Marx: Selected Writings,* 329–55. New York: Oxford University Press.

Marx, Karl and Friedrich Engels. 1998 [1848]. *The Communist Manifesto.* New York: Signet Classics.

McAdam, Doug. 1999. *Political Process and the Development of Black Insurgency 1830-1920.* Chicago: University of Chicago Press.

McCarthy, John D. and Mayer N. Zald. 1977. "Resource Mobilization and Social Movements: A Partial Theory." *American Journal of Sociology* 82(6): 1212–41.

Micheletti, Michele. 2004. "'Put Your Money where Your Mouth Is! The Market as an Arena for Politics." In Christina Garsten and Monica L. de Montoya (eds.), *Market Matters: Exploring Cultural Processes in the Global Marketplace,* 114–34. New York: Palgrave Macmillan.

Mishel, Lawrence and Alyssa Davis. 2015. *Top CEOs Make 300 times More than Typical Workers.* Economic Policy Institute Issue Brief No. 339.

Monbiot, George. 2007. *Heat: How to Stop the Planet from Burning.* Cambridge, MA: South End Press.

Morris, Aldon D. and Suzanne Staggenborg. 2004. "Leadership in Social Movements." In David A. Snow, Sarah A. Soule, and Hanspeter Kriesi (eds.), *The Blackwell Companion to Social Movements,* 171–196. Oxford: Black-well.

Parsons, Talcott. 1971. *The Systems of Modern Societies.* Englewood Cliffs, NJ: Prentice-Hall.

Pinckney, Darryl. 2016. "Black Lives and the Police." *The New York Review of Books* 63(13). http://www.nybooks.com/articles/2016/08/18/black-lives-and-the-police/

Ritzer, George. 2010. *The McDonaldization of Society.* 6th ed. Thousand Oaks, CA: Pine Forge.

Robnett, Belinda. 1997. *How Long? How Long? African-American Women in the Struggle for Civil Rights.* New York: Oxford University Press.

Schnaiberg, Allan and Kenneth Alan Gould. 1994. *Environment and Society: The Enduring Conflict.* New York: St. Martin's.

Stephen, Bijan. 2015. "Get Up, Stand Up: Social Media Helps Black Lives Matter Fight the Power." *Wired,* November. https://www.wired.com/2015/10/how-black-lives-matter-uses-social-media-to-fight-the-power/

Szasz, Andrew. 2007. *Shopping Our Way to Safety: How We Changed from Protecting the Environment to Protecting Ourselves.* Minneapolis: University of Minnesota Press.

Tesh, Sylvia N. 2000. *Uncertain Hazards: Environmental Activists and Scientific Proof.* Ithaca, NY: Cornell University Press.

Victor, Daniel. 2016. "Why 'All Lives Matter' Is Such a Perilous Phrase." *New York Times,* July 15. https://www.nytimes.com/2016/07/16/us/all-lives-matter-black-lives-matter.html?_r=0

Weber, Max. 2010 [1905]. *The Protestant Ethic and the Spirit of Capitalism.* Translated by S. Kalberg. New York: Oxford University Press.

Related Websites

Center for Media and Democracy: www.prwatch.org
Center for Responsive Politics: www.opensecrets.org
International Labor Organization: www.ilo.org
National Research Council: www.nationalacademies.org/nrc
Southern Poverty Law Center: www.splcenter.org
Union for Concerned Scientists: www.ucsusa.org
World Economic Forum: www.weforum.org

LESSON 8, PHOTO REFLECTION:

The People's Climate March in front of Trump International Hotel, New York City.
Photo by Ken Gould.

The People's Climate March was the largest climate change protest in history, with over 300,000 people participating. Frontline communities, those most vulnerable to the impacts of climate change, led the march. The ability of social movements to focus public attention on social problems such as racial discrimination, gender inequality, the AIDS epidemic, and economic inequality is a key factor in generating social change. Social movements often take problems that people experience as individual troubles (e.g., hate crimes, HIV infection, environmental illness, limited access to employment or housing, etc.) and reframe them as social problems that must be addressed by public policy. We chose this photo because it represents a recent, high-profile collective effort at generating social change to address a global social problem. If you were the photographer, what picture would you take to represent the forces of social change?

What indicators of globalization can you identify in this photo?

9

Global Dynamics

Kenneth A. Gould

INTRODUCTION

You use a smart phone made in China, from materials mined in Africa and Latin America, for a company based in the United States or Europe. You wear a shirt made in Central America from cotton grown in the Middle East. You drive a car assembled in Mexico and Tennessee for a company based in South Korea. You wear sneakers designed in Oregon and produced in Thailand. You eat lunch that contains Mexican tomatoes from seeds genetically engineered in the United States, soybean oil from Argentina (also from seeds genetically engineered in the United States), and beef raised in the former rainforests of Costa Rica. You grew up watching the same animated TV shows as your peers in the Philippines, France, and Columbia. You might even think that The Weeknd is an American. And you think of all of this as normal. The reason that the vast transnational networks, international **commodity chains**, and worldwide cultural flows that you are immersed in and that are manifest in most of the products you consume don't phase you is because you were born in a global era, and this era is relatively recent and very different from any that have come before it.

Sociologists have called the time period of the late twentieth century and early twenty-first century an era of "globalization." Human society is now global in a number of interesting ways. The people and societies across the globe have never been more interconnected, interdependent, and in close contact than they are now. The world has never been smaller in terms of the insignificance of great distance. Both the speed and ease of travel and the ability to instantaneously communicate across space are unprecedented. The planet has never been more crowded nor more environmentally threatened by human society than it is at this moment. Culture and ideology has never been more globally homogenous (uniform, similar). National and continental economies have never been more vulnerable to each other. Food systems have never been more transnationally interreliant. Populations have never been more mobile. And energy demand to fuel all of this has never been higher. Humans have thus generated a global society the likes of which has never been tried before and the long-term consequences of which are unknown.

Will the era of globalization usher in a world of unity, peace, and harmonious sharing in which our deep interdependence upon one another requires us to find ways to resolve our ancient quarrels? Or will the global competition for increasingly scarce resources on an ever-smaller and more crowded planet launch us into a world of violent conflict, expanding inequality, and ecological destruction? It would not be difficult to identify broad social trends indicating either or both global social trajectories. For example, at the same time that 195 countries came together to produce the United Nations Framework Convention on Climate Change in an effort to solve a global ecological crisis, world leaders failed to find a means to resolve the Syrian civil war, which has caused over four million Syrians to flee their country seeking refuge abroad. The era of globalization is rife with competing and diverging social trends and tensions, which tells us that the future of globalization is in many ways contested and up for grabs. Globalization is a social fact. What kind of global society our species will ultimately construct is yet to be seen.

If, as C. Wright Mills (1959) wrote, sociology is about the intersection of history and biography, it would be impossible for you to make sense of your life without understanding the ways in which your experiences are shaped by the historical era of globalization into which you were born. As previously noted, you may take the unique experiences of a life being lived in a globalized society as normal, and so you should. You take as normal the social world into which you have been socialized. Your expectations, hopes, dreams, norms, constraints, and opportunities are largely shaped by the particular social order and historical era in which you happen to find yourself. What is harder to realize, and what takes a sociological imagination, is that things could be, have been, and will be in the future quite different as society changes over time. The hopes, dreams, norms, constraints, and opportunities presented to you by your particular position in this era of globalization are historically specific, socially constructed, and changeable as the social forces and processes that gave rise to globalization generate social tensions and dynamics that are contested and in flux. Your capacity to text your friend on the other side of the country, follow the Twitter feed of some celebrity in Europe, and listen to reggaeton on your ear buds, all while eating a kiwi from New Zealand is a function of the social world into which you were born, no matter how much you may feel that your text, your celebrity choice, your musical taste, and your fruit preference reflects your own individual uniqueness. That you are likely to worry more about a terrorist attack or a global disease epidemic than about total global thermonuclear war (as your parents or grandparents probably did) is a reflection of social changes on a global scale and their impacts on your individual perceptions and consciousness. That you or a friend are more likely to want to occupy Wall Street than shut down the Pentagon or be a hedge fund manager than an astronaut is a reflection of your historically specific social era.

Understanding globalization and how it will shape your individual life and life course requires that you apply your sociological imagination in a nested analysis. That is, to make sense of the ways in which your life is "globalized," you will have to be able to locate yourself in a time and in a place that is at once local, regional, national, continental, and global. If you and your family have been experiencing economic hardship, perhaps it is due to the loss of manufacturing or service employment in your town. That employment, whether a call center or a factory, might have been moved to another state or another country by a corporation based many states away or even overseas. The ability of companies to move production and service so quickly, easily, and profitably is due to changes in communications and transportation technology developed elsewhere. That the employment that left your town was attracted by cheap labor rates in Southeast Asia or Central America reflects corporate access to global labor markets. And so, changes in global labor markets reduced national employment options in the United States, which is manifest in the deindustrialization of formerly industrial regions of the country, which led an employer to close a plant in your town, which caused someone in your family to become unemployed, which forced you to take out additional college loans so that you are now in much more debt. After graduation, that debt may lead you to take the better paying job that you don't really have a passion for rather than the lower paying one that you do feel a passion for, and in that way your life course is altered by a series of decisions made at local, regional, national, and global levels by people who you don't know and who don't know you. Of course, individual results may vary. The interrelated series of social changes that have led us to an era of global social dynamics are complex, and they impact countries, towns, families, and individuals differently. Understanding the patterns of difference and similarity in outcomes that emerge from the actions of global social forces, at every level of analysis, is a job for sociologists.

Sociologists are especially interested in understanding the group of related social changes connected to globalization, as the discipline of sociology itself emerged from the effort to make sense of sweeping, rapid, widespread social realignments. In many ways, the changes associated with globalization are similar in scope and depth to those associated with the European Industrial Revolution that first inspired Marx, Weber, and Durkheim to ponder and posit how and why societies change. The industrial revolution changed how and where goods were produced, expanded access to products and ideas, shifted the spatial distribution of populations, reorganized the relationships between continents, and called into question the goals of economies and the proper functions of governments. The era of globalization raises similar questions for sociologists but on an even grander scale. What is the dynamic between cultural diversity and global mass communication? How can people make a local living when economies shift rapidly and globally? What are the functions and meanings of terrestrial borders for people when information and capital (money and manufactured goods) are decreasingly effected by them? What is the relationship between labor and capital when capital can move so much more easily and quickly than labor can? What is the ideal balance of power between corporations, states, and civil society? How can a growing population of higher-demand consumers have their needs and aspirations satisfied from a limited global resource base? What impacts will destabilizing the Earth's ecosystems have on our social systems? How do we manage the relationship between individual freedom and global responsibility? The era of globalization poses new and old questions for sociologists, and it does so on a planetary scale. Such questions require us to create a global sociology that both transcends and accounts for the specifics of particular national societies. And sociologists, as they have in the past, have jumped into this sea of difficult and pressing questions with both feet.

THE INFRASTRUCTURE AND INSTITUTIONS OF GLOBALIZATION

The social trends, patterns, forces, and processes that have led us to the fact of globalization are not new by any means. Most of the social developments that have brought us to this era have been at work for many centuries and have been identified by sociologists in earlier times and disparate places. Certainly, the compression of space and time that results from the emergence of instantaneous point-to-point and mass communication has been developing since the first telegraph transmission and the first radio broadcast. Developments in telecommunications are fundamental to many of the elements of globalization that we now take for granted. The late-twentieth-century development of communications satellites placed in geostationary orbits around the Earth first allowed every point on the planet to be viewed and to be put in immediate and direct contact with every other location on earth. Not only did the space age of the 1960s provide human society with an image of the earth as a single object, it also allowed us to communicate as a single community in unprecedented ways. The Internet age followed in the 1990s, creating an increasingly global network of institutional and personal computers that allowed for the exchange of vast amounts of information in real time. The growing mobility of ever smaller digital electronic data transfer devices like smart phones and tablet computers in the early twenty-first century has produced a social world in which nearly anyone can be in touch with nearly anyone else, nearly anywhere, at nearly anytime. Although you may take such capabilities for granted as a simple social fact of the world into which you were born, there has been nothing like this ever before in the long human history of communication. And the time it took to get from the first live transcontinental television transmission in 1951 to the first smart phone sold to the public in 1993 is less than one-tenth of the time it took to get from the first book printed with moveable type in 1439 to the first telephone call in 1876 (see Table 9–1). Technological developments in communication have come faster than in previous eras, and the transformative social impacts of those developments have been changing societies rapidly and repeatedly. More than anything else, it is changes in information and communication technology that has facilitated globalization.

Table 9–1 Changes in Communication Technology

Year	Communication/Information Technology
1450	Gutenberg movable type printing press
1843	Long-distance electric telegraph line
1876	Telephone first exhibited
1901	Radio transmission
1914	Cross continental telephone call
1916	Radios with station tuners
1925	Television signal
1939	Scheduled television broadcasts
1951	Computers sold commercially
1963	Geosynchronous communications satellite
1966	Fax machines
1971	ARPANET e-mail
1979	First cell phone network
1981	Laptop computers commercially sold
1984	Apple Macintosh
1985	Car phones
1994	Worldwide Web
1994	Text messaging
1996	GPS for civilian use
2004	Facebook
2006	Twitter
2007	iPhone
2010	Instagram

The social institution that has transformed the most, and been the most transformative in the era of globalization, is the corporation. Digital information and communications technology allowed businesses to operate on a global scale, organizing resource extraction in one corner of the planet, primary production in another corner, assembly yet elsewhere, advertising in the remotest reaches of the Earth, and distribution to markets scattered across the globe. While intercontinental trade, extraction, production, and distribution have been occurring in various forms and places since ancient times, the ease and speed of institutional organization on a global scale facilitated by developments in electronic communication have allowed for the first truly global corporations to emerge as the wealthiest and most powerful social institutions on the planet. These rich and powerful social institutions include Exxon-Mobil, JP Morgan Chase, Apple, Royal Dutch Shell, Samsung, Bank of America, PetroChina, Berkshire Hathaway, Wells Fargo,

Table 9–2 The World's One Hundred Largest Economic Entities (Selected)

Rank	Country/Corporation	GDP/Revenues (US$ million, 2012)
1	United States	15,685,000
2	China	8,227,000
3	Japan	5,964,000
4	Germany	3,401,000
5	France	2,609,000
28	Walmart	469,000
29	Royal Dutch Shell	467,000
30	Exxon Mobil	421,000
31	Sinopec-China Petroleum	412,000
35	BP	371,000
40	PetroChina	309,000
47	Volkswagen	254,000
52	Total	241,000
54	Toyota Motor	232,000
55	Chevron	225,000
63	Samsung Electronics	196,000
69	Apple	169,000
70	ENI	165,000
71	Berkshire-Hathaway	164,000
73	Daimler	153,000
74	AXA Group	153,000
75	General Electric	148,000
76	Petrobras	147,000
77	Gazprom	144,000
78	Allianz	144,000
80	ICBC	138,000
81	AT&T	135,000
83	Nippon Telegraph & Tel	127,000
84	Statoil	127,000
85	BNP Paribas	127,000
87	China Construction Bank	119,000
88	Banco Santander	113,000
89	JPMorgan Chase	109,000
90	HSBC Holdings	108,000
91	IBM	105,000

92	Agricultural Bank of China	105,000
93	Nestlé	103,000
94	Bank of America	101,000
95	Bank of China	100,000
98	Wells Fargo	92,000
99	Citigroup	91,000
100	China Mobile	89,000

Sources: Transnational Institute, State of Power 2014 (https://www.tni.org/en/publication/planet-earth-a-corporate-world).

and Petrobras. According to the Institute for Policy Studies, of the 100 largest economic entities on earth, 63 are corporations and 37 are countries, with Walmart having global sales roughly equivalent to the gross domestic product of Australia (see Table 9–2). The ability of corporations to move billions of dollars from point to point on the planet with a simple keystroke allows for an unprecedented exercise of power over the fate of local, regional, national, and continental economies. Governments are bounded by territorial limits and have jurisdictions that extend only to their physical borders. Electronic communications allowed multinational corporations to largely escape the constraints imposed upon them by governments by being able to move vast sums of money and information instantaneously across borders and with that money and information, production, jobs, and economic growth. Because these social institutions are not bounded by physical territorial limits as are governments, the emergence of instantaneous point-to-point communication and real-time data transfers allowed corporations to jump scale to a global level and thus largely escape the limits placed upon them by democratic (or nondemocratic) governments. The result is that the era of globalization is an era of enormous, powerful corporations that operate more autonomously, everywhere, and with less social accountability for the consequences of their actions than ever before (Barnet and Cavanagh 1995). Global corporate power is one of the key social facts of the era of globalization, and the responses of governments and civil society to the shift in institutional power in favor of **transnational corporations** is one of the central global dynamics of our time.

CULTURAL GLOBALIZATION

Perhaps in no other field is the corporate capacity for global production and distribution more apparent than in the field of culture. It is not surprising that little more than a decade after the first live transcontinental TV broadcast, the Beatles became the first truly global superstars, followed quickly by the Rolling Stones and other bands with a distinctly British take on African-American music that would have people rocking out in Asia by the mid-1960s. Cultural products *are* communications, so it is not surprising that a global culture has rapidly emerged from the linking of societies through global mass and point-to-point communications systems. Hip-hop may be a distinctly New York City contribution to the world, but it is a global phenomenon now with hundreds of national and regional flavors. American movies no longer rely on American markets for their success. American sports icons are increasingly recognized throughout the world, just as soccer has become more popular in the United States. Muhammad Ali's death was mourned on every continent, something that might have seemed quite unlikely when he was born in Louisville, Kentucky, in 1942 into a world that was much less technologically capable of being culturally homogenized. We celebrate cultural diversity more consciously and overtly than ever before, and perhaps that is because we are more immediately in contact with that diversity through a global media network. But cultural diversity is in decline worldwide, as the cultural products of the dominant culture-producing corporations saturate a truly global media. Fewer languages are spoken on Earth now than in the twentieth century, even if you recognize more words from more languages than your parents do.

One of the central tensions in the era of globalization is that between global cultural uniformity and local cultural specificity. On the one hand, being linked together across societies and cultures by a global media system has created tendencies toward what some sociologists have called "McDonaldization." Every one in every corner of the earth may soon find themselves drinking Coca-Cola, eating at McDonald's, and listening to hip-hop. In this scenario, local and regional cultural differences appear to decline as people across societies share common cultural products through global media. More than ever before, people on this planet see the same movies, listen to the same music, and purchase the same products across cultures. As transnational corporations seek out expanding markets for their products, cultural and otherwise, they benefit from the creation of consumer uniformity. Burger King may sell lamb burgers in India instead of beef burgers to adjust to regional culture, but PepsiCo wants Indians to drink Pepsi and not lassi and has been pretty successful at marketing this "foreign" beverage abroad. Sociologists refer to the adjusting of global products to local cultures and the mixing and blending of elements from a range of cultures as "hybridity." And while some sociologist see the emergence of widespread cultural hybridity as increasing cultural diversity, others see this as a superficial response to widespread **cultural homogenization**. Some social critics have articulated this global cultural homogenization as "Americanization," as the United States has been a dominant producer and distributer of cultural products and mass consumer goods. Certainly, American movies have a global audience, American popular music is heard worldwide, and Coca-Cola is far from a local soft drink in Atlanta. How deep the cultural influences of global consumption are is a point of debate. The corporate-produced, secular, materialistic, consumer culture that is marketed globally has its detractors in every society, including the United States. As local cultures are threatened by a global culture, there

FOOD FOR THOUGHT
AGRICULTURE, FREE TRADE, AND UNDOCUMENTED IMMIGRATION TO THE UNITED STATES
Justin Sean Myers

Immigration is generally a hot topic during elections. Candidates are expected to have a position on the "immigration issue"—code for the Mexican border and the Latinization of the United States. The debate is largely centered on how the United States should prevent undocumented immigrants from crossing the border: build a bigger fence, enforce existing laws, or pass new laws. Every once in a while the possibility of amnesty is discussed. Little discussion actually takes place about why undocumented immigration occurs in the first place. As a result, the role that the United States and its political and economic policies play in motivating undocumented immigration is ignored. To recenter the debate on how undocumented immigration is socially produced by free trade policies, we have to go back to President Clinton's signing of the North American Free Trade Agreement (NAFTA), its activation on January 1, 1994, and its effects on the staple foodstuff of Mexicans, corn.

For Mexico, NAFTA's free trade policies required the elimination of all "trade-distorting" tariffs on imported foods, state assistance to small farmers, and public funding of the agricultural sector. This meant the privatization of state sectors that produced farm inputs (seeds, fertilizers, etc.), marketed farm inputs, and farm products as well as the privatization of crop insurance, grain storage, and the irrigation infrastructure. NAFTA's logic followed that of other free trade programs implemented throughout Latin America during the 1980s and 1990s. Market signals would force Mexican farmers to embrace its "competitive advantage" of a winter growing season and a cheap labor force to engage in export of fruits and vegetables to the United States and Canada. This would generate positive trade balances for Mexico, increase government revenues, and provide income to fuel industrialization, enabling Mexico to follow in the path of the United States.

Instead, the rural economy of small farmers was hard hit. Small farmers lacked social, political, and economic access to the land, capital, technology, and marketing channels to engage in this conversion, access dominated by foreign and domestic corporations and large-scale farmers. In addition, the private companies that took over the agricultural services previously provided by the state did not want to assist small farmers, only large farmers and corporations, because this is where the major money is made. Moreover, this logic of competitive advantage presumes small farmers wanted to make the conversion in the first place. NAFTA's market-centric logic not only fails to understand but also rejects the reality that farming and corn is an important part of Mexican culture and a way of life that cannot be easily reduced to the principles of price signals or profit maximization.

Either way, due to the lack of access, the denial of access, or cultural resistance, many of these farmers were pushed out of farming altogether when cheap US imports of heavily subsidized corn flooded the Mexican market after NAFTA. The inability to sell their corn produced a mass migration of over 1.3 million rural families to urban areas within Mexico as well as to the dangerous border crossings into the United

Food for Thought *continued*

States. Upon arrival in the United States, the peasant farmers become the farmworkers subjected to the brutal working conditions discussed earlier. They also become the day laborers on street corners, the cooks in restaurant kitchens, the workers in slaughterhouses, the gardeners mowing lawns, the janitors cleaning office buildings, the takeout deliverymen, ad infinitum. They fill low-wage jobs that many US residents are able to refuse.

The outcome in Mexico is similar to the rest of Latin America where a free trade agro-export model has been erected: increasing poverty and unemployment, social unrest, urban shantytowns, and out-migration northward. Millions of people from Latin America have fled to the United States in search of work because they are displaced by free trade agricultural policies favoring international corporations, factory farms, and the dumping (i.e., the sale of a commodity below its cost of production) of US agricultural commodities globally. As a result, the undocumented immigration issue that is frontline news in the United States is largely produced by its own agricultural and trade policies, a relationship generally absent from the same news reports that sensationalize the Mexico–US border as a fault line of racial politics.

Sources

Bello, Walden. 2009. *The Food Wars*. New York: Verso.
Green, Duncan. 2003. *Silent Revolution: The Rise and Crisis of Market Economics in Latin America*. New York: Monthly Review.
Holt-Gimenez, Eric, Raj Patel and Annie Shattuck. 2009. *Food Rebellions! Crisis and the Hunger for Justice*. Oakland, CA: Food First Books.
Wright, Angus. 2005. *The Death of Ramon Gonzalez: The Modern Agricultural Dilemma*. 2d ed. Austin: University of Texas Press.

are numerous signs of backlash. Cultural identity movements may respond by deepening commitments to local cultural difference and traditional cultural values, rejecting assimilation into a global corporate consumer culture (Barber 1995). Christian fundamentalists in the United States may reject the permissive sexual norms popularized in global media products like movies, music, and TV shows. Islamic and Jewish fundamentalists may do the same. There is certainly a strong element of cultural backlash, assertion of local cultural integrity, and rejection of McDonaldization, Americanization, and corporate, secular values evident in militant calls for jihad. The September 11, 2001 terrorist attacks on the World Trade Center in New York City and the more recent rise of ISIS cannot be separated from the cultural threats felt worldwide from the globalization of a decidedly Western culture transmitted through the global media as part of world trade or globalization. World trade and local culture are in dynamic tension in the global era.

One aspect of the emerging world culture and the emerging cultural responses to it is that, in a global communications system, ideas, trends, and movements spread more quickly between societies than ever before. Whether it is the movement for gay marriage (legalized in 23 countries between 2000 and 2016), the notion of equating freedom with shopping, or Bieber fever, the speed and audience for new memes to go viral is truly unprecedented. Two hundred years ago, to popularize an idea required spreading the word by mouth or printing pamphlets and distributing them by hand to the minority of people who could read and who you could physically reach. Today, you can tweet an idea with a potential instant audience of millions. For better or worse, a global culture is emerging (with great local and regional variation), and that culture reflects both the dominant position of culture producing corporations noted above, and the globally dispersed access to the Internet. The tension between the democratizing self-expression of your Pinterest site and the ideological dominance of News Corporation (which owns the *Wall Street Journal*, Fox News, Twentieth Century Fox, and hundreds of other media outlets) is another key global dynamic of our time. In the era of globalization, media-producing corporations have merged and consolidated, meaning that fewer and fewer and larger and larger corporate entities control the vast share of cultural products (e.g., movie companies, TV programming, radio stations, newspapers, magazines, book publishers, etc.). Some analysts have termed this a "media monopoly" in which a handful of corporations control the vast majority of cultural products that you consume (Bagdikian 1983). The five largest media conglomerates in 2016 were Comcast, 21st Century Fox, Walt Disney, Viacom/CBS, and Time Warner, and they are all based in the United States. What this means is that a very small number of people in a very small number of organizations decide what you will and will not read, see, hear, and know. In a world in which information is power, that type of consolidation of control over information and culture is a massive exercise of power. However, the countertrend in this global dynamic is your ability to enter ideas, information, and cultural products of your own into the World Wide Web without the filters and gatekeepers that limited entry to culture in the era before globalization. You can "publish" without peer review or editors, you can distribute music without a contract from a record label, and you can upload an indie film without an executive producer. The result is a world in which a dynamic tension exists between "any idiot" being able to publish anything he or she wants on the Internet, and no dissident being able to publish anything through a major book publisher. How the battle of ideas and culture will play out in a conflict between consolidated corporate control and dispersed individual access remains to be seen.

ECONOMIC GLOBALIZATION

World Trade

Systems of world trade are not a late twentieth-century development. The Indian Ocean trade of the thirteenth century put Asian and African societies in contact with each other and linked their economies. The European-centered world system that started to emerge in the fifteenth century eventually set in place an international division of labor (Wallerstein

1974). In the European-centered world system of the colonial era, in which much of Asia, Africa, the Americas, and Oceania was under direct European political and military control as formal colonies, the colonies were developed for primary natural resource extraction and agricultural production. That is, plantations were established to provide food and textiles (like cotton) for Europe, and minerals were mined and forests were cut to provide raw materials for European production. These colonial (now postcolonial) areas of the world are often referred to as the "global south," since they are to the south of the colonizing powers (which are now often referred to as the "global north"). The raw materials provided by the global south under colonialism served the technology and capital-based manufacturing in the global north (Europe and North America) for centuries. In the nineteenth century in Latin America and the twentieth century in Asia and Africa, the era of formal colonialism, where European nations directly ruled the peoples of the global south, would give way to a **postcolonial** era of economic dependency.

The rise and fall of the Soviet Union throughout much of the twentieth century would generate a **cold war** in which two nuclear superpowers competed for the allegiance of the rest of the nations of the world, especially those that became newly independent following colonialism. The newly independent nations of the global south were encouraged to take on enormous international debt to finance their development in the late twentieth century. Guided by what sociologists call "**modernization theory**," the nations of the global south were loaned large sums of money by **international financial institutions** such as the World Bank to invest in large-scale infrastructure projects. The idea was that the postcolonial nations could go through the same development stages that Europe and North America did in earlier eras. Often, the key to this effort was the construction of large hydropower dam projects to provide the nation with a source of electric power. The belief was that providing electric power plants would lead to the emergence of heavy industries, which would create working-class jobs and paychecks and thus spawn a local market for goods. That local market would generate economic multiplier effects as industrial workers would represent economic demand for household goods and eventually cars, all of which would be provided by secondary industrial developments in the nation. It was the modernization theory view that all countries everywhere, regardless of natural resource endowments, culture, or international economic relations, could be sent through these stages. The expected result was that soon everyone everywhere would be working in an industrial or related job, living a middle-class lifestyle, with a house, cars, a big TV, sitting in a La-Z-Boy and watching the Super Bowl. Needless to say, it didn't quite work out that way. The world of the late twentieth century was different from the eras in which Europe and North America developed. International competition from multinational corporations, years of colonial exploitation, and the emergence of global resource pools and markets meant that national-level development would take very different paths in different times and different places. **Dependency**

theorists argued that modernization failed because the nations of the south were dependent on northern capital, northern technology, and northern markets. The countries of the south therefore developed to serve the needs and interests of the north, rather than those of their own people. Dependent development, it was said, would lock these dependent countries into a role in the world economy in which they would always be subservient to the economic power of northern countries, unless they focused their development internally. In other words, national development in an era of globalization would have to take a very different path than development in the eras that came before.

The debt that accumulated in failed modernization schemes was used by international financial institutions such as the International Monetary Fund to forcibly restructure indebted countries in ways that powerful northern nations desired. Under an ideology of **neoliberalism**, countries secured repayment plans or debt forgiveness under a series of conditions. These conditions adhered to the ideology of neoliberalism in which public sector industries and jobs were privatized—that is, sold by the governments to private corporations. In addition, government subsidies (or "big government spending") for things like food, energy, transportation, education, and health care were reduced or eliminated. While this created economic opportunities for transnational corporations to invest in the global south, it greatly increased the cost of food, energy, transportation, education, and health care for most people. Economic inequality rapidly increased and food riots or austerity protests swept throughout the global south. In fact, one indicator that we had established a truly global neoliberal economic regime was the near universality of austerity protests in countries on different continents, with different languages, cultures, and ecosystems from the 1970s on. Privatization and austerity measures continue as part of the global economy to this day, even in the United States and Europe. The structural adjustment of the global south was a way of integrating countries into a global economic system designed by and for the former colonial and neocolonial powers. It is the post-cold war entrance of all nations and places into a single global financial network and economy that makes this an era of a truly global economy that is distinct from the world systems of the past.

One of the consequences of the ability of corporations to organize the production and distribution of goods globally has been that the advantages of local production with local labor for local markets have been greatly reduced. In earlier eras, it made little sense for a company based in London to produce goods in Guangdong, China, to be sold in Kansas. Organizing and overseeing production, guaranteeing consistent quality, and maintaining supply lines for raw materials from five thousand miles away across languages and cultures presented too many difficulties. The problems involved in managing the volume of production in Guangdong to match demand in Kansas and to get those goods to market in time as demand fluctuated made such global systems of production and distribution less appealing than simply making goods closer to where they would be sold.

World Production

Sociologists often contrast the delocalization of production that has occurred under globalization with **Fordism**. Fordism is a term used to describe the centralization of production that typified the heavy industry of the first half of the twentieth century. It is named for the automobile maker and industrial production innovator, Henry Ford, who is often credited with inventing the assembly line. In Fordism, the production of materials, component parts, accessories, and final assembly of a product is centralized as locally as possible. This centralization and localization of production allows for greater coordination between the various elements of making a final product and easier control over labor, facilitates oversight of quality, and allows management to directly intervene at all stages and in all aspects of production. That is, prior to the emergence of global communications and information systems, space, distance, and proximity were very important factors in the organization and coordination of production. In the case of Ford Motors, automobile parts production was located near final assembly plants in southeast Michigan, which was in close proximity and easy transportation access to steel production in Gary, Indiana and Pittsburgh, Pennsylvania, and rubber tire production in Akron, Ohio. The cars produced were initially primarily sold in US markets. One marker of the emergence of the era of globalization was the delocalization of automobile manufacturing in the 1980s, when Detroit-based car companies like Ford and General Motors closed plants in southeast Michigan and moved various components of car manufacturing throughout the globe in search of cheap labor and low environmental standards. The result was the devastation of the Detroit-area economy and the depopulation of Detroit, as workers and their children migrated away in search of economic opportunity. In the 1950s, Detroit was the model, modern, industrial, corporate city based on heavy industrial production of what was perhaps the defining American product. In the early twenty-first century, Detroit is the poster child for the loss of local economic stability in the global economy. With the globalization of the auto industry, Detroit's population went into decline as automobile-related economic opportunity dried up. The city went from a population of nearly two million in the 1950s to under 700,000 in 2016. Detroit lost nearly 25 percent of its population between 2001 and 2010 and is now smaller than it was when Henry Ford first built the River Rouge auto plant in 1917.

Real time global communications, the emergence of a global business culture, containerized transshipment, and giant corporate distribution and retailing networks like Walmart, have made global production for global markets economically viable. The use of containers for shipping goods, starting in the post-World War II era, allowed larger ships to carry more goods further and to load and unload them with large cranes directly to and from trucks and trains. In addition to eliminating most longshoreman jobs and displacing smaller ports and waterways, the containerization of shipping allowed for rapid improvement in the ease and cost of shipping a growing volume of goods great distances. It now makes good business sense to find the cheapest raw materials anywhere on earth, ship them to the cheapest workers anywhere on earth, and ship the goods to consumers anywhere on earth. Space and time have been made almost inconsequential in the production and distribution process. Global communications and global corporations have altered the comparative advantages of place. Where in the past there might have been obvious economic advantages to making goods in the United States and selling them to consumers in the United States, in a globalized economy, it is actually cheaper to produce the goods on the other side of the planet where wages, benefits, environmental regulations, and worker safety standards are all lower, and ship them to consumers in the United States. That is an enormous change that increases the physical and social distance between producers and consumers, management and labor, and ecosystems and the society that draws upon them.

Global Labor

In a global economy, there is little chance that you will ever meet the people that work in the fields and factories that produce the goods you consume. Knowing, or having the possibility of knowing, some of the people who produce some of the products you use can make the production process, the relationship between making things and owning things—between working and having—more socially apparent. Although you may not work in the toy factory, knowing someone who does might change the way you think about wages, safety standards, and benefits. Let's face it, it is easier to worry about your cousin Frank's working conditions than it is to worry about the working conditions of an anonymous stranger in another part of the world with another language, another culture, and whose face and family you will probably never see. Globalization may make the world smaller in some ways, but it can also make the people we are directly economically connected to more anonymous. And, as a worker, you may feel differently about the quality and safety of the toy you are producing if you think your niece Aisha will be playing with it. The increased distance between producer and consumer in a global economy has real social consequences for how we think about, feel about, and imagine each other.

Similarly, there is a real difference between working for someone who lives in your community, your city, your state, or your country than working for someone who you will never see, whose society is very different and distant from yours. As an employer, firing people who live in your town might feel differently from firing people who live on the other side of the planet. Cutting their wages, reducing their family's access to health care or reducing their safety protections might be more problematic if you thought that your workers lived within driving distance of your family, went to the same house of worship as you, and rooted for the same baseball team. The greater the distance between corporate headquarters and the subcontracted factory door, the harder it is to sustain a sense that we are all in this together, as a team, working for our mutual common good. Of course, local producers have not necessarily treated their local employees well. Karl Marx and Friedrich Engels wrote extensively about that. However, the consequences of treating local employees poorly for a local employer might be more acute, and the ability of workers to effectively respond with significant consequence was clearly much greater. And without the emergence of global production, employers could not always believably threaten to simply move production elsewhere. It is hard to imagine the carriage plant owner in late nineteenth-century Phoenix, Arizona, plausibly threatening to move his carriage making to Thailand. He would have to stay in Phoenix and deal with his local labor issues. Once employers gained the plausible threat of moving production out of state or out of country, workers became subject to a level of job blackmail that was unprecedented prior to the era of globalization. In a real sense, globalization put every worker on earth in competition with every other worker on earth. And every place, every country, every city, and every town became locked in a global economic competition to retain and attract employers and investors to sustain their local economies in a global system. The result is that nearly every place has bent over backward to make itself more attractive than the next to locate production and employment. Part of that effort to make places economically attractive to employers is to depress wages, benefits, and safety standards. That has meant a dramatic assault on labor unions that were created specifically to protect workers' wages, benefits, and safety standards (Derber 1998). Capital looks to locate where production costs are lowest, and labor is a primary cost of production. The lower the labor costs, the higher the profits in producing a good, so finding places with very low wages, no benefits, and no worker protections is a priority. And it is hard for folks in Dearborn, Michigan, to compete for jobs with places where people get paid less than $1 an hour. The era of globalization has been an era in which the relative power of organized labor has dramatically declined. When the power of labor declines, economic inequality increases.

In an effort to attract foreign direct investment (capital from corporations based in other countries), many countries of the global south established "free trade zones" where cheap, nonunion labor would be supplied for the production or assembly of goods to be exported. These zones are areas in which companies are exempt from export taxes as well as many labor regulations. Entrance to the zones is usually tightly controlled by security, and workers are paid low wages, work long hours, and have few rights. Factories in the free trade zones are often run as sweatshops and owned and operated by local firms who assemble goods like electronics, sneakers, and other items for larger transnational corporations like Nike, Apple, Reebok, GAP, and J. C. Penny. By subcontracting production to local firms, large, name-brand companies hope to avoid legal and public relations liability for poor labor practices. For example, Nike manufactures no sneakers. Nike subcontracts sneaker-making to a range of smaller local subcontractors who assemble shoes for Nike based on Nike's specifications. The result is that Nike

SOCIOLOGY AT WORK
WORK AND GLOBAL DYNAMICS: MAKING IPHONES AND IPADS
Arne L. Kalleberg

Apple Inc.'s iPhones and iPads are two of the most successful products of modern times and have contributed greatly to the company's record profits in recent years. While Apple is an American company based in Cupertino, California, all of its iPhones and iPads are currently assembled in China (though Apple is now negotiating building them also in India). There are various reasons for Apple's globalization strategy. The wages paid to Chinese workers are low compared to those in the United States. There are also large networks of equipment suppliers in China that can be relied on to provide needed materials, and Apple is able to pressure these suppliers to keep prices low. Thus, Apple Inc. is able to obtain high-quality iPhones and iPads at low cost.

The consequences of this business strategy for workers are illustrated by the case of Foxconn, the world's largest contract electronics manufacturer. It assembles about 40 percent of the world's consumer electronics and serves a range of high-profile customers in addition to Apple such as Dell, Hewlett-Packard, Sony, and Amazon. Foxconn is China's leading exporter and one of its largest employers, with over one million workers, most of who are relatively young migrants from the rural areas of China.

The working conditions at the Foxconn plants are harsh (Duhigg and Barboza 2012). Workers are required to work long hours, often seven days a week and for extended periods of overtime. Banners on the wall of one factory proclaimed "Work hard on the job today or work hard to find a job tomorrow." Basic salaries are relatively low, and workers earn the bulk of their salaries through overtime work. Workers live in crowded dormitories, with sometimes as many as 20 people in a three-bedroom apartment. There is also a military-style management culture as Foxconn hires many security guards who discipline employees, often by using verbal abuse or physical violence to control workers. These working conditions and low pay led to widespread feelings of frustration and misery among the workers. Discontent with working conditions has surfaced in various ways. Most dramatically, between January and May 2010, 13 young workers attempted suicide at two production plants in southern China, and 10 were confirmed dead. This led the company to install nets to catch people jumping out of dormitories. The suicides aroused intense media attention and public outcry, bringing public attention to the issue of the poor quality of working life among migrant workers.

Since then, Apple has switched some of its production to another Chinese supplier, Petragon, which offers an even cheaper labor cost alternative to Foxconn. Working conditions at Petragon are also very poor, as workers there also live in cramped housing, receive very low wages, and receive inadequate job safety training (China Labor Watch 2015). Apple has also shifted some of its production to various sites in India.

These examples illustrate a dark side of globalization: to reduce costs and maximize profits, companies such as Apple seek out places to manufacture their products that have the cheapest labor costs. and maintaining these low labor costs often motivates suppliers like Foxconn and Petragon to cut corners as much as possible, forcing workers to toil in poor working conditions.

Sociology at Work *continued*

Sources

China Labor Watch. 2015. *Something's Not Right Here: Poor Working Conditions Persist at Apple Supplier Pegatron.* China Labor Watch Report No. 109. http://www.chinalaborwatch.org/report/109

Duhigg, Charles and David Barboza, 2012. "In China, Human Costs are Built into an iPad." *New York Times,* January 25.

employs nobody who makes Nike sneakers and has claimed at times that the abuse of sneaker workers is beyond their control, since they are employees of a bunch of small companies owned by other people in other countries. When it comes to sneaker manufacturing, Nike just doesn't do it. Nike focuses its operations on producing TV ads that make you want to own their products.

Governments in the global south establish the free trade zones in which the subcontractors operate to attract foreign investment that creates jobs for growing populations. Transnational companies use the free trade zones because they can minimize production costs by **outsourcing** production to subcontractors and because they can avoid legal responsibility for sweatshop conditions. Retailers in the United States, like Walmart, like free trade zone production because it allows them to offer cheaply made imported products to consumers at low prices, while still yielding high retail profits. So the **commodity chain** (the path of social connections that leads backward from your consumption through product manufacturing) for your new pair of jeans may lead from a retailer like Walmart to a clothing label like Faded Glory to a subcontractor you've never heard of operating a sweatshop (a *maquiladora*) in a free trade zone in Mexico to a worker working 12-hour days, six days a week without bathroom breaks in physically hazardous conditions, being harassed by an abusive supervisor, and getting paid just enough to starve to death slowly. While the global economy allows for the construction of these long-distance commodity chains, most of the unpleasant action behind the TV ads for new products, and the wide aisles and broad parking lots of the retail outlets, remains socially invisible to consumers. It is only through the efforts of labor and human rights activists who work to bring information about the plight of workers on the production end of the commodity chains to the consuming public that broader social action to address the problems with free trade zones and *maquiladoras* becomes possible.

Transnational efforts to end the labor abuses of sweatshop production in the global economy are the object of study of the University of California Riverside-based sociologist Ralph Armbruster-Sandoval (2005) in his book *Globalization and Cross-Border Labor Solidarity in the Americas: The Anti-Sweatshop Movement and the Struggle for Social Justice.* In this qualitative comparative analysis, Armbruster-Sandoval uses data collected through in-depth interviews with workers and activists and personal observation to compare the organization and outcomes of efforts to improve working conditions in *maquiladoras* in four Central American countries. Comparing his qualitative case studies of labor struggles in Guatemala, El Salvador, Honduras, and Nicaragua, Armbruster-Sandoval seeks to explain why some transnational campaigns were more successful than others in raising worker wages and improving their working conditions. In constructing his analysis, he applies the theoretical framework of the "boomerang effect" developed by Margaret Keck and Kathryn Sikkink (1998). Because the commodity chains of goods produced in the era of globalization reach across borders, addressing problems associated with production requires organizing transnationally. When workers in sweatshops appeal to their governments to intervene for better wages, governments are often resistant since it is cheap labor that provides their countries with a **comparative advantage** over other countries with whom they are in a global competition to attract foreign investment. If your employer and your government won't respond to your needs, who will? With a transnational commodity chain, you might be able to appeal to consumers in the countries into which the products you produce are imported. In exposing bad labor practices to consumers, they may in turn put pressure on the name-brand companies who are subcontracting production to *maquiladoras*. That is, once consumers of Nike sneakers start to understand that the teenage girls who actually make their sneakers get paid terrible wages and work in atrocious conditions so that Nike can make a huge profit by selling them very expensive shoes that only cost $5 to produce, they may start to look at Nike differently. If what Nike primarily produces is brand identification, that is, the idea that owning Nike sneakers is "cool," then the company can be threatened by a campaign that promotes the idea that, because of their bad labor practices, owning Nike sneakers is "uncool." So the transnational organizing strategy is to chase power up the commodity chain to threaten the interests of the transnational corporate decision makers. The boomerang effect is when the name-brand corporation responds to the labor–consumer campaign by putting pressure on governments hosting free trade zones, and on subcontractors manufacturing products for them, to address labor issues. That is, if direct worker pressure on subcontractors and governments fails, activists can go outside of the country, up the commodity chain, and have pressure "boomerang" back into the country from outside (Keck and Sikkink 1998). Sometimes this pressure can come from retailers of name-brand products as well, such as Macy's and Walmart who may not want their stores implicated in labor abuses. One of Armbruster-Sandoval's findings in his study of how well this worked in four Central American labor campaigns is that some companies are more vulnerable to what we might call "public shaming" than others. The more recognizable the name brand and the more highly focused the corporation is on brand identity, the more likely the company is to respond to such campaigns. Where a company like GAP is highly vulnerable, a company like Chentex is not. What Armbruster-Sandoval's sociological study makes clear is that, in a global economy with a **post-Fordist** organization of production, addressing local labor issues requires global action.

THE GLOBAL ENVIRONMENT

Environmental Regulation

Capital can move globally to places where labor is cheap and forming labor unions is hard. Labor regulation is not the only form of government intervention that corporations attempt to avoid in their global quest to find places where the cost of production is cheapest. Environmental protection can also increase the cost of production. By requiring producers to treat toxic waste before dumping it into the local water supply or requiring producers to add scrubbers to smokestacks to capture carcinogens before they are released into the air, governments raise the costs of making products. As we previously noted, governments are "local" in the sense that their jurisdictions have physical boundaries or borders. Environmental regulations are established and enforced by governments and vary greatly from country to country. The result of having few global environmental standards, regulations, or enforcement mechanisms is that corporations can seek out the lowest regulation scenarios, that is, the places with the worst environmental standards to locate their production facilities and therefore keep their production costs as low as possible. Again, this puts every place on earth in competition with each other to establish the lowest environmental standards to attract investment, production, and jobs. The ability of private capital to relocate production globally creates real disincentives for any place to establish higher environmental standards (Gould, Pellow, and Schnaiberg 2008). In that sense, economic globalization is an obstacle to improving environmental conditions. This is what sociologists have called the "race to the bottom" in environmental protection (which is a term also applied to labor standards in the global economy).

The distance between factory owners, boards of directors, and stock shareholders and the places where production actually occurs has real consequences for the willingness to sacrifice people, places, and communities in the pursuit of greater profits. If production were not easily globally mobile and owners and investors had to live relatively close to the production facilities they control, they might be less willing to poison the air they too must breathe and the water they too must drink. They might be less inclined to despoil the countryside that they also recreate in. And having to come into contact with the citizens whose water, air, and countryside they degrade might serve as a real check on their willingness to sacrifice the environment for their wealth. Globalization increases the distance between decision makers and the consequences of their decisions. And it renders those consequences socially invisible to them. If the environment is degraded by oil extraction in Nigeria, what difference does that make to an oil company executive living in the Netherlands? If workers in Thailand are exposed to deadly toxins at their workplace, what difference does that make to corporate shareholders in the United States or product consumers in Canada? Distance and difference can make the consequences of economic decisions feel more abstract to decision makers in much the same way that guiding drone strikes from thousands of miles away makes killing feel more abstract. In both cases, not having to look in the eyes of those who suffer the consequences of your decisions changes the way you experience the decision.

Environmental Threats

Another sense in which society has globalized is in its capacity to create environmental problems on a global scale, with truly planetary consequences. Socially created environmental disorganization is not new. The development of settled agriculture transformed local ecosystems from biodiverse natural habitats to biologically simplified, homogenous, synthetic systems created by societies to meet specific human needs. Fields were cleared; desirable, often nonnative, species of plants were planted; unwanted "pests" were exterminated; water flows were diverted; wetlands were drained; and forests were burned. As ecologically devastating as these impacts were, they were primarily local or regional. The scale of human alteration of the environment was limited by relatively small populations and relatively low technological capacity. Societies could undermine the environmental basis of their own survival by depleting soils, facilitating blights, denuding forests, and exterminating animal species on which they were dependent, but the environmental unsustainability of any particular society or culture did not threaten the integrity of the global biosphere as a whole. The earth marked their passing and moved on. It is only in recent times that the size of the human population, the levels and type of consumption, and the technologies of production (and destruction) have made it possible to disrupt ecosystems on a global scale and with irreversible global consequences for all living things.

In the global era, Monsanto creates a new species of soybean in a lab in the United States, and it is planted across millions of acres in the Americas, Africa, and Asia. Entire ecosystems are eliminated and replaced by those of corporate design, to be sprayed with chemical compounds with unknown environmental and human health consequences. Fossil fuels are burned to power industry, transportation, household gadgets, and heating on such a scale that the very chemical composition of the earth's atmosphere is altered, impacting climate and ecosystems in every part of the world. Agriculture and human settlement displace habitats at unprecedented rates, driving species and entire ecosystems to extinction. It is no coincidence that the era of globalization is also an era of the first great, human-induced mass extinction in the history of life on earth. When the Chinese plow their fields, they raise a cloud of dust into the atmosphere, and that pesticide-laden dust settles on North America and is found in the fish that we eat from the Great Lakes and increases our cancer risk. When the United States burns coal from West Virginia, it adds carbon to the atmosphere, which traps solar radiation that reaches the earth, raises global temperatures, and melts the glaciers of Greenland and the polar ice caps, and the sea levels rise in Bangladesh resulting in flooding and death. When Monsanto seeks expanding profits and markets, it sells genetically modified seeds and pesticides as a technological package in Brazil, incentives to expand agricultural production increase, forests are cleared, and the indigenous peoples of the Amazon rainforest lose their home. When global demand for oil rises rapidly, the relative value of places with oil reserves in the ground increases, states and corporations vie for control of oil fields, and war erupts in the Middle East, with all the associated carnage and cost. We live in an era of global environmental consequence. Having a global economy and a global society means that the environmental unsustainability of that society impacts everyone and everyplace in a way that earlier periods of human-induced ecological disruption could not.

One manifestation of globalization in the arena of environmental sustainability is the emergence of threats to, and concern for, tropical forests on a global scale. While tropical deforestation has occurred in various times and places for thousands of years, it is only in the current era that the future of the existence of tropical rainforests or "jungles" on the planet has come into question. And while concern over tropical deforestation has emerged in specific locales in earlier times, the emergence of a transnational movement and global consciousness of the ecological importance of, threats to, and concern for rainforests as a planetary ecosystem type is unique to the era of globalization. And as befits the era of globalization, we might mark the beginning of a global social movement for rainforest protection to 1989, when the international pop star Sting and his wife formed a foundation and sponsored a series of globally televised concerts to raise money for rainforest protection after visiting the Amazon. The leap in global consciousness generated by Sting built upon the local rubber tappers union organizing work of Chico Mendez in Brazil, whose campaign was made internationally visible by US-based environmental movement organizations. The assassination of Mendez by cattle ranchers in 1988 inspired Sting's attention to Amazonia.

Sociologists have studied the social causes and consequences of tropical deforestation since the 1970s. Thomas K. Rudel, a sociologist at Rutgers University in New Jersey, has dedicated much of his career to understanding the social processes that lead to rainforest destruction and the social policies that may reduce or prevent it. In his book *Tropical Forests: Regional Paths of Destruction and Regeneration in the Late Twentieth Century*, Rudel (2005) draws on hundreds of studies of tropical forest change across many decades to compare, contrast, and comprehend how global social forces impact tropical forest cover in different locations around the world. Rudel constructs a comparative, nested analysis exploring how changes in the global economy have impacted the mix of variables leading to deforestation in particular regions. Such global changes include the International Monetary Fund's structural adjustment programs, changes in global demand for cheap beef, plantation crop commodity booms, economic growth in China and India, and the increased demand for timber and pulp. Rudel demonstrates how global-level changes generated different sets of opportunities and constraints for countries, communities, and individuals who then engaged in activities that decreased or increased forest cover in their specific locale. His large number, cross-national comparative analysis examines the unique mix of social factors contributing to the global phenomenon of tropical deforestation in seven regions of the planet (Central America and the Caribbean, the Amazon Basin, West Africa, Central Africa, East Africa, South Asia, and Southeast Asia). One of his findings that cuts across all seven regions is that governments played a key role in creating policies that lead to deforestation in the 1980s with resettlement policies and road construction but that the role of governments as institutional actors in deforestation waned in the 1990s. As we might expect in the period of the rise of globalization, it was global corporations that played the key role in tropical deforestation in the 1990s, as logging firms, soybean producers, and others sought to expand production to serve global markets. By analyzing large amounts of data, from hundreds of locations, across three decades and seven regions of the planet, Rudel is able to provide an overview of global environmental change, while illuminating the specific nuances of regional variation in causes, outcomes, and possible public policy interventions.

GLOBAL SOCIAL MOVEMENTS

Globalization is a phenomenon filled with tensions and contradictions, tendencies and countertendencies. Globalization moves us farther apart and brings us closer together. While it increases the distance between owners and workers and consumers and producers and therefore allows us to impact the lives of people we will never meet with our consumption and production choices, it also creates conditions in which we may join up across great distances to make collective efforts to improve social conditions. The same communications systems that allow corporations to organize production globally and escape local labor and environmental regulations also allows workers, consumers, environmentalists, women's rights, and human rights advocates to organize across great distances to fight labor and environmental abuses. As previously noted in the cases of anti-sweatshop campaigns and rainforest protection struggles, the same communications and information systems that allow production to be moved to the remotest places on the earth also allows those most remote places to be brought into a global spotlight. In an era of globalization, corporations can run, but they cannot hide. And if the era of globalization is largely defined by the emergence of the global corporation as a dominant social institution, it is also defined by the emergence of global social movements that increasingly participate in a global culture.

Largely through the use of the Internet, environmental, human rights, labor, and women's rights organizations have transnationalized. Boycotts, protests, and a wide range of other campaigns to pressure corporations or states to alter their labor, environmental, and other behaviors can now reach across continents and oceans with relative ease. A human rights abuse (like police killing an unarmed African American in a routine traffic stop) in the United States can be exposed and discussed in an Internet café in South Africa on the same day. A Japanese company deforesting Southeast Asia can find itself facing a coordinated boycott and negative publicity campaign in North America and Europe very quickly. While global regulation may be slim, there is no question that global norms for human rights, environmental protection, and labor standards have started to emerge, largely as a result of global social movement activities and the inability of states and corporations to effectively shield their worst behaviors from a global public view. In the 1960s, with the growth of international television transmission, social movements adopted the slogan "The whole world is watching" to indicate to power holders that their actions would be viewed and judged by a global community. Certainly, the emergence of live television was crucial to the success of the US civil rights movement, as the beating of peaceful protesters was broadcast nationally and internationally. President John F. Kennedy was pressured to act when the brutality of local sheriffs became a visible embarrassment to the United States on a world stage. In the twenty-first century, the idea that the whole world is watching is even truer, and it is watching in real time, and it is not relying on large, professional, news corporations for its access to information. Anyone, anywhere with a smart phone and Internet access can potentially expose a social problem to billions of people across the planet in a very short span of time. And that capacity makes the era of globalization very different from all the eras that preceded it. The scale at which corporations and social movements are organized is now truly global, and the pace at which social events develop is faster than ever.

The capacity for real-time global communication increasingly means that an action in one part of the world can bring a response in another part of the world almost immediately. One hundred and seventy-five years ago, it might have taken months for news of an event in Cairo to reach people in San Francisco. Today, San Franciscans can watch events in Cairo unfold live on their mobile devices. Haitians abroad learn of events back home on the same day that they occur. And global responses to events may be learned back in the places in which the events occur nearly immediately as well, so that a human rights abuse in Syria can bring same day protests in New York, and images of those protests can be viewed by the human rights abusers on the day of the abuse. World events emerge and develop more rapidly than they have in the past. That means that some things might be stopped more quickly before they spin out of control. However, it also means that things can spin out of control more quickly, as the time in which options may be considered, responses may be framed, and decisions may be taken is greatly compressed. In an era of globalization, we are compelled to act fast, and acting fast usually means acting with less consideration, deliberation, and thoughtfulness.

THE GLOBAL MOVEMENT OF PEOPLE: MIGRATION

In an era of globalization, information, capital, and goods move more rapidly and freely across borders than ever before. The growing integration of a global society has also meant that people move more rapidly and freely as well. In 2015, roughly 250 million people (or 3.3 percent of the global human population) were living outside of the countries of their birth. However, national borders remain a greater obstacle to the free movement of people than to the free movement of capital, goods, or information, and international migration has been a growing point of conflict within and between countries in the twenty-first century. The decision to relocate to another country is not an easy one, and the costs and risks are high. People migrate internationally for a number of reasons including the search for economic opportunity and personal safety. Many of the causes of migration can be traced to the set of social changes associated with globalization.

As corporations have been liberated to decentralize production across the globe, local economies have become more volatile. Economic opportunities move across borders as factories are closed in one place and opened in another and as agricultural production shifts in method and locale. These shifts in global production change demand for labor, and job opportunities rise and fall across great distances. Within the United States, automobile production shifted from the Great Lakes states to the southern states in the 1980s, as corporations sought out cheaper, nonunion labor. Americans migrated from north to south in search of jobs (in a reversal of earlier migrations from the south to the north when the automobile industry took off in the 1920s and 1930s). This occurs on a global scale as well. When the North American Free Trade Agreement (NAFTA) allowed greater sales of US-produced corn in Mexican markets beginning in 1994, Mexican corn farmers went out of business. Displaced Mexican farmers sought agricultural and service work in the United States, increasing immigration from Mexico (see Food for Thought box in this chapter). Demand for higher-wage industrial workers in the United States declined as those jobs were moved out of the country by corporations, but demand for low-wage workers in the service sector (such as hotel workers) increased. However, international borders are legal obstacles to the movement of people. Free trade agreements free the movement of capital and goods, not the movement of people. While Texas had no legal recourse to slow the migration of Michiganders seeking work in the 1980s and 1990s, the United States government does have legal recourse to slow the migration of Mexicans to the United States. The desire to control the free movement of people is fueled by racial, cultural, and economic anxiety, stoked by globalization's threat to local values, traditions, and economies.

Many of the world's millions of migrants also move to escape war, famine, repression, and ecological collapse. The United Nations (UN) estimated that, in 2015, the world's population included 65.3 million people who had been displaced by human rights violations, persecution, violence, or conflict. The UN has projected that by 2020 there will be 50 million environmental refugees worldwide due to draught, desertification, sea level rise, and the disruption of seasonal weather patterns. Environmental degradation and violent conflict are not unrelated, as a rapidly expanding economy on a finite planet has amplified conflicts over access to natural resources like oil and water. Human-induced climate change has generated rising sea levels and more frequent extreme weather events. Low-lying small island states like the Republic of the Marshall Islands and Kiribati must now consider the possibility of disappearing all together. The government of Kiribati has purchased land on Fiji in case all of its 110,00 citizens must relocate due to climate change. As the number of the world's environmental refugees and refugees escaping armed conflict increases, the countries to which they emigrate struggle to absorb, accommodate, or repel the mass migration of people. The dynamic tensions of globalization are played out in political conflicts over whether to accept or reject refugees, whether to naturalize or deport undocumented immigrants, and whether to maintain or sever ties between countries. The xenophobia (fear of others not like you), ethnic nationalism, and racism evident in the United Kingdom's exit from the European Union (so–called Brexit), and Donald Trump's call for building a wall between the United States and Mexico are indications of backlash against globalization and the free movement of people across the planet.

CONCLUSION: THE CONTESTED FUTURE OF GLOBAL DYNAMICS

The era of globalization is one in which capital and information moves rapidly around the globe. Despite the increases in international migration that have accompanied globalization, capital and production are now much more mobile than people. Although people may move from North Africa to Paris or from the West Indies to Brooklyn where economic opportunity, human rights, or environmental conditions may be better, people and communities are simply not able to move as swiftly, easily, and constantly as data. The result is that, despite diasporas and improvements in transportation, people live their lives in places while dominant social institutions such as transnational corporations are increasingly "placeless." Even people who feel most socially connected to Internet "communities," by virtue of their bodies, must live life in a place that has real material and social conditions. And those places are increasingly subject to the economic, environmental, and political decisions of somewhat placeless, transnational organizations. This dynamic tension between place and placelessness is at the heart of sociological debates about the nature and future of globalization (see Table 9–3). Global society constructs a dynamic tension between forces of cultural homogenization on the one hand and local cultural identity, cultural hybridity, and cultural resistance on the other. Global society constructs a dynamic tension between forces of consolidated corporate control of the global information environment on the one hand and the information-democratizing possibilities of independent media and decentralized information sourcing on the other. Global society constructs a dynamic tension between forces of transnational corporate dominance on the one hand and the power of global social movements on the other. Global society constructs a dynamic

Table 9–3 Dynamic Tensions in the Era of Globalization

Cultural homogenization/McDonaldization	Local cultural identity, hybridity, cultural resistance
Consolidated corporate control of information/media monopoly	Information democratization, independent media, decentralized sourcing
Transnational corporate power	Global social movements
Post-Fordist production, capital mobility, job blackmail	International migration
Race-to-the-bottom, global competition for low wages and weak environmental regulation	Global/universal social norms for human rights, labor rights, environment
Global environmental threats	Sustainable development goals

tension between forces of globalized production, local economic insecurity, job blackmail, and capital flight on the one hand and the increased ability of peoples to cross borders on the other. Global society constructs a dynamic tension between the social structural forces that incentivize a global race-to-the-bottom in labor and environmental standards on the one hand and those producing global social norms for human rights on the other. And global society constructs a dynamic tension between forces of environmental destruction and those inspiring efforts at achieving **sustainable development** trajectories. Global society is now a social fact, but global society is also in flux and contested. The outcomes of these global social processes, forces, and dynamic tensions will be shaped by the social structures, institutions, movements, and norms that we create. You and I and everyone else are all social actors actively creating, participating in, and responding to global dynamics as we live our daily lives in a globalized social world.

Lesson Take-Aways

- Changes in information and communication technology in the late twentieth century made globalization possible.
- Because there is little global-level governance, the ability to operate globally has granted corporations enormous freedom and power relative to governments.
- The reduced importance of time and space as barriers has facilitated a homogenization of culture and the rapid spread of ideas.
- Globally decentralized production has made local economies more volatile and insecure.
- A global economy has generated global ecological threats like climate change and mass extinction.
- Although migration has increased, globalization has freed the movement of capital and goods more than the movement of people.

Discussion Questions

1. How does the breakfast you ate this morning reflect the globalization of the economy? What labor and environmental issues can you connect to the food you ate?
2. How do the dynamics of a global society impact the kinds of jobs that you anticipate having over the course of your life? How do you think these might change over time?
3. How can you, working with others, have an impact on one or more of the global social issues examined in this chapter? What technologies might you use in these efforts?

Sources

Armbruster-Sandoval, Ralph. 2005. *Globalization and Cross-Border Labor Solidarity in the Americas: The Anti-Sweatshop Movement and the Struggle for Social Justice*. New York: Routledge.

Bagdikian, Ben H. 1983. *The Media Monopoly*. Boston: Beacon.

Barber, Benjamin R. 1995. *Jihad vs. McWorld: How Globalism and Tribalism are Reshaping the World*. New York: Ballantine Books.

Barnet, Richard J., and John Cavanagh. 1995. *Global Dreams: Imperial Corporations and the New World Order*. New York: Simon and Schuster.

Derber, Charles. 1998. *Corporation Nation: How Corporations Are Taking Over Our Lives and What We Can Do about It*. New York: St. Martin's Griffin.

Gould, Kenneth A., David N. Pellow, and Allan Schnaiberg. 2008. *The Treadmill of Production: Injustice and Unsustainability in the Global Economy*. Boulder, CO: Paradigm.

Keck, Margaret E. and Kathryn Sikkink. 1998. *Activists Beyond Borders: Advocacy Networks in International Politics*. Ithaca, NY: Cornell University Press.

Mills, C. Wright. 1959. *The Sociological Imagination*. New York: Oxford University Press.

Rudel, Thomas K. 2005. *Tropical Forests: Regional Paths of Destruction and Regeneration in the Late Twentieth Century*. New York: Columbia University Press.

Transnational Institute. 2014. *State of Power 2014*. Amsterdam: TNI. https://www.tni.org/en/publication/planet-earth-a-corporate-world

Wallerstein, Immanuel. 1974. *The Modern World-System I: Capitalist Agriculture and the Origins of the European World Economy in the Sixteenth Century*. New York: Academic Press.

Related Websites

Corporate Accountability International: www.stopcorporateabuse.org
Global Environmental Facility: www.thegef.org
United Nations Conference on Trade and Development: www.unctad.org
United Nations High Commissioner for Refugees: www.unhcr.org
World Economic Forum: www.weforum.org
World Social Forum: www.forumsocialmundial.org.br

LESSON 9, PHOTO REFLECTION:

Food choices in Manhattan's Chinatown.
Photo by Ken Gould.

Manhattan's Chinatown is known, in part, for its high density of Chinese restaurants, but Chinese food it not your only culinary option while walking along its crowded streets. The universally recognizable golden arches corporate logo conveys its message of fast, cheap, unsurprising, global food products effectively if the corporate name is written in English or Mandarin (or is it Cantonese?). The corporate giant is faced off by the individual entrepreneur meeting an increasingly globalized demand for cheap, fast, Halal food (food prepared according to Islamic religious requirements). We chose this photo because it illustrates two globalizing forces: multinational corporations and religious ideologies. The irony is that these forces are at work in an ethnic enclave, which itself is representative of global migrations past and present. If you were walking down this street, what would you choose to eat for lunch? If you were the photographer, what picture would you take to represent global dynamics?

What are the different ways that the lessons of sociology can be communicated to the public?

10

Public Sociology: The Task and the Promise

Michael Burawoy

I was telling my nephew, a schoolteacher in England, about **public sociology** and the idea of making sociology comprehensible to people like himself. I told him that I had become an evangelist for pubic sociology. He looked at me quizzically, trying to imagine his uncle as an evangelist, and then asked: "What's the big deal? Sociology for the people? Isn't that what sociology is for? Isn't it supposed to shed light on people's lives, shouldn't they be able to comprehend it?" He shrugged his shoulders, at a loss to understand what the fuss was about.

CHANGING THE WORLD

My nephew was not the only one! When I travel to South Africa, India, or Brazil and speak about public sociology to sociologists, they too look bored and bemused. If sociology is not "public," then what on earth is it? Why would anyone bother to do sociology if it did not have a public mission? In each of these countries, sociology has been deeply implicated in social movements. In South Africa during the anti-apartheid struggles, for example, sociology demonstrated that violence could only be averted if conflict was institutionalized, if workers were given the right to organize into trade unions, if Africans were given residence rights in the cities, and, in the final analysis, if they were given the vote. Now sociologists are involved in the reconstruction of the post-apartheid state, or in accounting for xenophobic violence, debating these matters in the media.

In Brazil, during the dictatorship, sociologists around Fernando Henrique Cardoso and his colleagues at his Center for Social Science Research, known locally as CEBRAP, developed connections to social movements, fostering the demand for the expansion of rights. Today Brazilian sociologists continue to work with trade unions and invent new forms of democracy, such as the now-famous scheme of participatory budgeting, whereby citizens collectively decide how to spend municipal funding—for schools, roads, parks, better services, and so on. Similarly, in India, sociologists are actively promoting the rights of indigenous people against predatory capitalists—both national and international—who want to expropriate the land of the peasantry, or they work with populations displaced by government-sponsored dams. Many Indian sociologists assume they will partake in people's struggles by offering interpretations that demonstrate the broader social, economic, and political forces that are responsible for their plight. So obviously, sociology has to be public!

After all, that is why many of us became interested in sociology in the first place. Perhaps we had read Mills's (1959) *The Sociological Imagination*, and it stirred us to recognize that the world is made up of more than individuals; that there are social, political, and economic forces that control our destiny; and that we need to understand those forces if we are to improve our society. That was certainly why I became a sociologist. In this lesson, I want to illustrate Mills's idea by showing how I made my own life as a sociologist not freely but under the influence of forces beyond my control. Sociology, says Mills, enables us to "grasp history and biography and the relation between the two within society" (6). Sociologists cannot be the exception to their own rules. Sociologists are social beings, too, living lives at the intersection of the history of the world and their own biographies. My history and my biography would eventually lead me to become the president of the American Sociological Association and to call for sociologists to practice "public sociology."

LOSING NAIVETÉ AND BECOMING A SOCIOLOGIST

Let us begin when I was a student like you. It was in 1965. I was a mathematics student at the University of Cambridge in England, and that meant you did nothing but mathematics for three years. I hated both Cambridge and mathematics. They seemed irrelevant to the pressing problems of the world that the student protests of that era brought to public attention.

One of the virtues of Cambridge education, however, was the brevity of the terms: eight weeks. This gave me long summer vacations, which I exploited by traveling to distant lands on money I saved up during the year from my government scholarship. Just imagine that—money saved on a grant! That's history indeed. These travels—hitch-hiking through Africa, for example, at the end of my first year—opened my eyes not just to the meaning of underdevelopment and the problems it defines; meeting people on the roads, in the villages and in the towns of Africa, also made me optimistic about the human capacity and ingenuity to overcome those problems.

This was, indeed, an era of optimism—the era of the Beatles, who were my symbolic neighbors. For me, the optimism took a particular direction. Despite my own negative experience at university, or perhaps because of it, I thought that education could save the world. So, at the end of my second year in Cambridge, having nearly flunked the exams, I packed my bags and went off to India to study what seemed to be an important problem: the medium of instruction in university education. Should it be English (the inherited language of the colonizer), Hindi (the controversial national language spoken by 30 percent of the population that put people from southern states at a disadvantage), or one of the 14 official regional languages (of which 10 were spoken by more than 15 million people).

Who was I, a 20-year-old mathematics student, to go off to India to investigate this matter? You may well ask. Fools march in where angels fear to tread. I thought this problem of medium of instruction was a technical issue—which language would be the most effective as a medium of instruction—and so I went around India by third class rail (an experience by itself) dividing university economics classes into two and giving them the same comprehension test in English and the regional language. This was a very crude randomized controlled experiment.

Well, I learned my first and most important sociology lesson: technical problems often turn out to be political problems. The medium of instruction in university education held all sorts of implications for different groups— the national elite who already spoke English could lose privileged access to the best universities, and thus the best jobs, if the medium of instruction became the regional language or Hindi. Regional elites, on the other hand, might reap the benefits of regional language. They would appeal to their people—Bengalis, Tamils, Marathas, and Gujaratis—to oppose the imposition of a colonial language (English). In south India, however, there were riots when the north threatened to make Hindi the language of the civil service examination. If they could not secure the legitimacy of their own regional languages, then non-Hindi speakers preferred English. In short, this was and has always been a political struggle of intersecting class and regional interests, conducted in the idiom of nationalism. There were many other issues involved in this apparently simple question of the medium of instruction, such as the availability of texts in the regional language, and the brain drain that might follow if the best students were taught in English. But there was no doubt that this was far more than a simple technical issue— far more than whether students were more competent in their regional language, Hindi, or English. The result was that I lost my political naiveté and became a sociologist.

POLICY SOCIOLOGIST

I managed, somehow or other, to complete my mathematics degree and immediately quit England for Africa, hoping somehow, someday to become a sociologist. It was 1968, the year of student rebellions. After a period in South Africa, working as a journalist, I ended up in Zambia penniless. Zambia had been a British colony until 1964. On the advice of South African sociologist in exile, Jack Simons, I looked for a job on the Copperbelt, with one of the two major multinational mining corporations. Jack said that we knew about the conditions of workers, but we didn't know what the mining companies were up to and how they were reacting to the new Zambian government installed after independence. With my skin color and my Cambridge degree—my

cultural capital, as sociologists say—I landed a job in the copper industry's personnel research unit.

As it turns out, I could not have been better situated to investigate the policies of the mining companies through what sociologists call **participant observation**. At the time the mining companies were trying to develop an integrated wage scale to replace the two segregated wages scales that existed before independence—a wage scale for whites and a wage scale for blacks. They were trying to develop a single job evaluation scheme that would bring the jobs of 50,000 employees under a single rank ordering, based on the ranking of 20 key jobs, representative of the industry as a whole. Each job was evaluated on a range of factors (e.g., skill, responsibility, training, education, etc.). The task was to develop a system of evaluation that would award every job, black and white, a number of points that would translate into pay differentials and to do so without upsetting the existing wage hierarchy. Well, the only way this could be accomplished was through manipulating the weights accorded to each factor with a mathematical technique known as linear programming. Once again, I saw how a technically neutral mode of evaluation concealed a political determination upon which it was based, namely the choice and ranking of key jobs that had to conform to the previous wage structure. Here I was, unexpectedly crowned as a policy sociologist, deploying my expertise to serve a very clear goal defined by the mining companies.

I didn't exactly see myself as a policy sociologist. All I knew was that the mining companies were dependent on my mathematical skills. It gave me not only entry into the high-level negotiations with the trade unions but also access to all sorts of company information. I even milked the companies for resources to run a social survey of miners, my imagination of what a sociologist should do. The companies were very pleased with my work and awarded me a scholarship to go to the University of Zambia, where I got my first degree in sociology.

The mining companies may have been happy with me, but I was not happy with them. I was appalled by their complicit maintenance of the "color bar," defined as a racial division of labor in which no black employee has any authority over any white employee. This had characterized the colonial division of labor, but it was expected to disappear with independence whose central plank, after all, was the struggle for racial equality. But first the colonial and postcolonial context needs filling out, as this is part of the history that shaped my biography and the biographies of those around me.

THE PUBLIC SOCIOLOGIST AS ORGANIC INTELLECTUAL

I arrived in Africa at one of its most exciting moments. During the late 1950s and the 1960s, country after country had secured its independence from colonial rule. The people of Africa were no longer governed from Paris, London, or Lisbon but governed themselves, bringing equality to all citizens, allowing them to vote in their own elections, have access to education, and live where they had the means. The racial despotism of colonialism had largely disappeared, except in southern Africa, namely, Southern Rhodesia (now Zimbabwe), South Africa, Mozambique, and Angola. Zambia had achieved independence in 1964, and four years later the shine was still on, the country was breathing optimism, and President Kaunda was preaching Zambian humanism, a form of African socialism. Among social scientists, debates raged about development, dependency, neocolonialism, class, socialism, and tribalism. Sociologists engaged in the debates from different vantage points, but everyone thought their analysis really mattered. If only the right policies were pursued, Africa would be a beacon to the whole world, transcending the cold war dividing the United States and the Soviet Union and the capitalist and communist worlds. For an aspiring sociologist, this was indeed an exciting time and place to be—an experience deeply seared into my sociological mindset.

I was especially influenced by the writings of Frantz Fanon, author of *The Wretched of the Earth* (Fanon 1962), a book that took Africa by storm. Fanon was an intellectual organically connected to the colonized and their struggles for freedom, but he was much more than that. He offered a powerful sociological analysis of the postcolonial predicament. Born in Martinique of Creole parents, he trained to be a psychiatrist in France after World War II and left for Algeria to head up a psychiatric hospital in 1953. There he despaired of treating his patients—black and white—suffering from the traumas of the violence of the Algerian war of independence. He joined the liberation struggle, only to be deported from Algeria in 1957; he then became an ambassador for the Algerian National Liberation Front. He dictated *The Wretched of the Earth*, an encomium of colonial revolution, while dying from leukemia at the age of 36. That was 1961, a year before Algeria won its independence from France.

In his lyrical analysis, Fanon identified two struggles. The first was to overthrow colonial rule, and here he argued violence had to be met with violence—violence unified, violence was redemptive of the century of violence suffered by the colonized, violence was cathartic. It delivered the colonized from internalized oppression. Important as this struggle was, far more important was a second struggle among the colonized themselves, a struggle between two visions of independence—on the one hand, an independence in which black simply replaced white as the rulers of the postcolony, becoming a national bourgeoisie, and, on the other hand, an independence that involved liberation, not a racial succession that left the class structure untouched but a revolution that would abolish class domination and inaugurate socialism based on collective, participatory democracy. Such a revolution would not be made by a working class, which Fanon regarded as pampered and parasitic, but by the peasantry, the overwhelming majority of the population who had lost so much of their land to the colonizers that they had nothing more to lose. Fanon argued that the first road, the national bourgeois road, imitative of Western democracy, would be unable to sustain itself due to economic backwardness. It could only be an appendage of Western capital, and, as a result, the multiparty democracy would degenerate into one-party rule and then one-man dictatorship. The only alternative was a revolutionary struggle that would liberate human energy and creativity, hold Western capital to ransom, and build a new socialist order.

So which road would Africa take? Fanon interrogated the strength and the interests of the classes among the colonized. The interests of the middle classes and working class on the one side and the peasantry on the other were quite clear, but the interests of the traditional leaders, the *lumpenproletariat* (unemployed migrants, living in squatter settlements in the urban periphery), and the intellectuals were far more ambiguous and contradictory. Would they support the bourgeois road or the socialist road? Fanon examines the pressures that might push them in one direction or another, hoping that a symbiosis of dissident intellectuals and a volcanic peasantry would capture the imagination of the vacillating classes.

Well, we know what happened. He was tragically right about the bourgeois road: Africa has taken great leaps in the direction of dictatorship. As to the national liberation road, this was a phantasm that could not be realized. Where settler colonialism held out and engendered violent struggles, as in Algeria, Mozambique, Zimbabwe, and South Africa, the upshot has been more violence and less revolution. The idea of blackmailing the West or canceling Africa's past through struggle were pious hopes. Still, it was the phantasm—the vision of an alternative—that drove his prophetic analysis of Africa's future and that has inspired so many in their struggles against all manner of oppressions.

So, what sort of sociology is this? Certainly, it was not intended for *professional sociologists*, yet it did offer an original analysis of colonialism and postcolonialism that has influenced professional sociologists. But influence is not enough to make it **professional sociology**. More important, Fanon would have to worry about the empirical basis of his claims, such as, in the colonial context, the revolutionary character of the peasantry or the conservative impetus of workers. Evidence is simply lacking. At best, it represents a hotly disputed hypothesis. If it is not professional sociology, perhaps it is **critical sociology**, aimed against the more evolutionary, reformist models of development that took little account of the legacy of colonialism and even less account of class. That may have been how it has been seen in some quarters, but, still, it was not Fanon's intent. He couldn't have cared less about professional sociology—whether to develop it or to criticize it.

Equally, it is hard to think of *The Wretched of the Earth* as policy sociology. Fanon was not paid to write this for some client, and, yet, paradoxically, it has been read by governments to forearm themselves against revolution. More to the point, one could say that it was a form of **policy sociology** for the liberation movement. It was meant to serve the liberation struggle, even if the liberation struggle did not contract Fanon to write it, even if parts of it are quite critical of the liberation struggle.

Confining attention to professional, critical, and policy sociologies misses *The Wretched of the Earth*'s enormous influence on much wider publics. In dictating

FOOD FOR THOUGHT
BECOMING A SOCIOLOGIST OF FOOD
Justin Sean Myers

It was the summer of 2008. My wife and I, newlyweds, were driving up the coast of northern California and southern Oregon on our honeymoon. During our two-week trip, we would see grey whales, sea otters, and sea anemone; become engulfed by millions of monarchs in migration; go white-water rafting on the Klamath River; and swim in Crater Lake—which, at 42 degrees, was quite a refreshing or chilling experience, depending on your point of view. To top off the trip, everywhere we stopped had fresh local food to eat: fruits, veggies, greens, and fish. All of it was delicious. Grown by small farmers. Grown without pesticides. Harvested locally. On the surface, it was amazing, but in talking to the people growing the food, I heard story after story about how difficult it was to be a small farmer today. From the cost of land, to getting credit from banks, to finding reliable outlets for their produce, most didn't make enough money to be only farmers and were dependent on a family member working a regular nine-to-five job too.

These comments were local echoes of the major argument of the book I was reading on our trip, *Earth Democracy* by Vandana Shiva (2005). In the book she documents the global struggle for food sovereignty. Peasants, small farmers, and the indigenous are struggling to maintain their livelihoods against national governments, transnational corporations, and international agencies, such as the World Bank and International Monetary Fund. I learned how trade policies, land theft, and the privatization of seeds were dispossessing millions from the land base and consolidating the food system under the power of factory farming and for-profit corporations. By the end of the book, it was clear that a global struggle today is occurring over *who* controls the preconditions for life—water, land, and seed—and *how* they are used to feed people or to feed profit rates.

It was this trip that woke me from the slumber of being a critical armchair sociologist and pushed me to become a public sociologist engaged in the food justice movement. When I got back to New York City, I engaged in a self-directed crash course in the sociology of food and agriculture, found professors who supported my interests, and began to volunteer at a local food justice organization, East New York Farms! (ENYF!), which exists to promote community-led economic development through urban farming in a low-income black, Caribbean, and Latina/o community in Brooklyn, New York. Emerging out of an asset-based participatory planning project between community and borough stakeholders, ENYF! privileges grassroots organizing and class-conscious interracial politics as central to addressing institutional racism in the food system and the wider society.

In my time there, I have engaged in the basic building blocks of a community food system by being a community garden member, facilitating community garden meetings, volunteering at the farmers market, and helping to build raised beds and harvest crops. I have also participated in intercultural potlucks and anti-oppression workshops at ENYF! to build the people-to-people relations necessary to building community-level power. In the former activity, people bring a cultural dish that is personally

Food for Thought *continued*

meaningful and share this food and its story with others. In the latter, people engage in interactive skits to address internalized and interpersonal oppression, discrimination, and ageism, among other inequities. The purpose of both is to tell stories, share knowledge, and build relations by working together across and through difference to confront attitudinal and institutional racism through the cultivation of antiracist sentiments and practices. Finally, in my time at ENYF! I have been involved in a citizen science project run through the Cornell Cooperative Extension that worked to strengthen the agroecological knowledge and practices of community gardeners to improve soil fertility and reduce crop loss to insects. This asset-based project specifically sought to empower gardeners to come up with locally based solutions to environmental problems by working with extension actors rather than relying solely on technical inputs or external specialists as solutions.

Based on my experiences at ENYF! I have documented the conflicts emerging between the food justice movement and the economic aspirations of Walmart, the development priorities of City Hall, the market-centric politics of the alternative food movement, and the limited funding structures of philanthropic funding organizations. All of these issues raise questions about the ability of ENYF! to realize its aspirations in an environment where low-wage neoliberalism, gentrification, political consumerism, and austerity predominate. Alongside this descriptive work, I have written about the need to change existing practices within urban planning, philanthropic funding, labor market policies, and food assistance and diet-related health programs to create a just and sustainable food system premised on the empowerment of the marginalized rather than paternalistic top–down solutions.

All of these experiences have been central to my development as a public sociologist who is theoretically working through the successes of, barriers to, and conflicts that emerge within the food justice movement as he lives them. Such insights benefit my scholarship as well as my activism and most hopefully the long-term success of the food justice movement.

Sources

Shiva, Vandana. 2005. *Earth Democracy.* Cambridge, MA: South End.

---

what became a bible of revolution for and by the marginalized, Fanon started a conversation among and within liberation struggles everywhere about possible postcolonial trajectories and radical transformations, a conversation that took on a life of its own soon after he died. Whatever Fanon's intentions, *The Wretched of the Earth* generated debate about the nature of colonial oppression not just in Africa but also among French intellectuals divided over France's role in Algeria; in the United States, among the Black Panthers and other groups over the revolutionary potential of ghettoized African Americans; and in Italy, where it informed Gillo Pontecorvo's masterful film, *Battle of Algiers*. The circulation of *The Wretched of the Earth* generated worldwide discussion that still continues.

That makes it public, but does it make it public *sociology*? Certainly, its analysis was profoundly sociological, linking the experience of the colonized to the wider social structures in which they were entangled, but did the analysis have sufficient empirical veracity? I tried to demonstrate its empirical and analytical power by adapting his scheme to Zambia. Let me explain.

PUBLIC SOCIOLOGIST OF A TRADITIONAL STRIPE

Fanon's class analysis was rooted in his experience of Algeria, a settler colony with a strong agrarian base. There were peasant rebellions and the independence struggle did have a rural base. Zambia, on the other hand, was dominated by its industrial base, its copper enclave. Zambian humanism was a socialist cloak that concealed a raw capitalist reality. Zambia had clearly taken the national bourgeois road of racial succession. So the sociological question was, how did this succession work—why did it end up reproducing the old racial hierarchy, the color bar?

Let's begin with the government's perspective. When I arrived in 1968, the government had just put out a report on Zambianization, that is the localization of the labor force, that is, the displacement of white by black. It was a congratulatory report that spoke of great success of Zambianization. I reproduce the table that captured the progress made since independence (see Table 10–1). Sure enough, the number of Zambians in expatriate positions had increased over fivefold. At the same time, the number of expatriates had fallen. No doubt about it this was a great success story. But do you notice anything about the numbers? The increase in the number of Zambians (2,967) exceeds the number of expatriate displaced (2,597), which suggests that managerial hierarchy was getting bloated. Why might that be the case? That would require careful investigation of the microprocesses of Zambianization.

I couldn't interview management about Zambianization—this was such a delicate matter that I would have been chased off the mine immediately and that would have been the end of the research. I had to undertake *covert* research of a particular sort: what sociologists call participant observation,

Table 10–1 Progress of Zambianization

	Total Expatriates (*n*)	Total Zambians in the Field of Expatriate Employment (*n*)
December 1964	7,621	704
March 1966	6,592	1,138
September 1966	6,358	1,884
October 1967	5,671	2,617
June 1968	5,024	3,671

Source: Government of the Republic of Zambia (1968, 9).

research conducted in the time and space of the subjects themselves. In other words, I had to watch the process of racial succession as it unfolded over time. To do that I solicited the help of fellow (Zambian) students at the University of Zambia who worked in the mine. So what happened?

I focused on instances of Zambianization, that is, cases in which a Zambian succeeded a white (expatriate) employee. Take the position of mine captain, which was the highest level of managerial supervision underground and just beginning to be Zambianized. What happened when a black shift boss (the next level down in the hierarchy) was promoted to replace the white mine captain? Perhaps you can guess? The white mine captain was displaced but not removed. He was displaced upward, that is, promoted into a newly created position, called assistant underground manager.

This, of course, effectively protected the color bar but at the cost of creating all sorts of tensions within the organization. The former white mine captain took with him into the new position many of the resources and influence that he had previously possessed, while the new black mine captain had the same responsibilities as his predecessor but not the organization support to carry them out. The job of the immediate subordinate of the mine captain—the black shift boss—was, thereby, made more difficult, and he came to resent his new black supervisor, even to the point of wishing for the return of the previous white mine captain. The tensions reverberated all the way down the hierarchy so that the Zambian successors were seen to be an "uppity class" in thrall to white management. The Zambian successor himself therefore led a very insecure existence and sought to alleviate his anxiety by an ostentatious lifestyle (e.g., sporting fancy cars), which only intensified class hostility.

Still, why did Zambianization happen this way on the Copperbelt when in government it would take place from top down as well as bottom up? The answer lay in developing the distinctive Millsian method, linking microprocesses to macroforces, moving beyond everyday common sense of the participants to the structural forces at work. What did this mean in this case? I examined the postcolonial class structure to tease out the interests of different classes. The African working class—the miners—was not interested in Zambianization, the creation of a new class of Zambian overlords but in improving their wages and bettering the conditions of work. White management—and management was still largely white—was even less interested in removing the color bar since they wanted to cling on to their lucrative jobs (their skills were often specific to the Zambian copper mines so they wouldn't be able to find such rewarding jobs elsewhere). Corporate management, on the other hand, found itself in a quandary: on the one hand, it was interested in promoting Zambianization and dismantling the color bar as this would lower labor costs; on the other hand, they did not want to upset the apple cart by alienating white mine management that were not easy to replace, having developed special skills to run the mines.

As I discovered, corporate management did not have a fixed strategy or plan but would wake up every morning and see which way the winds were blowing. They found themselves in a very uncertain environment—political (government), economic (price of copper), and technological (always facing new unexpected problem of excavation)—and so adopted a flexible decision-making process. It let government take the lead on the matter of Zambianization, and the government was not interested in removing the color bar, or so it seemed, because they did not want to jeopardize the foreign revenue that came from the mines. More than that, having expatriates running the mines was preferable to Zambians who might pose as a political opposition to government—expatriates on three-year contracts could be removed at any time if they presented any threat. And, then, of course, there was the question of whether there was a sufficient number of Zambians who were equipped to take over the mines. In other words, none of these "class" entities, with the exception of the Zambian successors themselves, had a clear interest in removing the color bar—that is, in demolishing the colonial racial order. In moving from the microprocesses to the macroforces, I identified the class interests behind racism.

Having undertaken this analysis, all covert—unbeknownst to the mining companies but based on company data and on four years of detailed observations of successions—I had to decide whether to turn this local problem into a public issue and, if so, how. Mills writes as though the sociological imagination linking micro to macro automatically brings about the move from personal troubles into public issues. Nothing could be further from truth. When people are confronted with the macroforces shaping their lives, they are as likely to withdraw into cynicism as they are to take public action. Turning the sociological imagination into a public project requires **political imagination**.

Having written my report on Zambianization, I decided to seek permission from the mining companies to publish it, even though I realized this might spell the end of social science research on the mines. The corporate executives were both shocked and annoyed by what I had done and flatly opposed publication. "It's all based on your data," I pleaded. That may be, they said, but we don't agree with your interpretation. Faced with my insistence that this was too important to keep quiet, they sent me to the Zambianization department of the Ministry of Mines, on the grounds that the mines had recently been nationalized. My attack on the government was even more severe than on the companies, so they knew, and I knew, the government would turn down my request even more forcefully than they. But we were both wrong. The person responsible for Zambianization (ironically, an expatriate) read the report with enthusiasm and instructed me to get it published as quickly as possible. I was astonished. It refuted my claim that the state was a monolithic entity not interested in disrupting the color bar—there were clearly different interests within the state. I would have to revise my theory.

The report was published, and when it appeared, it was subject to lively discussion in newspapers and television. I was not aware of any vitriolic feeling from the mining companies or government, even though this was a condemnation of the class structure of postcolonial Zambia. As is usually

SOCIOLOGY AT WORK
WORK AND PUBLIC SOCIOLOGY: PROFESSIONAL SOCIOLOGISTS
Arne L. Kalleberg

Professional sociologists are one of four types of sociologists in the sociological division of labor that Michael Burawoy identifies in this chapter, the others being public, critical, and policy-oriented sociologists. Professional sociologists seek to obtain instrumental knowledge: they try to solve puzzles or social problems by discovering new methods, theories, or conducting new empirical research using these methods and theories. Professional sociologists regard themselves as social *scientists* and thus use rigorous scientific methods to try to answer questions and solve problems in a dispassionate and apolitical way. They publish their results primarily in academic journals or books, thereby speaking to audiences consisting mainly of other professional sociologists and students in universities. Publishing in academic journals and books and teaching students are key requirements to establish one's career as a professional sociologist. Most PhD sociologists in the United States can be classified as professional sociologists, as about 70 percent teach in colleges and universities. In other countries, public, policy, and critical sociologists might be the dominant type.

Sociologists often move among the four types over the course of their careers. As Burawoy discusses in this chapter, some people are drawn to sociology because they want to be critical or public sociologists and then become professional sociologists as they attend graduate school and begin their careers in academia; finally, they become critical or public sociologists again later on (as Burawoy did). Others are motivated to become sociologists mainly because of an interest in understanding particular puzzles (such as my desire to understand the causes behind overtraining) and then later seek to disseminate their findings to policymakers and various publics. Their scientific discoveries may also lead them to become highly critical of the social and economic systems that account for the phenomena they are studying and thus turn to public or critical sociology. Professional sociologists need not check their values at their office doors nor hesitate to study important critical, policy, and public issues. However, professional sociologists should conduct their research objectively according to rigorous scientific standards and not set out to prove a particular result a priori.

Professional sociologists are thus complementary to, not inconsistent with, the other three types of sociologists in the sociological division of labor. The four types of sociologies are interrelated, mutually dependent, and reinforcing. At the same time, professional sociology is in many ways the heart of the discipline of sociology, since it creates the high-quality research and basic knowledge that is necessary to address and understand significant social issues, problems, and puzzles. In addition, the research that professional sociologists conduct and publish provides the scientific authority and basis of scientific expertise that helps public, policy, and critical sociologists to be persuasive in reaching and convincing their respective audiences. Good public sociology depends on good professional sociology.

Sources
Clawson, Dan, Robert Zussman, Joya Misra, et al. 2007. *Public Sociology: Fifteen Eminent Sociologists Debate Politics and the Profession in the Twenty-First Century.* Berkeley: University of California Press.

the case with public debates, it is not possible to measure their influence; what is important is the debate itself. Still, I do know that the mining companies, ever flexible, exploited the opportunity and used my Fanonite report to discipline their own mine managers, ordering them to get their Zambianization house in order. Once again, I had to face my own political naiveté—knowledge, however progressive, does not create its own impetus for self-realization, and it is easily used by those with power for their own ends. Once more, chipping away at my political naiveté was all part of becoming a sociologist.

Just as class analysis applied to the processes of Zambianization, so now it also applied to the dissemination of knowledge. In such **traditional public sociology**, a report, a book, or a commentary is broadcast, sent out into the public arena where, if it commands any attention at all, it is subject to a political struggle over its interpretation, and the stronger party usually wins. An alternative strategy is the method of **organic public sociology**, in which the sociologist develops a direct unmediated relation to a given public and in that way contests the balance of forces in society. Thus, I could have made the young Zambian personnel officers, with whom I worked closely on the project, the interlocutors or audience for my research. The danger of such *unmediated* engagement, however, is that the reciprocal conversation dissolves either in the direction of the sociologist who leads or dominates the public— Fanon's revolutionary intellectuals—or, the other way around, wherein the sociologist is dragged on to the terrain of the public, thereby losing autonomy. These are, indeed, the political dilemmas of public sociology, dilemmas that can divert it from its goal—two-way conversation between sociologist and public.

THE CRITICAL SOCIOLOGIST

Chastened by my first experience of public sociology and thinking I needed further training in sociology, I applied to graduate school in the United States. Why the United States? Because, in the English-speaking world and beyond, the United States was the home of sociology, not least of what I regarded as the deeply flawed theories of underdevelopment that attributed African backwardness to traditional mores and primordial attachments. I arrived at the University of Chicago in 1972 (the only department that accepted me) ready to dedicate myself to the fundamentals of sociology. I was shocked, however, by the poverty of the courses—the trivial accounts, the tedious abstraction, the smug complacency, and their remarkable irrelevance, mired in provincialism. There was no sniff of Marxism or feminism; even the famed ethnography had disappeared. I had come all this way for this? This is a common experience for many graduate students, but it was in a sense worse for me as I knew from Zambia that it didn't have to be this way. While it would eventually change, at this moment in time, US sociology was marked by its conservativism.

It was in my second year that I stumbled across a political science course on contemporary Marxism. I was not the only one. Indeed, it seemed the whole university wanted to squeeze into Professor Przeworski's seminar. At the time, I didn't realize that there was a pent-up demand for some form of critical thinking to bring sociology into line with contemporary realities— the Vietnam War, the civil rights movement, the student movement. Critical thinking aimed at self-congratulatory functionalism was on the agenda in many sociology departments, at least among graduate students and some forward-looking teachers, such as Maurice Zeitlin at the University of Wisconsin, Immanuel Wallerstein at Binghamton University, and Barrington Moore at Harvard University. A new generation of insurgent sociologists had been born on the waves of the 1960s social movements and was now delivering body blows to the reigning mainstream sociologists. Although in Chicago, such critical analysis was rather thin on the ground. In response to changes in society, individual sociologists shifted the topics they studied and the questions they asked. This led to a gradual reorientation of the field as sociology changed with the times.

This was when I first met Erik Wright. We were both opposing mainstream sociology with Marxist analysis, he against stratification theory and I against industrial sociology. He used statistical analysis of survey data to demonstrate the explanatory power of a Marxist theory of class that was rooted in **relations of production**, relations between those who own the means of production and those who don't, that is, between capitalist and workers. He added a third category, "the **petty bourgeoisie**"—individuals who owned their own means of production but didn't employ wage laborers (e.g., shop keepers, independent craft workers, etc.). Between each pair of fundamental class positions, he identified three intermediate positions— supervisors and managers, small employers, and semiautonomous workers (e.g., teachers, lawyers, and others who were between wage laborers and petty bourgeoisie). He called them "contradictory class locations." He tried to show that this paradigm of class analysis was superior to the conventional models of status attainment that strung occupations on a continuum or to the economists' models of human capital, superior in its capacity to explain variations in income inequality.

While Erik was developing his analysis of national class structure based on relations of production, I was focused on a microanalysis of social *relations in production* at one factory in South Chicago where I worked for a year. I tried to develop the ideas of a politics of production to explain why workers so actively participated in the production of profit for their employers. Hitherto Marxists were more focused on the objective features of work organization, what they called the labor process, but I was focused on the subjective dimensions, the way workers were constituted as citizens with rights and obligations by what I called the "internal state" and the "internal labor market." I began with a criticism of industrial sociology, which had the interests of employers in mind, focusing on why workers are so lazy, why they don't work harder whereas I wondered why they worked so hard, given that the benefits accrued to their employer not to themselves. Marxists had answered this question by emphasizing the coercive element of the employment relation, namely, fear of being fired, whereas I focused on the organization of consent, albeit backed up by force.

At the time, we, the young Turks, suffered from illusions of grandeur. We thought we would conquer sociology with our new Marxist science. We were using the tools of sociology—regression analysis and participant observation—against sociology. Our work was definitively not aimed at "publics" beyond sociology, but we naively thought that to revolutionize sociology would somehow challenge capitalism. Thus, when I worked at Allied I was not concerned with converting my fellow workers to Marxism or even working with them to build a stronger trade union; my goal was to use my experiences as a worker as the basis of a critique of mainstream sociology. My audience was undoubtedly other sociologists. I was not a public sociologist but a **critical sociologist**.

THE PROFESSIONAL SOCIOLOGIST

As we became established sociologists, our work lost its critical edge and became part of mainstream sociology—Erik's elaborations on the Marxist theories of class have become part of the canon, and my notion of production politics has been systematically criticized and developed by a succession of graduate students. Over time, interest in class analysis on the one side and in the labor process on the other has waned, and in their stead younger generations of sociologists have been interested in class formation, classes acting to make history. They have become interested in social movements, in particular new directions in union organizing. They have become less interested in transforming sociology and more interested again in building close connections to the union movement. Like Dan Clawson (2016), who has studied United Students against Sweatshops, and Ruth Milkman, who has examined immigrants' roles in the US labor movement, for example, they have become practitioners of public sociology. Indeed, the labor section of the American Sociological Association has become a beehive of creative public sociology that has inspired new directions for research.

Through the 1980s and 1990s, Erik and I grew into the professional world, which entailed teaching and researching within the framework of academic norms. For me, the transition to teaching had been traumatic and the tenure battle draining. Our research followed parallel routes: he organized surveys in different countries to map out national class structures, while I turned to a comparative analysis of production regimes in different countries. We wanted to understand just how peculiar was the United States, whether in terms of its class structure or its politics of production. Our students were no less critical but less passionate about Marxism, especially as it became more mainstream. But this was also because the world beyond had become more quiescent under the assault of the market that was depleting the labor movement and exhausting the civil rights movement. Again, history mattered for the direction of sociology.

We took stock of the situation and in our different ways sought to enliven the sociological imagination by reflecting upon alternatives to capitalism. I turned to the study of actually existing socialism, working in factories in socialist Hungary and post-Soviet Russia, trying to understand what had become of the greatest social experiments of the twentieth century, how and why it had deviated from the ideals that motivated it, and, above all, how workers lived in what was called the "workers' state." Erik, on the other hand, developed an interest in other types of experiments, surviving in the interstices of capitalism, such as participatory budgeting, cooperatives, Wikipedia, and the universal income grant. All contained the seeds of alternatives to capitalism, alternatives he calls "real utopias." He called it a sociology of the possible as opposed to a sociology of the actual or of the impossible. Against the idea of a value-neutral sociology, Erik has advanced a sociology that is self-consciously founded on values—equality, democracy, freedom— and their institutional expression. He had made the return to critical sociology from where he had come and then created a science of real utopias that was and is energized by moral concerns.

In the meantime, my own biography took an unexpected twist. Desperate to find someone to chair their department, my colleagues at UC-Berkeley turned to me. The department had been rather fractious for many years, reflecting and inheriting the turmoil on the Berkeley campus, but in the mid-1990s, peace reigned. We asked ourselves what sort of vision Berkeley sociology had of itself, and what collective identity might we develop. I had always admired the way my colleagues had transmitted their ideas to broader audiences—Erving Goffman's (1959) *Presentation of Self in Everyday Life* or his book on stigma, Robert Blauner's theory of internal colonialism, Arlie Hochschild's sociology of emotions and the gender division of labor, Kristin Luker's study of the politics of abortion, Todd Gitlin's account of the 1960s and the student movement, Robert Bellah's work on civil religion and then his collaborative work on American individualism, and Jerry Karabel's work on educational inequalities and the history of quotas at Ivy League universities. They all reached out to audiences way beyond sociology. When I became chair, my colleagues Claude Fischer, Mike Hout, Martin Sánchez Jankowski, Sam Lucas, Ann Swidler, and Kim Voss had just completed *Inequality by Design* (Fischer et al. 1996), a book aimed at dispelling biogenetic views of inequality then being popularized by Murray and Hernstein's (1996) *The Bell Curve*. Experts in different areas, they put their heads together to produce what was intended to be a prototype of traditional public sociology.

So that is how the public sociology project began—we defined the department as engaged with the world, addressing big issues in public ways. We ran a colloquium series on public sociology and with Jonathan van Antwerpen, then a graduate student, I wrote a history of the department from the standpoint of public sociology. At the time, it seemed quite harmless to all concerned.

PUBLIC SOCIOLOGY LIVE!

When I was elected president of the American Sociological Association, it was natural to take the public sociology theme to a national level, and I criss-crossed the country giving talks and having debates with faculty and students in different universities. Now the battle lines were being drawn. The professional sociologists, the leaders of our profession, many residing in the top universities, professionals who publish articles in the *American Sociological Review* (important articles but accessible and of interest to the few) disapproved of public sociology. They feared it might question the sacrosanct nature of their science. If sociology is made accessible to broad publics, then perhaps, after all, it is no more than common sense. It has no right to claim to be a discipline competing with other disciplines for a place in the sun or, more precisely, for funds, for positions, and for a space in the university. There is the view, hotly contested by C. Wright Mills, that for sociology to be a science it must create its own language, its own methods, its own style of arguing that clearly demarcates it from common sense.

While public sociology garnered a lot of support from sociologists in non-elite departments, or at least those that did not aspire to climb the disciplinary totem pole, and from those parts of the discipline that felt marginalized, it was given the cold shoulder by the guardians of our profession. As far as the professionals were concerned, even the critical sociologists were more acceptable than the public ones. However harsh their criticism, the critical theorists rarely targeted broader publics and, therefore, did not threaten the credibility of the discipline as a whole. The professionals, however, were most at home with policy sociology, because policy sociology was the mobilization of sociology's scientific status to solve problems defined by clients. Besides, it often brought in hefty funds. For their part, policy sociologists, seeking to influence government agencies with their "neutral" science, were even more avid than the professionals in their disavowal of public sociology for fear it would politicize their craft and leave them without any clients.

So now, finally, you can see why something so obvious and natural—public sociology—should be so controversial. It's because, in the United States, sociology has such a strong presence in the universities, where the status of disciplines as academic enterprises rules the roost. Of course, we do need a professional sociology that accumulates bodies of research findings and makes possible the sort of book you are reading and to which I'm contributing. Without an established body of research, there simply cannot be any public sociology, not to mention critical and policy sociology. So, while public sociologists such as C. Wright Mills might rail against the irrelevance and obscurity of professional sociology, they are actually attacking its pathological forms and not its essence. Mills was himself, for much of his life, a professional sociologist writing for fellow academics. Indeed, it requires substantial investment in scientific research before one can become an effective public sociologist or else you simply reinvent the wheel or draw erroneous conclusions from sloppy research. Training in methods, accumulating knowledge, and grasping social theory are all not only essential for the advance of professional sociology but also good public sociology. Still, professional sociology can be taken too far, becoming self-referential and dismissive of public engagement. Where there is a more balanced relation—as in Brazil, India, and South Africa—between public and professional sociologies, they can inspire each other.

Let me give you some examples from an experimental course called Public Sociology Live! The idea was to bring Berkeley undergraduates into conversation with sociologists engaging with publics in different places in the world. We did this over Skype—the sociologist in question would lecture for 15 minutes or so and then there would be a discussion for the next 40 minutes. (You can watch these conversations at www.isa-sociology.org/public-sociology-live.) Classes around the world have discussed them and posted their own comments on Facebook. You can look at those and contribute your own.

The seminars start with the famous Spanish sociologist Manuel Castells talking about the way media control the very space public sociology seeks to enter. We move on to Nandini Sundar, talking about her work with indigenous groups in India faced with land expropriations and caught in a field of violence between left-wing guerrillas and a state-sponsored special police force. Having spent many years studying the adivasi of Chhattisgarh, she now seeks to bring their plight to public attention through media and bringing a case before the Supreme Court. César Rodríguez Garavito describes a similar situation for indigenous groups in Colombia, only he works with human rights nongovernmental organizations that are seeking leverage through the application of international law. Sari Hanafiworks with Palestinians in Lebanese refugee camps, describing their fate to the media, drawing attention to rights of employment and education that they have been denied. Marta Soler and Ramon Flecha show how their critical communicative methodology, a form of organic public sociology, gives voice to marginalized groups in Spain, such as the Roma, and how their work has influenced social policies. Walden Bello, now a politician, describes a public sociology that borders on political activism, an investigation into the role of the World Bank in upholding the Marcos dictatorship in the Philippines. Karl von Holdt describes the frustrations of policy-oriented sociology concerned with the transformation of the post-apartheid state, in particular one of the world's biggest hospitals. Michel Wieviorka recounts the challenges of public sociology in France where he has been concerned with questions of anti-Semitism, racism, and terrorism—topics that are fraught with political divisiveness—again based on detailed sociological research. Finally, we talked with Frances Fox Piven about her theory of disruptive power and how that has influenced the way she has fostered movements for the defense of the welfare rights and voting rights of marginalized populations in the United States.

What we learn from all these examples is the fortitude and commitment required by public sociology. First, venturing into the public sphere armed with sociology can, indeed, prompt violent reactions. Even in the

United States, Frances Fox Piven, for example, was subject to a barrage of public vilification from Glenn Beck of Fox News, and with that came death threats. For this reason and more generally to develop method and strategy it is important that public sociology be conducted collectively. Second, each public engagement is based on a wealth of prior research undertaken by themselves or by others. There is no warrant for naively stumbling into a political battlefield. Third, the context within which public sociology operates varies a great deal. Here too professional sociology can help us explore the nature of that context so that we are better equipped to negotiate its terrain.

All of these points were captured in the seminar presentation of Pun Ngai, a Chinese sociologist based in Hong Kong. She reported on the appalling conditions of work at Foxconn, one of the world's biggest multinational corporations that makes the parts for Apple Computers, iPhones, and iPads. Foxconn employs a million young workers in China, half of them in one city, Shenzhen. Pun Ngai herself had worked in one of Shenzhen's electronics factories as a participant observer narrating her experiences of China's despotic labor system in her book *Made in China* (Ngai 2005). She began our seminar with a 6-minute film made by herself and other sociologists associated with the nongovernmental organization, Students and Scholars against Corporate Misbehavior, contrasting the enormous profit of Apple with the impoverished conditions of Foxconn workers. She went on to describe the military organization necessary to run factories with over 100,000 workers and the resulting anomie and alienation that in 2010 led to a spate of 17 suicides. Her account was based on the undercover research of students who became workers at Foxconn factories to conduct interviews and observe conditions there. Some of her, along with her colleagues, work is detailed in "Worker-Intellectual Unity: Trans-Border Sociological Intervention in Foxconn" (Ngai et al. 2016).

We felt very uncomfortable as we listened to the gruesome details of the labor that produced the shining Mac computers lining our seminar tables, all made visible on camera. Unlike so many of the other seminars that were about distant places with which students had little direct connection, this seminar brought home their connection to the very public issues being discussed. Even though China was far away, students benefited directly from the degradation and exploitation of Chinese workers. Pun Ngai was urging the students to get involved in protesting Apple's connection to Foxconn. Students shrugged their shoulders—Apple products are part of everyone's life, there's no way of getting rid of them. She said that the campaign was more to shame Apple into giving up $1 on each product sold, by revealing how Foxconn depends on indentured student apprentices as cheap and insecure labor. She was appealing to their identity as students. They responded defensively: "But this is capitalism, you can't reform it without overthrowing the whole system." Sociological imagination—that is, tying lived experience to its wider determination—was mobilized to justify inactivity rather than to move forward with political imagination to public sociology.

After the seminar, students wondered whether Pun Ngai had strayed into political activism. Indeed, the line between public sociology and political activism can be a very fine one. Public sociology is primarily accountable to the community of sociologists; it operates in the fields of sociology whereas political activism operates in the field of politics. When the two fields overlap, they can be indistinguishable, but the principle of public sociology must prevail: namely, it is a two-way conversation between sociologist and public. This means that we have to recognize that everyone is a sociologist and carries with him or her a theory of how the world works. We call it common sense, and it is with common sense that public sociologists converse.

Just as my nephew, outstanding teacher that he is, knows he must start with the lived experience of his students so public sociology does something similar: it elaborates common sense. I can see him laughing again, shrugging his shoulders: "So public sociology is just common sense?" Yes and no. Public sociology is the *elaboration* of a particular part of common sense, what we can call the *good sense*, composed of the sociological imagination that ties biography to history, that recognizes the source of personal ailments as lying with wider societal forces. At the same time, the public sociologist seeks to delete the other part of common sense, the *bad sense*—the mythologies of individualism, the ideologies of success, the falsehoods of conventions, the distortions of stereotypes, the blindness to injustice—that bombard us from all sides and that we inherit from the past. So, yes, public sociology is a form of teaching in which common sense is cultivated and society itself becomes a classroom, a classroom for developing a critical social consciousness that strives for what could be rather than adapting to what is.

Lesson Take-Aways

- Sociologists approach their research with different goals that can vary over the development of a career. Burawoy shifted from a policy sociologist, to a critical sociologist, to a professional sociologist and finally to a public sociologist.
- Public sociology aims to make sociology relevant and understandable to a broader audience (not just sociologists), with a goal of engaging the general public with social issues.
- In the same way that we use the sociological imagination to understand an individual in relation to his or her history and biography, the field of sociology must be understood in the context of its history. The field shifts over time as historical events raise new questions and challenges that sociologists address.

Discussion Questions

1. What is public sociology, and does it differ from political activism?
2. What are the relations among public sociology and critical, policy, and professional sociologies? Give an example of each.
3. What public sociology project could you imagined pursuing?

Sources

Bellah, Robert. 1975. *The Broken Covenant: American Civil Religion in a Time of Trial*. New York: Seabury.

Bellah, Robert, Richard Madsen, William M. Sullivan, Ann Swidler, and Steven Tipton. 1985. *Habits of the Heart: Individualism and Commitment in American Life*. Berkeley: University of California Press.

Blauner, Robert. 1972. *Racial Oppression in America*. New York: Harper-Collins.

Burawoy, Michael. 1972. *The Colour of Class on the Copper Mines, from African Advancement to Zambianization*. Manchester, UK: Manchester University Press for University of Zambia, Institute of African Studies.

Clawson Dan. 2016. "Excerpt from *The Next Upsurge: Labor and New Social Movements* (2003)." In Kenneth A. Gould and Tammy L. Lewis (eds.), *Thirty Readings in Introductory Sociology*. 2d ed. New York: Oxford University Press.

Fanon, Frantz. 1962. *The Wretched of the Earth*. New York: Grove.

Fischer, Claude, Michael Hout, Martín Sánchez Jankowski, et al. 1996. *Inequality by Design: Cracking the Bell Curve Myth*. Princeton, NJ: Princeton University Press.

Gitlin, Todd. 1987. *Sixties: Years of Hope, Days of Rage*. New York: Bantam Books.

Goffman, Erving, 1959. *Presentation of Self in Everyday Life*. New York: Anchor Books.

Government of the Republic of Zambia. 1968. *Progress of Zambianization in the Mining Industry*. Lusaka, Zambia: Government Printer.

Hernstein, Richard J. and Charles Murray. 1996. *The Bell Curve: Intelligence and Class Structure in America Life*. New York: Free Press.

Hochschild, Arlie. 1983. *The Managed Heart*. Berkeley: University of California Press.

Hochschild, Arlie. 1989. *The Second Shift*. New York: Viking.

Karabel, Jerome. 2006. *The Chosen*. New York: Mariner Books.

Luker, Kristin. 1985. *Abortion and the Politics of Motherhood*. Berkeley: University of California Press.

Mills, C. Wright. 1959. *The Sociological Imagination*. New York: Oxford University Press.

Ngai, Pun. 2005. *Made in China: Women Factory Workers in a Global Workplace*. Durham, NC: Duke University Press.

Ngai, P., S. Yuan, G. Yuhua, et al. 2016. "Worker-Intellectual Unity: Trans-Border Sociological Intervention in Foxconn (2014)." In Kenneth A. Gould and Tammy L. Lewis (eds.), *Thirty Readings in Introductory Sociology*. 2d ed. New York: Oxford University Press.

Wright, Erik Olin. 2010. *Envisioning Real Utopias*. London: Verso.

Related Websites

Association for Applied and Clinical Sociology: www.aacsnet.net

Public Sociologies: http://burawoy.berkeley.edu/PS.Webpage/ps.mainpage.htm

Public Sociology, Live!: https://isapublicsociology.wordpress.com

LESSON 10, PHOTO REFLECTION:

Sociology professor leading students on a field trip to a local brownfield.
Photo by Tammy Lewis.

There are many ways to teach about the intersection of biography and history. In the photo, a sociology professor is leading his class on a walking tour of a toxic brown field not far from campus. Many of the students pass by this site on a regular basis, not wondering much about what goes on here. Walking the site, learning its social history, and knowing its present, students are better able to understand the neighborhood around it: why it smells so bad, why low-income housing has been placed there, and why there's been an ongoing political battle over what to do about the site. Using our sociological imaginations to examine the everyday places in our lives, we have the potential to imagine whether and, if so, how we can shape the future. Students can ask, what should be done here? Who are the winners and losers if we decide to clean this site up? What are the social consequences? What outcomes would I advocate for, and how? If you were the photographer, what picture would you take to represent public sociology?

Index / Glossary

Page numbers followed by *f* or *t* indicate a figure or table, respectively

Ethics and Compliance Office at GAbookethics@oup.com. This book is traceable.

339

double consciousness: Term used by W. E. B. DuBois to explain how African Americans perceptions of themselves was through two lenses-one their own and the second through the eyes of others, 42

dramaturgical theory (of Goffman): as aid in understanding "self," 66, 68; described, 66, 67, 76–77; and impression management, 76–81, 83–84; and social construction of gender, 223

Dream Defenders, activist organization, 276

"driving while black" ("DWB"), 133

dropout rates, 20

drug abuse, 18, 20, 193

dual citizenship, 137

DuBois, W. E. B., 41–42, 132

DuPuis, Melanie E., 269, 271

Durkheim, Emile, 18; book on religion and suicide, 37; co-founding of sociology by, 34; concerns about class inequality, social instability, 181–182; concerns on social change, 289; concerns with maintenance of social order, 37–38; *The Division of Labor in Society*, 37, 253; economic writings of, 37; functionalist theory of, 38–39; social fact concept of, 38; view of society as a social organism, 253. *See also* evolutionary model of social change; social fact; structural functionalism

Earth Democracy (Shiva), 323

East New York Farms! (ENYF!), 323–324

economic globalization, 297–302; global labor, 301–302, 304–305; in largest economic entities (selected list), 292*t*–293*t*; modernization schemes, 298–299; vulnerabilities of, 287; world production, 300–301; world trade, 297–299

Economy and Society (Weber), 35–36

economy life: scientific work embedded within, 100

education: anxiety and dropout rates, 20; charter schools, 107–108; and class, 7, 16, 186; as core social institution, 97, 98; cultural capital and, 65, 188, 203; dropout rates and anxiety, 20; efforts at green lunch programs, 40; efforts at rewriting American history in textbooks, 144; for-profit colleges and universities, 108–109; and functionalism, 38–39; hegemony in, 86; interactions of nonprofits, for-profit corporations, the state, 107–108; limitations of multicultural education, 143–144; media's impact on, 103; meso-level organizations in, 106; nested analysis findings, 25; race and access issues, 15–16; relations to social class, 7, 128, 173, 176; school lunch program issue, 104–105; scientific work embedded within, 100; social interactions in classrooms, 101–102; teacher-student interactions, 103

The Eighteenth Brumaire of Louis Napoleon (Marx), 247

"electronic profiling," 89

The Elementary Forms of Religious Life (Durkheim), 37

Ellis, Emily, 232

emotions, sociology of (Hochschild), 332

employment: class structure and, 183, 185–186; corporations, deregulation, and, 20; discrimination against LGBTQ, 212; economic globalization and, 201, 204–205; education and, 183–187; family structure changes and, 23, 106; food access and, 13–14, 139; gender and, 230–233; gender-based pay gap, 128, 229–230; globalization's impact on, 289, 297–298; global labor, 301–302, 304–305; health care and, 116, 119–120; post-World War II data, 22*t*; reconciling parenthood with, 24*f*; in the restaurant industry, 184–185; sexuality and, 230–233; workplace discrimination, 194, 212, 228, 233, 238

employment discrimination, 194, 212, 238

Employment Non-Discrimination Act (ENDA), 233

Engels, Friedrich: critique of capitalism, 34–35; on "haves" and "have nots" in society, 35; on the mutual common good, 302; optimism of, 36; stratification as understood by, 37

England, Dawn, 215

Enloe, Cynthia, 228

environment: concerns for ecosystem destabilization, 290; degradation concerns, 44; regulation in the global environment, 306–307; threats in the global environment, 307–309. *See also* rainforests

Environmental Defense Fund, 266

environmental sociology, 53

Ethiopia: family income distribution data, 178*t*

ethnic conflict. *See* interracial and ethnic conflict

ethnicity, 6, 10; association of race and nationality, 136–137, 142; class conflict and, 160; economic relevance of, 164; and employment discrimination, 146; and friendship and marriage selection, 151; interracial and ethnic conflict, 158–164; and social structure, 159

ethnic violence, 159

ethnocentrism: judging the behaviors of others through one's own value system, 64

ethnographic approach: An approach to research also known as participant observation and fieldwork in which the researcher immerses him or herself in the community they are researching and lives the lives of those being studied to gain insights into the social meanings of their actions, 48; hospital study findings, 116–118; study of black middle-class neighborhood, 157; study of three Washington, DC suburbs, 157–158

ethnomethodology: An approach used by Garfinkel to understand how people learn about and reproduce the unspoken rules of everyday life, 77, 83, 223, 257

Europe: civilizing mission of, 135; colonial era systems, 298; Euro debt crisis, 9; feudal system in, 197; health care, social services in, 106; Industrial Revolution in, 289; rich *vs.* poor income gap, 35; rise of industrialization in, 34; south-central Eastern (SCE) emigration, 134

European Economic Community (EEC), 148

evolutionary model of social change: The model that claims that social change has an adaptive process that maintains the stability of society, 253–254; dialectical model comparison, 255

experts, as agents of social change, 267–268

exploitation: A set of social relationships where one group of people are treated unfairly for the benefit of another group., 135

ExxonMobil, 262*t*, 291

Facebook, 80, 262, 274

Fahs, Breanne, 230

Fair Housing Act (1968), 144

families: alternates to two-parent heterosexual model, 220; cultural norms in, 12, 14; England, Descartes, Collier-Meek's studies of, 215; income in select countries, Gini index, 178*t*; influence of social forces on, 25; and intimate partner violence, 225; nested analysis findings, 23–25, 24*f*, 25*t*; as social institution, 97, 98; structural changes in, 106. *See also* marriage and the family

Families That Work: Policies for Reconciling Parenthood and Employment (Gornick and Meyers), 22*f*, 23–25, 24*f*, 25*t*

Fanon, Frantz, 321, 322–324

fast-food revolution (U.S.), 13–14

Feagin, Joe, 81

Fearon, James, 161

Federal Bureau of Prisons, 108

Federal Housing Authority, 153–154

Federal Reserve study, on race-based mortgage lending, 153

feminist anthropology, 213

feminist movement, 80, 91

feminist sociology, 42–43, 211–212, 213, 224

feminization of poverty The rise in the percentage of women who are poor, 194

Ferguson, Missouri, police violence, 133

feudalism, 35

Fischer, Claude, 332

FiveThirtyEight blog, 54

Flecha, Ramon, 334

Flint, Michigan, contaminated water crisis, 271

food apartheid, 138

food desert, 138

food (fast-food) consumption, U.S., 13–14

food justice, 323–324

food-related self, 73–74

food swamps, 138

Ford, Henry, 87–88, 300

Fordism: A system of mass production typical of advanced capitalist societies in the twentieth century based on assembly-line production, centralization of component

manufacturing, scientific management, and stimulation of relatively high wages, low pricing, advertising, and consumer credit, 87–88, 300. *See also* post-Fordism

foreclosure crisis, 153

Foucault, Michel, 258

Fox News, 335

"framing" notion (of Goffman), 81, 83

France: family income distribution data, 178*t*; large economic global entity ranking, 292*t*; parent employment data, 24*f*; public sociology challenges in, 321

Frankfurt School: A theoretical perspective that integrates aspect of Marxist theory with cultural theories to understand the power of culture to socialize people and to hold a system of economic class privileges in place, on "false choices" of consumers, 66; interest in a "culture industry," 86; on power of culture to socialize people, 85–86

free trade zones, 302, 304–305

Freud, Sigmund: on gender identity, 219; Mead's comparison with, 70; psychoanalytic theory of, 218; "sublimation" idea of, 87

front-stage/backstage: performance concept (of Goffman), 77, 79–80, 93

Fujimori, Alberto, 136

Fukumura, Yoko, 228

functionalism: A school of thought that examines how the various social parts work together for the good of the whole by examining their uses (their "functions") for society; argues that shared social values are the glue that holds society together, 254; capitalism comparison, 39; conflict theory comparison, 39*t*, 41; development of, 41; Durkheimian tradition structural functionalists views on, 181–182; inequality as viewed by, 182; Merton's and Parson's belief in, 39; types of functions in, 38–39; U.S. racial inequality and, 254

Gaddis, Michael, 150

Gagnon, Valère Philip, 161

Gamson, William, 269

Gang Leader for a Day (Venkatesh), 158

Gans, Herbert, 195, 197

GAP Corporation, 302

Garfinkel, Harold, 77, 223–224

Garner, Eric, 133, 275

Gay Asian Pacific Alliance, 230

gay marriage, 98, 110, 112, 114, 211, 296–297

gay people: activism by, 228, 230; domestic partnerships, 114; fear of coming out, 211; and workplace harassment, 233. *See also* lesbians; LGBTQ

gay rights, 191

gemeinschaft to *gesellschaft* societal shift, 34

gender: looking-glass self and, 68–69; social scripts and, 68

gender: The socially constructed and unequal division into femininity and masculinity that

CPSIA information can be obtained
at www.ICGtesting.com
Printed in the USA
BVOW06s1648250917

495784BV00003B/17/P